Implementation and Public Policy

Implementation and Public Policy

with a New Postscript

Daniel A. Mazmanian
Claremont Graduate School

Paul A. Sabatier
University of California at Davis

UNIVERSITY
PRESS OF
AMERICA

Lanham • New York • London

Copyright © 1989 by

University Press of America®, Inc.

4720 Boston Way
Lanham, MD 20706

3 Henrietta Street
London WC2E 8LU England

Printed in the United States of America

British Cataloging in Publication Information Available

Copyright © 1983 by
Scott, Foresman and Company

Dedicated to the understanding and encouragement of
Jenny, Melissa, Mary, and Pooh

Library of Congress Cataloging-in-Publication Data

Mazmanian, Daniel A., 1945–
Implementation and public policy, with a new postscript /
Daniel A. Mazmanian, Paul A. Sabatier.
p.   cm.
Reprint. Originally published: Glenview, Ill. : Scott, Foresman, ©1983.
Includes bibliographical references.
1. Policy sciences. 2. United States—Economic policy. 3. United
States—Social policy. 4. Social justice. I. Sabatier, Paul A. II. Title.
H97.M39   1989   361.973— dc20   89–36189 CIP

ISBN 0–8191–7526–9 (pbk.)

Preface to the University Press of America Edition

Identifying the key ingredients in what is needed for governments to deliver on the promises they make to their citizens is the heart of implementation analysis. Scholars and practitioners alike have agreed on the importance of knowing what these ingredients are, which accounts for the explosion of implementation studies over the past two decades. This book presents a synthesis of the scholarly work on the factors that have emerged from this inquiry, viewed across a wide range of public programs.

Implementation analysis begins with formal public policy pronouncements that legislatures—and sometimes the courts—adopt and the President and Governors are expected to carry out. What are the crucial components of a statute or directive in helping to ensure successful imlementation? Who in the executive branch should be made responsible? What kinds of resources should be devoted to the effort? What are the hurdles one can expect to find in a program's path? Is the goal being sought beyond our technical or social capabilities? These are the questions that implementation analysis asks.

There is a high degree of consensus on the questions that must be asked and the range of leading factors central to successful implementation. Sometimes the factors can be affected quite directly by the way a program is formulated. For example, the implementation task can be turned over to a new and energetic agency versus one well set in its ways and interested in doing other things. Other times it cannot. Public support, also important to program success, is usually beyond the reach of those designing a program and must be taken as a given.

The body of this book was written, at the beginning of the 1980s, in an attempt to present within a comprehensive framework the range of relevant factors that must be considered, and questions that must be answered about any major implementation effort. Since that time, few new questions or relevant factors have been added to the list, despite the volume of studies that have followed. In this sense, then, we believe that the book has captured the perennial questions and key analytical issues of implementation analysis today. And this is the justification for a second edition.

The specific programs examined—air pollution, desegregation, coastal land management, new towns, and compensatory education—have continued to unfold over the past seven years. The implementation process is always evolving and today we might not reach the same conclusions about their degree of success as we did based on developments through 1982. We faced a difficult choice, therefore, in deciding whether to begin writing the case material anew. Since our primary objective is to provide a coherent analytical perspective on the process of implementation, with cases serving to clarify and make concrete the analytical discussion, we have resisted the temptation to revise and extend the case material.

The field of implementation, and more broadly speaking policy studies, has not stood still during the 1980s. Three avenues of inquiry have moved our understanding of and analytical approaches to implementation beyond the boundaries of this book. First, just as this book represents a significant advance over the preceding single case approach to analysis, subsequent efforts have been made at better quantifying and gauging the relative importance of implementation variables more systematically (and empirically). Several examples, such as the work of Goggin et. al. and McFarlane, are noted in our new postscript. Second, the limited time-frame, often from only a couple of years to a decade, within which most cases of implementation are studied has proved simply too short. It cannot capture the learning that takes place within policy arenas by advocates on all sides, nor does it provide sufficient time to fully appreciate the unfolding dynamics of the process. The emerging emphasis on long-term policy change is highlighted by Paul Sabatier in his call for a synthesis of the "bottom-up" and "top-down" approaches to implementation through his "advocacy coalition framework," outlined in the postscript. Finally, in an effort to fit the best "means" of implementation to a particular situation, attention is now being given to fitting the most appropriate "tool" or "policy instrument" to the program context, as reflected in the recent work by scholars such as Lester Salamon, Anne Schneider, Helen Ingram, Richard Elmore and Lorraine McDonnel.

To our pleasant surprise, the first edition of this book proved to be equally useful as an undergraduate level introduction to the implementation field and as a guide for graduate and professional level discussion and research. We presume this will continue to be the case with the second edition. The support and cooperation of the University Press of America has made this rerelease possible, and for this we are grateful.

Daniel A. Mazmanian   Paul A. Sabatier
Claremont California   Davis California

Preface

Ours is an era of considerable pessimism and concern about government. Following four decades of unprecedented government expansion into commerce and business, foreign affairs, and domestic issues of social policy, more and more Americans have come to believe that our government has exceeded its fundamental charter, whether it is the charter granted in the Constitution or the "living" charter founded on what most Americans consider an appropriate and necessary level of government involvement in the lives of its citizens. The controversy over the proper scope of government is not new; it has emerged as a central topic of debate in each of the periods of governmental activism throughout our two-hundred-year history.

Today's pessimism and concern stem from government's seeming inability to deliver, even in the case of programs with strong public backing which have been legitimately enacted into law. This holds for programs as diverse as health care for the poor, the young, and the elderly; jobs and job training for the unemployed; our military defense and preparedness; equal rights protection for women and minorities; occupational health and safety; and the protection of our precious natural resources. This is the "crisis of implementation" that we currently face in the United States. It has precipitated a skepticism on the part of many that government may be inherently incapable of performing any but the most routine and noncontroversial tasks. Again, the concern is not with the objectives of the programs *per se;* rather, even if the programs are enacted, the ability to translate stated goals into reality may be beyond the capacity of government as we know it.

The primary focus in this book is on the ability of government to deliver — to implement—the specific objectives that are set forth in constitutionally adopted public policies. The substance of programs to be implemented is obviously important to us, but secondary in the sense that the focus of implementation analysis is on "how well" executed. Consequently, our interest in policy formulation, whether through legislative enactment or presidential or judicial directive, is limited to understanding how the formulation process and the mandate that results enhance or detract from program implementability. We therefore ask, how well does a statute or directive define objectives and structure the implementation of those objectives? Whose responsibility is it to see that the policy is implemented? What resources are they given? What impediments are placed in their path? And, what does the variety of recent implementation efforts, both good and bad, tell us about the general factors central to success or failure?

Gauging the effectiveness of policy implementation against goals and objectives articulated in formulating statutes and guidelines may seem an obvious way to proceed. However, several alternative approaches to the study of policy implementation and evaluation have achieved prominence today. In one approach, the outcomes of the implementation process are judged by some external standard, despite the fact that such standards may not be reflected in the goals of a program as envisioned by legislators or other formulators. In this approach the analyst brings to bear his or her own normative values of what public programs ought to be accomplishing. A good example is the adoption of the Rawlsian criterion, implicit if not explicit in much research today, that the justification of any public program must be that it enhances the position of the least-well-off persons in society.

Another approach to implementation analysis is to view the formulation and enactment documents of a program not as a benchmark against which to assess the effectiveness of the implementation effort, but as a starting point of an unfolding process. This approach is frequently used in studies of locally implemented federal government programs in areas such as education and community development. From this perspective the articulation, clarity, and accomplishment of specific goals is less important than their symbolic import. Program enactment is simply the starting point of an evolving process of experimentation and search for the implementation strategy best suited to the local circumstance. The effectiveness of implementation is judged by a number of criteria pertinent to a particular site as the implementing agency finds its own way of responding to the generalized federal mandate of the program. Evaluating the degrees of creativity and implementation in each case must therefore largely be left to the particular analyst and local community. One difficulty with this approach is determining whether either the specific or general goals of the program as set by its enactors are being met.

By juxtaposing these three approaches to implementation analysis we do not mean to suggest that each is mutually exclusive of the others. Conceivably, one can examine whether program objectives are met and why (as well as whether) the results enhanced the less-well-off. Even when the focus is primarily on the prescribed goals of the program, unanticipated outcomes (positive or negative) that result from implementation at the local level must be considered in any analysis. However, to the extent that it is important to determine the effectiveness of an implementation effort in light of the objectives of the policy formulators, who typically are elected political officials, the focus on accomplishment of specified goals and objectives would appear to be of greatest importance.

Given this orientation, we have not written a text in the traditional sense of an encyclopedic and neutral coverage of the subject. Instead, we present in *Implementation and Public Policy* a comprehensive framework of the implementation process through which specific policy objectives can be analyzed and evaluated. We also outline the six conditions we consider most necessary for effective implementation. These conditions can not only be used as a checklist to judge program effectiveness, but may also be regarded as a set of tasks program enactors must accomplish to ensure the success of any implementation effort. The utility of the framework and the six conditions is tested through an in-depth analysis of five cases, ranging from the relatively unsuccessful New Communities program to the largely successful coastal land use regulation in California.

Finally, we have written this text because we are at heart traditionalists, possibly even idealists, in viewing the public policy process; we believe that legislators, as the preeminent representatives in our system of government, should set policy and do so in a manner that ensures the proper and intelligent implementation of established programs. Yet we are also realists in appreciating that the implementation of any but the most routine and mundane policy is an extremely complex and precarious undertaking. We have observed over the past several decades a significant shift in real power over policymaking from the legislative to the executive branch of government. It is our hope that a thorough understanding and appreciation of the implementation process, and the capabilities and limits of legislators to guide it, will help turn the tide against the ever expanding executive power. Yet that will occur only when legislators and the public come to appreciate what actually takes place in that mysterious void between enactment of a program and its ultimate impact on people and events.

We have been extremely fortunate throughout the preparation of the book to have the counsel and assistance of numerous friends, colleagues, and participants in the policy process. To all we owe a debt of gratitude. For comments and assistance in the preparation of drafts of several of the specific chapters we would especially like to thank the following persons: For Chapter 3 on New Communities—Raymond Burby, Jack Underhill, Helene Smookler, and, our research assistant, Alison Whalen; for Chapter 4 on Automotive Emissions Control—Bob Faoro, Karl Hellman, William Chapman, Ron Wada, Richard Lifoff, and Angus MacIntyre; for Chapter 5 on School Desegregation—Charles Bullock, III; and for Chapter 6 on Compensatory Education—Richard Jung, Don Burnes, Richard Elmore, and Jerome Murphy. For their encouragement throughout the project, we thank series editors Arnold Meltsner and Mark Moore.

Daniel A. Mazmanian

Paul A. Sabatier

Contents

Implementation
and Public Policy

Chapter 1
An introduction to policy implementation

In 1970 Congress passed and President Nixon signed into law the Urban Growth and New Communities Development Act. It was hailed as the cornerstone of a bold new urban growth policy to lead the nation into the twenty-first century. The act promised a dramatic change in the way communities were organized and allowed to develop, away from the classic cycle of rampant urban sprawl encircling a decaying center city to relatively self-contained, planned communities large enough to support a range of living styles and economic opportunities within their borders. These "new towns" would provide a mix of industrial, commercial, residential, and public facilities and open spaces all sensibly laid out during the planning stage. Greenbelts would surround the towns and density limits would be imposed to limit physical size and population. Through careful planning under federal tutelage, new communities would succeed where so many previous programs had failed; they would achieve both social and racial integration within their borders. The actual construction of new communities would be done by private enterprise, but the federal government would provide financial support, planning assistance, and general guidance. This was to be the beginning of a new positive public-private partnership in all aspects of urban living.

In four short years these dreams were dashed, leaving behind a series of partially begun new communities, many unmet promises on the part of the federal government, recriminations and disappointment on all sides, and, ultimately, neglect of the program by the Department of Housing and Urban Development (HUD). Barely a murmur of protest was heard from Congress.

As citizens and taxpayers we have the right to know how this could have happened. Could the outcome have been different? Can we learn from the experience and avoid similar problems in designing future public programs? These are the challenges of policy implementation analysis.

Separate but equal is not equal under the Fourteenth Amendment of the United States Constitution declared the Supreme Court in its 1954 decision, *Brown* v. *Board of Education of Topeka, Kansas.* In the words of Chief Justice Warren, "Separate educational facilities are inherently unequal. Therefore, we hold that the plaintiffs . . . are, by reason of the segregation complained of, deprived of equal protection under the laws." The implication was profound. The several thousand dual school systems in the South and border states would have to change their deeply rooted and long-standing practice of school segregation. In later decisions, the courts ruled that racially motivated boundary drawings, pupil placements, and other school policies that resulted in segregated schools—techniques used most often in the North which did not have formal dual school systems—also must be eliminated. Ten years after *Brown* Congress passed the 1964 Civil Rights Act, which stipulated, "No person in the United States shall, on the ground of race, color, or national origin, be excluded from participation in, be denied the benefits or, be subjected to discrimination under any program . . . receiving Federal financial assistance." The meaning of the mandate was unmistakable; desegregation in all school systems receiving public funds was to be ended.

Mechanisms were established in the Department of Health, Education and Welfare (HEW, reorganized into the Department of Health and Human Services) to ensure that this provision of the Civil Rights Act was applied to public schools across the nation. Yet it was not until the end of the 1960s—a decade and a half after the historic *Brown* decision and several years after the passage of the Civil Rights Act—that dual school systems in the South were actually dismantled under HEW supervision. Why did it take so long? Why had the law of the land established by the Supreme Court and Congress gone unimplemented for so many years? And what turned the picture around dramatically at the end of the 1960s? In the North, though some strides have been made through private efforts, the full powers of the federal government have never been brought to bear on segregated schools. Why not? What factors are responsible for desegregation where it has occurred and segregation where it remains?

For several years the California legislature turned back bills to provide comprehensive land use regulation and environmental protection for the state's 1100-mile coastline, despite growing public sentiment in favor of coastal protection. While local governments had full jurisdiction over coastal land use, it appeared that these local jurisdictions were unable or unwilling to curtail the rapid spread of urbanization along the coast. In the southern portion of the state urbanization threatened nearly 250 miles of coastline extending from Santa Barbara south through Los Angeles, Orange, and San Diego counties to the Mexican border. Little was being done to keep open for the general public the visual and physical access to the beach. There were few attempts to coordinate home building, commerical and industrial developments, and roads and other services to mitigate their adverse effects, or to protect the state's few remaining wetlands so critical to coastal marine life. In 1972, a coalition of environmental groups brought before the state's voters an initiative that was an interrelated package of proposals for coastal protection, planning, and management. The initiative, Proposition 20, called for establishment of state authority over every proposed development within 1000 yards of the coast and state power to veto any project that would adversely affect the coast or preclude future public usage. It also required that within three years a plan be drawn up for the long-range protection and use of the coastline, spelling out in detail the steps that would be needed to protect the resources of the coast and the type of permanent state authority over the coastline that would be necessary. After a hard-fought battle between the environmental coalition and many businesses, developers, and local interests, Proposition 20 was enacted into law in November 1972.

To this day the Coastal Act stands as the most encompassing, powerful, and innovative land use program in the nation. The Coastal Commissions, established by Proposition 20 to carry out its mandate, by and large have executed their function in an effective and timely manner. Their decisions on proposed developments have shown a sensitivity to environmental impacts, a long-range plan for the coastline was developed true to the protectionist mandate of the initiative, and the Coastal Commissions were reconstituted on a permanent basis by the state legislature in 1976 and have continued to function in a manner generally consistent with the goals of the 1972 Act.

Why was the Coastal Act so well implemented, particularly in comparison with the less successful attempts to implement the new communities and desegregation programs? Are there lessons of a general nature that can be learned from the coastal protection program to help us better understand and improve public policy implementation? We will argue throughout this book and illustrate with these and other case studies that the basic components of policy implementation are the same across most policy areas and that effectiveness of their implementation results from the presence of more, or less, of the relevant factors. We will elaborate on just what those factors are in the following chapter. But first we will sketch out briefly a few general observations on the emerging field of policy implementation analysis.

Who has been paying attention to implementation?

Despite the many obvious differences in the new communities, school desegregation, coastal protection, or any other programs undertaken by government, they share one important feature: Knowing the objectives set for the program by Congress, the Supreme Court, or the president usually gives only a general hint of what will actually be done by the agency responsible for carrying out the program and how successful it will be at winning the cooperation and compliance of persons affected by it. To understand what actually happens after a program is *enacted* or *formulated* is the subject of *policy implementation:* those events and activities that occur after the issuing of authoritative public policy directives, which include both the effort to administer and the substantive impacts on people and events. This definition encompasses not only the behavior of the administrative body which has responsibility for the program and the compliance of target groups, but also the web of direct and indirect political, economic, and social forces that bear on the behavior of all those involved, and ultimately the impacts—both intended and unintended—of the program.

Surprisingly, both practitioners and students of government are only beginning to appreciate the full importance and general characteristics of the implementation process. Scholars outside the field of public administration have traditionally dismissed problems following enactment of a program either as trivial or viewed them in terms of rational and impartial program administration. When objectives were not being met, the solutions sought were thus those of better—more rational, scientific, efficient, hierarchically controlled—administrative systems. This attitude reflected the belief in the constitutionally prescribed division between the legislature's role of formulating policy and the executive's role of doing no more than faithfully carrying out the wishes of the legislature. For most observers of the governmental process the salient issues were those raised at the point of legislative enactment. Nevertheless, in two distinct lines of inquiry, the literature reflected a movement toward a greater appreciation of the importance of policy implementation.

One field of inquiry was that of classic public administration. While there may well have been a period of innocence during which the administration of a statute was viewed as nonproblematic, as simply a matter of handing over a settled legislative decision to civil servants to be carried out faithfully and efficiently, such a view did not long withstand serious scrutiny. On the one hand, a number of important studies in the decade before and after World War II[1] revealed that administrative agencies were affected not only by their legal mandates but also by the pressures of concerned interest groups, by the intervention of legislators, and by a variety of other factors in their political environments. Moreover, during the 1950s and early 1960s organization theorists expressed serious doubt about the degree of hierarchical control in even private bureaucracies operating in relatively stable environments. They identified the now familiar phenomena of subunit loyalty, cognitive limits on rationality, distorted communication flows, and difficulties in monitoring subordinates' behavior.[2]

The second body of theory important in the creation of a distinctive literature on policy implementation was the development of a systems approach to political life.[3] Systems theory allowed policy analysts to break out of the organizational perspective of public administration and start thinking in terms of inputs from outside the administrative arena, such as new legislative and administrative policy directives, changing public preferences, and new technologies. This, in turn, directed attention to what have become the standard questions of implementation analysis: To what extent are the policy outputs of the administrative agencies and the subsequent outcomes of these decisions consistent with the original policy objectives? What effects, in turn, do these outcomes have on subsequent legislative decisions, i.e., on policy feedback and reformulation?

The literature in these two fields provided many of the conceptual and empirical insights upon which implementation research was built. But it was the perceived failure of many Great Society programs of the 1960s, and the related phenomenon of problematic compliance with the Supreme Court's desegregation and school prayer decisions, that provided the essential intellectual, emotional, and financial spur to the investigation of the relationships between pronounced public policies and subsequent administrative performance. Just as much of the best empirical work in the years around World War II had sought to explain the tendency of New Deal regulatory agencies to become dominated by their clientele,[4] so it was the desire to investigate the anatomy of failure which prompted the vast majority of early implementation studies: Title I of ESEA;[5] President Johnson's cherished "new towns in-town" program;[6] job creation programs;[7] and desegregation in the South.[8]

The seminal study of the reasons behind the government's inability to attain its stated policy objective, Pressman and Wildavsky's analysis of the failure of federal agencies to create 3000 new jobs for unemployed inner-city residents of Oakland, California, set the tone for much of the implementation literature to follow.[9] It focused on the factors that were to distinguish the mainstream of implementation analysis from the antecedent literature on public administration:

1.   An explicit concern with policy evaluation as well as with political behavior, with examining the extent to which various policy objectives were achieved as well as the reasons for the performance.
2.   A focus on what Pressman and Wildavsky termed "the complexity of joint action," i.e., the myriad of actors in various public and private institutions involved in the implementation of a decision rather than the more limited traditional concern with the actors within a single agency and its immediate political environment.
3.   A careful analysis of the (often implicit) causal assumptions behind the original policy decision which would have to be met if policy goals were to be attained.

For the scholarly community to give inadequate attention to implementation until the perceived collapse of the Great Society programs may be understandable, but what of the members of Congress and state legislators who presumably have had a long-standing interest in overseeing the programs that they have enacted? Indeed, democratic creed provides that one of the most important checks on inappropriate and ineffective administrative action will be the watchful eye of the elected representative. Some rather extra-ordinary legislators have in fact overseen implementation, especially over legislation which they have sponsored, but most have not. And although Congress has incorporated greater oversight responsibilities within its standing committees in recent years, most members find little payoff in devoting time to the effort. The reasons why legislators fail to oversee remain as valid today as when first enumerated by Scher nearly twenty years ago in his analysis of Congress.[10] Scher points to seven reasons:

> *1. Congressman tend to see opportunities for greater rewards in the things they value from involvement in legislative and constituent-service activity than from participation in oversight activity.*
> *2. Committee members tend to view the agencies as impenetrable mazes and to believe that any serious effort at penetrating them poses hazards for the inexpert Congressman which outweigh any conceivable gain to him.*
> *3. Congressmen who have established mutually rewarding relationships with agency people tend to be reluctant to initiate or become actively engaged in a close review of that agency's affairs.*
> *4. Congressmen tend to view their personal contacts with the agencies as more efficient than committee investigations for serving constituents and group needs.*
> *5. Committee members will tend to avoid agency review if they expect it will provoke costly reprisals from powerful economic interests regulated by the agencies.*
> *6. Congressmen who perceive that gains to themselves can be had by loyalty to the President can be expected to avoid close examination of the performance of agency officials appointed by the Executive.*
> *7. As committee routines become fixed . . . in ways that make no regular provision for agency oversight, in the absence of powerful external stimuli, they [committee members] tend to resist change.*

Furthermore, no recent president has been able to devise an effective system of control over the vast federal establishment which the president ostensibly heads, though several have tried some form of agency reorganiza-tion in addition to planting loyal partisans among the ranks of top department and agency officials.[11] While selective monitoring has been accomplished by the president's White House staff and Office of Management and Budget, these are notable exceptions. Apparently, the reality of being the chief executive of the nation, or for that matter of a state, today, is that there are far greater rewards in promoting new programs than in tending to the far less glamorous task of monitoring ongoing ones.

However, in the face of an unprecedented failure to deliver, which was the case with many Great Society programs,[12] both scholars and practitioners turned their attention in the 1970s to implementation, to an examination of how to devise more efficient and successful programs. While the investigators agreed that there were serious problems in implementation, several different perspectives emerged from the disagreement over how best to analyze the problem.

Critical issues in policy implementation

While we hope to demonstrate shortly the efficacy of our approach to viewing and studying the implementation process, it is important to keep in mind that there is a good deal of divergence in the field over several key issues. We shall therefore identify some leading questions that have arisen and suggest how choices on these issues have tended to direct research in the field.

The relationship between formulation and implementation

Certainly most scholars have assumed that a reasonably clear distinction can be drawn between (1) the formulation/adoption of a policy, usually in the form of a statute or a landmark court decision; (2) its implementation by one or more administrative agencies and perhaps the courts and subordinate/ peripheral legislatures; and, in many recent studies, (3) its reformulation by the original policymaker based in part upon the successes and difficulties of the implementation experience.[13] This view, based on the definition of implementation as the carrying out of a policy decision made by a public authority, is reaffirmed by Americans' traditional belief in the separate functions of legislatures as enactors and administrative agencies as executors of public policy. It is also the approach taken in several studies of the implementation of various innovations by public bureaucracies.[14] Finally, while Rein and Rabinovitz have called attention to the need to distinguish the development of general policy guidelines from their "routine" administration and enforcement, they view these as substages in the implementation of major statutes.[15]

However, the conceptual distinction between formulation and implementation has been implicitly challenged from two sources. The first source is what has been termed the "adaptive" or "interactive" approach to implementation, which emphasizes the adjustments that take place between goals and strategies among various actors throughout the process to the point of rendering the formulation-implementation distinction meaningless. This approach is perhaps best illustrated by Bardach and by the Rand study by Berman and McLaughlin of the adoption and implementation of educational innovations in local school districts.[16] The second and similar challenge comes from Majone and Wildavsky. While they regard as illegitimate any effort by implementing officials to alter basic goals and strategies, they nevertheless advocate a view of policymaking in which goals and programs are continuously modified to adjust to various constraints and to changing circumstances. They state:

> *Policies are continuously transformed by implementing actions that simultaneously alter resources and objectives. . . . It is not policy design but redesign that goes on most of the time. Who is to say, then, whether implementation consists of altering objectives to correspond with available resources or of mobilizing new resources to accomplish old objectives? . . . Implementation is evolution. . . . When we act to implement a policy, we change it.[17]*

This latter view serves as a useful reminder that statutes and appellate courts decisions are elaborated and often modified as they go through the implementation process. Moreover, there may well be occasions when the distinction between formulation and implementation is quite blurred. These include cases in which the original policy decision is so ambiguous as to be vacuous, for example, the legislative directive to "regulate in the public interest," thereby forcing implementing officials to actually formulate a "policy" if there is to be one. Other problematic cases involve those occasions when the formulation of a reasonably coherent policy involves numerous interchanges among courts, legislators, and administrative agencies over a number of years. This has recently been the case, for example, between the Court of Appeals in the District of Columbia and the Environmental Protection Agency in the attempt to develop regulations for initiating formal safety reviews of pesticides.[18] A third type of problematic case involves the gradual evolution of a small experimental program into a major policy innovation.[19]

Nevertheless, there are several reasons why the distinction between formulation and implementation should be maintained. First, the fact that most implementation scholars have made the distinction suggests that the problematic cases are the exception rather than the rule. Second, if we accept Majone and Wildavsky's argument that objectives evolve *continuously* as a result of the interaction among a myriad of actors or as a response to new circumstances, then evaluation of goal attainment becomes impossible. Third, and perhaps most importantly, viewing policymaking as a seamless web obscures one of the principal normative and empirical concerns of scholars interested in public policy, namely, the division of authority between elected public officials (principally legislators) on the one hand, and appointed and career administrative officials on the other.[20]

Moreover, we need not reject the formulation-implementation distinction in order to incorporate legitimate concern with the evolution of policy over time as value priorities change. In fact, the division into three basic stages of *formulation, implementation,* and *reformulation* directs attention to this distinction by focusing on the extent to which the legislature or the court modifies its original policy as a result of the implementation experience. For example, as we shall argue in Chapter 4, an analysis of the implementation of the automotive-related provisions of the 1970 Clean Air Act reveals that the 1977 Amendments essentially retained the original goal of a 90 percent reduction in new car emissions but (1) reduced it to 75 percent in the problematic area of nitrogen oxides, (2) extended the unrealistic timetables in the original legislation, (3) clarified the originally implicit constraints on EPA's efforts to reduce vehicle miles traveled through transportation control plans, and (4) greatly increased the sanctions available to EPA in its effort to convince states to enact automobile inspection and maintenance programs.

Likewise, viewing policymaking as an iterative process of formulation, implementation, and reformulation—rather than a seamless web of continuous evolution—helps focus on the traditional concern with administrative discretion. One can ask such questions as the following:

1. At what substage of the implementation process did the important discretionary decisions occur? During guideline writing by central authorities? During the subsequent processing of cases? As a result of performance gaps revealed by audits, formal evaluation studies, or other feedback mechanisms?
2. Did the exercise of discretion involve efforts to make sense out of conflicting statutory mandates, modification of statutory intent in order to accommodate the objections of important political actors, or the development of policy initiatives in an area on which the original statute was silent?
3. How significant was the discretionary authority exercised by implementing officials? Did it fundamentally modify the basic objectives of the legislation or merely the strategies for achieving them?
4. Were the policy adjustments made during implementation the result of administrators' preferences or a response to court decision or legislative oversight?
5. To what extent were these adjustments subsequently affirmed, modified, or rejected by the original policymaker (usually the legislature) in the course of formal reformulation?

In short, while the formulation-implementation-reformulation distinction may be difficult to apply in some instances, it can certainly incorporate most of the concerns of those advocating a "policy evolution" approach to the study of implementation. On the other hand, obliteration of this distinction jeopardizes the ability to assess both the extent of goal attainment and the distribution of authority between elected and appointed officials.

Criteria and focus of program evaluation

All implementation studies seek to evaluate program performance, though they can differ markedly in the evaluative criteria employed. They can also be distinguished by where they focus on either policy outputs or eventual outcomes (or both).

On the issue of evaluative criteria, most research has begun with the formal objectives enunciated in the original statute or appellate court decision. This is to be expected, given the historical preoccupation of much implementation research with assessing the extent of goal attainment and analyzing the reasons for the inability of major policy initiatives to actually attain their stated objectives. This focus on legal objectives has also revealed their frequent ambiguity and inconsistency and the consequent adjustments that must be made during the implementation process. Finally, in focusing on the original policymakers' intent, one can ask both was the optimum level of objectives attained? and, even if not attained, did the program result in more of those values than would have been the case without the program? The latter approach involves some thorny methodological problems in specifying what might have occurred without the program, but it nevertheless may be precisely the sort of analysis that policymakers need in a world where optimal solutions are few and far between.

Another frequently employed evaluative criterion, particularly in regulatory policy, is benefit-cost analysis. In most cases, the benefits of the program are calculated in terms of the legislation's stated goals, e.g., the effects of reduced pollution emissions on health and property values, while the costs involve both administrative expenses and the time and monetary costs borne by groups being required to comply. While such studies sometimes simply seek to arrive at a net benefit/cost figure, they frequently also compare the present program with an alternative, e.g., deregulation or a system of emissions fees.[21] Although such approaches invariably run into problems of accurately estimating both benefits and costs and of estimating the probable effects of alternative programs, they have the advantage of highlighting explicitly the fiscal constraints which are, at least implicitly, part of most policy decisions.

Finally, studies sometimes use an evaluative criterion largely unrelated to prescribed goals. This may be taken from the researcher's own value preferences, such as the program effects on the poor[22] or from the program's effects on other societal goals. For example, Ingram and Mann suggest that, while U.S. immigration policy has obviously failed to reach its stated objective of stemming the flow of illegal aliens from Mexico, the policy also should be evaluated in terms of its overall effect on maintaining friendly relations with that country.[23]

A second and related topic concerns whether the focus of analysis is on policy *outputs* or the ultimate *outcomes* of a program. On the one hand, Van Horn argues that implementation analysis should only be concerned with measuring the extent to which the policy outputs of the implementing agencies conform to legal objectives—with, for example, the extent to which the Comprehensive Training and Employment Act (CETA) agencies provide jobs for the hard-core unemployed—rather than with the policy's ultimate impacts on target groups, e.g., the extent to which the long-term employment and earnings potential of low-income people are affected by enrollment in CETA programs.[24]

Such a circumscribed approach, however, often precludes some of the most interesting and important aspects of implementation analysis, namely, the adequacy of the theoretical assumptions underlying a program and, in regulatory programs, the degree of compliance by those affected by agency decisions. For example, an inquiry confined to the extent to which various social services were delivered to Aid to Families with Dependent Children (AFDC) recipients under the 1962 welfare amendments would have missed the program's inherently limited ability to achieve its basic goal of reducing the welfare roles because such an inquiry would have ignored the program's inability to affect the number of jobs available.[25]

Of course, there certainly are instances in which statutes make absolutely no pretense of doing anything more than delivering a specific service or regulating a specific type of behavior. But if a statute also seeks to attain an objective, it is entirely appropriate for implementation analysis to ask whether the statute incorporates an adequate understanding of the factors affecting that objective and gives implementing officials sufficient authority to have at least the possibility of attaining it. Many implementation studies make their greatest contributions by revealing the inadequacy of the underlying theory or the limited ability of regulatory agencies to bring targeted groups into compliance.

This wider view is accepted by many if not most people in the field, including Pressman and Wildavsky; Bardach; Majone and Wildavsky; and Browning, Marshall, and Tabb.[26] In fact, there may even be a consensus that implementation analysis should examine both the extent to which major legal objectives have been achieved and any other program impacts—intended and otherwise—which affect the amount of support and opposition to the program and eventually the reformulation process. Furthermore, one might consider the role of formal evaluation studies in the reformulation process, as there is now a fairly extensive and rather discouraging literature on the use made of formal impact assessments in the policy process.[27]

From whose perspective: center, periphery, or target groups?

The implementation of any program involves the effort of some policymaker to affect the behavior of what Lipsky has termed "street level bureaucrats" in order to provide a service to, or regulate the behavior of, one or more target groups.[28] Among the conceptually simplest cases, as it involves a single organization, would be the efforts of a local school board to alter the practices of classroom teachers. Of course, most implementation efforts involve more than one organization, e.g., a city council and local bureaucracies, and many involve more than one level of government. In fact, most implementation studies have probably dealt with the most complex intergovernmental cases, i.e., the efforts of Congress or federal appellate courts to affect the behavior of classroom teachers, local social service caseworkers, or private industrial firms throughout the nation.

Thus the implementation of any program—but particularly those involving many organizations or several levels of government—can be viewed from three quite different perspectives: (1) the initial policymaker, the *center;* (2) field-level implementing officials, the *periphery;* or (3) the private actors at whom the program is directed, the *target group.* From the standpoint of the center, implementation involves the efforts of higher-level officials or higher-level institutions to obtain compliance from peripheral or lower level institutions and officials in order to provide a service or to change behavior. If the program is not working, then either adjustments have to be made in the program or sanctions have to be invoked or the basic policy has to be reformulated. But the basic concerns from the center's perspective are, first, the extent to which official policy objectives have been met and, second, the reasons for attainment or nonattainment. This appears to be the dominant approach in implementation research.

From the standpoint of the periphery, however, implementation focuses on the manner in which local implementing officals and institutions respond to the disruptions in their environment caused by the efforts of outside officials to achieve a new policy. For example, the study by Browning, Marshall and Tabb of the implementation of three federal programs (General Revenue Sharing, Community Development Block Grants, and Model Cities) in ten San Francisco Bay Area cities focuses on the extent to which local political officials and groups used the federal funds to pursue their own goals.[29] Similarly, the Rand study of the implementation of educational innovations dealt primarily with factors affecting the adoption of federally sponsored innovations in local school districts and, even more so, with the manner in which those innovations were modified by local school officals and classroom teachers in order to meet the particularities of their specific situations.[30] Other examples of this approach would include the Huron Institute's study by Cohen and Farrar of the experimental school voucher program in Alum Rock, California, and the analysis by Weatherly and Lipsky of the coping behavior of local school officials involved in the implementation of a Massachusetts special-education law.[31]

Finally, implementation can be viewed from the perspective of the target group—for example, the poor in social welfare programs or sources of emission in pollution control programs. When target groups are the principal beneficiaries of a program, their perspective may be quite similar to that of central authorities: To what extent are the intended services actually delivered?[32] But target groups are likely to be even more concerned with whether the services make any real difference in their lives, i.e., does participation in CETA significantly improve the long-term flow of income? In regulatory programs, the target group perspective is likely to focus on the difficulties encountered in complying with program rules and regulations.

Understanding the perspective of target groups is also likely to be important to central authorities. Such understanding enables them to anticipate political feedback and to be aware of the behavioral assumptions upon which the program is based. For example, a study of welfare recipients in New York City and Chicago concluded that the work-incentive program is based on the erroneous assumption that AFDC mothers do not perceive any negative status to being on welfare and thus need to be prodded into seeking work. While this may be true of some, for many others their expectations of remaining economically dependent result more from past inability to find work or unwillingness to leave small children in day-care centers.[33] In short, the ability to change the behavior of target groups is contingent upon an adequate understanding of their incentive structure.

Detailed case studies of the implementation of local programs or of intergovernmental programs in a few selected areas have been able to combine two or more of these perspectives.[34] Unfortunately, though the ideal reseach design involves both a comprehensive evaluation of the extent to which central objectives are attained and an analysis of the activities and perspectives of central authorities, local implementing officals, and target groups, this is usually precluded by the limited availability of resources for research. When choices have to be made, it would appear that the center-focused perspective is appropriate in those cases when the researcher wishes simply to obtain a general idea of the extent to and the reasons for which official objectives are attained and when the basic policy decision provides reasonably clear objectives and coherently structures the implementation process. But as central objectives become ambiguous and peripheral officials are given more discretion, it becomes more and more crucial to understand the perspectives of the periphery.[35] Likewise, an appreciation of the target group's perspectives becomes critical when the program is based upon assumptions about the target group's motivation.

Conclusion

Keeping in mind the various issues and approaches in implementation analysis, we believe that any thorough implementation analysis must address three major issues:

1. To what extent are the policy outputs of the implementing agencies and/or the outcomes of the implementation process consistent with the official objectives enunciated in the original statute, court case, or other authoritative directive? Are there other politically significant impacts?
2. To what extent were the objectives and basic strategies outlined and anticipated in the original directive modified during the course of imple-

mentation or during the period of policy reformulation by the original policymaker?

3.   What are the principal factors affecting the extent of goal attainment, the modifications in goals and strategies, and any other politically significant impacts?

The emphasis throughout this book is on developing a general conceptual framework within which an implementation analysis focusing on these issues can take place. The applicability of the framework across a diverse range of public programs is illuminated through an examination of five major public programs.

Structure and organization of this book

Chapter 2 presents our framework of the implementation process. It distinguishes three sets of factors that affect implementation: (1) the inherent tractability of the program being addressed, e.g., the amount of behavioral change intended; (2) the extent to which policy formulators legally structure the implementation process by establishing priorities of goals, the assignment of activities and powers to implementing agencies in order to ensure that goals will be accomplished, and the provisions for supportive constitutencies to participate in policy administration; and (3) factors such as the activities of relevant interest groups, the commitment and leadership of implementation officials, and the socioeconomic conditions within which implementation occurs. Such factors are usually beyond the reach of policy formulators but nevertheless are of substantial importance to effective implementation.

In addition to identifying these key variables, the framework subdivides the overall implementation process into five analytically distinct and manageable stages. These stages are: (1) the policy outputs of the implementing agency— what the implementing agency asks or demands of those coming under its jurisdiction; (2) the extent of compliance by those affected—the target groups—with the angency's directives; (3) the perception of agency outputs and the agency's impacts on people and events by both the informed and the mass public; (4) the actual impacts of the program (both intended and unintended); and, finally, (5) the formulators' revisions or attempted revisions of the policy. Following reformulation, the process again goes through the five stages of implementation in what becomes a series of formulation-implementation-reformulation cycles.

In chapter 3 through 7 the framework is applied in the analysis of five specific implementation efforts. The cases were selected on the basis of four criteria:

a.   They vary from relatively unsuccessful efforts (new communities in Chapter 3) to moderately successful efforts (school desegregation in the South in Chapter 5 and compensatory education in Chapter 6) to a fairly successful effort (the California Coastal Commissions in Chapter 7).

b. They vary according to the tractability of the problem being address. The problems range from air pollution, which is an extraordinarily difficult problem from technical, economical, and political standpoints (Chapter 4) to coastal protection and new communities, areas which pose far fewer problems of basic knowledge and size of the target groups (Chapters 7 and 3, respectively).

c. They span programs as diverse as education, housing, aid to the poor, civil rights, and environmental protection.

d. While the programs examined are predominantly those of the federal government, federal-state differences are highlighted with the inclusion of the California Coastal Commissions study.

It is our hope that the amount of detail provided on each case is sufficient both to acquaint the reader with the program and enable useful comparisons across programs. Chapter 8 draws together the lessons of the five implementation efforts both in terms of the utility of our framework and, more broadly, in furthering understanding of the implementation process.

For further reflection ·

1. What theories of politics and power (e.g., Marxist, pluralistic, exchange, bureaucratic, general systems) *most* and *least* emphasize the point that implementation is a very problematic consideration in the policy process?
2. Identify two public programs that in your estimation are being successfully implemented today and two that are not. What are the principal factors affecting that success? How are you defining "success"?
3. It cannot be assumed that persons directly responsible for policymaking are always sensitive to problems of implementation. Find out for yourself. In a policy issue of interest, seek out a state legislator or city council member who helped set that policy and determine how well acquainted he or she is with its implementation—the extent to which policy objectives are being achieved, and why.
4. What attention does the print media give to public policy formation versus its implementation? For a two-week period trace first the number and scope of stories devoted to program enactment, and second stories on the implementation of existing programs. Repeat the exercise for both the *New York Times* (or *Washington Post*) and your leading local newspaper.

Notes
1. Pendleton Herring, *Public Administration and Public Interest* (New York: Russell & Russel, 1936); Avery Leiserson, *Administrative Regulation* (Chicago: University of Chicago Press,

1942); Marver Bernstein, *Regulating Business By Independent Commission* (Princeton, N.J.: Princeton University Press, 1955).

2. James March and Herbert Simon, *Organizations* (New York: John Wiley, 1958); Daniel Katz and Robert Kahn, *The Social Psychology of Organizations* (New York: John Wiley & Sons, 1978); Anthony Downs, *Inside Bureaucracy* (Boston: Little, Brown & Co., 1967).

3. David Easton, *A Systems Analysis of Political Life* (New York: John Wiley & Sons, 1965); Charles Jones, *An Introduction to the Study of Public Policy,* 2nd ed. (North Scituate, Mass.: Duxbury Press, 1977).

4. Herring, *Public Administration;* Leiserson, *Administrative Regulation;* Bernstein, *Regulating Business.*

5. Stephen Baily and Edith Mosher, *ESEA: The Office of Education Administrators a Law* (Syracuse, N.Y.: Syracuse University Press, 1968); Jerome Murphy, "Title 1 of ESEA," *Harvard Educational Review* 41 (February 1971): 35–63.

6. Martha Derthick, *New Towns In-Town* (Washington, D.C.: The Urban Institute, 1972).

7. Jeffrey Pressman and Aaron Wildavsky, *Implementation* (Berkeley, Calif.: University of California Press, 1973).

8. Fred Wirt, *Politics of Southern Equality* (Chicago: Aldine, 1970).

9. Pressman and Wildavsky, *Implementation.*

10. Seymour Scher, "Conditions of Legislative Control," *Journal of Politics* 25 (August 1963): 526–51.

11. Hugh Heclo, *A Government of Strangers: Executive Politics in Washington* (Washington, D.C.: The Brookings Institution, 1977); Richard Nathan, *The Plot That Failed* (New York: John Wiley, 1975); Ronald Randall, "Presidential Power versus Bureaucratic Intransigence," *American Political Science Review* 73 (September 1979): 795–810.

12. A noted exception to the critique of the Great Society is found in Sar Levitan and Robert Taggart, "The Great Society Did Succeed," in *Making Change Happen?* ed. Dale Mann (New York: Teachers College, Columbia University, 1978).

13. Pressman and Wildavsky, *Implementation;* Murphy, "Title 1 of ESEA"; Erwin Hargrove, *The Missing Link* (Washington, D.C.: The Urban Institute, 1975); Carl Van Horn, *Policy Implementation in the Federal System* (Lexington, Mass.: D. C. Heath, 1979); Martha Derthick, *Policy Making for Social Security* (Washington, D.C.: The Brookings Institution, 1979); Paul Sabatier and Daniel Mazmanian, "The Conditions of Effective Implementation," *Policy Analysis* 5 (Fall 1979): 481–504.

14. Richard Nelson and Douglas Yates, *Innovation and Implementation in Public Organizations* (Lexington, Mass., D. C. Heath, 1978).

15. Martin Rein and Francine Rabinovitz, "Implementation: A Theoretical Perspective," Working Paper No. 43, MIT-Harvard Joint Center for Urban Studies.

16. Eugene Bardach, *The Implementation Game* (Cambridge, Mass.: MIT Press, 1977); Paul Berman and Milbrey McLaughlin, "Implementation of Educational Innovation," *Educational Forum* 40 (March 1976): 345-70.

17. Giandomenico Majone and Aaron Wildavsky, "Implementation as Evolution," in *Policy Studies Review Annual, 1978* ed. Howard Freeman (Beverly Hills, Calif.: Sage Publications), pp. 109, 111, 114.

18. Angus MacIntyre, "The Politics of Nonincremental Domestic Change: Major Reform in Federal Pesticide Control Policy" (Ph. D. diss., University of California at Davis, 1980).

19. Ladislav Cerych and Paul Sabatier, *The Implementation of Higher Edcuation Reforms* (Paris: Institute of Education, 1981).

20. Kenneth Culp Davis, *Discretionary Justice* (Urbana: University of Illinois Press, 1969); Theodore Lowi, *The End of Liberalism: The Second Republic of the United States,* 2nd ed. (New York: W. W. Norton & Co., 1979).

21. Almarin Phillips, *Promoting Competition in Regulated Markets* (Washington, D.C.: The Brookings Institution, 1975); Ann Friedlaender, *Approaches to Controlling Air Pollution* (Cambridge, Mass.: MIT Press, 1978).

22. Frank Levy, Arnold Meltsner, and Aaron Wildavsky, *Urban Outcomes* (Berkeley Calif.: University of California Press, 1974); Rufus Browning, Dale Marshall, and David Tabb, "Implementation and Political Change: Sources of Local Variations in Federal Social Programs," in *Effective Policy Implementation,* ed. Daniel Mazmanian and Paul Sabatier (Lexington, Mass.: D. C. Heath, 1981): 127–46.

23. Helen Ingram and Dean Mann, "Policy Failure: An Issue Deserving Analysis," in *Why*

Policies Succeed or Fail, ed. Helen Ingram and Dean Mann (Beverly Hills, Calif.: Sage Publications, 1980), p. 15.

24. Van Horn, *Policy Implementation,* pp. 9–10.
25. Leonard Goodwin and Phyllis Moen, "The Evolution and Implementation of Family Welfare Policy," in *Effective Policy Implementation,* ed. Mazmanian and Sabatier, pp. 147–68.
26. Pressman and Wildavsky, *Implementation;* Bardach, *Implementation Game;* Majone and Wildavsky, "Implementation as Evolution"; Browning, Marshall and Tabb, "Implementation and Political Change."
27. Martin Rein and Sheldon White, "Policy Research: Belief and Doubt," *Policy Analysis* 3 (Spring 1977): 239–71; Daniel Mazmanian and Paul Sabatier, "The Role of Attitudes and Perceptions in Policy Evaluation by Attentive Elites: The California Coastal Commissions," in *Why Policies Succeed,* ed. Ingram and Mann, p. 107.
28. Michael Lipsky, "Street Level Bureaucracy and the Analysis of Urban Reform," *Urban Affairs Quarterly* 6 (June 1971): 391–409.
29. Browning, Marshall, and Tabb, "Implementation and Political Change."
30. Milbrey McLaughlin, *Evaluation and Reform: The Case of ESEA, Title I* (Cambridge, Mass.: Ballinger Publishing Co., 1975).
31. David Cohen and Eleanor Farrar, "Power to the Parents: The Story of Education Vouchers," Public Interest 48 (Summer 1977): 72–97; Richard Weatherly and Michael Lipsky, "Street Level Bureaucrats and Institutional Innovation: Implementing Special-Education Reform," *Harvard Educational Review* 47 (May 1977): 171–97.
32. Raymond Burby and Shirley Weiss, *New Communities U.S.A.* (Lexington, Mass.: Lexington Books, 1976), Chapter 19.
33. Goodwin and Moen, "Family Welfare Policy."
34. Wirt, *Southern Equality;* Pressman and Wildavsky, *Implementation;* Jerry Mechling, "Analysis and Implementation: Sanitation Policies in New York City," *Public Policy* 26 (Spring 1978): 263–84.
35. Paul Berman, "Thinking About Programmed and Adaptive Implementation: Matching Strategies to Situations," in *Why Policies Succeed,* ed. Ingram and Mann, pp. 205–27.

Chapter 2
A framework for implementation analysis

There are two extremes among those concerned with understanding policy implementation. On the one hand are practitioners who want to know about the implementation process in order to decide which levers they need pull to make a program work. Or, if a program is in the design and formulation stage, they want to know which features should be included in a statute or authoritative directive to best ensure goal attainment. For the implementation analyst to suggest, therefore, that what is really needed to attain a particular goal is to overcome longstanding cultural values or basic tenets of human nature is of little use or interest to practitioners. Their view of implementation is an extremely practical and proactive perspective. If the nuts and bolts answers cannot be provided by implementation analysts, then they have little to offer the real world of policymaking.

On the other hand, social scientists are ever sensitive to the fact that much of what occurs in the course of an implementation effort cannot be changed by policy formulators and implementors. For example, the elimination of theft and fraud may require a change in human nature. Elimination of growing world hunger and poverty may require draconian measures of population control combined with a monumental redistribution of wealth and resources among nations. For most social scientists, then, we are captives of social, economic, and political circumstances that may, with concerted effort over time, be mitigated but never fully erased. Their focus is on the broad picture and a search for general propositions about human behavior and social organizations, rather than on the specific levers that policymakers can manipulate in a particular situation.

Good implementation analysts must appreciate both perspectives; they must: (a) be fully aware of the characteristics of the society within which implementation takes place; (b) know the range of access points where formulators and implementors can influence the course of events; and (c) recognize which overarching social and institutional factors in a specific implementation effort cannot easily be affected through present action, and those, such as increasing the resource base of implementors and stiffening the legal sanctions for noncompliance, which are more amenable to short-term intervention.

Our framework for implementation analysis incorporates those basic, yet usually uncontrollable, factors deemed critical by general social system theorists in determining the capacity for, and constraints on, self-conscious social change. Such factors include available resources, economic capacities, technological know-how, and prescribed (constitutional) political rules. A useful way of thinking about these factors is provided in Hofferbert's general systems model of policy formation which portrays systemic capacities/ constraints as a series of narrowing filters through which a policy must travel in moving from conception to actualization.[1] A policy is explained as the result of four general filters extending from the most distant and encompassing historical and geographical setting, to contemporary socioeconomic composition, the beliefs and political behavior of the mass public, and formal/constitutional structure.

The general importance of the several filters is widely recognized. In the words of Eulau and Prewitt, though a community's socioeconomic and other background characteristics may not cause or predetermine policy in a literal sense, nor even be sufficient to "set governance in motion," they do establish the boundaries of possible action. In the broadest sense, then, policymaking is "a purposive response to challenges from the physical and social environment."[2] The limited empirical evidence available suggests, furthermore, that about half of the variance in policy output can be directly accounted for by the four filters identified by Hofferbert.[3] In recognition of their importance, the broad social, economic, and cultural factors are incorporated into our framework through variables such as socioeconomic conditions and technology, public support, attitudes and resources of constituency groups, hierarchical integration (of administrative agencies), and support of agency sovereigns (a chief executive, legislature, or the courts).

A general systems theory approach, however, takes us only so far in understanding the policy process. An adequate understanding of policy implementation must also be based on the contributions which organization theorists and others have made concerning policymaking within those bodies immediately responsible for implementation, that is, public bureaucracies.[4] In particular, it is generally accepted that governmental agencies are concerned not only with legally mandated goals but also with organizational maintenance and survival. And while these agencies want to maximize their autonomy, tension is created by the fact that they are heavily dependent upon external institutions—notably their legislative, executive, and judicial sovereigns—for essential legal and financial resources. Furthermore, in any specific policy area, such as education or pollution control, policy formulation and implementation are normally dominated by a "policy subsystem" composed of the relevant agencies, legislative committees, and interest groups at one or more levels of government, all of which may be more or less tightly coupled.

The work on policy subsystems and on resource interdependencies within them explains the emphasis in our framework on sovereigns and interest groups, as well as on the former's potential ability to structure the behavior of implementing agencies. On the other hand, repeated evidence of "loose coupling" (modest hierarchical integration) within and among the agencies in a policy subsystem contributes to our awareness of just how difficult it is to obtain compliance from "street-level" bureaucrats (lower-level bureaucrats in an agency who are in direct contact with the persons a program is intended to affect), not to mention the external target groups themselves.

Finally, within these broad historical, cultural, and economic conditions and organizational "imperatives," we posit that the energizing force of the implementation process is the rational pursuit by individuals of their desires for power, security, and well-being. Much of the general theory of organizational behavior, from Simon to Downs, is couched in these terms. Working from this premise, Mancur Olson, Jr., has persuasively demonstrated why it is so difficult for large numbers of people to organize in pursuit of their self-interest.[5] And virtually every study of legislative behavior assumes that legislators seeking their own reelection work within the constraints and exploit the resources provided in the legislative arena. The preferences of those having the most direct bearing on the implementation process are incorporated into the framework through variables dealing with attitudes of constituency groups, the support of sovereigns, and the commitment of implementing officials.

A conceptual framework of the implementation process

We turn now to the task of spelling out more systematically the crucial variables affecting the policy implementation process.[6] This begins with a formal definition:

> Implementation *is the carrying out of a basic policy decision, usually incorporated in a statute but which can also take the form of important executive orders or court decisions. Ideally, that decision identifies the problem(s) to be addressed, stipulates the objective(s) to be pursued, and, in a variety of ways, "structures" the implementation process. The process normally runs through a number of stages beginning with passage of the basic statute, followed by the policy outputs (decisions) of the implement-*

ing agencies, the compliance of target groups with those decisions, the actual *impacts—both intended and unintended—of those outputs, the* perceived *impacts of agency decisions, and, finally, important revisions (or attempted revisions) in the basic statute.*

In our view, the crucial role of implementation analysis is the identification of the variables which affect the achievement of legal objectives throughout this entire process. These variables can be divided into three broad categories: (1) the tractability of the problem(s) being addressed; (2) the ability of the statute to structure favorably the implementation process; and (3) the net effect of a variety of political variables on the balance of support for statutory objectives. In the remainder of this section, we shall examine each of the component variables and their potential effects.

The entire framework is presented in skeletal form in Figure 2.1. It distinguishes the three categories of variables (what might be best thought of as "independent" variables) from the stages of implementation (which can be thought of as the "dependent" variables in the process). It should be noted that each of the stages affects subsequent ones; for example, the degree of target group compliance with the policy decisions of implementing agencies affects the actual impacts of those decisions.

Tractability of the problem(s)

Totally apart from the difficulties associated with the implementation of government programs, some social problems are simply much easier to deal with than others. Preserving a neighborhood in Davis, California, from noise pollution is inherently a far more manageable problem than the safe generation of electrical power from nuclear energy. In the former situation, unlike the latter, there is a clear understanding of the technical aspects of the problem; the behavior to be regulated is not very varied (primarily fraternity parties) and involves only a small subset of the town's population; and the amount of behavioral change required among target groups is quite modest. The specific aspects of a social problem which affect the ability of governmental institutions to achieve statutory objectives are discussed below. While each is a separate variable, they can be aggregated—at least conceptually— into a summary index of (inherent) tractability.[7]

Technical difficulties   The achievement of a program goal is contingent upon a number of technical prerequisites, including an ability to develop relatively inexpensive performance indicators and an understanding of the principal causal linkages affecting the problem. While in some cases, such as the elimination of 'dual school systems in the South, the attainment of legal objectives posed few technical problems, this is often not the case. As we shall see in Chapter 4, for example, federal air pollution policy has been plagued by difficulties in monitoring ambient air quality and in relating emissions from

Figure 2.1
Variables Involved in the Implementation Process

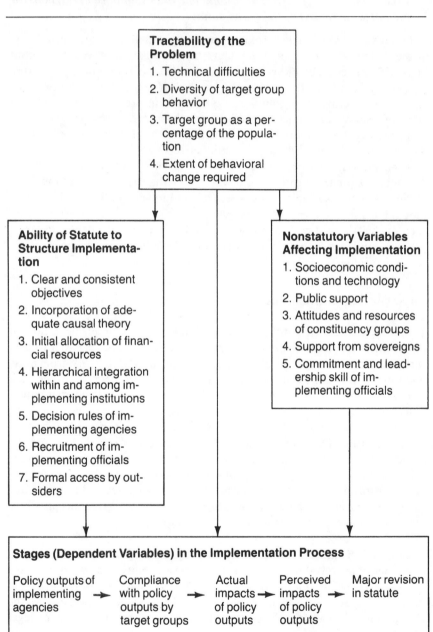

Tractability of the Problem
1. Technical difficulties
2. Diversity of target group behavior
3. Target group as a percentage of the population
4. Extent of behavioral change required

Ability of Statute to Structure Implementation
1. Clear and consistent objectives
2. Incorporation of adequate causal theory
3. Initial allocation of financial resources
4. Hierarchical integration within and among implementing institutions
5. Decision rules of implementing agencies
6. Recruitment of implementing officials
7. Formal access by outsiders

Nonstatutory Variables Affecting Implementation
1. Socioeconomic conditions and technology
2. Public support
3. Attitudes and resources of constituency groups
4. Support from sovereigns
5. Commitment and leadership skill of implementing officials

Stages (Dependent Variables) in the Implementation Process

Policy outputs of implementing agencies → Compliance with policy outputs by target groups → Actual impacts of policy outputs → Perceived impacts of policy outputs → Major revision in statute specific pollution sources causally to ambient air levels and, in turn, to health effects on specific subsets of the population.

Moreover, many programs are predicated upon the availability or development of specific technologies. For example, reduction in sulfur emissions from power plants is contingent upon finding a reliable and relatively inexpensive technology for removing sulfur from coal either before or after it is used in power generation. There has been considerable dispute between the utilities and the Environmental Protection Agency over whether such a technology is presently available. Other social problems beset by serious technological difficulties include pollution emissions from automobiles, the storage of nuclear waste, and agricultural pest control.

The absence of the requisite technology for carrying out new programs poses a number of difficulties for the successful implementation of statutory objectives. First, any program involves costs to taxpayers (in the form of program administration) and to target groups. To the extent that these costs cannot be justified by measurable improvements in the problem being addressed, political support for the program will probably decline and thus statutory objectives will be either ignored or modified. Second, disputes over the availability of the requisite technology will produce strong pressures for delaying deadlines for achieving statutory objectives and considerable uncertainty over the most effective means of encouraging technological innovation—as the problematic implementation of the "technology-forcing" provisions of the 1970 Federal Clean Air Amendments (discussed in Chapter 4) demonstrates.

Diversity of proscribed behavior   The more diverse the behavior being regulated or the service being provided, the more difficult it becomes to frame clear regulations and thus the greater discretion which must be given to field-level implementors. Because of the differences in their commitment to statutory objectives, discretion is likely to result in considerable variation in program performance. For example, one of the major obstacles confronting the implementation of the 1972 Federal Water Pollution Control Amendments has been the extreme diversity in the type and seriousness of discharges from the nation's estimated 62,000 points of major sewage discharge. Such variation makes the writing of precise overall regulations essentially impossible, with the result that regulations for each industry and firm have to be negotiated on an *ad hoc* basis and considerable discretion is left to field personnel in state and local pollution control agencies. On the other hand, there is some indication that this aspect of tractability can sometimes be ameliorated through greater emphasis on economic incentives, e.g., the levying of pollution taxes, rather than the imposition of detailed cleanup regulations.[8]

Target group as a percentage of the population   In general, the smaller and more definable (capable of being isolated) the target group whose behavior needs to be changed, the more likely the mobilization of political support in favor of the program and thus the more probable the achievement of statutory objectives. For example, the successful implementation of the 1965 Voting Rights Act derived in large part from the fact that it applied to a fairly specific set of abuses among voting registrars in only seven southern states. This facilitated the formation of a strong constituency in support of the legislation. In contrast, civil rights measures have been much less successful in dealing with widespread problems such as housing discrimination and *de facto* school segregation. Likewise, the success of the California Coastal Commissions (see Chapter 7) can be partially attributed to the fact that the principal target group (coastal property owners) comprised a much smaller percentage of the state's population than did the potential beneficiaries of the program.

Extent of behavioral change required   The amount of behavioral modification required to achieve statutory objectives is a function of the (absolute) number of people in the ultimate target groups and the amount of change required of them. The basic hypothesis is, of course, that the greater the amount of behavioral change, the more problematic will be successful implementation.

In short, some problems are far more tractable than others. This brief review of the variables involved suggests that problems are most tractable if: (1) there is a valid theory connecting behavioral change to problem solution, the requisite technology exists, and measurement of change in the seriousness of the problem is inexpensive; (2) there is minimal variation in the behavior which causes the problem; (3) the target group constitutes an easily identifiable minority of the population within a political jurisdiction; and (4) the amount of behavioral change required is modest. For example, the success of the 1965 Voting Rights Act in drastically improving the percentage of blacks voting in the South can ultimately be traced largely to the first and third reasons, even though the amount of behavioral change required of southern voting officials was considerable. In contrast, the implementation of federal occupational health and safety legislation has been exacerbated by the extreme diversity of the practices being regulated, the extensive amount of behavioral change required (particularly in small manufacturing establishments), and, to a lesser extent, problems in actually measuring health and safety benefits.

Nevertheless, one should be cautious about placing too much emphasis on the tractability of the problem being addressed. After all, one of the goals of policy analysis is to develop better tools—for example, a greater reliance on economic incentives—for addressing heterogeneous problems which demand substantial behavioral change. It is also conceivable that more adequate causal theories, better methods of measurement, and the requisite technologies can be developed during the course of program implementation. Finally, one of the purposes of our framework is to show how even relatively difficult problems can be ameliorated through a more adequate understanding of the manner in which statutory and political variables affect the mobilization of support necessary to bring about rather substantial behavioral change. It is to an examination of these variables that we now turn.

Ability of policy decision to structure implementation

In principle, any statute, appellate court decision, or executive order can structure the implementation process through its delineation of legal objectives, through its selection of implementing institutions, through the provision of legal and financial resources to those institutions, through biasing the probable policy orientations of agency officials, and through regulation of the opportunities for participation by nonagency actors in the implementation process. In general, legislatures have more potential capacity to coherently structure the process than do appellate courts, although they have considerable difficulty in actually doing so.[9] Nevertheless, our basic argument is that original policymakers can substantially affect the attainment of legal objectives by utilizing the levers at their disposal to coherently structure the implementation process.

Precision and clear ranking of legal objectives   Legal objectives which are precise and clearly ranked in importance serve as an indispensable aid in program evaluation, as unambiguous directives to implementing officials, and as a resource to supporters of those objectives.[10] With respect to the last, for example, implementing officials confronted with objections to their programs can sympathize with the aggrieved party but nevertheless respond that they are only following the legislature's instructions. Clear objectives can also serve as a resource to actors both inside and outside the implementing institutions who perceive discrepancies between agency outputs and those objectives (particularly if the statute also provides them formal access to the implementation process, e.g., via citizen suit provisions).

While the desirability of unambiguous policy directives within a given statute is normally understood, it is also important that a statute to be implemented by an already existing agency clearly indicate the relative priority that the new directives are to play in the agency's programs. If this is not done, the new directives are likely to be delayed and be accorded low priority as they are incorporated into the agency's operating procedures. In short, to the extent that a statute provides precise and clearly ranked instructions to implementing officials and other actors—controlling for required departure from the *status quo ante*—the more likely that the policy outputs of the implementing agencies and ultimately the behavior of target groups will be consistent with those directives.

Validity of the causal theory   Every major reform contains, at least implicitly, a causal theory of the manner in which its objectives are to be attained. In fact, one of the major contributions of implementation analysis—as opposed to simply public administration and organization theory—is its emphasis on the overall theory for obtaining desired changes.

An adequate causal theory requires (a) that the principal causal linkages between governmental intervention and the attainment of program objectives be understood; and (b) that the officials responsible for implementing the program have jurisdiction over a sufficient number of the critical linkages to actually attain the objectives.[11] For example, if the major objective of school desegregation in the South was simply the elimination of dual school systems, then the causal theory was relatively simple and basically involved bringing sufficient incentives and sanctions on southern school boards. But to the extent that the objective was to provide equal educational opportunity to children regardless of race, then the theory became much more problematic both in its cognitive and jurisdictional aspects. Not only was there considerable dispute over the factors affecting—and indeed the means of measuring—educational achievement, but the implementing agencies (principally the Office of Education and local school boards) had practically no jurisdiction over the host of factors outside the schools affecting educational achievement.

In fact, inadequate causal theories lie behind many of the cases of implementation failure. Of the cases discussed in this volume, the following were all plagued by serious difficulties in this regard: new towns, automotive pollution control, Title I of ESEA, and—depending on the interpretation of objectives—school desegregation. In fact, only the California Coastal Act provided a generally adequate causal theory. Even in that case, it did so more for some objectives than for others, and program performance was strongly correlated with adequacy of the causal theory.

Initial allocation of financial resources   Money is obviously critical in any social services program. It is also required in classical regulatory programs to hire the staff and to conduct the technical analyses involved in the development of regulations, the administration of permit programs, and the monitoring of compliance. In general, a threshold level of funding is necessary if there is to be any possibility of achieving statutory objectives, and the level of funding above this threshold is (up to some saturation point) proportional to the probability of achieving those objectives.[12]

The initial (basic) policy decision establishes the general level of funding. An inadequate level can doom a program before it begins. Conversely, an adequate level (as in Title I of ESEA) can help, but not guarantee, that a program gets off to a decent start. But, except in cases of guaranteed funding (e.g., the California coastal commission and the highway trust fund), any program must come back to the legislature periodically for renewed funding. Thus the appropriations process also serves as an important indicator of the degree of legislative and executive support for a program over time.

Hierarchical integration within and among implementing institutions One of the best-documented findings in implementation literature is the difficulty of obtaining coordinated action within any given agency and among the numerous semiautonomous agencies involved in most implementation efforts.[13] The problem is particularly acute in the case of federal statutes which rely on state and local agencies to carry out the details of program delivery in a very heterogeneous system. One of the most important attributes of any statute is the extent to which it hierarchically integrates the implementing agencies. To the extent that the system is only loosely integrated, there will be considerable variation in the degree of behavioral compliance among implementing officials and target groups as each responds to the incentives for modification within their local setting.

The degree of hierarchical integration among implementing agencies is determined by (a) the number of veto/clearance points involved in the attainment of legal objectives; and (b) the extent to which supporters of those objectives are provided with inducements and sanctions sufficient to ensure acquiescence among those who have a potential veto. Veto/clearance points involve those occasions on which an actor has the capacity (quite apart from the question of legal authority) to impede the achievement of legal objectives.[14] Resistance from specific veto points can, however, be overcome if the statute (or other basic policy decision) provides sufficient sanctions or inducements to convince the actors (whether implementing officials or target groups) to alter their behavior. In short, if the sanctions and inducements are great enough, the number of veto points can delay—but probably never ultimately impede—compliance by target groups. In practice, however, the compliance incentives are usually modest enough that the number of veto/clearance points become extremely important. Thus the most direct route to a statutory objective, such as a negative income tax, to provide a minimum income level for all Americans, may be preferable to complex health, welfare, and employment programs administered by numerous semiautonomous bureaucracies.

Decision rules of implementing agencies In addition to providing clear and consistent objectives, few veto points, and adequate incentives for compliance, a statute can further influence the implementation process by stipulating the formal decision rules of the implementing agencies.[15] To the extent, for example, that the burden of proof in permit/licensing cases is placed on the applicant and agency officials are required to make findings fully consistent with legal objectives, the decisions of implementing institutions are more likely to be consistent with those objectives. In addition, when multi-membered commissions are involved, the statute can stipulate the majority required for specific actions. In the case of regulatory commissions which operate primarily through the granting of permits or licenses, decision rules making permit grants contingent upon substantial consensus, e.g., a two-thirds majority, are obviously conducive to stringent regulation.

Officials' commitment to statutory objectives   No matter how well a statute or other basic policy decision structures the formal decision process, the attainment of legal objectives which seek to significantly modify target group behavior is unlikely unless officials in the implementing agencies are strongly committed to the achievement of those objectives. Any new program requires implementors who are sufficiently persistent to develop new regulations and standard operating procedures and to enforce them in the face of resistance from target groups and from public officials reluctant to make the mandated changes.

In principle, there are a number of ways in which the framers of statutes can reasonably assure that implementing officials have the requisite commitment to statutory objectives. The responsibility for implementation can be assigned to agencies whose policy orientation is consistent with the statute and which will accord the new program high priority.[16] This procedure is most likely when a new agency is created specifically to administer the statute, as the program will necessarily be its highest priority and the creation of new positions opens the door to a vast infusion of statutory supporters. Alternatively, implementation can be assigned to a prestigious existing agency which perceives the new mandate to be compatible with its traditional orientation and is looking for new programs. The statute can often stipulate that top implementing officials be selected from social sectors which generally support the legislation's objectives. For example, several studies of state and regional land use agencies have shown that local elected officials are generally more likely to approve developments than appointees of state officials.[17]

The choice of implementing officials is, however, often severely constrained in practice. In many situations, e.g., education, implementation must often be assigned to existing agencies which may be ambivalent or even hostile. And most positions in any agency are held by people with civil service protection. In fact, it is the generally limited ability of program designers to assign implementation to agency officials committed to the program's objectives which probably lies behind many cases of failure to achieve legal objectives.

Formal access by outsiders   Another factor affecting implementation is the extent to which opportunities for participation by actors outside the implementing agencies are biased toward supporters of legal objectives. Just as a statute can influence the implementation process through design characteristics of implementing agencies, it can also affect the participation of two groups of actors external to those institutions: (a) the potential beneficiaries and/or target groups of the program; and (b) the legislative, executive, and judicial sovereigns of the agencies.

In most regulatory programs, for example, the target groups do not have problems with legal standing nor do they generally lack the financial resources to pursue their case in court if displeased with agency decisions. In contrast, the beneficiaries of most consumer and environmental protection legislation *individually* do not have a sufficiently direct and salient interest at stake to obtain legal standing and to bear the costs of petitioning adverse agency decisions to judicial and legislative sovereigns. Thus statutes which permit citizens to participate as formal intervenors in agency proceedings and as petitioners in judicial review (in mandamus actions requiring agency officials to comply with statutory provisions) are more likely to have their objectives attained.[18]

Statutes can also affect the scope and the direction of oversight by agency sovereigns. On the one hand, as we shall see in the case of Title I of ESEA, requirements for formal evaluaion studies by relatively independent observers are probably conducive to the achievement of legal objectives. On the other hand, provisions for legislative veto of administative regulations in regulatory programs probably hinder achievement of those objectives simply because the target groups are likely to be much better organized and to have more incentives for appealing to legislators than are the beneficiaries of regulation.

In sum, a carefully drafted statute (or other basic policy decision) can substantially affect the extent to which its objectives are attained. More precisely, legislation which seeks to significantly change target group behavior in order to achieve its objectives is most likely to succeed if (a) its objectives are precise and clearly ranked; (b) it incorporates an adequate causal theory; (c) it provides adequate funds to the implementing agencies; (d) there are few veto points in the implementation process and sanctions or inducements are provided to overcome resistance; (e) the decision rules of the implementing agencies are biased toward the achievement of statutory objectives; (f) implementation is assigned to agencies which support the legislation's objectives and will give the program high priority; and (g) participation by outsiders is encouraged through liberalized rules of standing and through provisions for independent evaluation studies.

We recognize, of course, that statutes and other basic policy decisions often do not structure the implementation process very coherently. This is particularly true at the federal level, where the heterogeneity of interests effectively represented, the diversity in proscribed activities, the multiple vetoes and weak party system in Congress, and the constitutional and political incentives for implementation by state and local agencies make it extremely difficult to develop clear goals, to minimize the number of veto points, and to assign implementation to sympathetic agencies. Moreover, adquate causal theories are often either unavailable or unincorporated into legislation. Thus, many programs may, from their inception, be doomed to failure or only modest achievements by the intractability of the problems they address or by the inability of the legislature to structure coherently the implementation process. The importance of tractability and statutory variables in explaining program success or failure needs to be more adequately examined than has often been the case in implementation research.

Nonstatutory variables affecting implementation

While a statute establishes the basic legal structure in which the politics of implementation take place, implementation also has an inherent dynamism driven by at least two important processes: (1) the need for any program which seeks to change behavior to receive constant or periodic infusions of political support if it is to overcome the delay involved in seeking cooperation among large numbers of people, many of whom perceive their interests to be adversely affected by successful implementation of statutory objectives; and (2) the effect of changes in socioeconomic and technological conditions on the support for those objectives among the general public, interest groups, and sovereigns. In addition to these changes over time, there is usually variation in the antecedent factors identified by Hofferbert—e.g., historical events, socioeconomic conditions, public opinion—among the governmental juris-dictions in which a statute is being implemented.

The policy outputs of implementing agencies are essentially a function of the interaction between legal structure and political process. Whereas a statute which provides little institutionalized bias leaves implementing officials very dependent upon variations in political support over time and among local settings, a well-drafted statute can provide them with sufficient policy direction and legal resources to withstand short-term changes in public opinion. Such a statute also provides considerable capacity to bring about the desired behavioral changes in widely different local jurisdictions.

In this section we will discuss the major nonlegal variables affecting the policy outputs of implementing agencies, target group compliance with those decisions, and ultimately the achievement of statutory objectives. We will begin with clearly external variables, e.g., changes in socioeconomic condi-tions; move through essentially intervening variables, e.g., attitudes of sovereigns and constituency groups; and deal finally with the variable most directly affecting the policy outputs of implementing agencies, namely, the commitment and leadership skill of agency officials.

Socioeconomic conditions and technology   Variations over time and among governmental jurisdictions in social, economic, and technological conditions affect the attainability of statutory objectives. There are at least four ways in which variation in such conditions can substantially affect the political support for statutory objectives and, hence, the policy outputs of implement-ing agencies and eventually the achievement of those objectives.

First, variation in socioeconomic conditions can affect perceptions of the relative importance of the problem addressed by a statute (or other basic policy decision). To the extent that other social problems become relatively more important over time, political support for allocating scarce resources to the original statute is likely to diminish.[19] Second, successful implementation is rendered more difficult by local variation in socioeconomic conditions and, as indicated previously, in the seriousness of the problem being addressed. Such variation produces enormous pressures for "flexible" rules and considerable administrative discretion by local units. In such cases, the policy outputs of implementing agencies are likely to mirror the degree of local support for statutory objectives. Any attempt to impose uniform standards on jurisdictions with widely different situations will only increase opposition from those who must bear costs which appear unjust. In either case, statutory objectives are less likely to be achieved. Third, support for regulation aimed at environmental or consumer protection or worker safety seems to be correlated with the financial resources of target groups and the groups' relative importance in the total economy.[20] The more diverse an economy and the more prosperous the target groups, the more probable the effective implementation of statutes imposing nonproductive costs on them. The lower the target groups' economic diversity and prosperity, the more likely the substitution of subsidies for policing regulation. Finally, in the case of policies (such as pollution control) which are directly tied to technology, changes or the lack of changes in the technological state of the art over time are obviously crucial.

In short, as Hofferbert points out, social, economic, and (we add) technological conditions are some of the principal external variables affecting the policy outputs of implementing agencies and ultimately the attainment of legal objectives. These conditions are linked to implementation through changes in interest group and public support for those objectives or through the legislative and executive sovereigns of the implementing agencies. Implementing officials may also respond directly to changes in environmental conditions, particularly if they perceive that those changes support their programs or preferences.

Public support   Variations over time and jurisdiction in public support for legal (statutory objectives) is a second variable affecting implementation. Anthony Downs has argued that public (and media) attention to many policy issues tends to follow a cycle in which an initial awakening of public concern is followed by a decline in widespread support as people become aware of the costs of "solving" the problem, as other issues crowd it off the political agenda, or as scandals arise in program administration.[21] Conversely, public support may be temporarily reawakened by dramatic new evidence that the problem persists, e.g., another oil spill or nuclear power accident. The episodic, or perhaps cyclical, nature of public concern creates difficulties for the successful implementation of any program requiring periodic infusions of support from sovereigns, either in the form of large budgetary allocations (e.g., Title I of

ESEA) or protection from opponents' counterattacks (e.g., federal pollution control policy).

Variation among political jurisdictions in public support for a particular program is likely to result in pressures for ambiguous regulations and considerable discretion to local officials—both of which probably contribute to the difficulty in changing behavior in a systematic manner.

The general public can influence the implementation process in at least three ways:

1.   Public opinion (and its interaction with the mass media) can affect the political agenda, i.e., the issues to be discussed by legislatures.
2.   There is substantial evidence that legislators are influenced by their general constituents on issues salient to those constituents, particularly when opinion within the district is relatively uniform.[22]
3.   Public opinion polls are often employed by administrators and sovereigns to support particular policy positions. For example, in 1973-74 the Environmental Protection Agency sponsored a survey to refute the belief that the Arab oil embargo had substantially undermined public support for pollution control measures; when the poll essentially confirmed the agency's position, the EPA used this information extensively in an effort to convince Congress not to weaken the 1970 Clear Air Amendments.[23]

Attitudes and resources of constituency groups   Changes in the resources and attitudes of constituency groups toward statutory objectives and the policy outputs of implementing institutions play a part in the implementation process. The basic dilemma confronting proponents of any program that seeks to change the behavior of one or more target groups is that public support for the program will almost invariably decline over time. Normally, statutes are the result of heightened public concern with a general problem, such as environmental quality, consumer protection, or achievement scores of low-income schoolchildren. Such concern wanes as the costs of such programs on specific segments of the population draw away previous supporters and intensify opposition and the public and the media turn to other issues. The essential—and very problematic—task confronting proponents is translating the original widespread support which helped pass the initial legislation into organizations with sufficient membership, cohesion, and expertise to be accepted as legitimate and necessary participants in important policy decisions by both implementing officials and their legislative and executive sovereigns.

On the other hand, opponents of the mandated change—though they may not dominate the implementing agencies—generally have the resources and incentives to intervene actively in the implementation process. Their organizational resources and access to expertise enable them to present their case effectively before administrative agencies and, if displeased with their decisions, to initiate appeals to the legislative sovereigns, to the courts, and to public opinion. Because opponents can generally intervene more actively over a longer period of time than proponents, most regulatory agencies eventually recognize that if a program is to survive in an unstable political environment, some compromise with the interests of target groups and thus less departure from the status quo than that envisaged by the original statute will be necessary.[24]

Constituency groups interact with the other variables in our framework in a number of ways.[25] First, their membership and financial resources are likely to vary according to public support for their position and the amount of behavioral change mandated by statutory objectives. Second, constituency groups can intervene directly in the decisions of the implementing agencies by commenting on proposed decisions and by supplementing the agency's resources. Finally, such groups have the capacity to affect agency policy indirectly through publishing studies critical of the agency's performance, through public opinion campaigns, and through appeals to the agency's legislative and judicial sovereigns.

Support from sovereigns Sovereigns of implementing institutions provide support for statutory objectives through (a) amount and direction of oversight; (b) provision of financial resources; and (c) the extent of new (i.e., after original statute) and conflicting legal mandates. The sovereigns of an implementing agency are those institutions which control its legal and financial resources. They will normally include the legislature (and, more specifically, the relevant policy and fiscal committees); the chief executive; the courts; and, in intergovernmental programs, hierarchically superior agencies.

One of the major difficulties in the implementation of intergovernmental programs is that implementing agencies are responsible to different sovereigns who wish to pursue different policies. Often, in such situations, when an intergovernmental subordinate is faced with conflicting directives from its intergovernmental superiors and its coordinate sovereigns, it will ultimately lean toward the directives of the sovereigns who will most affect its legal and financial resources over the longest period of time. For example, when a state agency is faced with conflicting directives from a federal agency and the state legislature, primary loyalty is given to the sovereign most likely to affect the agency's vital resources—which, in almost every case, will be the state legislature. In relations between a local agency and its state superiors, however, the situation is not nearly so predictable. Local governments generally have less constitutional autonomy compared with states than do the states compared with the federal government.

Sovereigns can affect the policies pursued by implementing agencies through both informal oversight and formal changes in the agency's legal and financial resources. Oversight refers to the continuous interaction between an agency and its legislative (and executive) sovereigns in the form of formal oversight hearings, consultation with staff and legislators on the key committees, routine requests from legislators concerning constitutent com-

plaints, etc. On the one hand, legislative policy committees become increasingly sympathetic to target groups over time, in part as a reflection of changes
in the balance of interest group support and in part because constituency
casework appears to be weighted toward complaints. On the other hand,
legislative sovereigns who support a controversial program can play a crucial
role in the achievement of statutory objectives if they have the resources and
the desire to do so. Here we come to Eugene Bardach's extremely interesting
concept of a "fixer," i.e., an important legislator or executive official who
controls resources important to crucial actors and who has the desire and the
staff resources to monitor closely the implementation process and to intervene
on an almost continuous basis.[26]

On a more formal level, sovereigns have the authority to alter the legal and
financial resources of implementing agencies. There have, for example been
statutes which have been essentially destroyed by the courts or through the
appropriations process.[27] Legislatures also have the authority to revise
substantially and even revoke statutes; in fact, the first major effort to do so
marks the end of what we have termed the short-term implementation
process. But the most frequent effects may well be of a more indirect nature.
As indicated previously, almost any statute is affected by policies outside its
specific domain. Changes in any of these can strongly affect support for
statutory objectives and/or the number of veto points involved in statutory
implementation. An agency and its legislative supporters must be aware of
these ramifications and make sure that they are explicitly addressed by
(subsequent) legislation. In short, the interrelatedness of policy areas in any
complex society greatly increases the monitoring responsibility of the
protectors of any particular statute and thus the probability that the statute
will gradually be undermined through subsequent tangential legislation.

Commitment and leadership skill of implementing officials   We come finally
to the variable that affects most directly the policy outputs of implementing
agencies, namely, the commitment of agency officials to the realization of
statutory objectives. This comprises at least two components: first, the
direction and ranking of those objectives in officials' priorities; and, second,
officials' skill in realizing those priorities, i.e., their ability to go beyond what
could normally be expected in using the available resources. The importance
of both attitudes and skill will, of course, vary with the amount of discretion
afforded administrators.

The commitment of agency officials will partially—and, in some cases,
largely—be a function of the capacity of the statute to institute a bias in the
implementing agencies through selection of institutions and top officials. It
will also be a function of professional norms, personal values, and support for
statutory objectives among interest groups and sovereigns in the agencies'
political environment. In general, the commitment of agency officials to
statutory objectives and the consequent probability of their successful
implementation will be greatest in a new agency with high visibility which was
created after an intense political campaign. After the initial period, however,

the degree of commitment will probably decline over time as the most committed people become disillusioned with bureaucratic routine and are replaced by officials much more interested in security than in taking risks to attain policy goals.[28]

Commitment to statutory objectives will contribute little to their attainment unless implementing officials display skill in using available resources to that end. Usually discussed under the rubric of "leadership," this skill comprises both political and managerial elements.[29] The former refers to the ability to develop good working relationships with sovereigns in the agency's subsystems, to convince opponents and target groups that they are being treated fairly, to mobilize support among latent supportive constituencies, to present effectively the agency's case through the mass media, etc. Managerial skill involves developing adequate controls so that the program is not subject to charges of fiscal mismanagement, maintaining high morale among agency personnel, and managing internal dissent in such a way that outright opponents are shunted to noncrucial positions.

On the whole, however, leadership skill remains a rather elusive concept. While everyone acknowledges its importance, its attributes vary from situation to situation. Thus it is extremely difficult to predict whether specific individuals will go beyond what could reasonably be expected in using the available resources to achieve program objectives.

Stages (dependent variables) in the implementation process

The discussion thus far has focused on factors affecting the implementation process as a whole. But that process must be viewed in terms of its several stages: (1) the policy outputs (decisions) of the implementing agencies; (2) the compliance of target groups with those decisions; (3) the actual impacts of agency decisions; (4) the perceived impacts of those decisions; and finally, (5) the political system's evaluation of a statute in terms of major revisions (or attempted revisions) in its content. All these stages are often lumped together under the general heading "feedback loop." But there are two separate processes. If one is concerned only with the extent to which actual impacts conform to program objectives, then only the first three stages are pertinent. In our view, however, one should also consider the political system's summary evaluation of a statute, which involves the latter two stages in addition.

Each of these stages can be thought of as an end point or dependent variable. Each is also, however, an input into successive stages. For example, compliance of target groups with the policy decisions of the implementing agencies clearly affects the actual impacts of those decisions. Likewise, the perceived impacts of agency decisions are probably the crucial variable affecting revisions (or attempted revisions) in the statute.

Policy outputs of implementing agencies Statutory objectives must be translated into substantive rgulations, standard operating procedures for processing individual cases, specific adjudicatory (permit, licensing) decisions, and enforcement of those adjudicatory decisions. This process normally requires considerable effort on the part of officials in one or more implementing agencies to provide technical analyses of the manner in which general rules apply to successively more concrete situations and then the actual application of those rules in thousands of specific cases. While most administrative officials can generally be expected to follow legal mandates, some discretion is invariably involved. In many cases—particularly in intergovernmental programs—some implementing officials may be opposed to program goals and thus seek to undermine them.[30] One way to deal with these problems is to issue increasingly detailed regulations to limit officials' discretion. However, such "red tape" has its own costs and may be quite harmful to program effectiveness in cases that require the *active* commitment of street-level bureaucrats, particularly those with professional autonomy.[31] For these and many other reasons, the translation of statutory objectives into the policy decisions of implementing agencies in individual cases is an exceedingly problematic process.

While some discrepancy between statutory objectives and policy decisions is almost inevitable (if for no other reason than disagreements about how general rules apply to specific cases), such differences can be reduced if the statute stipulates unambiguous objectives, assigns implementation to sympathetic agencies who will give it high priority, minimizes the number of veto points and provides sufficient incentives to overcome resistance among recalcitrant officials, provides sufficient financial resources to conduct the technical analyses and process individual cases, and biases the decision rules and access points in favor of program objectives. Conformity of policy decisions with program objectives also depends upon the ability of constituency groups and legislative and executive sovereigns who support the program to intervene actively in the implementation process to supplement the agency's resources and to counter resistance from target groups.

Even under such favorable conditions, however, implementing agencies and the entire political system find it difficult to sustain, over an extended period of time (e.g., more than five years), the tension and conflict inherent in a program that mandates substantial behavioral change. Moreover, as indicated previously, the balance of constituency group support for such a program almost invariably declines over time. For these reasons, we hypothesize that—in the case of such programs—within five to seven years the sovereigns or the implementing officials will (a) change, delay, or ignore the statutory objectives in order to require less change in target group behavior; or (b) reduce opposition through payments of various sorts (e.g., subsidies, tax breaks). In fact, it is probably only through supplementing legal directives with such payments that the policy outputs of implementing agencies can be maintained in a manner consistent with stringent statutory objectives over an extended period of time.[32]

Target group compliance with policy outputs   Although most Americans generally profess to be law-abiding, several studies of compliance with judicial and administrative decisions have demonstrated that, in practice, behavioral compliance is generally related to individuals' assessment of the relative costs and benefits to them of following legal directives. These same studies have suggested that the decision to comply is, in turn, a function of (a) the probability that noncompliance will be detected and successfully prosecuted; (b) the sanctions available to penalize noncompliance; (c) target group attitudes concerning the fundamental legitimacy of the rules; and (d) the costs to target groups of compliance.[33]

In the context of our framework, the probability that substantial sanctions will follow noncompliance is affected by the variety and magnitude of sanctions provided by statute; the resources available to implementing agencies to monitor noncompliance; the ability of constituency groups to supplement agency resources in monitoring compliance and bringing enforcement actions; the commitment of agency officials to prosecuting noncompliance; and the number of veto points involved in actually bringing enforcement actions. With respect to the perceived legitimacy of the rules, the entire literature on civil disobedience certainly indicates that some individuals will risk jail rather than submit to fundamentally unjust laws. On the whole, however, most individuals will modify even behavior based upon deeply held beliefs if the probability that severe sanctions will be invoked is sufficiently high.[34]

Apart from such instances of rule-rejection, however, any program that seeks to substantially modify target group behavior will involve cases of extreme hardship in which the cost-bearers will vehemently oppose rather than comply. It is precisely to minimize the incidence of such debilitating battles—and the possibility that they will result in court suits which endanger the entire program—that police-power programs need to be supplemented by the provision of side-payments.

Actual impacts of policy outputs   Throughout this discussion we have been concerned with the achievement of program objectives. It should now be clear that a statute will achieve its desired impacts if: (a) the policy outputs of the implementing agencies are consistent with statutory objectives; (b) the ultimate target groups comply with those outputs; (c) there is no serious "subversion" of policy outputs or impacts by conflicting statutes; and (d) the statute incorporates an adequate causal theory linking behavioral change in target groups to the achievement of mandated goals.

Although our main concern is the conformity of impacts to legal objectives, there are two other aspects of this stage of the implementation process which merit brief mention. First, the implementation of a statute may—perhaps because of changing socioeconomic conditions or technologies—have substantive impacts not envisaged in the legal objectives. A second important category of impacts concerns long-term changes in the political strength of competing interests. For example, the mobilization of constituencies as part of program implementation can result in the growth of local political organizations which then elect some of their members to local office and eventually change a wide variety of local programs.[35]

Perceived impacts of policy outputs   While policy analysts and administrators may be primarily interested in the *actual* impacts of the policy outputs of implementing agencies, these are often very difficult to measure in a comprehensive and systematic fashion. Moreover, what may be of most concern in the evaluation of the program by the political system are the impacts *perceived* by constituency groups and sovereigns in the policy subsystem. These perceived impacts may lead eventually to changes in the statutory mandates.

It is our contention that perceived impacts will be a function of actual impacts as mediated by the values of the perceiver. In general, we expect a high correlation between initial predisposition toward a statute and perception and evaluation of its impacts.[36] Moreover, in keeping with cognitive dissonance theory, an actor who does not approve of the perceived impacts of a statute will either (a) view those impacts as inconsistent with statutory objectives, (b) view the statute as illegitimate, and/or (c) question the validity of the impact data.[37]

Major revision in statute   Just as the passage of a statute (or other basic policy decision) should be viewed as the starting point for an analysis of implementation, so the revision/reformulation of that statute should be viewed as the culminating stage of the process (although the process may be repeated several times). The amount and direction of changes—or attempted changes—in the legal mandates of implementing agencies will be a function of the perceived impacts of past agency activities; changes in policy priorities among the general public and policy elites as a result of changing socioeconomic conditions; the political resources of competing groups; and the strategic positions of supportive and opposing sovereigns.

In this regard, a few observations are pertinent. First, in the five to seven years after passage of the basic statute, a "fixer" (to use Bardach's term) can play an absolutely crucial role in preventing destruction of—although not necessarily revisions in—an agency's statute. But after ten to fifteen years, it is the balance of constituency forces—and, behind them, changes in social, economic, and technological conditions—which prevail. The reason is simply that any particular fixer, no matter what his or her resources or skill in employing them is, after all, subject to electoral defeat, retirement, or death.

Also, as we have mentioned, because of the declining balance of constituency support for stringent regulatory programs over time and the inability of our political system to tolerate intense opposition from legitimate interests over sustained periods, stringent regulatory statutes will invariably be revised to substitute side-payments for some of the more onerous police-power decisions. The result is, then, that only by mixing distributive with regulatory policies can substantial changes in target group behavior be achieved.

Implementation as a dynamic process

Identifying individually the many varibles involved in implementation is an important first step in understanding its complexity and in developing an appreciation of the enormity of the task of changing the status quo through governmental action. Moreover, grouping variables by whether they are amenable to statutory manipulation helps distinguish between factors that can be manipulated (in the short term) through formulation and design by policymakers. Yet this provides only a static picture.

Bringing the various facets of the implementation process together and depicting it as the dynamic process that it is, is complicated by the sheer number of variables involved and the fact that interaction among them continues throughout the process. For example, the amount of change one hopes to bring about in a target population will affect the precision required in spelling out policy directives, the adequacy of the causal theory needed, the degree of needed public support, the severity of sanctions required, and so on. Each of these factors is linked to the others so that as one changes, there is a rippled effect throughout the system. In a two-dimensional space it is virtually impossible to depict *all* of the actual interaction patterns and the respective feedback loops. However, for illustrative purposes the major components of the picture are brought together in the flow diagram in Figure 2.2, which incorporates each of the tractability, nonstatutory, and statutory variables, and suggests through the use of arrows where each has a major bearing on the five stages of implementation. Though a truncated picture of the process, the diagram suggests the major linkages among variables, the direction of impacts, and the complexity of the overall process. Thus, we find that the diversity of target group behavior that policymakers wish to change, a key tractability variable, has an important and direct bearing on how a statute is to be written; whether it can be general and sweeping in language or whether it must specify a diverse range of activities and prescribe an equally wide range of remedies. Likewise, the figure highlights the direct influence of public support on sovereigns and constituency groups—both of which, in turn, have a major bearing on each of the stages of the implementation process. Finally, the extraordinary influence of a statute itself in shaping the implementation process—through establishing goals, priorities, incorporating a causal theory, providing adequate resources, etc.—is clearly shown through the series of arrows linking the statute with each major phase of the process.

Figure 2.2
**Flow Diagram of the Variables and Stages Affecting the Implementation
of a Statute**

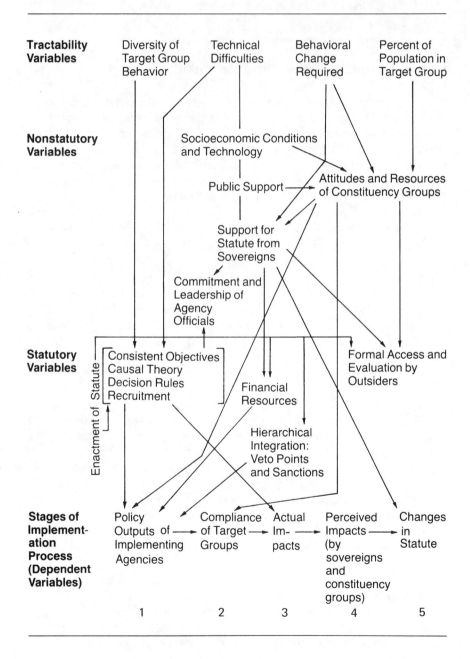

One must keep in mind that the diagram is only suggestive, however. Though not shown, public support also affects the degree of target group compliance and, ultimately, changes in the status quo. Indeed, the entire implementation process, if it is at all successful, will eventually feed back into the nonstatutory and tractability variables affecting, for instance, socioeconomic conditions and the percentage of the population in the target group. Although the implementation process may be difficult to comprehend fully and depict at this stage of our discussion, the dynamic nature of this process should become quite evident as we deal with specific implementation efforts in subsequent chapters.

Six conditions of effective implementation

While the full framework is designed to be of use to both practitioners and social scientists, we recognize that many students and practitioners would also like a checklist of specific factors to be considered in estimating the likelihood that a particular program will achieve its legal objectives. Chapter 8 contains some guidelines for making such "implementation estimates." We also recognize the list of factors to be considered is somewhat imposing. However, the statutory and political variables can be organized into a set of six sufficient conditions of effective implementation. In other words, a statute or other policy decision seeking a substantial departure from the status quo will achieve its desired goals if:

1. The enabling legislation or other legal directive mandates policy objectives which are clear and consistent or at least provides substantive criteria for resolving goal conflicts.
2. The enabling legislation incorporates a sound theory identifying the principal factors and causal linkages affecting policy objectives and gives implementing officials sufficient jurisdiction over target groups and other points of leverage to attain, at least potentially, the desired goals.
3. The enabling legislation structures the implementation process so as to maximize the probability that implementing officials and target groups will perform as desired. This involves assignment to sympathetic agencies with adequate hierarchical integration, supportive decision rules, sufficient financial resources, and adequate access to supporters.
4. The leaders of the implementing agency possess substantial managerial and political skill and are committed to statutory goals.
5. The program is actively supported by organized constituency groups and by a few key legislators (or a chief executive) throughout the implementation process, with the courts being neutral or supportive.
6. The relative priority of statutory objectives is not undermined over time by the emergence of conflicting public policies or by changes in relevant

socioeconomic conditions which weaken the statute's causal theory or political support.

Compared to the original variable list in Figure 2-1, this reformulation combines legal variables 4 through 7 into Condition 3. It deals with problem tractability by arguing that, while "high" ratings on all six conditions will always be sufficient to achieve legal objectives, they may not always be necessary. More specifically, while the first two conditions must always be met at least moderately well and all six are necessary in the case of really difficult problems (i.e., those involving significant behavioral change of a substantial subset of the population against its wishes), fairly low ratings on one or two of the last four conditions may not threaten programs involving less widespread change. This is, however, the sort of empirical issue that the case studies in this volume are designed to help answer. While the issue of problem tractability obviously complicates the utility of this approach, the fundamental implication is quite straightforward: the likelihood that legal objectives will be attained is essentially a function of the extent to which the six conditions have been met.

In practice, of course, all six conditions are very unlikely to be attained during the initial implementation period for any program seeking substantial behavioral change. Policymakers sometimes have only a very partial understanding of the causal factors affecting program objectives. Goal conflict and multiple vetoes in the legislature often result in ambiguous objectives, inadequate financial resources, or assignment to one or more implementing agencies unsympathetic to program objectives. But these legal deficiencies can be gradually improved over time if the program has the strong support of key sovereigns (e.g., legislative committee chairmen) and active constituency groups and if evidence arises that program goals are not being attained. If the legislation was passed in a moment of public arousal but lacked the support of critical legislators and organized constituency groups, then proponents must seek to find a "fixer" among key sovereigns and to organize a supportive constituency if the program is to overcome target group resistance and to adjust creatively to changing socioeconomic conditions.[38]

In short, the list of six conditions can serve not only as a relatively brief checklist to account *post hoc* for program effectiveness or failure but also as a set of tasks which program proponents need to accomplish over time if statutory objectives are to be attained. In fact, the appropriate time span for implementation analysis is probably about seven to ten years. This gives proponents sufficient time to correct deficiencies in the legal framework, and it also tests their ability to develop and maintain political support over a sufficient period of time to actually be able to bring about important behavioral or systemic changes. It also gives the political system sufficient experience with the program to decide if its goals are really worth pursuing and to work out the conflicts with competing values.

Conclusion

In their essay, which was one of the first efforts at conceptual integration of the implementation literature, Rein and Rabinovitz suggested three basic forces or "imperatives" affecting the implementation process: the legal (with its emphasis on statutory intent), the rational-bureaucratic (with its emphasis on workability, consistency, and organizational maintenance), and the consensual (with its emphasis on reaching a *modus operandi* with major interest groups).[39] While our framework has incorporated all three factors, it has placed greater emphasis on the legal imperative than have other conceptualizations.[40] There are at least two reasons for this approach, one empirical, the other normative. On the one hand, we feel that scholars in the so-called behavioral era have tended to ignore the importance of legal variables. Our argument is not with their behavioral focus but rather with their failure to realize that much of bureaucratic behavior may be explained by the legal structure (or lack of such structure) imposed by the relevant statutes. The second reason for focusing on the legal imperative stems from our conviction that, insofar as possible, policy decisions in a democracy ought to be made by elected officials rather than civil servants. Thus, one of our objectives has been to demonstrate the mechanisms whereby legislators and chief executives can formally affect the implementation process through statutory design, as well as to identify the nonstatutory variables which can substantially undermine the attainment of those objectives.

The framework divides the implementation process into five stages and then identifies three groups of independent variables which operate within the context of general causal assumptions taken from general systems theory, principles of organizational behavior, and individual strategizing behavior. Its focus is on the potential for legal structuring of the implementation process and on the need to maintain continuous (or periodic) infusions of political support in the fact of changing social and economic conditions.

For further reflection

1. It has been argued that implementation analysis is simply a new term for public administration. Is this true? Compare the factors examined in one or more of the classics of the administration of public programs [e.g., Philip Selznick, *TVA and the Grass Roots* (Berkeley: University of California Press, 1949); Herbert Kaufman, *The Forest Ranger* (Baltimore, Md.: Johns Hopkins Press, 1960); Pendleton Herring, *Public Administration and Public Interest* (New York: Russell and Russell, 1936)], with the factors enumerated in this chapter.

2. There is more than one view of the best way to conduct an implementation assessment. Compare and contrast the factors emphasized in this chapter with those presented by Eugene Bardach, *The Implementation Game: What Happens After a Bill Becomes a Law* (Cambridge, Mass.: MIT Press, 1977); Carl Van Horn, *Policy Implementation in the Federal System* (Lexington, Mass.: D. C. Heath and Company, 1979); and Richard Elmore, "Backward Mapping: Implementation Research and Policy Decisions," *Political Science Quarterly* 94 (Winter 1979–80): 601–16.

3. Which of the following actors are more likely to have the resources and commitment necessary to serve as a "fixer"? Identify those resources.

   ☐ The president (or governor)
   ☐ Chairman of the legislative committee overseeing the implementing agency
   ☐ A legislator not on an oversight committee
   ☐ The leader of an affected interest group
   ☐ A newspaper reporter or television journalist
   ☐ A district court judge

4. Charles Lave and James March in chapter 3 of their book, *An Introduction to Models in the Social Sciences* (New York: Harper and Row, Publishers, 1975), set forth three criteria for evaluating social science models:

   ☐ *Truth* That they are correct, consistent with reality.
   ☐ *Beauty* This is simplicity of assumptions, yet producing a large number of interesting predictions with interesting implications that are surprising to us.
   ☐ *Justice* That our models contribute to making better worlds.
      a. How would you rate the framework presented in this chapter in terms of the three criteria?
      b. Are there any good rationales for developing a conceptual framework that might not satisfy the Lave and March criteria?

5. Select a public program with which you are familiar and briefly sketch out its underlying causal theory. In your view, how adequate is the theory? Enumerate the principal veto points in this program's implementation. [For an illustration of veto point identification see Jeffrey Pressman and Aaron Wildavsky, *Implementation: How Great Expectations in Washington Are Dashed in Oakland* (Berkeley: University of California Press, 1973), Chapter 5].

Notes

1. Richard Hofferbert, *The Study of Public Policy* (Indianapolis: Bobbs-Merrill, 1974), especially chapter 7.
2. Heinz Eulau and Kenneth Prewitt, *Labyrinths of Democracy: Adaptations, Linkages, Representation, and Policies in Urban Politics* (Indianapolis: Bobbs-Merrill, 1973), p. 506.

3. Daniel Mazmanian and Paul Sabatier, "A Multivariate Model of Public Policy-Making," *American Journal of Political Science* 24 (August 1980): 439–68.

4. Among the major influences on our thinking have been Anthony Downs, *Inside Bureaucracy* (Boston: Little, Brown, 1967); James March and Herbert Simon, *Organizations* (New York: John Wiley, 1958); Daniel Katz and Robert Kahn, *The Social Psychology of Organizations* (New York: John Wiley, 1966); Jeffrey Pfeffer and Gerald Salancik, *The External Control of Organizations* (New York: Harper & Row, 1978); Ronald Randall, "Presidential Power versus Bureaucratic Intransigence: The Influence of the Nixon Administration on Welfare Policy," *American Political Science Review* 73 (September 1979): 795–810; Randall Ripley and Grace Franklin, *Congress, the Bureaucracy, and Public Policy* (Homewood, Ill.: Dorsey, 1976); A. Lee Fritschler, *Smoking and Politics*, 2nd ed. (Englewood Cliffs, N.J.: Prentice Hall, 1976); Karl Weick, "Educational Organizations as Loosely Coupled Systems," *Administrative Science Quarterly* 21 (March 1976): 1–19; Richard Elmore, "Organizational Models of Social Program Implementation," *Public Policy* 26 (Spring 1978): 185–228; and Harrell Rodgers and Charles Bullock, *Coercion to Compliance* (Lexington, Mass.: D. C. Heath, 1977).

5. Mancur Olson, Jr., *The Logic of Collective Action: Public Goods and the Theory of Groups* (Cambridge, Mass.: Harvard University Press, 1965).

6. This is a revised version of the framework developed in Daniel Mazamanian and Paul Sabatier, eds., *Effective Policy Implementation* (Lexington, Mass.: D. C. Heath, 1981), pp. 5–24. In addition to numerous editorial changes, the major modification is the deletion of media concern as a political variable. Throughout this framework, the "target group" will be defined as the private actors at whom the program is addressed. In regulatory programs, they are the objects of behavioral change, e.g., pollution sources. In social service programs, they are the intended beneficiaries, e.g., disadvantaged children in compensatory education programs.

7. By "inherent" we mean inherent in the nature of the problem itself, given technical and practical constraints that cannot be removed through human effort (at least not in the short term). Hence our focus on the availability of a valid causal theory, variation in target group behavior, and so on. We do not include the political resources of target groups, as these are included in the discussion of the political resources of constituency groups. For an excellent discussion of intractable problems, see Richard Nelson, "Intellectualizing about the Moon-Ghetto Metaphor," *Policy Sciences* 5 (December 1974): 375–414.

8. See, for example, Charles Schultze, *The Public Use of Private Interest* (Washington, D.C.: Brookings Institution, 1976); Giandomenico Majone, "Choice Among Policy Instruments for Pollution Control," *Policy Analysis* 2 (Fall 1976): 589–614.

9. Lawrence Baum, "Comparing the Implementation of Legislative and Judicial Policies," in *Effective Policy Implementation*, ed. Mazmanian and Sabatier, pp. 39–62.

10. We suggest that the clarity and consistency of statutory objectives be conceptualized along the following ordinal scale:

1. Ambiguous objectives. These include both meaningless injunctions to regulate "in the public interest" and mandates to balance potentially conflicting objectives, e.g., air quality and industrial employment, without establishing priorities among them.

2. Definite "tilt." This involves a relatively clear ranking of potentially conflicting rather general objectives, for example, "improve air quality even if it results in some unemployment."

3. Qualitative objectives. These involve a rather precise qualitative mandate to, for example, "protect air quality so as to maintain the public health, including that of susceptible populations." Note that this qualitative objective is considerably more precise than that under a "tilt."

4. Quantitative objectives, e.g., reduce automotive emissions from 1970 levels by 90 percent by December 31, 1975.

11. For analysis of different conceptualizations of causal theory, see Paul Sabatier and Dan Mazmanian, "Policy Implementation," in *The Encyclopedia of Policy Studies*, ed. Stuart Nagel (New York: Marcel Dekker, 1982).

12. Determining what constitutes adequate financial resources is, however, extremely difficult, except to note that it must be related to the seriousness of the problem(s) to be addressed (with per capita expenditures often used as a very crude indicator).
13. See, for example, Jeffrey Pressman and Aaron Wildavsky, *Implementation,* 2d ed. (Berkeley: University of California Press, 1979), chapter 5; Eugene Bardach, *The Implementation Game* (Cambridge, Mass.: MIT Press, 1977), chapters 2, 7; Elmore, "Organizational Models of Social Program Implementation," pp. 199–216; and Paul Berman, "Macro- and Micro-Implementation," *Public Policy* 26 (Spring 1978): 165–79.
14. In calculating the number of veto points, one should distinguish (1) the principal implementing agencies (those which are clearly and explicitly assigned a major role); (2) the secondary implementating agencies (those which can intervene on specific issues); and (3) the target groups. In federal pollution control policy, for example, the first would involve federal, state, and local pollution control agencies; the second would include a variety of land use, transportation, and energy agencies, as well as the federal and state attorney generals (in enforcement actions); and the third would include not only the major sources, e.g., steel mills, but also their unions and suppliers of critical equipment and production resources. Moreover, one needs to sum up the number of clearance points involved in (a) the development of general rules and operating procedures; (b) the disposition of specific cases; and (c) the enforcement of those decisions. It does not take much imagination to realize that the number can become truly staggering. For example, Pressman and Wildavsky counted about seventy clearance points in the EDA public works projects in Oakland, and our analysis of the implementation of the public access requirements of the 1972 California Coastal Initiative (see chapter 7) revealed a minimum of seven major decision points involving nine different institutions in order to open a coastal access or park.
15. On the importance of decision rules, see James Buchanan and Gordon Tullock, *The Calculus of Consent* (Ann Arbor: University of Michigan Press, 1972); and Charles Wright, "A Note on the Decision Rules of Public Regulatory Agencies," *Public Choice* 31 (Fall 1977): 151–55.
16. Downs, *Inside Bureaucracy,* chapter 3. For an example in which choice of the principal implementing agency was a major issue, see Zigurd Zile, "A Legislative-Political History of the Coastal Zone Management Act of 1972," *Coastal Zone Management Journal* 1 (1974): 235–74.
17. Judy Rosener with Sally Russell and Dennis Brehn, *Environmental vs. Local Control: A Study of the Voting Behavior of Some California Coastal Commissions* (Irvine: University of California, 1977).
18. James W. Wilson, "The Politics of Regulation," in *Social Responsibility and the Business Predicament,* ed. James McKie (Washington, D.C.: Brookings Institution, 1974), 135–68; Paul Sabatier, "Social Movements and Regulatory Agencies," *Policy Science* 6 (Fall 1975); 301–42; Karen Orren, "Standing to Sue: Interest Group Conflict in the Federal Courts," *American Political Science Review* 70 (September 1976): 723–41.
19. For example, the Arab oil boycott of 1973–74 undermined support for implementation of the 1970 Clear Air Amendments as both the general public and political elites became more aware of the effects air pollution control measures had on, for example, increased consumption of natural gas by utilities and the adverse impacts of automotive emission control on gasoline mileage.
20. For the relationship between economic diversity and ability to withstand perturbation (or, in the case of regulation, nonproductive costs), see Jane Jacobs, *The Economy of Cities* (New York: Vintage, 1970).
21. Anthony Downs, "Up and Down with Ecology—The Issue-Attention Cycle," *Public Interest,* Summer 1972, pp. 38–50.
22. Warren Miller and Donald Stokes, "Constituency Influence in Congress," *American Political Science Review* 57 (March 1963): 45–56; Charles Backstrom, "Congress and the Public," *American Politics Quarterly* 4 (October 1977): 411–35.
23. Joseph Viladas Co., *The American People and Their Environment,* A Report to the Environmental Protection Agency (Springfield, Va.: NTIS, 1973).
24. For the general argument, see Marver H. Bernstein, *Regulating Business by Independent Commission* (Princeton: Princeton University Press, 1955), Chapters 3–8.
25. Constituency groups can supplement an agency's resources by providing technical data and by helping to monitor compliance. See B. Guy Peters, "Insiders and Outsiders: The Politics

of Pressure Group Influence on Bureaucracy," *Administration and Society* 9 (August 1977): 191-218; Sabatier, "Social Movements and Regulatory Agencies," pp. 301-42.
26. Bardach, *The Implementation Game,* pp. 268–83.
27. Peter Woll, *American Bureaucracy* (New York: Norton, 1963), pp. 39–40. In general, however, courts are reluctant to overturn agency decisions.
28. Bernstein, *Regulating Business,* chapter 3; Downs, *Inside Bureaucracy,* chapters 2, 16.
29. For discussions of leadership and illustrations of its importance, see Frances Rourke, *Bureaucracy, Politics, and Public Policy,* 2d ed. (Boston: Little, Brown, 1976), pp. 94–101; Martin Levin, "Conditions Contributing to Effective Implementation and Their Limits," *1980 Proceedings of the Association of Public Policy Analysis and Management.*
30. See Carl Van Horn, *Policy Implementation in the Federal System* (Lexington: Heath, 1979); Helen Ingram, "Policy Implementation Through Bargaining: The Case of Federal Grants-In-Aid," *Public Policy* 25 (Fall 1977): 499–526; Christa Altenstetter and James Bjorkman, *Implementation of a Federal-State Health Program* (Berlin: International Institute of Management, 1977); Robert Thomas, "Intergovernmental Coordination in the Implementation of National Air and Water Pollution Policies," in *Public Policy Making in a Federal System,* ed. Charles Jones and Robert Thomas (Beverly Hills, Calif.: Sage, 1976), pp. 129–48.
31. Berman, "Macro- and Micro-Implementation," pp. 165–69; Richard Elmore, *Complexity and Control: What Legislators and Administrators Can Do about Implementing Public Policy* (Washington, D.C.: National Institute of Education, August 1980).
32. The response to the 1970 Clean Air Amendments has, for example, involved both actions: the deadlines for achieving the auto emission reductions have been repeatedly delayed, while payments have included tax credits and low-interest loans for the purchase of pollution and control equipment. Although such subsidies are generally criticized by economists for their inefficient allocation of resources, they are also fully in keeping with what Charles Schultze has termed the "no direct harm" rule of American politics. See Schultze, *The Public Use of Private Interest,* pp. 70–72.
33. Rodgers and Bullock, *Coercion to Compliance,* Chapter 1. See also the relative merits of penalties and incentives in *Law and Policy Quarterly* 2 (January 1980): 3–128. Nelson Rosenbaum and Michael Fix, *Enforcing State Land Use Controls* (Washington, D.C.: Urban Institute Working Paper 1236-01, September 1977); Don Brown and Robert Stover, "Court Directives and Compliance: A Utility Approach," *American Politics Quarterly* 5 (October 1977): 465–80.
34. For example, southern school districts failed to comply with desegregation orders for years, but compliance was achieved in a short period of time when administrative authority was vested in a specific agency and when the 1964 Civil Rights Act and a 1969 court decision enabled officials of that agency to bring very severe sanctions to bear on local districts—specifically, loss of about 67 percent of their total funding (Rodgers and Bullock, *Coercion to Compliance,* chapters 2–4.) Moreover, individual parents complied even though many continued to view desegregation rules as illegitimate; see Douglas Gatlin, Michael Giles, and Everett Cataldo, "Policy Support Within a Target Group: The Case of School Desegregation," *American Political Science Review* 72 (September 1978): 985–95.
35. Rufus Browning and Dale Marshall, "Implementation of Model Cities and Revenue Sharing in Ten Bay Area Cities," in *Policy Making in a Federal System,* ed. Jones and Thomas, pp. 191–216.
36. For evidence in support of this position, see Daniel Mazmanian and Paul Sabatier, "The Role of Attitudes and Perceptions in Policy Evaluation by Attentive Elites: The California Coastal Commissions," in *Why Policies Succeed or Fail,* by Helen Ingram and Dean Mann, Vol. 8 of Sage Yearbook in Politics and Public Policy (Beverly Hills, Calif.: Sage, 1980).
37. For example, about 60 percent of southern school officials who viewed the anticipated impacts of school desegregation as undesirable justified their noncompliance on the grounds that the federal court orders were illegitimate (Rodgers and Bullock, *Coercion to Compliance,* pp. 70–74). For a general review of cognitive dissonance, see Roger Brown, *Social Psychology* (New York: Macmillan, 1965), pp. 584–604.
38. For a slightly more extended discussion of strategies to meet initial program deficiencies, see Paul Sabatier and Daniel Mazmanian, "The Conditions of Effective Implementation," *Policy Analysis* 5 (Fall 1979): 502–4.
39. Martin Rein and Francine Rabinovitz, *Implementation: A Theoretical Perspective,*

Working Paper No. 43 (Cambridge, Mass.: Joint Center for Urban Studies, March 1977), p. 39.

40. See, for example, Bardach, *The Implementation Game;* Donald Van Meter and Carl Van Horn, "The Policy Implementation Process: A Conceptual Framework," *Administration and Society* 6 (February 1975): 445–88; Carl Van Horn, *Policy Implementation in the Federal System* (Lexington, Mass.: D. C. Health, 1979) chapter 1; Paul Berman, "The Study of Macro- and Micro-Implementation," *Public Policy* 26 (Spring 1978): 1957–84; and Paul Berman, "Thinking about Programmed and Adaptive Implementation: Matching Strategies to Situations," in *Why Policies Succeed or Fail,* ed. Ingram and Mann (Beverly Hills: Sage, 1980) pp. 205-27. For a brief review and critique of much of this literature, see Mazmanian and Sabatier, eds., *Effective Policy Implementation,* pp. 4–5. For a review of much of the case study literature, see Robert K. Yin, *Studying the Implementation of Public Programs* (Golden, Colo.: Solar Energy Research Institute, January 1980).

Chapter 3
New communities:
the promise unfulfilled

The basic idea was a very simple and compelling one. Assuming that the dilapitated state of mid-twentieth century American cities is the result of 200 years of more-or-less incremental, generally unplanned expansion, driven primarily by the dictates of commerce and industry, the logical solution to the urban problems created is an entirely new approach to urban living—a holistic approach that would detail a *de novo* preplanned, carefully considered and developed series of new communities (or, as they came to be known, new towns) across the land. Under this new approach community size and growth would be closely regulated and a better balance between the competing needs of residential and commercial uses and human development, environmental protection, cultural amenities, and recreation would be sought. Towns developed under the new plan would provide comprehensive and efficient transportation both within and between communities and, finally, if managed properly, would promote both racial and class integration.

This new approach was the latest in a long, though largely unsuccessful, history of plans to develop freestanding communities in the United States ranging from colonial Philadelphia and Williamsburg to the Mormon settlement at Salt Lake to industrial towns such as Pullman. During the decades of the twentieth century, however, especially during the post-World War II era, growth centered in and around the thirty or so major metropolitan areas of the nation, and memories of the past plans for new communities faded. The idea of new communities received renewed attention in the 1960s, however, for several reasons. First was the growing dissatisfaction with American's urban centers and interrelated health, crime, employment, education, and other urban problems that were not easily solvable, especially under the existing social, political, and economic conditions. Not only were these problems difficult to solve, but solutions attempted by the federal government were often frustrated by the failure of local governments to appreciate the effort as well as to coordinate solutions among themselves. Second was the suburbanization that occurred when 60 million Americans (approximately one third of the population) moved from the center-cities to the surrounding suburbs in the two decades following World War II.[1] The suburbs, while mostly planned subdivisions, were not designed as freestanding communities; rather, they served as bedroom and commuter communities surrounding the decaying commercial and industrial centers of the nation. They provided an escape for the white middle classes who could afford to move to them, but the escape proved to be shortlived. Contiguous to the older centers and soon penned in on all sides by similar bedroom communities, the suburbs soon encountered many of the same problems of transportation, pollution, education, and intergovernmental coordination plaguing the older cities. With their checkerboard and uncoordinated pattern of construction, limited political jurisdiction, and inability to affect the broader urban setting, they too were incapable of solving such problems. Third, and most distressing to many who looked to the near future, was the forecast by demographers that by the last quarter of the twentieth century the United States would have to absorb an additional 75 million people. Naturally, this one-third increase in population would add to the need for adequate housing, jobs, and recreation. If unrestrained, such a rise in population would inevitably increase the pressures on the already overtaxed metropolitan centers.

The professional planning community added a fourth reason for the renewed interest in new communities. Many planners believed that after a century of unremitting urban sprawl the time was ripe for launching a nationwide program of well-conceived, balanced, and integrated, new communities. The total community approach, in which planning would start from the ground up, would enable both policymakers and citizens to overcome the traditional and ineffectual piecemeal approach to the social, economic, and political problems facing urban America. Most urban planners thought a publicly sponsored new communities program would draw off at least some of the pressures associated with the anticipated population increase and the pressures that would be added on services in the existing urban centers. Urban planners also expected to establish the viability of new communities, which would be a model for community development into the twenty-first century.

These beliefs gained prominence in the late 1960s with release of a series of reports from planning organizations such as the American Institute of Planners, the Advisory Commission on Intergovernmental Relations (ACIR) and the National Committee on Urban Growth Policy. The reports called for large-scale government financing and management of new communities as at least a partial cure to the urban crisis. In the aftermath of widespread rioting in many cities and growing disillusionment with many of

President Johnson's Great Society urban programs, new communities appeared as an attractive alternative. The perceived success of a new towns policy in Britain after World War II that had resulted in twenty-two new communities led American planners to believe that with the proper level of government support, such a program could be replicated on a large-scale basis in the United States. According to urbanologist Eric Stowe, the British experience was extremely important in influencing the thinking of planners because it supposedly showed the great potential of preplanned, national government-sponsored intervention into what had been the purview of the market and local government. It also demonstrated to American planners the importance of the two factors critical to the success of a new towns effort:

> *First, the incorporation of an open-ended level of public financial support which would enable the pursuit of the ambitious goals of creating a series of totally new cities emphasizing a high "quality of urban environment"; secondly, assumption of a degree of national control which could coordinate urban development and avoid the adverse side effects of the ad hoc nature of the highly fragmented, uncoordinated conventional building industry.[2]*

As we will see, the failure of the new communities program in the United States in the 1970s is closely linked to the failure to satisfy either of these conditions.

Finally, the new towns idea gained attention because of the highly acclaimed experience of the two privately developed truly new communities of the 1960s—Reston, Virginia, and Columbia, Maryland. Both developments combined centrally planned, innovative architectural and spatial design to create attractive, well-planned, and, despite some financial setbacks, thriving living environments. They were roundly applauded as "the best of everything . . . [capable of] transforming not just the physical landscape, but the human affairs of millions of Americans as well."[3] James Rouse, developer of Columbia and outspoken new communities advocate, captured the mood of proponents in his lament that:

> *"suburban sprawl—i.e., the unplanned, polynucleated agglomerations of residential, commercial, and industrial land-uses—is an irrational process which produces "noncommunities . . . formless places without order, beauty or reason, places with no visible respect for people or the land."[4]*

His recommended alternative was adoption of the new communities concept as national urban policy.

Although nearly everyone could agree on the problem—urban sprawl— and could agree in concept, at least, on what would be a major contribution to the solution—new communities—a precise definition of a new community, in contrast to a traditional subdivision or extension of sprawl, was more difficult to come by. Probably the best definition came from a 1968 ACIR report:

A New Town is an independent, relatively self-contained, planned community of a size large enough to support a range of housing types and to provide economic opportunities within its borders for the employment of its residents. It is large enough to support a balanced range of public facilities and social and cultural opportunities. It is surrounded by a green belt of open space which serves to limit its size within a predetermined range regarding both population and area. Within reasonable limits the proportions of total area to be used for industrial, commerical, residential, public facilities, and open spaces are specified during the planning process. . . . New Towns are started on previously undeveloped land and are built by staged development over a period of time.[5]

Of course, federal, state, and local governments have been intimately involved in community development from the outset of the nation. Involvement has sometimes been indirect through, for example, such transportation programs as the canal building and railroad subsidization of the nineteenth century and, more recently, construction of the interstate highway system, which obviously has a large bearing on where communities will be located. Indeed, almost every major domestic government program, be it in education, health care, housing, zoning, or land-use, affects the nature and quality of urban life. By one recent count, there are more than 500 major domestic programs affecting the urban environment, and over 70 of them explicitly relate to housing and are administered by the Department of Housing and Urban Development (HUD).[6] The many government programs administered by local, state, and federal agencies provide assistance in each of their specific program areas, yet, unfortunately, the programs are often at cross-purposes and, in aggregate, seem to contribute to the unplanned and often chaotic problems called urban sprawl. This is clearly one case where the whole (of government aid) is far less than the sum of its parts. Greater coordination was needed before any concerted government effort to correct the multiple problems of urban America could hope to be successful.

New communities were hailed as a way of accomplishing this objective. They were professionally planned, coordinated among all relevant public and private parties in advance, moderately sized, self-contained, attractive, socially and racially integrated, and included sufficient business and industry. By moving away from the traditional pattern of urban growth and starting anew, they would break with the past unsuccessful approaches to solving urban problems. As a result, many social and economic problems of twentieth-century urban society would be resolved.

Attempts to develop a new communities program

Thus the impetus to federal action was provided both by the acknowledged failure of incremental urban growth and by the perceived success of the British model of government-sponsored new towns. The dominant characteristics of the British model were public financial support to create totally new communities and sufficient central government management and control to overcome the highly balkanized, uncoordinated, and locally controlled conventional development pattern. However, the nature of the American political tradition is such that policymakers were only able to adopt the goals of the British plan, without providing for the levels of government control and expenditure necessary for effective implementation.[7]

The Americn new communities program began on a small scale in 1965 when President Johnson, who had initiated a variety of housing and social programs to revitalize urban communities, called for a federal mortgage insurance program for land acquisition for new communities and aid to state land development agencies for land acquisition, installation of facilities, and resale to private developers. These proposals were ultimately amended and passed in 1966 as Title X of the National Housing Act, which empowered the secretary of HUD to insure loans of up to $25 million to private developers for new community development. The act, however, included no other incentives to private developers and the loan insurance was not attractive enough to induce private capital to participate in the program. The lack of private participation can be attributed to a combination of factors, including the tight money market of 1965–67, the high financial risk inherent in the creation of entirely new communities, the reluctance of private developers to provide for racial and economic integration as required by the federal government, and the unwillingness of local governments to allow the creation of whole new political entities.[8] In fact, no loans were ever insured under Title X.

Nevertheless, committed to the new towns concept, in 1967 Johnson again tried to initiate a new community policy by diverting funds already appropriated for various community development purposes within HUD to the development of new communities *within existing urban centers* on government-owned land. Johnson hoped that these "new-towns-in-town," though they diverged from the original ideal, would demonstrate the feasibility of new communities to private developers and would provide desperately needed good housing within urban centers. Unfortunately, the program was killed by opposition from local political leaders who saw creation of a new community within their jurisdiction as a political threat. After a fairly extensive examination of the several unsuccessful efforts initiated by Johnson's special task force to promote the new-towns-in-town, Martha Derthick concluded that a good deal of the opposition probably could have been circumvented if HUD had paid proper attention to local politicians.[9] However, since this was an executive program, it had no regular staff or resources of its own, either in the White House or at HUD, and relied heavily on the endorsement of the president for its political security. As presidential interest waned, so did the program, until it was quietly abandoned in 1968.

By 1968 only two large subdivisions had been completed and not a single new community project was in progress under the existing program. In response to this situation. Congressman Thomas Ashley (Dem., Ohio) initiated another call for a national urban policy by introducing legislation specifically designed to address the problems of new community development. He began with the premise the new community developers face a broad range of problems that conventional developers do not. First, the building of an organically whole community is a concept alien to the development industry. Few developers have attempted it successfully, and those who have tried it have been forced to adopt a trial and error approach that required considerable financial backing. There is no proven method of success to guide developers of new communities. Thus, while returns on new community development are potentially quite high, there must be a wide financial margin for error. Second, initial "front-end" costs for a new community are enormous. Large-scale land acquisition,[10] site preparation, provision of a public services infrastructure, debt maintenance, and overhead all require tremendous capital outlay with no prospect of any financial return until several years after project initiation. The paucity of "patient capital," or investment money willing to wait for payment of both interest and principal until development reached a profitable point, was perceived as the greatest stumbling block to private development of new communities. Few investors are willing or able to commit the tremendous amount of cash needed for new community development at such high stakes. One developer estimated overhead costs at $10,000 a day (in 1970 dollars). Land acquisition costs for one project could easily reach $50 million, while installment of site improvements guaranteed a negative cash flow for at least five years after the project started.[11] In his bill, Congressman Ashley presented an innovative proposal for private financing. The government would guarantee $50 million worth of bonds and indentures. Thus, private investors previously unwilling to risk loans to new community developers at the market interest rate would now be given an incentive to financing developers. Terms set would recognize the lag between investment and returns. Such an arrangement, it was thought, would substantially enlarge the pool of available private capital. Also, with the federal guarantee, small developers who would not normally qualify for substantial loans in the private market could participate in the program, which was supposed to encourage innovation and was in keeping with the social objectives of the National Housing Act.

The loan guarantee program was intended to cover most of the costs of land acquisition and the initial provision of a public services infrastructure. However, development of a good infrastructure would be extremely expensive and returns on investment would be marginal. First, public services must be provided to new community residents from the outset. Schools must be built and sewers installed to accommodate maximum residency capacity, although maximum capacity would not be reached for ten years or more. Provision of these services is traditionally the responsibility of local government, which is usually unprepared to make the financial commitment required unless it has a large tax base from which revenues can be raised. Second, one of the attractions of a new community was to be the centralization and superior quality of its public services. Local governments, saddled with the burden of financing superior public services for a community not yet inhabited found this prospect both politically and economically unappealing.

The Ashley bill attempted to solve this problem by offering a supplementary grant program as an incentive to local government agencies. Fifty percent categorical grants normally available to local governments would be supplemented by up to an additional 20 percent. In total, up to 70 percent of the cost of infrastructure would be borne by the federal government. Supporters of the bill viewed the application of supplementary grants to three grant programs as a modest step toward the ultimate goal of supplementing all categorical grants to new communities. The Ashley bill was passed as Title IV of the 1968 Housing and Community Development Act.

Only four communities were launched under Title IV: Jonathan, Minnesota; St. Charles, Maryland; Park Forest South near Chicago; and Flower Mound, Texas. Title IV failed to stimulate the anticipated new community growth for several reasons. To begin with, the program was to be implemented through the Office of New Community Development (ONCD) within HUD, yet the statute did not include any provisions for organization of the program or guidelines by which ONCD could make allocation decisions. Since Congress had not provided resources for a separate staff, the program assumed a low priority within the HUD bureaucracy. These factors, combined with the change to a Republican administration in 1969, ensured that the program, understaffed and without adequate resources, was largely ignored. Also, few developers participated in the program, partly because of the apparent chaos within HUD, and more significantly, because of the adverse economic conditions during 1969–70, which made it difficult for developers to raise necessary funds even with a government guarantee. Furthermore, money for supplemental grants was never appropriated and local governments were predictably unenthusiastic about negotiating new community plans for their jurisdictions. Thus Title IV never really got off the ground within the bureaucracy, although Congressional interest in new communities remained fairly constant.

In early 1970, the National Committee on Urban Growth Policy issued a report which pinpointed the problems confronting new community development. The report concluded that few new communities had been launched because of (1) inadequate funding for large-scale capital investment; (2) the difficulty of assembling large sites at economically feasible locations; and (3) poor coordination of arrangements between private and public organizations for site improvement. The problems, then, were primarily financial; given the appropriate economic incentives, new community development would succeed. Consequently, the report recommended that existing new community policy be expanded through a program of federal direct long-term loans and additional supplementary grants.

The committee's report, called "The New City," was in the form of a legislative proposal which was signed by Congressional leaders of both parties. It called for the creation of 100 new towns with an average size of 100,000 residents and 10 new cities with populations of at least 1 million to accommodate 20 million people by the year 2000.[12]

Three types of new communities were envisioned. First, freestanding communities would serve as "accelerated growth centers"; these would encourage growth in small towns, making the new communities program attractive to legislators with rural constituencies. Second, new-towns-in-town were to receive more federal attention to pacify urban mayors concerned with the suburban character of new communities. Third, "satellite communities," located near major urban areas would absorb a good portion of the population increase of 75 million projected for the end of the century and were expected to house 20 million people by 1980. These would differ from conventional suburbs, however, in that they would be self-sustaining urban entities, not merely bedroom communities for the greater urban area.

The report also recommended the creation of an Executive Council on Urban Growth, similar to the President's Council of Economic Advisers, and a Community Development Corporation (CDC) within HUD to facilitate implementation. The CDC would offer technical and planning assistance to state and local agencies and would coordinate interagency policy regarding new communities. Concern over past bureaucratic inaction prompted the recommendation for the establishment of both the CDC and the Urban Growth Council. Thus, the CDC was intended to promote the new communities program within HUD, while, at the same time, creating a bureaucratic constituency for the program.

The National Committee's report was incorporated into a second bill submitted by Congressman Ashley in late 1970. As initially introduced, the bill had four titles. The first adopted the idea of an Urban Growth Council from the committee's report but gave states and counties a more active role in policy recommendations. The second title set up the CDC to clarify Congressional intent. Hugh Mields, advisor to Ashley, stated that "the preceding Title IV program, in the Metropolitan Development Division of HUD, had no visibility or accountability to Congress. As a result, Congress had no way of keeping heat on the Administration."[13] The third and fourth titles provided authorization for certain classes of land acquisition under urban renewal programs and federal planning assistance to the states. The Ashley bill also provided grants for needed public services to a new community during the early phases of development. These grants were limited to three years and only a nominal amount of money was made available, but it was felt that new communities would be much more attractive to potential residents if these services were offered. Another provision of the bill authorized the CDC to undertake demonstration projects in regions where the need for new communities was not being filled by private developers. This provision was politically astute because it indicated that big, medium, and small cities would all benefit from the legislation.[14]

To win support for the bill, Ashley held public hearings under the auspices of an ad hoc subcommittee on urban growth. In general, reactions to the bill were positive; mayors of big cities responded favorably this time, and various public interest groups testified in support of the bill. However, traditional interest groups concerned with urban legislation were notable in their absence. The AFL-CIO, the National Association of Homebuilders, the National Association of Real Estate Boards, and savings and loan associations, all of whom usually lobby extensively on housing legislation, virtually ignored the Ashley bill.

The Nixon administration registered strong opposition to the program from the start. While HUD Secretary Romney seemed to be personally sympathetic to program goals and remained fairly noncommittal in his testimony, advisors to President Nixon argued against the bill for several reasons. First, the Office of Management and Budget (OMB) questioned the propriety of the Urban Growth Council on the grounds that Congress should not try to organize the White House. Second, OMB saw the direct loan program and public service grants as inflationary and the supplementary grants as undermining the President's new revenue-sharing plan. Third, creation of the CDC as an independent office within HUD was opposed because of Nixon's reluctance to have a strong agency implementing a program which his administration opposed.[15]

However, Congressional support for the bill was strong, and the executive branch was forced to compromise with supporters of new communities. As a result, the direct loan program was modified to one of loan guarantees; the independence of CDC was limited and it was placed under greater executive control; and the demonstration project provision of the program was dropped, although a provision requiring that any government program to build homes for government employees be cleared through the CDC remained. After a compromised form of the bill passed both the House and Senate, the bill went to conference, from which it emerged retaining most of the key provisions of the original bill. However, only by attaching the bill as a rider to the Housing and Urban Development Act of 1970 could the bill's sponsors assure Nixon's signature.[16] The bill became law on December 31, 1970.

In its final form the Ashley bill—the Urban Growth and New Community Development Act of 1970, Title VII of the Housing and Urban Development Act of 1970—expanded the loan guarantee program under Title IV of the 1968 act to $500 million and extended the guarantee to public development agencies. It mandated the creation of the CDC but authorized no separate funds for CDC, thereby placing the agency under HUD's control. Title VII also offered several categories of grants and loans to local governments and new communities developers. First, the supplementary grants originally incorporated into Title IV were increased from three to fourteen, which combined categorical and supplementary grants to subsidize up to 70 percent of public infrastructure costs in new communities. Second, planning assistance to cover two thirds of the costs of social and environmental planning was authorized to private developers. Technical assistance grants were also included to encourage innovation in development. Third, direct loans could be made to developers to pay off interest accruing on bonds and debentures during the first fifteen years of a project; these loans were designed to solve the problem of "patient capital" and developer liquidity. Fourth, the act included the much-debated public service grants to local governments for the first three years of a development project. And finally, the act authorized an interest differential grant to compensate local development agencies for their loss of tax-exempt status on bonds guaranteed under the act.

Implementation of the Urban Growth and New Community Development Act of 1970

The goals of the 1970 Act were numerous, general in nature, and not ranked in order of importance. Basically, the goals were a list of objectives that Congress lumped together into a single program. Ten were given:

> 1. *Encourage the orderly development of well planned, diversified, and economically sound new communities, including major additions to existing communities, and to do so in a way that will rely to the maximum extent on private enterprise;*
> 2. *Strengthen the capacity of State and local governments to deal with local problems;*
> 3. *Preserve and enhance both the natural and urban environment;*
> 4. *Increase for all persons, particularly members of minority groups, the available choices of location for living and working thereby providing a more just economic and social environment;*
> 5. *Encourage the fullest utilization of economic potential of older cities, small towns, and rural communities;*
> 6. *Assist in the effective production of a steady supply of residential, commercial, and industrial building sites at reasonable cost;*
> 7. *Increase the capability of all segments of the home building industry, including both small and large producers, to utilize improved technology in producing the large volume of well-designed, inexpensive housing needed to accommodate population growth;*
> 8. *Help create neighborhoods designed for easier access between the residence, work, and recreation;*

9. *Encourage innovation in meeting domestic problems, whether physical, economic, or social;*
10. *Improve the organizational capacity of the Federal government to carry out assistance programs for development of new communities and the revitalization of the Nation's urban areas.*[17]

Title VII was to be administered through HUD's New Communities Administration (NCA), formerly the Office of New Community Development (ONCD). Because of the complexity of the program, it was operated principally by the HUD staff in Washington, and the HUD secretary had substantial discretion for working out details. Few regional offices were willing to assume the burden of program participation without the promise of additional staff resources. A statutory attempt was made to avoid the various bureaucratic pitfalls encountered under Title IV of the 1968 act. For instance, Title IV had been administered through a large bureaucratic division of HUD which had little time for the program. Major policy decisions, however, had been centered primarily in the Urban Affairs Council's interagency subcommittee on land use and development, an arrangement that caused problems because other agencies were reluctant to surrender any autonomy to HUD. The program was severely understaffed—an original staff of three was only later expanded to seventeen. (The staffing problems give some indication of the relative importance that was placed on the program within the bureaucracy.) Finally, administration of Title IV had put heavy emphasis on the financial and managerial aspects of the program largely to the exclusion of the program's social objectives. Under Title VII the CDC was to be the overall decision-making and coordinating body of the program. The CDC was statutorily independent, under the administrative jurisdiction of HUD but with independently appointed personnel, largely because of the bias within the Ashley subcommittee against HUD's "banker mentality" and its tendency to ignore social goals. The statute assigned the governance of the CDC to a board of directors; however, despite the Congressional desire to assure CDC's independence, the CDC board consisted of the secretary of HUD, a general manager appointed by the president, and three additional appointments by the secretary. Resources for additional ancillary and technical staff were to be drawn from a revolving fund established to cover administrative costs and loan defaults, which would consist of developer fees paid into HUD.

While the CDC assumed decision-making responsibility for the program, actual implementation was left to the NCA. The NCA was hierarchically structured, with the secretary of HUD at the top, followed by the general administrator and that staff. Beneath the general administrator were the Office of Program and Policy Evaluation, which received preliminary applications from potential new community developers, and the Office of Program Development and Management, which had responsibility for assisting developers in meeting program goals. Beneath these were the Office of Finance, which conducted financial analysis and monitoring, and the

Office of Technical Analysis, which provided developers with technical assistance while coordinating various interagency programs to facilitate new community development. In total, maximum staff of the NCA was approximately thirty-five people.

The application process and HUD's administration

Establishment of application procedures for federal assistance under the act was left to the discretion of HUD; applications for assistance were first accepted in early 1971. The first step in the application process was the developer's informal statement of goals, which included a decision on site location, social objectives, and an extremely rough prediction of financial returns. The developer then met with HUD officials to discuss the project and either received encouragement to apply or was given an unqualified rejection. The next step was the preapplication proposal, which outlined the project in terms of the general legal requirements for assistance (for example, tentative proposals for subsidized housing) and included a physical plan, a discussion of environmental issues, potential political difficulties, and proposed methods to achieve social goals. If the preapplication was accepted by HUD, the developer was urged to submit a full application. Here, the developer had to provide a detailed range of background studies, environmental analyses, financial surveys and forecasts, and social impact studies. The financial aspects of the project received considerable attention during the application process; economic models to determine market feasibility were combined with fairly sophisticated market surveys to develop a comprehensive picture of financial viability. Relatively little attention, however, was directed toward ways to attain social objectives.[18] A formal environmental impact statement was submitted at this point but, because of the resources already committed in terms of time and money by both HUD and the developer, HUD was often willing to place more emphasis on the developer's initial (preapplication) estimates about environmental and social goals. After the application was submitted, HUD sent notification of pending projects to local and regional agencies for comment. This was the one opportunity HUD provided for local involvement in the federal decision-making process. Usually, however, local authorities did not offer any input and the application process continued without them.

The application was then submitted to the CDC for a final decision. It is worth noting that this procedure effectively subverted the legislative intention to create an independent CDC. Since the really crucial decisions were made at the preapplication level and since the CDC considered only formal applications, the CDC merely rubber-stamped decisions made at the lower levels of the NCA hierarchy.[19]

If the CDC offered a guarantee commitment, the developer had 120 days in which to find brokers to float the guarantee bonds and was required to pay a .5 percent commitment fee into HUD's revolving fund. A "project agreement," or binding legal contract, and trust indenture, were then negotiated and the developer paid another 3 percent fee. Proceeds from the bond sale were meanwhile placed in an escrow fund pending HUD approval for their withdrawal. However, applications seldom moved rapidly through the bureaucracy and money was not always released when scheduled; yet even as short as a three-month delay in the release of promised funds could scuttle a planned development. The complexity of the application process and the uncertain availability of funds once a commitment was offered made the developer's planning task much more difficult. The two separate negotiations of the application process could cost the developer as much as $650,000 and take twenty-one months; many developers argued that such detailed review of projects was unnecessary. What was needed, according to Mark Freeman, Executive Director of the League of New Community Developers, was a set of "easily reviewable standards [that could] be set in recognition of each project's uniqueness and not as part of an arbitrary and unified set of standards to be indiscriminately applied to all new communities."[20] Because of the tenuous nature of HUD's commitments, most developers did not participate in the Title VII program unless financial considerations forced them to rely on the federal guarantee. William Nicoson, director of ONCD (NCA) from 1969 to 1971 observed that " . . . because of lack of money and low levels of staff, developers who had the financial capability to go it alone without government support would do so, while those who were attracted to the program would be those who could not make it without a government guarantee and therefore would be the greatest risk to the government".[21]

The financial weakness of many HUD clients was not initially detected partly because the long lead time often concealed difficulties for several years. However, HUD's initial screening process was also fairly weak. First, studies determining the existence of a market were often questionable because HUD relied on developers to assess their own market prospects; HUD had no independent analysis team to check developers' findings. Consequently, HUD guaranteed $77 million worth of bonds for four projects and only later discovered that three fourths of the studies submitted by these developers were either outdated or lacked vital information. For example, Jonathan, Minnesota, a project guaranteed for $21 million, was approved in 1970 on the basis of a market feasibility analysis made in 1966. Second, financial feasibility studies, including estimates of costs and anticipated expenditures, were inadequate. Developers often submitted unrealistic or inaccurate estimates that went unchallenged by HUD. Jonathan's developers, for example, provided cost information for only half of the development period; cost projections for Park Forest South, Illinois, were unrelated to the eventual development plan adopted; and projections for Flower Mound, Texas, were based on the development and sale of land that its developers did not own.

HUD failed to fully evaluate these analyses and was unable to get a clear picture of each project's financial feasibility.

One reason the goals of the act were not successfully met was the act's focus on problems of physical design and cash flow and its failure to include local government participation in the planning process. Title VII substantially increased the demand for public services from local governments, which were poorly equipped to provide them. Although local governments hold legal responsibility for services and Title VII mentions "strengthening the capacity of state and local governments" to provide them, no provision for effective integration between federal, state, and local governments was spelled out in the act or created by HUD. Further complicating the problem of intergovernmental coordination, neither national nor local governments had major responsibilities for the implementation of the new communities program. Rather, those responsibilities were in the hands of private developers. Local governments, particularly those affected by satellite new communities, were extremely "ill-prepared to cope with developmental imperatives" and were frequently unwilling or unable to cooperate with other local agencies in providing a well-coordinated public service program.[22]

The act did anticipate the financial difficulties that local governments would encounter when faced with their own "front-end" costs; Section 715 provided local impact aid, particularly through special supplementary facility and planning grants and provision of grants for initial costs of educational, health, and safety services. However, Congress failed to allocate a large portion of these assistance funds, and OMB impounded all appropriated new community funds except those pertaining to the guarantee program.[23] This created a situation in which the federal government was supporting the front-end costs of the private developer through loan guarantees while denying similar assistance to local governments impacted by new communities. Consequently, most local governments were understandably resentful of "instant urbanization" and were unwilling to encourage development of new communities within their jurisdictions. Aggravating the situation was the fact that private developers had to rely on local governments for decisions that could determine the success of their projects, yet there was no single agency within the NCA delegated to coordinate implementation with local governments.

The statutory disregard for the ramifications of the policymaking autonomy allowed local governments is also reflected in HUD's disregard of the necessity of organizational interdependence at the local level. Perhaps it is too much to expect of any national program, but if projects as complex as those envisioned by Title VII are to succeed, the public/private partnership must extend to the local level through a complete vertical integration of policy. Without such integration, decisions vital to the new community had to run a gauntlet of functional veto points within the local government, each one perfectly capable of ruining the entire project.

Problems facing private developers

The developer encountered several difficulties during the application process. From initiation to completion, the average process took approximately thirty-eight months, and a developer could anticipate expenditure during this period of at least $1 million in planning costs. While theoretically there was only one negotiating round for project objectives, there were in fact two separate bargaining procedures. The first procedure, which took place in the Application Review Division under the Office of Technical Analysis, constituted a complete and comprehensive review during the preliminary and formal application stages. The process took approximately twenty-one months and cost the developer between $500,000 and $650,000. After CDC commitment, however, there was a renegotiation of terms before the signing of the project agreement. This was done through the Negotiation and Monitoring Division, which did not necessarily feel itself bound by previous agreements. The entire developer proposal was thus opened up to a second general review which was frequently a duplication of the first, saddling the developer with additional costs of up to $500,000.[24] Moreover, once a binding agreement was finally reached, staff shortages could cause funds to be tied up in escrow for an indefinite period.

The lack of clear guidelines on what was expected of them accounted for part of the difficulty encountered by developers in their dealings with HUD. As Smookler pointed out in reviewing accomplishments of the first five years under the 1970 Act, "after five years there are still no regulations or handbooks setting the ground rules. This has resulted in an ad hoc review of applications and virtually no monitoring of projects."[25] The sense of urgency that followed Title IV's (the 1968 act) record of inertia contributed in some part to the confusion surrounding early implementation of Title VII; over 200 requests for information were received by HUD during the first month of the new program. The paucity of professionals within NCA added to the confusion; most staff members, while extremely dedicated to the new communities program, did not have the financial expertise necessary to undertake analyses of such complex projects, and virtually none had ever been associated with the development industry in a managerial capacity.[26] Consequently, no one really knew what criteria should be used to measure the feasibility of a new community. Attempts were made to glean information for guidelines by reviewing applications pending under Title IV and by submitting tentative regulations to major developers for comment. In formulating guidelines, HUD was caught in a crossfire between those urging broad standards that would recognize the uniqueness of each project, and those arguing for a clear and detailed set of rules that could be applied uniformly to every application, thereby eliminating the uncertainty characteristic of the application process. HUD responded by stressing quantitative measures of economic feasibility at the expense of other aspects of the project. By 1973,

TABLE 3.1
New Communities Projects Approved by HUD Under Title VII

Projects Guaranteed	Location	Date of HUD Commitment	Guarantees Commitment (in millions of dollars)
Jonathan, Minnesota (S)	20 miles southwest of Minneapolis	2/70	21.0
St. Charles Communities, Maryland (S)	25 miles southeast of Washington, D.C.	6/70	24.0
Park Forest South, Illinois (S)	30 miles south of Chicago	6/70	30.0
Flower Mound, Texas (S)	20 miles northwest of Dallas	12/70	18.0
Maumelle, Arkansas (S)	12 miles northwest of Little Rock	12/70	7.5
Cedar-Riverside, Minnesota (NTIT)	Downtown Minneapolis	6/71	24.0
Riverton, New York (S)	10 miles south of Rochester	12/71	12.0
San Antonio Ranch, Texas (S)	20 miles northwest of San Antonio	2/72	18.0
The Woodlands, Texas (S)	30 miles north of Houston	4/72	50.0
Gananda, New York (S)	12 miles east of Rochester	4/72	22.0
Soul City, North Carolina (FS)	45 miles north of Raleigh	6/72	14.0
Harbison, South Carolina (S)	8 miles northwest of Columbia	10/72	13.0
Shenandoah, Georgia (S)	35 miles south of Atlanta	2/73	40.0
Newfields, Ohio (S)	7 miles northwest of Dayton	10/73	32.0
Radisson, New York (S)[a]	12 miles northwest of Syracuse	—	NA
Roosevelt Island, New York (NTIT)[a]	East River between Manhattan and Queens	—	NA

SOURCE, Helene Smookler, "Administration Hara-Kiri: Implementation of the Urban Growth and Development Act," *Annals* 422 (November 1975): Table 1 Status reports provided by the new Community Development Corporation, Department of Housing and Urban Development.

[a]State Land Development Agency Projects. Obligations will not be guaranteed by HUD, but project is eligible for other program benefits.

S   = Satellite new community
NTIT = New-town-in-town
FS   = Free-standing new community
NA   = Not applicable; loan guarantee not requested

Projected Population	Development Period (Years)	Population, 1980 (% Minority)	HUD Acquired (Year)	Disposed of or in Process of Disposition (Year)
50,000	20	2970 (2)	1980	1980
75,000	20	9180 (5)		
110,000	15	6000 (30)	1977	1981
64,000	20	1800 (3)	1977	1981
45,000	20	1784 (2)		
30,000	20	3100 (28)	1980	1980
26,000	16	1200 (2)	1978	1981
88,000	30	—		
150,000	20	9500 (3)		
56,000	20	—	1977	1979
44,000	20	160 (89)	1981	
23,000	20	1500 (15)		
70,000	20	750 (17)	1981	
40,000	20	225 (20)	1979	1981
18,000	20	1860 (2)		
18,000	7	5500 (30)		

HUD had attempted to compromise the demands for ad hoc review with those for rigid criteria by concentrating almost exclusively on financial analyses, while retaining only a vague commitment to social goals.

Outcome of the New Communities Program

By January 1975, when HUD closed its door to further new community applications, fourteen had been approved for $361 million in federally guaranteed assistance (with one subsequently dropped), and two had received eligibility certification, placing them in favorable position for future federal assistance.[27] The communities were planned to include more than 300,000 residential units, accommodating nearly 1 million people by 1995; see Table 3.1. While these figures were well below the 100 new towns and 10 new cities to accommodate 20 million people envisioned by the National Committee on Urban Growth Policy and congressional leaders of both parties as late as 1969, or even the promise of 10 federally guaranteed new communities per year,[28] the plans still offered the program an opportunity to prove itself.

While the new community program fell short of its promised scope, it did achieve, to a limited degree, some Congressional objectives. Yet the overall picture is discouraging. A case in point is Jonathan, Minnesota, launched by the first HUD loan guarantee under the 1970 Act. First envisioned in 1966 by state senator, landowner, and new town proponent Henry McKnight, the plan for Jonathan went through several revisions and expansions.[29] The agreement signed with HUD in February 1970 called for development of 8000 acres of relatively isolated rolling hills and farmlands 25 miles southwest of downtown Minneapolis, just off a major freeway. It called for accommodating a population of 50,000 residents within twenty years, to be located in five villages of approximately 7000 persons apiece and a town center with 15,000 persons. Almost a quarter of the site was to be used for industrial development in four industrial parks, which would eventually provide 23,000 jobs. Another 20 percent of the land was allotted for open space: lakes, wildlife preserves, greenbelt, and pathways.

Distinctive features of the plan for Jonathan were (a) McKnight's commitment and HUD concurrence that low- and moderate-income housing would receive uppermost attention and, therefore, become an integral part of the community—6500 such housing units out of a projected 15,000; (b) the provision of an infrastructure of health, educational, and other public services early in the development; and (c) the active role to be taken by residents in governing the course of development and the community. Jonathan was also equipped with a novel Community Information System that provided two-way communications via cable television lines between a central computing facility and hospitals, schools, offices, businesses, and homes. And it was one enough period so that the developer can anticipate adverse economic conditions, and projects can be postponed or canceled. The twelve- to twenty-

Despite the development of a plan that adhered to nearly every aspect of the new community concept, several factors converged within a few years to place Jonathan in a precarious financial situation, forcing it to scale down its broad development scheme and ultimately fall into HUD receivership. To begin with, revenues from land sales started off poorly, reaching only 65 percent of what was anticipated and almost $2 million short of expectations in 1971 and 1972. The net loss on the development for both 1971 and 1972 was nearly $500,000 over estimated losses despite the fact that these were still boom years for the nation's economy and new home purchases. Adding to these financial woes, OMB had impounded the service and planning money that the developers had been led to believe would be forthcoming once development began. Meanwhile, plans for local schools were delayed time and again due to hesitancy on the part of the local school district to build before the population warranted it, and other disagreements remained among Jonathan's management and residents. Finally, Jonathan's visionary, chief lobbyist, and benefactor Henry McKnight died unexpectedly in December 1972, and the development fell into the hands of a more financially oriented manager.

By late 1974 the development had defaulted on federally guaranteed debentures, was forced to dissolve its development staff, and had decided to seek a buyer for the development. Subsequently, development proceeded more like that of privately sponsored new communities, responding more to the dictates of the housing market than to the goals of a mix of housing for both the affluent and less-well-off, of a racially balanced community, of quality public services, and of publicly sponsored social and cultural amenities. In 1980 HUD was forced to foreclose and dispose of Jonathan as a Title VII new community.

Evaluation of Title VII

In view of the problems that were beginning to surface with new communities and the continued recalcitrance of the Nixon administration to carry out provisions of the act, in 1975, Congressman Ashley commissioned the Academy for Contempory Problems to survey available studies and report on the status of the act. Meanwhile, Burby and Weiss had undertaken a comprehensive assessment of the new communities concept as it had been implemented in fifteen developments in the U.S. through 1973, including two of the federally assisted new communities. And HUD undertook its own exhaustive assessment of Title VII projects in 1976.[30] Based on the results of these studies, as the following summary suggests, the picture for federally assisted new communities is gloomy but not entirely negative.

Program successes

New communities per se have been most successful in enhancing and preserving the local environment. Nearly all studies of both privately and federally funded new communities agree that planned, preserviced, large-scale projects are superior to incremental growth in conserving the quality of the physical environment.

New communities have also been fairly successful in encouraging innovation in planned community development and in the provision of housing and social services. Developers have demonstrated considerable creativity in design, waste disposal, and transportation, while providing better access to recreational facilities, schools, health care, and shopping centers. Innovation in mass transit in new communities has apparently had some effect on residential behavior; a significantly higher proportion of residents in new communities were reported to use public transit than were residents of conventional communities. To some extent, however, developer innovation in these areas was limited by local and regional governments. For example, county government preferred regional, rather than communal (within the new community) recreation centers; school districts were hesitant to undertake school construction for a projected but nonexistent population; local governments were unable or unwilling to finance the front-end cost of public services to new communities without a substantial tax base in place. Nevertheless, overall, new communities have still managed to offer services superior to those of conventional communities.

New communities, both privately and federally funded, also appear to have made substantial contributions to the welfare of the surrounding areas. Despite some conflicting assertions, it appears that new communities far enough along in their development to make a difference have generated fiscal, social, and environmental benefits for local areas and have returned more dollars than they received in services from local governments.[31] It is worth questioning, however, whether federal guarantees are necessary to ensure environmental enhancement, innovative design, and economic contributions to the surrounding area. While it has been argued that "without special incentives, it is difficult to encourage innovative planning in dealing with private developers,"[32] the success of nonfederally sponsored new communities suggests otherwise.

Federally supported new communities have been more successful in inducing developers to include subsidized housing as a means of achieving racial and economic balance within the community, though the record is not uniform. This appears to be an important result of HUD's guidelines and incentives. By comparison, privately developed new communities show much less mixing; there is little perceived market demand for integrated neighborhoods and consequently, except for Reston, Columbia, and a handful of others, little subsidized housing exists.[33] Local governments view low-income residency as unprofitable because it presents a burden in services without any tax revenue return. Thus, local governments have often used zoning and density laws to discourage the building of low-income housing.

HUD targeted federal new communities, on the other hand, to allot 27 percent of their residential units for low-income tenants.[34] The rationale for a policy of economic and class integration in new communities was partly based on the premise that these new towns could provide a mechanism for demonstrating that housing for low- and moderate-income families could be designed, grouped, and distributed in such a way as to overcome middle-class resistance.[35] However, even in the federally assisted new communities, of all the units completed through 1976, two thirds of the low- and moderate-income housing was located at Cedar-Riverside and Roosevelt Island, the two projects located in inner-city areas.[36] As Table 3.1 indicates, the only new community of any size to realize anything close to HUD's minority population target figure was Park Forest South. Moreover, the experience with public and private new communities suggests that whenever it is to be provided, subsidized housing should be built before there is a substantial number of residents in the new community, or middle-class homeowners may form strong opposition. If this is not feasible, prospective white middle-class residents must be fully apprised of the intention to provide racial and economic integration and allowed to opt in or out accordingly.

Federally assisted subsidized housing in new communities (and elsewhere) was quite adversely affected by the 1975 executive moratorium on subsidized building and the general slowdown of renewal money initiated by OMB under the Nixon administration. The moratorium was especially damaging for new communities because it came at a time when construction was just beginning. The exclusion of subsidized housing at the outset of development probably means that such housing will never be built and that the long-term projected levels for low-income populations will not be reached.

Burby and Weiss did find that new communities with a substantial class and racial mix report that minority residents are generally highly satisfied with the "livability" of their communities. Minorities seemed particularly satisfied with schools, safety, and the neighborhood as a place to raise children; they perceived new communities as vehicles of social mobility. This would seem to indicate that not only the letter but the spirit of the law was being met in this instance.

Program failures

Beyond these successes, however, the Title VII record is rather dismal. On the whole, with limited exception, the new communities have not met the ten statutory goals established for the program. To begin with, the new community program has not "encouraged" full utilization of the economic potential of older cities, small towns, or rural communities. Thirteen new communities are satellites, effectively commuter communities for the urban centers they surround, two are new-towns-in-town, and only one is freestanding. There are a variety of reasons why developers have chosen not to locate new communities in cities or rural areas. First, the statute directive to "utilize" urban centers was vague and offered no guidance on how that utilization should be accomplished, or what priority should be given it in the implementation process. Second, city governments were not interested in building tracts of low-cost housing; they much preferred programs that promised amenities and an attractive physical environment to lure the middle class, with all its revenue potential, back into the inner city.[37] Beyond this issue, however, was the simple logic of economics; undeveloped land is much cheaper than land already developed. To realize substantial land appreciation, developers had to locate outside of established cities. Since new-towns-in-town are both economically and politically more difficult to build, substantial incentives would have to be offered to private developers, yet few were included in the act. Section 741 of the act merely amended Title I of the Housing Act of 1949 to allow for new-towns-in-town. Finally, HUD's emphasis on financial viability and its political need for a quick, visible record of success, discouraged development of new-towns-in-town.

Nor could private developers build in rural areas far away from cities without encountering local rural governments incapable of financing the kind of quality services required by the new community. Remote rural locations also raised the issue of whether there was or would ever be sufficient demand to populate a freestanding new community once built, and if not, how jobs would be provided to attract the envisioned population? Provision of employment—a goal articulated by the statute but difficult to achieve— requires the creation of an industrial or commercial base in the community. The single freestanding new community, Soul City, has experienced this problem of "concurrent development"; to attract a population, the community must be able to offer jobs, yet without workers, no community can attract commerce or industry. "It's the chicken and the egg stuff," said Floyd McKissick, developer of Soul City.[38] Furthermore, what claim can such an isolated experimental community make on national priorities? Innovation of design and financing might be interesting, but it would have been politically unwise for HUD to commit large amounts of valuable national resources to such experiments.

Satellite communities, on the other hand, offered maximum autonomy as the developer did not have to negotiate with as many jurisdictions, districts, and agencies as found within an established city. At the same time, they offered greater promise of financial success because of the access to jobs in the metropolitan area. Thus, for the most part, new communities quickly became alternative suburbs, replete with centralized services, environmental compatibility, and superior amenities, but suburbs nonetheless.

Title VII new communities have not lived up to the goal of accommodating the nation's burgeoning population through "assisting in production of a steady supply of building sites over the next twenty years." When completed, the new communities now under construction are projected to house one million people, only about 7 percent of the population increase projected for the year 2000. Furthermore, critics such as William Alonso argued from the outset of the program that these and like projections are inherently misleading in that 80 percent of new community growth is taking place in existing urban areas, while 90 percent of all our housing is being built there anyway. Thus, Alonso contended, even given the most optimistic estimates for new communities capacity, the ability of these communities to chart a new course in community living and set a new pattern of autonomous self-contained population centers for the nation will actually "affect only a small part of our population and an even smaller part of our housing production."[39]

New communities have not been able to provide neighborhoods with better access to employment. As noted, most new communities, at least during their early stages of development, are serving as "bedroom communities" within the metropolitan area.[40] The economic base and self-sufficiency envisioned by program proponents has not materialized in most instances. That the new community has become a functional suburb has undermined the transportation objectives of the act. In terms of their spill-over impact on urban centers—adding to transportation congestion, air pollution, etc.—there has been little difference between the planned new communities and the traditional practice of incremental growth.

The act looked to new communities as a means to provide comprehensive and innovative solutions to problems of poverty and unemployment. Clearly, such a goal was unrealistic; the construction of new communities could never, in and of itself, make significant contributions toward solving the nation's social ills simply by creating a more attractive physical environment or offering better public services. Not surprisingly, new communities contain the same human and social problems found in any other community. It is probably naive to have expected new communities, even with all their advantages, to solve such problems through "innovative treatment," where most other government and community efforts have had only limited success.

While new communities did "increase the capability of large and small developers to engage in new community development and to use new technology in the provision of housing," and in this sense met the statutory goal, the program has been criticized for this very achievement. The initial capital investment required for new community development was estimated to be between $26.2 and $88 million. Large corporations are usually the only organizations with this kind of capital available for investment, and they purposely avoided Title VII assistance because of "red tape, fickleness, and the overburden of social objectives."[41] Consequently, the main participants in the government program were small developers who had to rely on assistance.[42] However, most grants promised under the program never materialized. Thus, reliance on illusory federal assistance combined with the unavailability of alternative sources of capital made the financial status of projects initiated by small developers quite tenuous, with the result that several have gone bankrupt or HUD has taken over their projects. The severe recession of 1974 had a devastating effect on virtually all of the Title VII communities. For example, in 1974 HUD was nearly saddled with a $12 million obligation when Riverton, New York, came close to financial collapse.[43] A series of financial crises led HUD, in January 1975, to suspend further processing of additional applications in order to concentrate fully on keeping the existing communities financially solvent.[44] When its attempted solutions proved only to be stopgap, HUD was ultimately forced to foreclose on seven projects between 1977 and 1981; see Table 3.1. In short, the program attracted clients who were financially weak to begin with, forced them to incorporate costly social goals into development plans, and then failed to deliver much of the promised assistance.[45] When a project failed financially, HUD finally had to step in to manage and eventually dispose of it.

New communities were supposed to "provide an alternative to disorderly urban growth" by exemplifying the benefits of a planned community. However, few state or local governments followed the example and established the necessary land use regulations for areas surrounding new communities.[46] It could be argued that new communities are merely well-planned enclaves in the midst of urban sprawl. Few localities formulated any urban growth policy. Antiquated zoning laws and jurisdictional methods of development restricted innovative planning and allowed discrimination to continue. "Without a larger regional policy framework to provide a context for the new community as a device to reshape the patterns of urban growth, the new communities impact on overall development can only be marginal."[47] *The new community is not an element in a larger plan, as the statute had originally intended it to be; it is simply an isolated development initiated wherever a developer can manage to assemble large tracts of land.* The statute, while encouraging states to formulate comprehensive growth policies, did little to provide incentives toward that end. Few states have tried. And HUD was unable to coordinate a coherent, interagency urban policy. Consequently, whatever impact new communities might have had on urban development was minimized.

New communities were intended to "help reverse patterns of rural outmigration" by acting as a "way-station" to a migrant population. The statute made no mention of how this reversal was to take place, nor did it define the characteristics of a "way-station." However, because most new communities are satellite communities, it is safe to say that no new community is now serving as a "way-station." This is partly due to the fact that over the past several decades rural outmigration has slowed to an insignificant trickle, and there is really no need to reverse it. Thus the statutory goal in this instance was apparently based on a faulty premise; new communities could not stem a tide of rural outmigration if such a tide did not exist.

The act cited the "improvement of the organizational capacity of local, state, and federal governments to carry out a national urban policy" as another goal. This was not met for several reasons. First, the long lead time for new community development subjected a developer to the authority of several different local administrations, each free to disregard the promises of its predecessor. Second, HUD was unwilling to intervene and to integrate a development plan coordinated through all levels of government. Third, statutory incentives for public planning were inadequate. The act attempted to induce program participation from public developers at the state and regional level by expanding its loan guarantee to public agencies. However, only New York participated in the program through its Urban Development Corporation (UDC), and the financial difficulties encountered by the UDC discouraged other states from becoming actively involved in development planning. Fourth, NCA was unable to prevent Title VII planning aid to local and regional governments from falling victim to other priorities of the Nixon administration. A chief example of this occurred in 1974 when Congress passed a Community Development Act that was meant to simplify federal grants-in-aid by replacing them with the Community Development Bloc Grant (CDBG). Bloc grants were intended to give state and local governments more responsibility, but the new plan did not address the need for better coordination between different levels of government. Indeed, the CDBG program severely hampered the efforts of the NCA, since much of NCA's ability to induce local governments' participation in the development process was contingent on the promise of a supplement to grants-in-aid. CDBG grants were awarded on the basis of population; thus, the unpopulated new communities were pitted against established communities during their initial development period when funds for infrastructure were needed most desperately. Finally, HUD was unable to coordinate its various programs to assist new community development and eliminate conflicting objectives. For example, a much-discussed problem that faced new communities was securing financing for public facilities. Local governments would not pay for these; the costs were usually absorbed by the developer and eventually reflected in higher selling prices for homes. A noted exception was the case of Columbia, Maryland, where the developer obtained permission from the Federal Housing Administration to place a permanent lien on all taxable property that would take precedence over mortgage claims on the property. The security provided enabled the developer to borrow funds for infrastructure, instead of having to pass on costs to the new home buyers. Unfortunately, HUD was unable to convince the Federal Housing Administration to apply this exception to other new communities.[48]

Another failure was HUD's inability to keep new communities afloat financially. The basic tractability of the enterprise accounts for part of this failure. Development of a community as an organic whole has never before been attempted in this country on a large scale; consequently, developers did not know what kind of planning was necessary for success. Traditional incremental development usually takes from five to seven years. This is a short enough period so that the developer can anticipate adverse economic conditions, and projects can be postponed or canceled. The twelve- to twenty-year lead time for new communities precludes developers that option; developers could only work financial contingency plans into their overall development scheme and hope that the project would not be wiped out by a recession. Even without a recession, the vicissitudes of inflation, combined with the requirement for vast capital reserves, would probably necessitate some form of refinancing.

Another major reason for the failure of Title VII was the exeuctive branch's hostile response to the act. The Nixon administration opposed the act from its inception; only because of Congressman Ashley's acumen in attaching the bill as a rider to a larger and more important piece of legislation was the act ultimately passed. During the oversight hearings conducted by Ashley in 1973 witnesses cited executive hostility as the primary reason that HUD had made only marginal progress toward realization of the act's goals. For example, because of an internal OMB veto, HUD never formally requested from Congress funds for the act's provision of Section 715 grants. As emphasized earlier, infrastructure grants were imperative to the success of new communities because of their incentive effect on local governments. Without them, developers were forced to levy higher assessments on property throughout the community, an action which served as a deterrent for relocation of industry, commerce, and home buyers. OMB also rejected requests to fund Section 716 of Title VII, which offered $240 million in loans to aid developers with short-term interest payments. Interest on these government loans could be deferred for 15 years, thus giving developers greater liquidity. Supplemental grants, authorized by Congress to provide a total of $70 million of aid in conjunction with categorical grants from other agencies, were never funded because of the administration's preference for the revenue-sharing plan. Technical assistance grants to encourage planning by both private and public developers were originally authorized for $10 million. When Congress appropriated only $5 million of this authorization, even this amount was impounded. Interest differential grants were intended to provide incentives for local government participation; since only taxable bonds could be guaranteed under the act, Congress authorized the "interest differential grant" to compensate public developers for the higher interest rates resulting from the loss of federal tax exemption. This provision, too, was never funded, in spite of the fact that it had virtually no impact on the budget.

The lack of support is probably best attributed to Title VII's place among executive priorities. As a holdover from the previous Democratic administrations, the program was viewed as incompatible with Nixon's concept of revenue sharing. Categorical grants were to be phased out, yet Title VII was designed to bolster grants-in-aid with an infusion of supplementary grants.

Inflationary concerns were also partly responsible for OMB's refusal to allow NCA any more than a skeletal staff. The complex nature of the program required specialists in architecture, the environment, social planning, land appraisal, and financial analysis, yet the maximum number of these professionals in the NCA was never very large, and at least at the critical outset of the program none of the specialists had ever had executive level experience within the private sector. In spite of the fact that substantial staff additions could have been paid for out of the self-sustaining revolving fund and therefore would have had no direct impact on the budget, OMB rejected nearly all NCA appeals for an expanded staff.

In short, the administration's opposition was evident at all levels of bureaucratic implementation. OMB not only refused to request funding for virtually all Title VII grant programs, but it impounded funds already appropriated by Congress without request, as well as $3.5 million in developer application fees earmarked for staff expansion. The CDC was never able to attain the independent status Congress envisioned for it. The statute did not give the CDC any independent source of staff or funds and it was forced to rely on HUD for these. The Nixon administration refused autonomy to an agency responsible for implementing an unwanted program; consequently, HUD dominated the CDC and the Congressional intent to use the program as an experiment in community planning gave way to HUD's "banker mentality."

The new communities program might have enjoyed a higher position among the priorities of a Democratic administration with a different ideological bent, but little changed after President Carter took office in 1977. However, Rabinovitz and Smookler believe that the program would have failed even had there been a sympathetic executive for several reasons.[49] Except for a few key supporters in Congress, there was little organized and powerful political support and the program was unable to generate a strong constituency during implementation. Mayors of big cities, while not opposed to the program, did not see enough benefits accruing to their cities to wield their political influence on behalf of the program. The two major natural constituencies of the program were private new community developers and new community residents (and potential residents). However, interested developers were usually too small in number and too unorganized and new communities residents were too few to have much political impact.

Closer scrutiny by HUD might have averted many of the financial problems that plagued new communities and subsequently led to their failure. Yet Rabinovitz and Smookler argue that the necessary critical evaluation is impossible in a bureaucracy responsible for monitoring and evaluating its own decisions, particularly in the absence of any statutory criteria for program success. Admitting defeat once agency resources have been committed presents the bureaucracy with the problem of extricating itself from a project that is financially unsound. The typical bureaucratic response is to stand one's ground, pump in more cash, and hope for the best, even if there is good evidence that abandoning the project would be the better course; HUD seems to have followed the traditional course.

A final problem plaguing effective implementation of Title VII was the statute's multiple and often conflicting goals. For example, new-towns-in-town were included in the 1970 Act in order to improve the condition of the inner-city poor by refurbishing the ghetto, yet new-towns-in-town were actually designed to attract the middle class back into the city, thus displacing the poor from the urban housing that was ostensibly being built for them. The act attempted to encourage, at least formally, the participation of local governments in the planning process, in spite of local government's traditional antipathy toward federally established goals of integration. The act stated its intent both to increase the volume of building sites over the next twenty years and to preserve the environment but made no attempt to reconcile these often conflicting objectives. The act promoted the development of a new technology for quality housing construction, while encouraging mass participation of small developers in the program, despite the fact that small developers typically do not have the resources for design experimentation. Statute goals were not ranked in order of importance, nor did the statute specify how HUD was to reconcile potential conflicts between goals. Consequently, HUD found itself applying different objectives to different projects, to the frustration of many developers. The Congressional emphasis on technical innovation, new-towns-in-town development, experimentation, and local government partici-pation was subordinated to financial considerations and, to a lesser extent, to the goal of class and racial integration.

New Communities viewed in light of the conceptual framework of implementation

How does the new communities program measure up to the requisite six conditions for effective policy implementation? We now turn to an examina-tion of this question.

Condition	Assessment
1. The statute contains clear and consistent policy directives.	The overall goal of the principal new communities legislation—the Urban Growth and New Communities Act of 1970—was to encourage construction of well-planned, diversified, and economically sound new communities in a manner that would rely to the maximum extent on private enterprise. Within this broad categorical statement of purposes was incorporated a body of formal statutory goals. Yet the ten goals established were neither ranked nor were they very specific. The act stated that new communities should

Condition	Assessment
	"develop means to encourage good housing for all Americans" while "treating comprehensively the problems of poverty and unemployment," yet provided no guidance on how such broad-ranging goals were to be achieved. When articulated goals are so comprehensive, it is likely that contradiction will emerge in specific application. The act did not indicate which objectives should be given priority in implementation. Considerable discretion was thus left to the HUD bureaucracy. The statute did attempt to indicate the relative priority of the new communities program within the HUD bureaucracy through the creation of the CDC and the expansion of the NCA. However, the CDC's governing board consisted primarily of HUD appointees and the NCA staff was recruited predominantly from within HUD. Title VII was perceived as a minor program by decision makers within HUD, and as a superfluous one by Nixon's White House advisors. Thus, Title VII did not command high priority among other HUD programs.
2. The statute incorporates a sound theory identifying the factors affecting program goals and gives implementing officials sufficient jurisdiction to attain those objectives.	The statute implicitly assumed that monetary incentives provided by the federal government would lead to the development of successful new communities. Its emphasis was therefore mainly on an economic remedy to the problems of new community development: certain levels of funding would lead to a realization of Congressional objectives, which would lead in turn to attractive, socially and racially integrated, self-sustaining new communities. The absence of new community development in the face of perceived need was seen as the result of market shortcomings; Title VII was a response

Assessment

to the argument that federal intervention was necessary for the attainment of federal goals. The validity of this theory was never really tested, since most of the incentive provisions of the act were never funded.

At the same time, the study by Burby and Weiss (*New Communities U.S.A.*) and the economic and racial assessment by Smookler (*Economic Integration in New Communities*) suggest that, with the important exception of achieving a fair amount of racial and class integration, federally supported new communities were no better than non-federally supported ones in enhancing the quality of life of their residents. Naturally, this conclusion does not negate the contention that new communities enhance the quality of life beyond that of traditional urban living; it simply questions the emphasis on a public means of bringing new communities into existence.

The basic theoretical assumption of the statute was that a financial incentive within the context of some broad federal guidelines would induce developers to serve the federal purpose by designing, planning, and, most importantly, negotiating with various local, regional, and state jurisdictions over a proposed community. Therefore, little attention was given to the mechanics of the actual implementation process. For example, the act did not provide HUD with any capability for continuing oversight and management of federally supported new communities. And HUD could not ensure delivery of the promised quality services; it could only provide a financial incentive (an added 20 percent to the federal share of a service) to local governments.

Condition	Assessment

3. The statute structures implementation to maximize the probability of compliance from implementing officials and target groups.

Since the act envisioned using the self-interest of developers to accomplish its implementation, little administrative infrastructure and authority was provided. And what little Congress did provide, the Nixon administration and HUD managed to undermine.

a. More specifically, Congress had little choice but to assign responsibility for the new communities to HUD. It was either that or create a new agency that duplicated HUD activities. Aware of the low priority new communities received under the 1968 act, Congressman Ashley incorporated into the 1970 act creation of the Community Development Corporation (CDC) to offer technical and planning assistance to state and local agencies. The New Communities Administration (NCA), which was intended to be semiautonomous within HUD, was also included, but because of the opposition of the Nixon administration, the CDC board consisted of four HUD appointees and a general manager appointed by the president.

The revolving fund established under the act was intended to provide resources for new community management staff and analytical work. By 1974 this revolving fund held over $8 million. Certainly this would have been an adequate amount to fund the increase in staff necessary to perform the many functions mandated by the program. The authors of the statute, then, at least attempted to provide an adequate level of resources for effective implementation. The administration, however, refused to release these funds and placed severe restrictions on staff hiring. Consequently, program analysis and monitoring were quite limited.

The statute's reliance for implementation on federal interagency coordination, local governments, and

Assessment

private developers seems to maximize, rather than minimize, the number of veto points in the program. State and local agencies were to play a key role in the success of implementation; however, the statute made no attempt to integrate them hierarchically into the process. Local involvement in the planning consisted mainly of negotiations between the developer and local agencies. This gave local officials, who may or may not have been sympathetic with the goals of the statute, considerable leverage over program decisions. The statute did provide supporters of the program with public service and categorical grants as inducements to facilitate local acquiescence; however, OMB rejected all requests to fund these grants.

b. The formal application process for loan guarantees called for the developer to submit a comprehensive plan outlining the means of goal achievement, a requirement which did suggest that decision rules within HUD were structured in a way to ensure achievement of those goals. While this requirement placed the "burden of proof" on the developer, unfortunately, the nature of the program was such that if goals were not achieved, HUD was relatively powerless to do much of anything about it. Thus, as a practical matter, a developer's burden of proof lightened with each federal dollar put into the project; as HUD's stake grew, so did its unwillingness to write off federal money. Consequently, HUD was lenient in enforcing strict adherence to statutory objectives until financial disaster was imminent.

c. The statute made no provision for the explicit participation of program proponents in HUD's decisions affecting new communities. The usual methods of lobbying Congress or the

Condition

Assessment

executive or the courts existed, but little more. To some extent, of course, this omission never became a major issue in the implementation process because of the general public's lack of interest in the program. Independent program evaluation and oversight, another avenue of success, was largely ad hoc.

4. Top implementing officials are strongly committed to attainment of statutory objectives and have the skills necessary to ensure achievement of the goals.

While the new units created in HUD to implement the act did give some visibility to the program, no dynamic and politically astute implementing officials were attracted to the program. Despite the enthusiasm of the initial staff assembled by William Nicoson, generally the program failed to attract a strong and effective staff to meet its objectives. Thus neither the NCA nor the nominally independent CDC had the requisite leadership and resources to command much attention within HUD. This may have resulted more from the Nixon administration's failure to make a strong commitment to the program rather than from an inherent lack of leadership or skills among HUD personnel. Those HUD officials given final authority over the program were thought to be mildly supportive, but outside of the NCA, the program was not assigned high priority even within HUD.

5. The program is actively supported by organized constituency groups and few key sovereigns (legislative or executive) throughout the implementation process.

The problem here was that no one in authority in HUD was particularly supportive of the program, and the White House was actively against it. No statutory provision was made for sovereign intervention or even systematic Congressional oversight. Ashley did attempt to act as a "fixer" and to monitor the program by allying with sympathetic elements within HUD, specifically former ONCD director Nicoson. However, Ashley was unable

Condition	Assessment

to overcome presidential and OMB hostility to get funding for the program's grant provisions; consequently, most statutory objectives went unrealized.

Ashley then turned to his legislative hearings which were designed to flush out latent support for the program. He was able to obtain support from some mayors of big cities, the National League of Cities, the U.S. Conference of Mayors, the American Institute of Planners, and a few governors. However, this support dissipated over time. And the "natural" clientele of the program—large real estate investors, property developers, and the building trades and unions—did not step forward and actively defend it. Local governments, the public constituents most likely to reap long-run economic benefits from new communities, were either skeptical about a federal/local partnership or were uninformed.

6. Changing socioeconomic conditions over time do not weaken the statute's causal theory or political support nor the priority of statutory objectives.

In the short span of four years that new communities was an active program within HUD, little technological change occurred to substantially alter implementability of the program. However, the recession of 1973–74 dramatically affected the financial viability of the new communities that were just getting underway at that time. Debt-service costs alone in 1975 exceeded 100 percent of all revenues in all but two cases, which was well over initial projections.[50] More than any other single factor, the dismal financial picture led to several refinancings and HUD takeovers in the mid- to late-1970s and early 1980s.

The program was also adversely affected by the changing public mood reflected in the changeover from an interventionist Democratic party, in

Assessment

power during the conception of the new communities program, to a Republican administration during the implementation phase. The change in administration also signaled a de-emphasis on programs targeted at the less-well-off in society, such as grant-in-aid housing subsidies vital to new communities, to allocation by population, e.g., bloc grants and revenue sharing.

Clearly, the statute was not written in a manner that would optimize its chances of implementation. It was a product of compromise and as such rather vague. The problem addressed by the statute was not intractable. The target group, defined as the private development industry, constituted only a small portion of the total population. Developer behavior was not particularly diverse; the statutory intent was to induce a single category of development. The extent of behavioral change required in the target group was not great; indeed, private new community development had already been undertaken and the statute merely attempted to accelerate and broaden this movement. Nevertheless, the new communities experience illustrates the extraordinary difficulty of attempting to devise the proper blend of regulations and incentives to entice private actors to serve the public weal.

Reviewing the new communities program, we find that it fell short on all six of the conditions required for effective implementation. A lofty and ambitious idea translated into a rather ambiguously worded statute with multiple objectives can conceivably be molded into an effective program, given strong support from sovereigns and constituency groups. Yet this was not the case. A loosely integrated statute with multiple objectives was assigned to an established agency which had many other missions to pursue. The program failed to command presidential attention, and it went underfunded by

Congress. Without an extremely potent lobby to resurrect the program and to push for more effective implementation, it simply fell by the wayside.

For further reflection

1. What might have been the fate of the New Communities Program if the liberal Democrat, Hubert Humphrey, had won the presidential election in 1968 rather than Republican Richard Nixon?
2. Assume that you were assigned to be chief program administrator for a new towns program today. What steps would you take to develop a more active and effective support constituency than that which existed during the implementation process of the 1968 and 1970 New Communities legislation?
3. It has been alleged that the program would have succeeded if responsibility for new towns had been placed in the hands of public housing officials, as was the case in the far more successful experience in Great Britain, instead of relying on the initiative of private developers. How do you react to this assertion? [For reference to the British new towns experience, see J. B. Cullingworth, *Town and Country Planning in Britain* (London: George Allen and Unwin, 1979), chapter 11; Marian Clawson and Peter Hall, *Planning and Urban Growth: An Anglo-American Comparison* (Baltimore, Md.: The Johns Hopkins University Press, 1973), chapter 6].
4. Assume the role of a policy analyst for a state governor committed to sponsoring new towns legislation. How would you design a program that would avoid some of the major pitfalls of the 1968 and 1970 New Communities legislation?

Notes

1. Carlos Campbell, *New Towns: Another Way to Live* (Reston, Va.: Reston Publishing Company, 1976), p. 5
2. Eric Stowe and John Rehfuss, "Federal New Towns Policy: 'Muddling Through' at the Local Level," *Public Administration Review* 35 (May/June 1975): 224.
3. Eleanore Carruth, "The Big Move to New Towns," *Fortune* 84, 3 (1971): 95–97.
4. Stowe and Rehfuss, "Federal New Towns," p. 223.
5. 1968 ACIR report, quoted in Stowe and Rehfuss, "Federal New Towns," p. 223.
6. Campbell, *New Towns*, p. 8.
7. Stowe and Rehfuss, "Federal New Towns," p. 224.
8. Thomas Ashley, "Congress and New Towns," *Public Administration Review* 35 (May/June 1975): 240.
9. Martha Derthick, *New Towns In-Town* (Washington, D.C.: The Urban Institute, 1972) p. 98.
10. In the early 1960s, for example, land acquisition cost alone ran $22 million for Columbia and $12 million for Reston. See Helene Smookler, "Administration Hara-Kiri: Implementation of the Urban Growth and New Community Development Act," *Annals* 422 (November 1975): 131, note 5.
11. U.S. Congress, House, Subcommittee on Housing, Committee on Banking and Currency, *Oversight Hearings on HUD New Communities Program*, 93rd Cong., 1st sess., 30–31 May 1973, p. 80.

12. Ashley, "Congress and New Towns," p. 241.
13. Hugh Mields, "The Politics of Federal Legislation for New Communities," in *New Community Development—Planning Process: Implementation and Emerging Social Concerns,* vol. 2, ed. Shirley Weiss et al. (Chapel Hill, N.C.: University of North Carolina, 1971), p. 246.
14. Mields, "Politics of," p. 248.
15. Francine Rabinovitz and Helene Smookler, "Rhetoric Versus Performance: The National Politics and Administration of U.S. New Community Development Legislation," in *New Towns—Why and for Whom?* ed. Harvey Perloff and Neil Sandberg (New York: Praeger, 1973), pp. 90–114.
16. Rabinovitz and Smookler, "Rhetoric Versus Performance," p. 94.
17. Urban Growth and New Community Development Act of 1970, Public Law 91–609, December 31, 1970, section 710 (f).
18. Jack Underhill, "New Communities Planning Process and National Growth Policy," in *The Contemporary New Communities Movement in the United States,* ed. Gideon Golany and Denial Walden (Urbana, Ill.: University of Illinois Press, 1974), p. 41.
19. Rabinovitz and Smookler, "Rhetoric Versus Performance."
20. *Oversight Hearings,* p. 55.
21. *Oversight Hearings,* p. 30.
22. Stowe and Rehfuss, "Federal New Towns," p. 225.
23. *Oversight Hearings,* pp. 17–19.
24. *Oversight Hearings,* p. 55.
25. Smookler, "Hara-Kiri," p. 137.
26. Campbell, *New Towns,* p. 247.
27. William Fucik, "The Challenge of Implementing Federally Assisted New Communities," *Public Administration Review* 35 (May/June 1975): 252.
28. Smookler, "Hara-Kiri," p. 130.
29. The description of Jonathan is drawn from Raymond Burby and Shirley Weiss, *New Communities U.S.A.* (Lexington, Mass.: Lexington Books, 1976) chapter 18, and Campbell, *New Towns,* chapters 7 and 14.
30. Academy for Contemporary Problems, "Report on New Communities" (Columbus, Ohio: unpublished monograph, 1975); Burby and Weiss, *New Communities U.S.A.;* New Communities Administration, *New Communities: Problems and Potentials* (U.S. Department of Housing and Urban Development, December 1976), Appendices A-D.
31. New Communities Administration, *New Communities,* Appendix D, pp. 41–42.
32. William Nicoson, "The Role of the Federal Government in New Community Development; Present and Projected," in *New Community Development Planning Process,* ed. Shirley Weiss et al., p. 454.
33. Burby and Weiss, *New Communities U.S.A.,* pp. 108–9.
34. Hugh Evans and Lloyd Rodwin, "The New Towns Program and Why It Failed," *The Public Interest* 56 (Summer 1979): 104.
35. Helene Smookler, *Economic Integration in New Communities* (Cambridge, Mass.: Ballinger Publishing Co., 1976), p. 131.
36. Evans and Rodwin, "New Towns," p. 104.
37. Rabinovitz and Smookler, "Rhetoric Versus Performance."
38. *Newsweek,* June 4, 1979, p. 15.
39. William Alonso, "The Mirage of New Towns," *The Public Interest* 19 (Spring 1970): 5.
40. Academy for Contemporary Problems, "Report," p. 5.
41. Academy for Contemporary Problems, "Report," p. 20.
42. *Oversight Hearings,* p. 30.
43. Smookler, "Hara-Kiri," p. 138.
44. Burby and Weiss, *New Communities U.S.A.,* p. 62.
45. Evans and Rodwin, "New Towns."
46. This was a central conclusion of the HUD staff evaluation of the program; see New Communities Administration, *New Communities,* pp. 78–95.
47. Academy for Contemporary Problems, "Report," p. 23.
48. Burby and Weiss, *New Communities U.S.A.,* p. 167.
49. Rabinovitz and Smookler, "Rhetoric Versus Performance," pp. 101–110.
50. Evans and Rodwin, "New Towns," pp. 97–98.

Chapter 4
Strategic retreat from stringent objectives: automotive emissions control, 1970-77

The automobile is a central feature of American society. Because of the convenience, comfort, and privacy it affords, it is by far our preferred mode of transportation. In 1975 over 80 percent of American families had at least one car, while about a third possessed two or more. In contrast, buses and trains accounted for only 4 percent of commuter trips and a lesser percentage of all transit.[1] The automobile provides mobility so more and more families can achieve the American dream of owning a home in the suburbs. Because of the drastic decline in intercity buses and trains since the end of World War II, the private car is virtually the only form of transportation in rural areas and for persons seeking temporary relief from the congestion and noise of urban areas by retreating to the mountains and other "quiet places."

The automobile is also one of the linchpins of the American economy. One job in six is dependent upon it, and 18 percent of the gross national product is related to it. In 1975, the three largest automobile companies employed 800,000 persons, exclusive of dealers, in 36 states. In addition, major portions of the steel, rubber, lead, oil, and aluminum industries are dependent upon the health of General Motors, Ford, Chrysler, and American Motors.[2]

For all of its benefits, however, the automobile is also a major contributor to some of our most serious national problems. In 1975 highway transportation (including trucks) accounted for 97 percent of all gasoline consumption and more than half the oil used in the nation. This is the equivalent of almost all of the nation's oil imports. The personal mobility which the automobile provides has been an important factor in the growth of the suburbs over the last thirty years, thereby contributing to both the decline of central cities and the loss of valuable farmland. About 50,000 Americans die in automobile accidents each year. Automobiles and trucks are the largest single source (by tonnage) of atmospheric pollutants. Throughout the 1970s, highway vehicles accounted for about 70 percent of all carbon monoxide emission, 36 percent of hydrocarbons, 27 percent of nitrogen oxides, and trace amounts of sulfur oxides and suspended particulate matter.[3]

Efforts to reduce vehicle emissions proceeded rather slowly, in part because their role in the formation of photochemical smog was not understood until the mid-1950s.[4] After the voluntary efforts of the automobile companies proved unsuccessful, the state of California and the federal government adopted some modest emission controls in the mid-1960s. This incremental approach was radically altered by the 1970 Federal Clean Air Amendments, which mandated a 90 percent reduction from 1970 levels of carbon monoxide and hydrocarbons emissions by 1975 and of nitrogen oxides emissions by 1976. Although the technology to achieve such substantial reductions was not then available, it was felt that the presence of clear legal requirements would force the automobile companies to develop the necessary innovations in engine design.

The seven years following passage of the 1970 amendments witnessed repeated postponements in these deadlines and a general inability of present emissions to meet prescribed levels. Not surprisingly, only rather modest improvements were registered in ambient air concentrations of carbon monoxide, hydrocarbons, nitrogen oxides, and photochemical smog. Finally, in 1977—a year *after* the 90 percent reductions in automotive emissions were supposed to have been achieved—Congress amended the Clean Air Act by (a) relaxing the final nitrogen oxides emission standard to require a 75 percent (rather than 90 percent) reduction from 1971 levels, (b) postponing the timetable for ultimate reductions until the 1981 model year, and (c) postponing the deadline for achievement of the ambient air quality standards (necessary to protect public health) from 1977 to 1982 and, in a few particularly severe areas, to 1987.

Efforts to control automotive emissions thus represent a classic example of what Aaron Wildavsky has termed "the strategic retreat from objectives."[5] The 1970 amendments established goals which may have been beyond the ability of any democratic government to achieve because they mandated extraordinary technological innovation in a critical sector of the economy, gave inadequate attention to other national priorities (e.g., fuel conservation), and entailed changes in the transportation habits of millions of citizens. Confronted with strong resistance from both automobile companies and commuters and with the manifest failure to achieve the objectives of the 1970 act, Congress in 1977 decided to adopt somewhat more limited goals and to relax the deadlines, while at the same time improving the prospects for compliance through more adequate sanctions and inducements.

In this chapter we will first review the history of efforts to control automotive emissions during the 1960s, which culminated in passage of the 1970 Clean Air Amendments. We will examine the implementation of those laws, focusing on the difficulties encountered in reducing emissions from automobiles and in altering the transportation habits of urban residents. The results of the implementation process—both in terms of changes in emissions and air quality over time, as well as the statutory changes incorporated into the 1977 amendments—will then be studied. Finally, we shall analyze the implementation of the 1970 Clean Air Amendments in terms of the analytical framework developed in chapter 2.

The background, history, and content of the 1970 Clean Air Amendments

Although the automobile is a major source of air pollution, it is by no means the only one nor, from a health standpoint, probably the most serious one. There are at least five air pollution "syndromes," with automobile emissions seriously implicated in the latter three:[6]

1. *Sulfur oxides (SO$_x$)/total suspended particulate matter (TSP)*. This is the oldest, best understood, and probably the most dangerous of the five. SO$_x$ and TSP result primarily from the burning of coal and fuel oil by residences and electrical utilities (primarily in the North and East), as well as emissions from steel mills, foundries, and other industrial processes. This is the syndrome primarily responsible for most of the famous air pollution "episodes"—Donora 1948, London 1952, New York 1962—and for which considerable evidence exists of serious adverse effects on human health and property for both short-term high-exposure and more long-term chronic conditions.

2. *Hazardous emissions from local point sources*. This refers to the release of extremely toxic chemicals such as cadium, mercury, and asbestos from a wide variety of industrial processes. Section 112 of the 1970 Clean Air Amendments required the Environmental Protection Agency to set extremely stringent emissions standards for such pollutants.

3. *Carbon monoxide (CO)*. This is the one pollutant for which the automobile is unquestionably the major source. Incomplete combustion of gasoline releases carbon monoxide and harmful concentrations tend to be found in downtown areas of large cities as a result of stop-and-go traffic. The adverse effects on human health of fairly high concentrations are fairly well documented.

4. *Photochemical smog (oxidant)*. Emissions of hydrocarbons (HC) and nitrogen oxides (NO$_x$) combine with sunlight in a very complex series of chemical reactions in the atmosphere to produce a number of oxidants, of which the two most important are ozone and PAN (peroxyacyl nitrate). There is ample evidence that the latter produces eye irritation and that oxidants have caused substantial crop damage. The effects of smog on human health have

been the subject of much dispute; in fact, EPA in 1979 loosened the oxidant standards originally adopted in 1970, at least partially because of errors in some of the original studies.[7] Ambient air concentrations in most urban areas exceed the old standard.

5. *Nitrogen oxides (NO_x).* In addition to their contribution to the formation of photochemical smog, nitrogen oxides on their own can adversely affect human health and property. As with oxidants, however, the health effects of specific concentrations have been the source of considerable controversy. While ambient concentrations in only a few cities exceeded federal air quality standards during the 1970s, there is some recent evidence implicating NO_x in acid rain.

Table 4.1 lists the principal sources for each of these pollution syndromes during 1970. Note that whereas highway vehicles were responsible for 69 percent of carbon monoxide emissions nationwide, they contributed only about 36 percent and 27 percent of hydrocarbon and nitrogen oxides emissions, respectively. Other major sources of hydrocarbons (or volatile organic compounds) include the chemical industry, oil and gas production, and a variety of organic solvent users (e.g., dry cleaning establishments). Likewise, stationary sources of nitrogen oxides (principally fuel combustion from utilities and industry) contributed 57 percent of nitrogen oxides emissions nationwide. However, in specific air basins, such as Los Angeles and San Francisco, mobile sources also contribute a majority of hydrocarbon and nitrogen oxides emissions.[8]

Background and early control efforts

In order to understand the history of automotive pollution control policy in the United States, we must know something about the principal factors affecting air quality levels of photochemical oxidants and carbon monoxide. Principally, ambient air concentrations result not only from emissions from manufactured sources but also from natural background concentrations, atmospheric dispersion processes, and, in the case of oxidants, sunlight. Pollution control agencies can, of course, affect only the first of these four factors. There are some regions—most notably, Los Angeles—where the combination of abundant sunlight, very poor air dispersion patterns, and moderate background levels of hydrocarbons and nitrogen oxides probably mean that the attainment of the primary (that is, health-related) air quality standards mandated by the 1970 Clean Air Amendments would require virtually zero emissions from manufactured sources.[9]

In terms of basic control strategy, it is also important to note that automotive emissions are a function of emissions per vehicle mile and the number of vehicle miles traveled. The former, in turn, is contingent upon the ability of the automobile companies to build, and motorists to maintain, emissions control systems in individual automobiles. In principle, pollution control agencies can affect both factors. On the other hand, reducing the number of vehicle miles traveled depends upon housing patterns and the availability of mass transit systems within an area. These matters have traditionally been under the jurisdiction of housing, land use, and transportation—rather than pollution control—agencies. Moreover, the dispersed housing patterns and strong preference of most Americans for the private automobile as a mode of transit mean that substantially reducing vehicle miles traveled would involve not only coordination among numerous autonomous agencies but also a rather fundamental change in the life-style of urban Americans.

It is hardly surprising, then, that efforts to reduce automotive emissions historically have focused on convincing automobile manufacturers to reduce emissions per mile rather than persuading motorists to travel fewer miles. There were, of course, other reasons for focusing on the automobile companies. They were highly visible and, at least during the 1950s and 1960s, quite prosperous impersonal corporations. Moreover, there was the hope or expectation that a change in automotive technology could significantly reduce emissions per mile without requiring any change in life-style. But probably the fundamental reason was the logical assumption that it is easier to change the behavior of the four major automobile makers than the behavior of millions of urban residents for whom the home in the suburbs and the privacy and comfort of the automobile are highly cherished values.

Neither the automobile companies nor motorists could, however, be expected *voluntarily* to change their behavior. In both cases the benefits to individuals (or individual firms) of pollution control were likely to be highly uncertain, given the problems of accurately assessing the health benefits of pollution control. Also, except in the case of individuals suffering from respiratory disease and farmers suffering crop damage, benefits might also be rather insignificant. In contrast, the costs of emissions reduction were much easier to predict and potentially quite substantial. For the automobile companies, the costs involved potentially lower sales due to the increased costs of pollution control systems and the inconvenience of changing production systems. For motorists, the inconvenience of using public transit or of moving closer to work in order to reduce vehicle miles traveled would almost certainly exceed the benefits received from the impact of any individual contributions to improved air quality. Hence significant reduction in automotive emissions could come about only if the government forced all members of the target group to bear the individual costs in order to attain the collective benefit of reduced damage to health and property from photochemical smog and carbon monoxide.[10]

Automotive pollution control policy during the 1950s and 1960s moved in small, hesitant steps.[11] Early efforts were concentrated in California, partly because that was the center of research on the dynamics of smog formation and partly because of the seriousness of the local problem, especially in Los Angeles. When repeated calls by local officials produced very little action by

TABLE 4.1
Percentage of 1970 Nationwide Emissions from Various Source Categories
(1,000,000 metric tons per year)

Source Category	SOx/TSP		Hazardous Pollutants	Carbon Monoxide	Photochemical Smog	
	TSP	SOx			HC[a]	NOx
Transportation			not presented			
Highway vehicles	3	1	because	69	36	27
Nonhighway	2	1	sources	10	5	11
Stationary fuel combustion	32	76	and	1	5	57
Industrial processes	54	21	specific	8	29	3
Solid waste	5	0	pollutants	6		1
Miscellaneous	4	1	so varied	6	19	1
Total	100	100		100	99	100

Source: U.S. Environmental Protection Agency, *National Air Quality, Monitoring, and Emissions Trends Report* Research Triangle Parks, N.C. 1 EPA, December 1978), Table 5-Z.

[a]Presently measured in terms of volatile organic compounds (VOC)

the automobile companies, California in 1961 required that crankcase ventilation devices be installed to reduce "blowby" emissions (about 25 percent of hydrocarbons from an uncontrolled car) and in 1963 required the installation of exhaust emissions systems in 1966 model year cars. These systems were designed to reduce hydrocarbon and carbon monoxide by an additional 25 to 30 percent. In both cases, similar standards were applied nationwide two years later by federal officials. But a limited understanding of the dynamics of smog formation and its effects on health and property hampered pollution control efforts throughout the 1950s and 1960s. In addition the automobile manufacturers repeatedly played down their contribution to the problem, stressed the difficulties of developing new technology, and quite possibly engaged in collusive activities to forestall the development and installation of such technology.

The 1970 Clean Air Amendments

By late 1969 and early 1970, however, the situation had changed considerably.[12] First, the automobile companies suffered a gradual loss of credibility with the publication of Ralph Nader's *Unsafe at Any Speed,* the subsequent inept effort by General Motors to discredit Nader, and the September 1969 out-of-court settlement of a suit brought by the Justice Department charging the four American automobile manufactures with suppressing the development of more effective pollution control systems. Second, and more important, the late 1960s witnessed a tremendous growth in public concern with environmental degradation. Although changes in general background factors such as improved living standards and a desire to forget the highly divisive issues of civil rights and Vietnam contributed, the rise in environmental consciousness was also due to specific events such as the 1969 Santa Barbara oil spill and to the quiet efforts of federal air pollution officials to disseminate information concerning the health effects of air pollution and to develop air pollution constituencies in large cities throughout the nation. A nationwide Gallop poll conducted in 1970 indicated that 53 percent of the respondents felt that air and water pollution was one of the three most serious issues facing the country, compared to 17 percent who answered that way on a similar poll taken in 1965. Throughout 1969 and 1970 the mass media were filled with stories about environmental damage, and the swell of popular concern reached a crescendo in the massive demonstration of Earth Day, April 22, 1970.

Although the situation was ripe for major new legislation, Senator Edmund Muskie (Dem., Maine), chairman of the Senate Subcommittee on Air and Water Pollution and the unchallenged Congressional expert on pollution control, introduced a bill in December 1969 which proposed only incremental changes in existing legislation. In contrast, President Nixon, who had no record of concern with environmental degradation, devoted much of his January 1970 State of the Union address to environmental issues. He created the Environmental Protection Agency (EPA) through an executive reorganization in July 1970 and introduced legislation in early 1970 which, among other things, would have required a 90 percent reduction in automotive emissions on new cars by 1980 and provided funds for reseach on low-polluting automotive technologies. A few months later the House of Representatives approved a slightly stronger version of Nixon's bill by a vote of 334 to 40. Whether recognizing that he had underestimated the public and Congressional mood for change or whether stung by this intrusion on his territory and by the highly critical review of federal air pollution policy published by a group of Nader's Raiders in April, Senator Muskie, together with members of his subcommittee, completely rewrote the bill over the summer. They advanced the deadline for the 90 percent reduction in new car emissions from 1980 to 1975 (1976 for nitrogen oxides), added a provision granting federal officials some authority to regulate land use and transportation habits, and greatly strengthened EPA's ability to set emission standards for new stationary sources, hazardous pollutants, and fuel additives. The Muskie bill was then approved by the Senate with a single dissenting vote, ratified by the House-Senate Conference Committee after minor changes, and signed into law by President Nixon on December 31, 1970.[13]

The 1970 Clean Air Amendments established a general goal of "protecting and enhancing the quality of the Nation's air resources so as to promote the public health and welfare and the productive capacity of its population."[14] This general intention was further clarified, first, by administrative actions indicating that air quality standards were to protect the health not only of healthy adults but also of susceptible populations (e.g., those suffering from respiratory disease) and, second, by the general absence of statutory language requiring that public health be balanced against economic costs and technological feasibility.

In order to achieve this basic objective, the 1970 amendments required the EPA administrator to set ambient air quality standards for major pollutants sufficient to protect public health with an adequate margin of safety and to set emission standards for new sources and for hazardous pollutants based upon adequately demonstrated state-of-the-art technology. State pollution control agencies were then to develop implementation plans to achieve these air quality standards by approximately May 1975 (with a possible extension to May 1977). Such plans were to include emissions standards for new and existing stationary sources, provision for adequate staffing and enforcement, and, where necessary to achieve air quality standards, land use and transportation control plans. The EPA administrator was to review the proposed implementation plans, to impose any revisions deemed necessary, and, in extreme cases, to substitute federal for state enforcement.[15]

The 1970 Clean Air Amendments also set emission standards for new cars, requiring a 90 percent reduction (from 1970 levels) in carbon monoxide and hydrocarbons by the 1975 model year and in nitrogen oxides by the 1976 model year.[16] The 90 percent figure was taken largely from an analysis by federal air pollution control officials of the reductions necessary to meet a peak oxidant standard of .06 ppm in *all* air basins by 1990, taking into account anticipated increases in automobiles and other factors. At a White House conference in 1969, the automobile manufacturers had committed themselves to achieving a 90 percent reduction by the 1980 model year, but in 1970 they expressed serious doubts about their ability to develop the new technology in time for the 1975–76 model years (as required by the 1970 amendments). Because of the uncertainties surrounding the attempt to accelerate technological innovation, the amendments also called for biennial reviews of auto pollution technology by the National Academy of Sciences and authorized the EPA Administrator to extend the emission deadlines for one year under certain conditions.

It should be noted, however, that the automobile emission standards could have only a very modest effect on the achievement of the ambient air quality standards by the mid-1975 deadline. Given the modest annual turnover in the automobile fleet, it might be another ten years, or 1985, before all cars on the road would supposedly meet the 90 percent reduction levels (assuming that cars met the emission standards for 50,000 miles as required by law). Thus, meeting the air quality objectives for oxidant and carbon monoxide by mid-1975 (or even mid-1977) would be contingent upon reductions in emissions from stationary sources (which accounted for about two thirds of the hydrocarbon and nitrogen oxides emissions—see Table 4.1) and in somehow reducing vehicle miles traveled through the use of land use and transportation controls. This topic received only a single sentence in the entire sixty-page bill, although a report by the Senate Committee on Public Works indicated implementation might require draconian measures.[17]

In order to promote compliance, the 1970 amendments provided civil penalties of $25,000 per violation-day for stationary sources and $10,000 per automobile for mobile sources and established a procedure enabling ordinary citizens to sue any government agency for noncompliance with nondiscretionary legal requirements.[18]

In sum, the 1970 Clear Air Amendments sought to achieve by mid-1977 nationwide ambient air concentrations that would be safe even for people suffering from respiratory diseases. While the basic objective of the program —protection of public health—was clear and some of the subsidiary objectives, for instance, the 90 percent reduction in auto emissions by 1975–76, were even more precise, these goals were also extremely ambitious. They essentially called for the use of state-of-the-art technology on all stationary sources, development and assembly-line production within five years of new technology to control automotive emissions, and probably a substantial change in the driving habits of millions of urban Americans. For these goals to have been achieved would have required a tremendous mobilization of national effort.

Not surprisingly, that effort was only partially forthcoming. Part of the problem resided in the legislation itself. In many respects, it did a coherent job of structuring the implementation process. The goals were clear. The statute contained a reasonably valid theory in which the general nature of causal relationships was understood—although not to the precise extent needed to develop quantitative models—and in which federal and state pollution control officials were given jurisdiction over sufficient causal factors (except, perhaps, in regions such as Los Angeles with extremely inhospitable meteorological and topographical features). The statute created an implementation system which, although it included numerous veto points in the preparation of implementation plans and the enforcement of regulations, also clearly left EPA with ultimate control over state programs. EPA was given apparently adequate sanctions to encourage compliance by automobile companies, stationary sources, and perhaps even motorists. And the legislation provided access for clean air advocates through public hearings in the development of implementation plans and through innovative provisions allowing suits to be brought by citizens; there were also requirements for independent review of many important technical questions by the National Academy of Sciences.

Nevertheless, with respect to the automotive pollutants—carbon monoxide, nitrogen oxides, and oxidants—the statute had at least two major flaws. First, it assumed that the automobile companies could be commanded to develop and produce new technologies within five years despite the lack of any sanctions or incentives for such dramatic behavioral change. The "nuclear deterrent" of closing down the auto manufacturers or imposing massive fines was simply not a reasonable option, given the economic importance of the industry. Second, the lack of fit between the 1975–76 new car emissions deadlines and the 1977 ambient air quality deadlines placed an enormous burden (prior to the mid-1980s) on reducing emissions from stationary sources and on reducing vehicle miles traveled. While the legislation attempted to give EPA some control over the latter, the legislative history suggests that most members of Congress did not understand the implications of those two deadlines. Had they realized that achieving the 1977 ambient air quality standards would entail a substantial restructuring of commuting habits and perhaps even land use patterns in many urban areas, the legislation would surely have been rewritten. In fact, much of the subsequent implementation process can be viewed as a gradual realization of the constraints which would have to be placed on the issue of "clean air."

Implementation of the 1970 Clean Air Amendments

Table 4.2 summarizes the major events affecting those portions of the 1970 Clean Air Amendments relating to automotive emissions. The table distinguishes actions principally affecting attempts to reduce emissions per vehicle

TABLE 4.2
Chronology of the Implementation of the 1970 Clean Air Amendments Relative to Automotive Emissions

Date	General	Event of Interest to	
		Reducing Emissions per Vehicle Mile	**Reducing Vehicle Miles Traveled (VMT)**
Dec. 1970	Passage of 1970 Clean Air Amendments.		
April 1971	EPA sets air quality standards for SO_x; TSP, HC, NO_x, and oxidants. States have until January 1972 to revise state implementation plans (SIPs) to meet standards by May 1975.		
June 1971		EPA publishes final regulations regarding 1975–76 auto emission standards and certification procedures.	
Aug. 1971	Promulgation of regulations for preparation of SIPs.		EPA grants one-year delay (until February 1973) for submission of transportation control plans (TCPs).
Jan. 1972	Department of Commerce publishes report on the costs of regulation on auto prices.		Deadline for submission of state implementation plans (SIPs).
April–July 1972	EPA approves 12 SIPs and revises deficient portions of 25 others—except for postponement with respect to TCPs.	EPA rejects auto manufacturers' request for a one-year postponement in emission standards (from 1975–76 to 1976–77). Auto companies appeal decision to courts.	EPA gives 18 states a two-year delay (from May 1975 to May 1977) to meet air quality standards.

Nov. 1972-Jan. 1973	In *Sierra Club* v. *Ruckelshaus*, superior court prohibits EPA from approving SIP permitting significant deterioration in air quality.		*Riverside* v. *Ruckelshaus and NRDC* v. *EPA* ruled that EPA lacked authority to grant one-year extension for TCPs and ordered EPA to prepare TCPs where necessary to meet air quality standards.
Feb.-April 1973	Arab oil embargo produces fuel shortages and heightens concern with fuel economy. President Nixon calls for relaxation of air quality and emission standards to ease fuel shortages. Formation of National Clean Air Coalition in response to attacks on Clean Air Act.	As a result of *International Harvester* v. *Ruckelshaus*, EPA ordered to reconsider its denial of extension of auto standards and to give more weight to economic and technical constraints. In April EPA delays auto emissions standards for one year (to 1976–77) while also setting interim standards for 1975–76. Ford Motor Co. fined $7 million for employee tampering with cars during pollution control tests; 2300 Chevrolets recalled for poor emission control systems.	In response to *Riverside* suit, EPA reluctantly prepares TCP for Los Angeles region calling for 80 percent reduction in VMT, probably through gasoline rationing. Arouses storm of protest throughout region.
June 1973		EPA releases data that NO_x not a widespread problem and thus that 90 percent reduction in auto emissions probably unwarranted.	EPA announces TCPs for 31 cities in June and another 22 in September.
July-Dec. 1973			In December, EPA orders delay in implementation of parking regulations as part of TCPs until January 1975 after emergency energy legislation imposing such bans had passed both houses of Congress. (Legislation subsequently vetoed by President Nixon for unrelated reasons.)

June 1974	Passage of Energy Supply and Coordination Act of 1974.	Energy Act extends EPA's interim standards for 1975–76 to 1976–77, as well as delaying final (90 percent) standards until 1977–78.
Aug.-Sept. 1974	NAS report, *Air Quality and Auto Emissions Control*, indicates (1) reasonable basis for air quality standard—with possible exception of oxidant—but major uncertainties in data; (2) TCPs of doubtful effectiveness; and (3) auto emission regulations would be more cost effective if NO_x emission standards relaxed for rural areas.	In *Pennsylvania v. EPA*, a federal appeals court upholds EPA's rationale for requiring TCPs. Energy Act requires postponement of any parking management plan until January 1975. EPA proposes new parking and other TCP regulations, in part to compensate for premature degradation of auto emissions control systems.
Dec. 1974-Jan. 1975	President Ford calls for relaxation of auto standards until 1982 on grounds of fuel economy.	Congress prohibits EPA from using funds to implement parking regulations as part of SIPs through fiscal year 1975 (i.e., until July 1975).
March-April 1975	EPA extends interim emission standards for CO and HC an additional year to 1977 and urges Congress to delay final standards until 1982, largely out of concern with alleged sulfate emissions from catalytic convertors. Subsequent studies a few months later suggested these fears to have been unfounded. California Air Resources Board requires final (90 percent) standards for CO and HC in that state for 1977 models.	

June–July 1975		At Congress' request, EPA indefinitely suspends implementation of parking regulations.
Fall 1975		*Brown v. EPA* casts doubt on EPA's authority to force states to enforce EPA-developed TCPs.
Summer 1975	Congressional consideration of amendments to Clean Air Act, due to expire June 1977. Bill killed by filibuster.	
Aug. 1977	Passage of 1977 Clean Air Amendments.	1977 Amendments continued restrictions on parking regulations.
		1977 Amendments (1) continued interim auto standards through 1979 and relaxed final NO_x standards, (2) strengthened requirement for auto inspection and maintenance.
June 1978	After proposing in June 1978 to relax the peak ozone air quality standard from .08 to .10 ppm, EPA in January 1979 officially raised it to .12 ppm.	

mile (with the goal of achieving 90 percent reductions by the 1975–76 model year) from those seeking to reduce vehicle miles traveled (principally via what came to be known as the transportation control plans).

The table indicates that the process proceeded on schedule during the first two years (1972–73) and in keeping with EPA Administrator William Ruckelshaus' basic strategy of relying as heavily as possible on reducing emissions from new automobiles and from stationary sources of hydrocarbons and nitrogen oxides, while being quite circumspect concerning any need to reduce substantially the number of vehicle miles traveled by urban Americans.[19] Thus in the spring and summer of 1972 Ruckelshaus rejected the automobile companies' request for a one-year extension of the 1975–76 emission standards and a few months later he made substantial revisions in the implementation plans submitted by most states. Those implementation plans dealt almost entirely with stationary sources, since Ruckelshaus had previously given the states a one-year delay (until February 1973) to submit transportation control plans (in those cases where they would be necessary to attain oxidant, hydrocarbons, or carbon monoxide air quality standards). He had also given eighteen states the two-year delay provided by law (from May 1975 to May 1977) to meet air quality standards, many of which dealt with areas where oxidant or carbon monoxide was the major problem.

By mid-1973, however, EPA's grand strategy began to unravel as a result of some adverse court decisions and the increased concern with fuel economy brought about by the Arab oil boycott. These, in turn, led to several delays in the deadlines for imposing automobile emission standards and in repeated actions by Congress preventing EPA from imposing parking restrictions, one of the critical components of transportation control plans. The program was also plagued by doubts about the validity of the data supporting some of the air quality standards (especially oxidant), by substantial resistance from the automobile companies and from motorists to reduce emissions per vehicle mile, and by a wide variety of very serious obstacles to reducing vehicle miles traveled.

Pressure of external events

Whatever the political merits of EPA's basic strategy, it was soon disrupted by events beyond the agency's control. First, responding to court suits brought by environmental groups using the citizen suit provisions of Section 304, a number of federal courts in the winter of 1972–73 ruled that Ruckelshaus had exceeded his discretion by granting the one-year extension in the submission of transportation control plans. Following the court's instructions in the *Riverside* case, EPA in the spring of 1973 reluctantly proposed a transportation control plan for the Los Angeles region designed to reduce vehicle miles traveled by 80 percent, largely through gasoline rationing, in order to meet the May 1977 deadline for achieving the oxidant standards. The proposal stirred a storm of protest in the region, as the public became aware of the requirements of the 1970 amendments—specifically, the need to alter transportation habits in some regions if air quality goals were to be achieved within the deadlines imposed by the legislation. Thereafter, Congress repeatedly prohibited EPA from requiring either gasoline rationing or any parking management scheme, thus eliminating one of the most effective ways of discouraging urban commuters from using private cars. After several efforts to revive transportation controls, particularly after it became evident that the expected reductions in emissions per vehicle mile would not be forthcoming, EPA in June 1975 simply gave up trying to implement any parking regulations and, by implication, abandoned any serious efforts to reduce vehicle miles traveled in urban areas.[20]

The second major court case involved the automobile companies' appeal of EPA's April 1972 decision not to postpone implementation of the final (90 percent) automobile emission standards for the 1975 model year (1976 for nitrogen oxides). In *International Harvester* v. *Ruckelshaus,* the District of Columbia Court of Appeals ordered EPA to reconsider its decision in the light of technological uncertainties and the potential for serious disruption of the nation's economy if one or more manufacturers were unable to meet the stringent 1975–76 standards and thus would be prohibited from marketing automobiles. In response, EPA in April 1973 granted the one-year delay in the final emission standards and set interim standards for the 1975–76 models requiring reductions from 1970 emissions of approximately 60 percent for carbon monoxide and hydrocarbons and 22 percent for nitrogen oxides. These standards, plus the strengthening of the standard for nitrogen oxides to require 50 percent reductions after 1977, were extended through the 1979 models by the 1977 Clean Air Amendments (see Tables 4.2 and 4.3).[21]

The third important judicial intervention in the implementation of the 1970 Clean Air Amendments concerned a series of cases dealing with the transportation control plans and specifically with EPA's authority to require state and local governments to enforce plans developed by EPA. Although a June 1974 decision *(Pennsylvania* v. *EPA)* by the U.S. Court of Appeals for the Third Circuit had upheld the justification for the transportation controls, two rulings made in fall 1975 by the courts of appeals in the ninth and fourth circuits *(Brown* v. *EPA* and *Maryland* v. *EPA)* asserted that the Clean Air Act did not authorize EPA to order state or other governments to implement plans designed by the federal agency. The U.S. Supreme Court decision in May 1977 ducked the issue by noting that EPA—often under informal Congressional pressure—had voluntarily withdrawn requirements that states adopt bus lanes, parking surcharges, and gasoline rationing and had admitted that it lacked statutory authority to force the states to enforce EPA-devised transportation control plans. In effect, the Court refused to rule on the constitutional issue and instead asked Congress to clarify its intent. Pending that clarification, the result of these cases was to cast very substantial doubt on EPA's ability to impose any sanctions on state and local governments which

Table 4.3
Changes in Automotive Emissions Standards, 1968–77

| | | Hydrocarbons | |
| | | Percent Change | |
	Amount (gpm)[a]	From pre-1968 car	From 1970 car
Baselines			
Uncontrolled pre-1968 car[b]	8.7	—	—
1970 car incorporating reductions required under 1965 federal law; baseline for 1970 Amendments	4.1	−53	—
Changes in Standards 1970–77			
Interim standards established by EPA in April 1973 for 1975 models (1976 for NO$_x$) and subsequently continued through 1978 models by 1974 Energy Act and 1975 EPA decision			
1975–76 models	1.5	−83	−63
1977 models and thereafter	1.5	−83	−63
Standards set by California Air Resources Board for cars sold in California[c]			
1975 models	.9	−90	−78
1977 models and thereafter	.41	−95	−90
Standards set by 1977 Clean Air Amendments			
For 1977–79	1.5	−83	−63
For 1980 models	.41	−95	−90
For 1981 models and thereafter	.41	−95	−90
The Original Goal			
Standards originally set by 1970 Amendments for 1975 models (1976 for NO$_x$)	.41	−95	−90

Sources: Mills and White, "Government Policies toward Automotive Emissions Control," p.353; U.S., House of Representatives, *Clean Air Amendments of 1977, Conference Report*, Report 95-564, 95th Cong., 1st sess., Aug. 3, 1977, p. 166.

[a]As measured by federal constant-volume sampling, cold and hot start test. Does not include evaporative emissions.
[b]Uncontrolled except for crankcase blowby device, required on all cars manufactured after 1960.
[c]California allowed to set stricter standards under Sec. 2096 of 1970 Clean Air Amendments.

Carbon Monoxide			Nitrogen Oxides		
	Percent Change			Percent Change	
Amount (gpm)[a]	From pre-1968 car	From 1970 car	Amount (gpm)[a]	From pre-1968 car	From 1970 car
87.0	—	—	3.5	—	—
43.0	−61	—	4.0	+14	—
15.0	−83	−56	3.1	−11	−22
15.0	−83	−56	2.0	−43	−50
9.0	−90	−74	2.0	−43	−50
3.4	−96	−90	—	—	—
15.0	−83	−56	2.0	−43	−50
7.0	−92	−79	2.0	−43	−50
3.4	−96	−90	1.0	−71	−75
3.4	−96	−90	.4	−89	−90

did not change their laws or programs to bring them into compliance with transportation plans formulated by EPA.[22]

Probably the most important event affecting the implementation of the 1970 Clean Air Amendments was the Arab oil embargo of the summer and fall of 1973 and the consequent quadrupling of gasoline prices that followed American support of Israel during the 1973 Arab-Israeli conflict. The increased concern with automotive fuel economy resulting from the temporary shortages in supply convinced Congress to extend for an additional year (to the 1976–77 models) EPA's interim standards. The pollution control systems selected by the automobile manufacturers during the 1970–74 period had had an adverse impact on fuel economy; subsequent systems, involving catalytic convertors, reversed this trend.[23]

The second important consequence of the rapid rise in gasoline prices was a gradual increase in the percentage of automobile purchases of foreign-made cars and domestic compacts and subcompacts up from abour 43 percent in 1973 to 54 percent in 1975. This trend had adverse effects on the economic welfare of the domestic manufacturers and on the number of jobs available in the automobile industry.[24] As a result, there was a significant shift in the degree of political support for stringent pollution control in the 1975–77 period, as both local automobile dealers and the United Auto Workers (UAW) actively supported relaxation of the final emission standards while Congress was considering comprehensive amendments to the Clean Air Act. Although there was no actual proof of the adverse effects of emission standards on automobile sales, both the dealers and the union were very sensitive to any factor which *might* negatively affect sales. The role of the UAW was particularly crucial, both because of its relationship with the Democratic Party and because of its previous support of stringent air pollution legislation. As the chief staff person for the Senate Environmental Subcommittee observed:

> *The auto companies never got to first base in persuading Congress to relax auto-emission standards until they got the support of the UAW on the issue of jobs. The UAW has credibility up here that the auto companies don't.*[25]

While the Arab oil embargo and the dramatic increase in fuel prices fundamentally changed the political context in which the 1970 Clean Air Amendments were implemented, there were a number of other problems plaguing that implementation.

Technical justification for air quality and emissions standards

The entire justification for imposing substantial costs on automobile manufacturers and consumers, urban motorists, and stationary sources of nitrogen oxides and hydrocarbons was to protect human health and welfare. Under the 1970 amendments, the EPA administrator was charged with setting two sorts of national air quality standards. The primary standards were to protect human health with an adequate margin of safety and the secondary standards were designed to protect the public welfare, chiefly by minimizing pollutant damage to crops and other materials. In general, two sorts of evidence were used in setting the standards: laboratory studies involving very high doses to animals in which toxic effects to specific parts of the organism could be ascertained and epidemiological studies of large numbers of people in which, for example, the incidence of respiratory diseases was correlated with air quality levels while alternative causes such as smoking or work-related exposure were controlled for.

Technical support for the air quality standards on sulfur dioxide and suspended particulates was fairly solid, but concern with oxidants, carbon monoxide, and nitrogen oxides was much more recent and there were serious reservations concerning the validity of both the epidemiological studies used in setting the criteria and the techniques of monitoring air quality. By 1973 the scientific community generally agreed that EPA had misinterpreted some of the key studies used to develop the oxidant standards, with the result that the standard was set at a more stringent level than justified by the evidence. EPA eventually acknowledged this conclusion, but not until February 1979 did the agency revise the peak oxidant standard from .08 ppm to .12 ppm (not to be exceeded more than one hour per year).[26]

Disputes between Los Angeles and EPA control officials over the proper techniques for measuring oxidants and nitrogen oxides compounded the problem. In the case of oxidants, for example, it was eventually recognized that the method used at EPA's request throughout most of the country—with the exception of Los Angeles—overestimated oxidant concentrations by about 25 percent. In 1977 several dozen air quality regions measured by the EPA technique violated the .08 ppm oxidant standard but only ten were above the standard when the more accurate Los Angeles method was used.[27] Similar disputes plagued the measurement of nitrogen oxides, with EPA admitting in June 1973 that its previously recommended technique had overestimated actual ambient levels; under the revised technique, few areas of the country violated the air quality standards, thereby undermining the rationale for the 90 percent reduction in nitrogen oxides emissions from automobiles.[28]

Finally, there was an extended debate within EPA over the potential seriousness of sulfate emissions from cars equipped wtih catalytic convertors.[29] The issue first surfaced in 1973, when preliminary tests by Ford Motor Company and EPA health researchers in North Carolina indicated potentially serious sulfate emissions from catalysts through oxidation of the trace sulfur in gasoline. This aroused alarm within the agency, as American automobile manufacturers had chosen convertors as the principal control technique to meet emissions standards scheduled to go into effect in 1976 in California and nationwide the following year. After a year of testing by EPA's health scientists, a report published in January 1975 concluded that the dangers from sulfate emissions would outweigh the benefits from carbon monoxide and oxidant control after about four years. Citing the sulfate threat, EPA Administrator Russell Train in March 1975 extended 1975–76 interim standards to 1978–79 and recommended that Congress delay the final (90 percent) standards until 1982. But the California Air Resources Board decided not to postpone the use of catalysts in that state, arguing that EPA's research was still preliminary and that alternative control strategies— including removing sulfur from gasoline during the refining process—were available. The skepticism of California officials was apparently justified a month later when an internal EPA report prepared by scientists at EPA's mobile source control laboratory in Michigan criticized the January study for overestimating (by a factor of two) sulfate emissions and for using unrealistic highway traffic patterns. Then, in April 1976, EPA acknowledged that a year of testing by EPA and General Motors researchers showed that the January 1975 report had used an atmospheric dispersion model which greatly overestimated sulfate concentrations near highways. The entire controversy was eventually resolved the following year when most of the manufacturers decided to install dual oxidation reduction catalysts as the preferred means of dealing with emissions of nitrogen oxides, carbon monoxide, and hydrocarbons.

All these controversies almost certainly undermined EPA's technical credibility. More importantly, they revealed the extent to which the entire air pollution control program was based on the highly complex effects of emission sources on air quality and those of air quality levels on human health. In several crucial areas, considerable uncertainty surrounded the validity of the raw data and the measurement techniques involved. As we saw, for example, estimates concerning whether transportation control plans were necessary in several dozen cities or only in ten hinged upon disagreements over the proper method of measuring atmospheric oxidant. And, in fact, depending upon the interpretation of the epidemiological studies and what constituted an appropriate margin of safety, the number of air quality regions requiring transportation control plans could be reduced to three or four. Moreover, uncertainties concerning ambient levels of nitrogen oxides and their precise role in the formation of photochemical smog raised very serious doubts concerning the necessity of requiring an eventual 90 percent reduction in nitrogen oxides emissions from new automobiles.[30]

Resistance from manufacturers and motorists

Title II of the 1970 Clean Air Amendments required automobile manufacturers to reduce emissions from new cars 90 percent by the 1975 models (for carbon monoxide and hydrocarbons) and by the 1976 models (for nitrogen oxides). In order to strengthen the legal requirements, Sections 203–205 prohibited cars which did not meet the standards from being sold in the United States and provided for fines of $10,000 per car. Section 202d of the amendments also sought to place as much of the burden as possible on automobile manufacturers, rather than on consumers, by requiring that the control systems be guaranteed for 50,000 miles. As we have seen, however, the new car standards were subsequently relaxed to require only about a 60 percent reduction in hydrocarbons and carbon monoxide and only 20 to 50 percent reductions in nitrogen oxides through the 1979 models. Moreover, it soon became evident that actual emissions by cars in use did not meet even these relaxed standards. What went wrong?

First, while the 1970 amendments permitted the automobile manufacturers to choose the control technology and seemingly gave them about four years to develop such technology, the auto companies actually had considerably less time to choose and develop a technology.[31] The three-year lead time required for designing and producing new cars meant that the manufacturers actually had less than two years to develop the new technology. Once the plan had been developed and certified by EPA, the manufacturers still had to find secure sources of supply (of, for example, platinum for the catalysts) and restructure their assembly lines. These time constraints and the apparent satisfaction of American consumers with large, high-powered cars encouraged the manufacturers to select a technology that minimized modifications to the internal combustion engine. Finally, the multiple emission standards posed two technically conflicting problems for the automobile manufacturers. Reduction of carbon dioxide and hydrocarbon emissions would essentially require more efficient fuel combustion; the higher temperatures involved in this combustion would *increase* the oxidation of nitrogen—and thus nitrogen oxides emissions—as indeed had happened in the 1968–70 period.

As a result of these constraints, by about 1973 the American manufacturers, following the lead of General Motors, decided to rely on an oxidation catalyst to reduce carbon monoxide and hydrocarbons emissions and to use either a second catalyst or exhaust gas recirculation systems to achieve the more problematic task of limiting nitrogen oxides emissions. But the choice of specific technologies was clouded by charges that one or both systems would affect fuel efficiency.

While EPA and many members of Congress had serious doubts about the intentions of some of the American manufacturers, most notably Chrysler, they ultimately had little choice but to accept the technological choices made by the automobile companies. Given the automakers' critical role in the economy, prohibiting the sale of cars which did not meet the original 1975–76 standards was simply not feasible. The ability to place effective pressure on the auto manufacturers was hindered by the lack of less severe and more graduated sanctions, the decline in car sales from 1974 to 1976, and the strong support the automobile companies received from the White House and, eventually, the United Auto Workers.[32]

Moreover, while Section 212 of the 1970 amendments mandated EPA research into low-emission propulsion systems the funds appropriated were not sufficient to develop a program by the 1975–76 deadline. Even if EPA had developed reliable low-emission prototypes capable of satisfying the American consumer, commercial production would still have required the active cooperation of private companies responsible for manufacture.[33]

In short, the limited choice imposed by the tight deadlines and an oligopolistic automobile market, the lack of effective sanctions against such a critical sector of the economy, and the fundamental constraints on government intervention posed by a capitalist economy meant that Congress and EPA could establish legal requirements and threaten sanctions but they would ultimately have to reach a negotiated settlement with the automakers. And that settlement—involving interim standards for 1975–79 and a relaxation of the ultimate nitrogen oxides standard (see Table 4.3)—was very similar to what the auto manufacturers had themselves reluctantly promised in 1969-70. In retrospect, then, the attempts to implement Title II of the 1970 amendments can be seen as a struggle to hold the manufacturers to their promise.

In addition to repeated relaxations of the emissions reduction timetable during 1973-77, there were also substantial problems concerning compliance with applicable standards by both the automobile manufacturers and, more importantly, car owners. Tests of in-use cars since 1972 have repeatedly shown that, in about 80 percent of the cases, actual emissions—while lower than those of the pre-1968 and 1970 baselines—violate at least one of the emission standards for the relevant model year . The problem is particularly severe for carbon monoxide emissions. For example, tests in five cities of nearly two hundred 1973 model cars after they had been a year in use and driven an average of 19,000 miles revealed mean hydrocarbons, carbon monoxide, and nitrogen oxides emissions to be 20, 60, and 10 percent over standards. Similar tests in 1976 on several hundred 1975 model cars revealed mean hydrocarbon and nitrogen oxides emissions to be lower than the standards, while mean carbon monoxide emissions exceeded standards by about 50 percent.[34]

Part of the blame for this lack of compliance can be attributed to poor surveillance by the automobile manufacturers and EPA. Until 1977 EPA relied almost entirely on the testing of prototypes for each model over simulated conditions of 50,000 miles, without also examining a sample of "standard" cars on the assembly line. Correction of manufacturer defects after certification was handled through recalls (about 10 million cars during the 1972-77 period). While such recalls undoubtedly encouraged manufacturers to improve emission system design and assembly-line quality control in order to minimize the costs and negative publicity of such recalls, as suggested by the better performance of 1975 over 1973 models in the tests cited above, the effect on emissions was limited by the rather modest (65 percent) rate at which recalled cars were returned to the dealers for corrective measures.[35]

But by far the largest share of the responsibility for the increasingly poor performance of emission systems over the life span of any car lay with the car owners themselves (and/or car service organizations). EPA estimated that only about 3 percent of emission system failures could be attributed to manufacturer design and performance. In contrast 47 percent of the failures were due to maladjusted engine settings, 25 percent to premature deterioration of parts (often because of the use of leaded fuels), 18 percent to outright tampering with emission systems, and the remaining 7 percent to inadequate maintenance.[36] EPA often mandated as part of the state implementation plans periodic inspections and maintenance of emission control systems to correct any problems. However, very few areas of the country required inspection and maintenance programs during the 1970–77 period. Part of the reason was the technical difficulty of developing a rapid, accurate, and inexpensive testing procedure, but a greater cause was the resistance of motorists to bearing the costs of inspection and any consequent engine readjustments and new parts. This is, in short, a classic example of the situation in which individuals are unwilling to bear potentially rather substantial immediate costs in return for a collective benefit of uncertain value toward which their individual contribution is insignificant.[37]

Efforts to reduce vehicle miles traveled

Unlike the specific standards and deadlines Title II of the 1970 Clear Air Amendments set for control of automotive emissions, Section 110(a) (b) simply listed "land use and transportation controls" as one of many measures which could be included in state implementation plans in order to reach and maintain air quality standards. Supplementary measures were clearly warranted since the requirements for 90 percent reductions in emissions from 1975 and 1976 model cars would have little effect in meeting the 1977—let alone 1975—deadlines for achieving the air quality standards because of the slow turnover in the automobile fleet. Thus the lack of fit between the emissions and air quality deadlines meant that achievement of the oxidant, carbon monoxide, and nitrogen oxides air quality standards by 1977 would have to come about primarily through reductions in emissions from stationary sources and in vehicle miles traveled.

EPA and state officials could choose from a wide variety of transportation and land use controls in order to reduce vehicle miles traveled, such as restrictions on parking places, parking surcharges, gasoline rationing, and the outright prohibition of auto use in some areas. They could develop incentives to use other forms of transit such as carpools, buses, trains, and bicycles. These would include such measures as special highway lanes for mass transit vehicles and bicycles, reduced bridge tolls and parking fees for such vehicles, and, of course, a variety of subsidies for the construction and operation of mass transit systems. Or, they could use land use restrictions designed to discourage urban sprawl and to regulate the location of so-called indirect sources of vehicle travel such as shopping centers. While all these measures could discourage use of the single-passenger automobile, transportation controls could also include a variety of methods designed to speed up traffic flow and thus reduce carbon monoxide and hydrocarbon emissions.[38]

By the mid-1970s, the importance of transportation controls had increased because of the slippage in automobile emissions controls due to the relaxation of deadlines and emissions standards for new automobiles and evidence that cars in use were not meeting those emission standards. As a result, about twenty urban areas were required to submit transportation control plans (TCPs) in order to meet the 1977 air quality objectives, and TCPs were required in ten to fourteen more areas in order to compensate for increases in population and automobile use by 1985.[39]

Unfortunately, the development of TCPs soon ran into a number of major difficulties which turned the entire process into a case study of the problems created by a poorly structured implementation plan. First, in part because of the inexperience of EPA and other air pollution control agencies with transportation and land use controls, there was considerable uncertainty over the available options and particularly the impacts specific measures would have on air quality. This, combined with the pressure to promptly implement the act resulting from several legal suits, led many states in 1973 to simply dump the problem on EPA.[40] Tremendous skepticism and wide opposition greeted EPA's hurriedly drafted proposals, partly because EPA often could neither justify the supposed benefits of specific measures on air quality nor dispel fears that the proposals would have disastrous economic consequences. For example, requirements for reserving certain freeway lanes for car pools and buses in Los Angeles and many other cities were criticized for causing considerable inconvenience to motorists without any corresponding benefit in air quality. Motorists often were simply displaced to arterial streets where accidents were more likely and where the increases in carbon monoxide and hydrocarbons emissions from stop-and-go traffic probably counterbalanced any reductions obtained from having fewer vehicles on the freeways. Likewise, EPA could not prove that the air quality benefits obtained from restricting parking in downtown areas (thereby reducing vehicle miles traveled by commuters) would not be counteracted by increased mileage from cars left at home. Again, the effects on air quality of spending millions of dollars on more bus and rail transit systems are quite uncertain, as there is considerable evidence that new mass transit patrons are replaced on highways by drivers who are new residents in the region. Finally, EPA did not have the evidence to answer the complaints of small business owners in many regions that restrictions on downtown parking supply would simply divert customers to other areas. The net results were a loss in EPA's credibility, substantial opposition to EPA proposals in most regions, and ultimately appeals by dissatisfied local officials and business owners to the courts and to Congress to restrict EPA's authority to require transportation control measures.[41]

The second major problem confronting EPA's efforts to reduce vehicles miles traveled was that the potentially effective options of gasoline rationing and restrictions on parking supply were withdrawn from active consideration. EPA rejected the first option as politically suicidal and inconsistent with the clear policy against gasoline rationing of Presidents Nixon and Ford, while

Congress repeatedly emphasized that it did not want EPA *requiring* the states to adopt parking surcharges or restrictions on parking supply. In addition, the entire status of TCPs was thrown into confusion beginning in the autumn of 1975 by conflicting appellate court decisions (most notably, *Brown* v. *EPA*) concerning EPA's authority to legally compel state and local governments to implement EPA-devloped transportation control measures.

A third difficulty involved in development of the transportation control plans was that implementation of almost all the control measures required the cooperation of several federal, state, and local agencies. For a variety of reasons, including other priorities and resource constraints, these agencies often exercised an effective veto. Parking control measures required the cooperation of numerous agencies—traffic and police departments for on-street parking, zoning authorities, municipal parking corporations, and private companies for off-street parking—within any local region. Moreover, local governments have been very sensitive to the competitive advantage which such restrictions may give commercial establishments in neighboring cities. EPA lacked effective incentives or sanctions to influence the behavior of any of these actors. Programs requiring additional bus or rail transit service were under the jurisdiction of federal, state, and local highway departments and transit authorities. Even when, as in the case of the Federal Mass Transit Administration, these agencies supported EPA's objectives, any expansion of service took time and, of course, depended upon obtaining additional subsidies from Congress or from state legislatures.

Implementation of TCPs took place in a very loosely coupled system in which there were numerous veto points and in which EPA was without effective incentives to force compliance. In such a situation, the only real alternatives were to ask Congress for more effective sanctions and to negotiate compromises with other actors. EPA eventually took both actions but was impeded in the latter by the lack of personnel with sufficient expertise to handle negotiations in the transportation subsystems throughout the country.

The final and, in many ways, most fundamental problem confronting the implementation of transportation and land use controls was that such measures threatened deeply held public values. People who have made a substantial investment in an automobile are unlikely to renounce the privacy, comfort, and mobility it provides in exchange for the inconvenience of carpools, trains, or buses. And the preference of many urban Americans for dispersed housing patterns creates problems concerning the development of improved mass transit systems or proposals to reduce commuting distances. As one author has observed:

> *A country whose land use patterns and lifestyle have developed in an era of unlimited personal mobility will not restructure itself in five years to meet a fixed standard, even for the preservation of public health.*[42]

Considering these difficulties, it is hardly surprising that, of the thirty air quality regions in which EPA required transportation control plans, in at least half of them there were sufficient delays in implementation or sufficient limitations in the effectiveness of adopted measures that the plans' contributions to meeting the 1977 air quality standards were not realized. There were some successes, most notably in Portland, Oregon, where a variety of traffic and parking controls combined with increased transit service and the strong leadership of the mayor helped to reduce carbon monoxide levels dramatically. In general, however, the major study of transportation controls concluded that controls were most effectively implemented in those cities where their adoption was independent of EPA efforts and had been initiated by local officials for reasons largely unrelated to air quality.[43]

Evaluation of the implementation of the 1970 Clean Air Amendments

The principal objective of the 1970 Clean Air Amendments was to improve the nation's air quality sufficiently that there would be no violations of the primary air quality standards (deemed necessary to protect public health) by the end of 1977. With respect to the principal automobile-related pollutants— oxidant, carbon monoxide, nitrogen oxides, and volatile hydrocarbons—this was to be accomplished through emissions controls on mobile and stationary sources and, where necessary, through reductions in vehicle miles traveled. The previous sections indicate that the implementation effort was confronted by many obstacles, including (1) adverse court cases and changes in economic conditions, (2) doubts concerning the technical justifications for some air quality and emissions standards, (3) resistance from automobile manufacturers and motorists in reducing emissions per vehicle miles, and (4) a whole series of difficulties plaguing efforts to reduce automotive use through transportation and land use planning.

Now we shall examine the outcomes of the implementation process, first, in terms of actual improvements in emissions and air quality during the 1970–77 period. Then we shall consider the political system's evaluation of the implementation process as manifested in the passage of the 1977 Clean Air Amendments.

Changes in emissions and air quality levels of auto-related pollutants, 1970–77

Table 4.4 indicates the changes in nationwide emissions of hydrocarbons, nitrogen oxides and carbon monoxide from highway vehicles and from other sources from 1970 through 1977. The portrait can hardly be termed encouraging. Instead of declining, nitrogen oxides emissions actually in-

Table 4.4
Changes in Nationwide Emissions of HC, NO$_x$, and CO from Highway Vehicles and Other Sources, 1970–77
(1,000,000 metric tons per year)

	1970	1971	1972	1973	1974	1975	1976	1977	Percent Change, 1970–77
Emissions of NO$_x$									
Highway vehicles	5.3	5.8	6.4	6.5	6.3	6.4	7.0	6.7	+ 26.4
Other sources	14.3	14.4	15.2	15.8	15.4	14.6	15.8	16.4	+ 14.7
Total	19.6	20.2	21.6	22.3	21.7	21.0	22.8	23.1	+ 17.9
Emissions of VOC (HC)									
Highway vehicles	10.6	10.6	10.9	10.7	10.0	9.8	10.0	9.9	− 6.6
Other sources	18.9	18.5	18.7	19.0	18.6	17.1	18.7	18.4	− 2.6
Total	29.5	29.1	29.6	29.7	28.6	26.9	28.7	28.3	− 4.1
Emissions of CO									
Highway vehicles	70.9	71.7	76.1	76.5	73.3	73.8	76.6	77.2	+ 8.9
Other sources	31.3	30.8	27.7	27.0	26.4	23.1	26.3	25.5	− 18.5
Total	102.2	102.5	103.8	103.5	99.7	96.9	102.9	102.7	+ 0.0
Gasoline Consumption by Highway Vehicles (billion gallons)	92.3	97.5	105.1	110.5	106.3	109.0	115.7	119.6	+ 29.6

Sources: EPA, *National Air Quality, Monitoring, and Emissions Trends Report, 1977*, Tables 5–2 to 5–9. U.S. Dept. of Commerce, Census Bureau, *Statistical Abstract of the U.S., 1980*, Table 1125.

creased 18 percent during this period, including a 26 percent increase from mobile sources. Carbon monoxide emissions were unchanged, a 9 percent increase from mobile sources counterbalancing a significant decrease from stationary sources. In fact, only the hydrocarbons (or VOC) picture is encouraging, as emissions from mobile sources declined about 7 percent, those from stationary sources slightly less.

With respect to mobile sources, much of this mixed record nationwide can be attributed to an increase of approximately 30 percent in vehicle miles traveled during the 1970-77 period (using gasoline consumption as a surrogate indicator).[44] Thus, on one hand, nitrogen oxides emissions rise almost in tandem with increased vehicle miles. On the other, suggesting that the automotive emission controls had some effect, emissions of carbon monoxide increased substantially less than did vehicle miles traveled, and hydrocarbons from mobile sources registered an almost 7 percent decrease in the face of the 30 percent increase in gasoline consumption.

Nevertheless, while it is difficult to relate these aggregated emissions data precisely to emissions from individual cars, it is obvious that the reductions in emissions per vehicle mile fell considerably short of the 90 percent figure prescribed in the 1970 Clean Air Amendments. Part of this shortfall was attributable to repeated relaxations of the standards for new cars, so that 1977 models (outside of California) were only required to incorporate reductions of 50 to 63 percent from the 1970 baseline (see Table 4.3). But another cause was the failure to maintain the emissions reductions for the 50,000 miles required by Section 202(d) of the 1970 amendments.

This failure is clearly shown in a study by Lawrence White in which he compares the average emissions from random samples of several hundred in-use cars in five cities with the federal emissions standards for that model year over the 1970–76 period. To begin with, the study shows that carbon monoxide emissions have consistently exceeded the applicable standard (even on one-year-old cars) and that the amount of slippage increased with car age. The record for hydrocarbons was slightly better, with cars generally not exceeding the applicable standard until the second year. On the other hand, mean nitrogen oxide emissions have almost always been within the relevant federal standard. Meanwhile, the more stringent 1975 emissions standards had a substantial effect on hydrocarbons and carbon monoxide emissions. For example, mean hydrocarbon emissions from one-year-old cars declined from 3.58 gms/mi for the 1974 model year to 1.72 for 1975 models. Similarly, carbon monoxide emissions declined from 41.8 gms/mi for 1974 models to 27.4 the following model year.[45]

One should remember, however, that the 1970 Clean Air Act was not directed principally at reducing nationwide emissions but rather at improving ambient air levels in areas where they exceeded the air quality standards. Therefore, failure to substantially decrease automotive emissions in general or in areas already meeting the air quality standards would not be a fundamental

TABLE 4.5
National Summary of Total Stations Reporting Data and Number Reporting Violations of Air Quality Standards, 1977

Pollutants	Data Record and standard exceeded	Number of stations	Percent of sites exceeding NAAQS
TSP	Valid annual data[a]	2699	
	Annual secondary		
	(guide only)	1070	40
	Annual primary	465	17
	At least minimal data[b]	4008	
	24-hour secondary	1424	36
	24-hour primary	314	8
SO_x	Valid annual data[a]	1355	
	Annual primary	19	1
	At least minimal data[b]	2365	
	24-hour primary	58	2
	3-hour secondary	30	1
CO	At least minimal data[b]	456	
	1-hour primary	11	2
	8-hour primary	211	46
OX/O_3	At least minimal data[b]	524[c][557][d]	86[c][57][d]
	1-hour primary	452[c][317][d]	
NO_x	At least minimal data[b]	1527	
	Valid annual data[a]	933	
	Annual primary	18	2

Source: EPA, *National Air Quality, Monitoring, and Emissions Trends Report, 1977*, Table 4-4.
Note: Recall that the primary air quality standards are designed to protect public health (including that of people already suffering from respiratory diseases), while secondary standards are designed to protect public welfare, i.e., generally crops and property.
[a]Valid annual data record must contain at least five of the scheduled 24-hour samples per quarter for EPA recommended intermittent sampling (once every 6 days) or 75 percent of all possible values in a year for continuous instruments.
[b]Minimal data consist of at least three 24-hour samples for intermittent sampling monitors or 400 hourly values for continuous instruments.
[c]Old standard of .08 ppm.
[d]New (1979) standard of .12 ppm. Data provided by EPA.

deficiency in the act's implementation. A more fundamental question, therefore, concerns the change in air quality in critical areas.

The critical areas data are provided in Table 4.5, which indicates the number of air quality monitoring stations violating specific air quality standards in 1977. In short, had the purpose of the 1970 amendments been completely realized, there would have been no violations of any of the primary standards at the end of 1977.

The actual record was, however, quite mixed. On the other hand, the data indicate that, with very few exceptions, 1977 sulfur dioxide and nitrogen dioxide levels did not violate the air quality standards. Moreover, only 8 to 17 percent of the stations violated the primary standards for suspended particulates. This was a substantial decrease from previous years.[46] On the other hand, 46 percent of the stations violated one of the short-term carbon monoxide standards; fully 86 percent violated the old oxidant standard of .08 ppm for a one-hour daily peak (not to be exceeded more than one hour per year), although only 57 percent of the stations exceeded the revised standard of .12 ppm. Clearly, these two pollutants continued to pose fairly widespread serious health problems as long as seven years after the passage of the 1970 amendments. Unfortunately, data indicating the distribution of the *number* of days per year on which the carbon monoxide and oxidant standards were violated are not readily available. This information would obviously be important in assessing the seriousness of the health threat.

Trends in levels of photochemical oxidants are somewhat difficult to interpret because of: (*a*) the limited number of monitoring stations outside California prior to 1972–73; (*b*) changes in the pollutant actually measured (from oxidant to ozone); and (*c*) the sensitivity of oxidant formation to variations in meteorological conditions, particularly the extent of solar radiation. With these caveats in mind, data from EPA indicate that oxidant concentrations were essentially unchanged over the 1972–77 period, with improvements in some California sites (including Los Angeles and San Francisco) negated by increases in concentrations in many sites outside that state.[47]

As for carbon monoxide, the relative lack of monitoring stations outside California prior to 1972 again makes longitudinal (time-series) analysis difficult. There appears, however, to have been rather steady improvement in ambient air concentrations between 1972 and 1977. Of 243 cities throughout the nation with sufficient data, 80 percent improved during this period, and, unlike the case for oxidants, the trend was fairly consistent nationwide.[48] Interestingly enough, this improvement occurred despite virtually static nationwide levels of carbon monoxide emissions (see Table 4.4). The answer appears to lie in the rather localized nature of the carbon monoxide problem. Thus, downtown areas already saturated with traffic would show some improvement (especially after 1975) because of improvements in emissions per vehicle mile, while increased emissions in suburban and rural areas (because of the greater number of vehicle miles traveled) would not be sufficiently concentrated geographically to result in noticeable deterioration in air quality.

Finally, analysis of trends in nitrogen oxide levels presents considerable difficulties, partly because monitoring in many areas of the country only began in the early 1970s and partly because the actual method of monitoring air quality (outside of Los Angeles) changed in 1973–74. Thus trends data are generally only available for the 1974–77 period.[49] The data show that the annual means have increased in most areas of the country, with the exception of the Northeast. This is hardly surprising, given the substantial increase in nationwide emissions over this period, as indicated in Table 4.4. Nevertheless, only about 2 percent of all stations exceeded the primary air quality standard in 1977 (see Table 4.5).[50]

In sum, this analysis of trends in emissions and air quality levels of the automobile-related pollutants during the 1970–77 period reveals a very mixed picture. While hydrocarbon emissions decreased slightly nationwide, oxidant air quality concentrations were generally quite stable—declines in some areas of California being offset by increased levels in almost a third of the stations in other areas of the country. At almost all stations, however, 1977 concentrations exceeded the old air quality standard. Carbon monoxide presented a similarly confusing pattern, with general improvements in air quality despite stable nationwide emissions, although almost half the stations continued to exceed one of the air quality standards. Only nitrogen oxide emissions and ambient concentrations presented a consistent pattern. Unfortunately the trend was in the wrong direction, although the ambient levels were not sufficient to endanger public health except in a very few areas (most notably, San Diego and Los Angeles).

It is clear, however, that proponents of the 1970 Clear Air Act had not anticipated any of these results. As we have seen, these mixed results can be attributed largely to (1) periodic relaxations of the deadlines and standards for new car emissions because of uncertain technology and increased concern with the potentially negative effects of emissions controls on fuel economy; (2) the failure of automotive emissions control systems to retain their efficacy over the 50,000 miles prescribed by law, largely because of improper maintenance and/or tampering by motorists and service dealers; (3) the mixed record in reducing emissions of nitrogen oxides, carbon monoxide, and hydrocarbons from stationary sources; and, perhaps most of all, (4) the utter failure to reduce or even stabilize the number of vehicle miles traveled through transportation and land use controls. Actually, the number of vehicle miles traveled increased approximately 30 percent during this period.

Statutory reevaluation: the 1977 Clean Air Amendments

Thus far we have been examining the extent to which the actual outcomes of the implementation process were consistent with the emissions and ambient air quality objectives of the 1970 Clean Air Act. It is also important, however, to evaluate the implementation process from the perspective of the political system. Ideally, we would like to have extensive interview data from important members of Congress, executive agencies, and affected interest groups, but such information is simply not available. Nevertheless, most important statutes are subject periodically to substantial and rather systematic amendment. These deliberations and their outcome can be viewed as a summary of the political system's evaluation of the implementation process. After X number of years of experience, was it deemed necessary to alter the relative priority of various objectives? What can be discerned from official documents concerning perceived impediments to effective implementation? Did the amendments incorporate more effective means of attaining the original (or revised) objectives? From such a perspective, then, we will now examine Congressional efforts to amend the 1970 Clean Air Act which began in 1975 and culminated in passage of the 1977 Clean Air Amendments.

Such reevaluation is not, however, based entirely (or perhaps even primarily) on the actors' perceptions of the impacts or of the deficiencies of the implementation process. It is also a product of changes in social and economic conditions and of the immediate context in which reevaluation takes place. In this respect, very few of the important social and political changes that occurred between passage of the 1970 Clean Air Act and that of the 1977 amendments were beneficial in protecting public health, which was the almost exclusive focus of the 1970 legislation. As previously indicated, the 1973-74 Arab oil embargo and the resultant quadrupling of petroleum prices and preoccupation with American dependence on unstable sources of petroleum imports had three very important consequences: First, it led to a substantial increase in Congressional concern with the automotive fuel economy and, more generally, with the potential impact of air pollution controls on petroleum consumption. This was reflected, for example, in passage of the 1974 Energy Supply and Coordination Act, which encouraged utilities and industrial facilities to switch from clean-burning natural gas to coal, as well as in approval of the 1975 Energy Policy and Conservation Act, which established minimum fuel economy standards for American-made cars beginning with the 1978 models. Second, consumer concern with fuel economy as a result of gasoline shortages and higher prices led to a noticeable increase in the sales of imports and smaller-sized American cars, with substantial adverse effects (especially in 1974–76) on the prosperity of the American manufacturers and on unemployment in the automobile industry. This, in turn, led to a critical reversal by the United Auto Workers. Formerly strong proponents of the 1970 Amendments, the union adopted a position which essentially mirrored the automobile companies' campaign for a relaxation of the automobile emissions standards. Third, the rise in inflation during the mid-1970s—reaching peaks of 11.0 percent in 1974 and 9.1 percent in 1975—prompted industry leaders and the White House to call repeatedly for relaxation of the inflationary aspects of environmental regulations; this campaign abated somewhat in 1976–77 as the annual inflation rate declined to 6 percent and studies showed that pollution control regulations contributed very little to overall inflation.[51]

In fact, from the standpoint of the original proponents of the Clean Air Act, the ony counterpoints to these unfavorable socioeconomic changes during the 1971-77 period were the formation of the National Clean Air Coalition in the fall of 1973 and the election of Jimmy Carter as president in November 1976. The NCAC was a coalition of environmental, public health, and civic groups organized in direct response to industry and presidential calls for relaxation of pollution control standards in the wake of the Arab oil embargo. The coalition was subsequently able to mobilize substantial grass-roots support against such measures and, together with the skillful efforts of Senator Muskie and some fortuitous political circumstances, probably saved the Clean Air Act from being emasculated during the economic crisis of 1973-75.[52] The election of Jimmy Carter as president in 1976 gave supporters of the 1970 act hope, as former president Gerald Ford had very close ties to the automobile manufacturers and a considerably less favorable rating by environmental groups than did Carter.[53]

Congressional consideration of comprehensive amendments to the 1970 Clean Air Act began in the summer of 1975 because of the need to deal with at least two major issues. The first was possible relaxation of the automobile emissions standards, as the automobile companies (backed reluctantly by the UAW) argued that meeting the 90 percent standards without incurring substantial fuel penalties for the 1978 models was technologically infeasible and would thus create economic havoc in the industry. The second was the need to clarify congressional intent concerning permissible deterioration of air quality in areas which did not violate the air quality standards; this issue arose as a result of a June 1973 court decision (*Sierra Club* v. *Ruckelshaus*) which interpreted the 1970 Clean Air Act as permitting no significant deterioration of air quality. Congress wrestled with these and other issues throughout the 1975 and 1976 sessions and had apparently agreed on a compromise which set interim automobile standards for 1978-80 and delayed the final standards (90 percent for hydrocarbons and carbon monoxide and 75 percent for nitrogen oxides) from 1978 until 1980. The conference committee report, though tacitly supported by the automobile companies and President Ford, was killed by a filibuster led by Senator Jake Garn (Rep., Utah) who was concerned with significant deterioration provisions.[54]

In a reflection of their economic and political power, the automobile companies subsequently announced that they would build 1978 models to the interim standards of the defeated bill on the gamble that the next Congress would legalize this and additional delays rather than have the automobile companies sell illegal cars—as they would in fact be doing were the 1970 Clean Air Act not amended. As the president of General Motors announced:

> *They can close the plants, put someone in jail—maybe me—but we're going to make [1978] cars to 1977 [i.e., 1975-77 interim] standards.*[55]

Not surprisingly, Congress backed down and passed the 1977 Clean Air Amendments in August with a slightly more relaxed automobile emissions timetable than in the 1976 bill and with sufficient softening of the significant deterioration provisions to avoid another filibuster.[56]

If we view 1977 amendments as Congress' evaluation of the nation's seven-year experience in implementing the 1970 Clean Air Act, what can we conclude? First, that the 1977 Amendments represented what Aaron Wildavsky (*Speaking Truth to Power*) would term a "strategic retreat on objectives" but not a fundamental reorientation of those objectives. Congress had to face the obvious fact that its attempt to increase substantially the pace of technological change in the automobile industry had only partially succeeded, in part because of uncertainties over what was technologically feasible given fuel economy constraints (particularly with respect to nitrogen oxide emissions). In addition, Congress had developed no effective sanctions against an industry upon which a sixth of the nation's economy depended, particularly when two of the four firms (Chrysler and Americn Motors) were in serious financial difficulties. Finally, there was little evidence that nitrogen oxide emissions presented a serious health problem, either by themselves or because of their contribution to oxidant formation. So the 1977 amendments relaxed the ultimate nitrogen oxide emissions standards from .4 to 1.0 grams/mile (or from 90 percent to 75 percent reductions from 1970 models), while keeping the interim 1975 standards through 1979 and not requiring full reductions in the three pollutants until the 1981 models (see Table 4.3).[57]

Likewise, Congress faced incontrovertible evidence that the fundamental objective of meeting the air quality standards by mid-1977 would not be achieved with respect to oxidants, carbon monoxide, and, to a lesser extent, suspended particulates. Congress then delayed the deadline for achievement of primary air quality standards until December 1982 and, for cities with particularly severe carbon monoxide or oxidant problems, until December 1987. This was, in part, a necessary consequence of the relaxed deadlines for automobile emission standards, but also a recognition that correcting the really severe carbon monoxide and oxidant problems would require substantial improvements in mass transit and other adjustments in urban transportation systems. Experience indicated such changes took considerable time to bring about in very fragmented political systems. On the other hand, Congress made relaxation of the 1982 deadlines to 1987 in a specific region contingent upon: (a) the inauguration of an inspection and maintenance program for automobiles; (b) the use of all reasonably available transportation funds to expand public transit service; and (c) a virtual lid on stationary source emissions by requiring any new stationary source to comply with the so-called offset policy.

While the relaxed timetable and a few other provisions in the 1977 amendments demonstrated a greater sensitivity than had the 1970 Act to potentially adverse effects on regulated industries, local economies, and fuel economy, the fundamental priority of the protection of public health was not basically altered. This basic focus was evident throughout, but perhaps no more clearly than in the offset policy and in the requirement that EPA set additional air quality standards for short-term nitrogen oxide exposure and for a number of particularly hazardous pollutants. The offset provision required any new source locating in an area violating the primary air quality standards to reduce emissions from existing sources (e.g., by buying them out) equivalent to its expected contribution. And the requirement mandating additional air quality standards—particularly short-term nitrogen oxide—demonstrated congressional willingness to initiate a process which would probably require additional controls in some areas in order to protect public health. Finally, the rather stringent policy regarding significant deterioration —especially around national parks—suggested that Congress had added aesthetics to its fundamental concern for public health.

Just as the 1977 amendments did not seriously alter the priorities established in 1970, so did they retain the 1970 act's basic (though tacit) strategy of placing the principal emphasis on reducing emissions from stationary sources and from new mobile sources rather than on altering the behavior of urban motorists. The continued emphasis on stationary sources was demonstrated in the offset provision, in detailed requirements concerning vapor (hydrocarbon) recovery from refineries and gasoline stations, and in the substantial attention paid to developing more effective enforcement. Methods to achieve better enforcement included increased civil (as well as criminal) penalties, the incorporation of a modified version of the "Connecticut Plan" to eliminate any economic advantage of delay and noncompliance, a substantially expanded citizen suit provision dealing primarily with stationary sources, the extension of criminal penalties to corporate officers, and a concerted effort to achieve better cooperation between Justice Department attorneys and EPA in litigation (almost all of it directed against stationary sources).[58] As for new mobile sources, the new legislation authorized other states to adopt the more stringent California standards for new cars. It also dealt much more forcefully with heavy-duty trucks and buses than had EPA under the discretionary authority vested in it by the 1970 act. Specifically, the 1977 amendments required a set of interim standards, a 90 percent reduction in carbon monoxide and hydrocarbon emissions by 1982, and a 75 percent reduction in nitrogen oxides by 1985; it also incorporated a version of the Connecticut Plan to remove any economic incentive to delay compliance. The amendments did not, however incorporate any new strategies to reverse the automobile companies' well-established pattern of seeking relaxation of more stringent standards.

In keeping with its predecessors' tacit strategy, the 1977 Congress was very reluctant to give EPA real authority to alter the transportation habits of urban motorists. While the 1977 amendments required EPA to publish information on the impacts of various transportation control strategies, they prohibited the agency from requiring states to regulate off-street parking or indirect sources (e.g., shopping centers, except with respect to federally-funded projects) and gave state governors the authority to suspend temporarily (until January 1979) any EPA-imposed requirements concerning on-street parking, gasoline rationing, or retrofit of pollution control devices on existing cars. In effect, the basic emphasis seemed to be on better information, increased cooperation with local authorities, additional funding for the development of transportation control plans, and some encouragement to use federal transportation funds for improved mass transit systems. Past experience suggested, however, that such an approach—without any corollary efforts to *discourage* automobile use—would be unlikely to significantly reduce vehicle miles traveled.

Similarly, Congress attempted to deal with the serious problem of the declining efficiency of automotive emissions controls systems over the life span of any car by strengthening the warranty provisions and by increasing the penalties for tampering. But it did not require inspection and maintenance (I&M) programs except in those regions requesting an extension of the carbon monoxide and/or oxidant deadline until 1987; in those cases, however, Congress did provide the potentially effective sanction of prohibiting EPA from approving any permit for new stationary sources in areas without an I&M program.[59]

The 1977 amendments did not alter the fundamental approach of federal air pollution law based upon requiring new automobiles and other pollution sources to meet specific (generally nationwide) emissions standards. By retaining this focus, Congress implicitly rejected the approach favored by numerous economists based upon emissions taxes/fees rather than specific emissions standards. Under the taxes/fees system, new automobiles would be assessed a fee (to be paid by the consumer) based upon the magnitude of their emissions. Such an approach, based on economic incentives, would give greater choice to both manufacturers and consumers, thereby supposedly permitting a more efficient allocation of costs and providing greater flexibility in technological innovation. While Congress did not substitute emissions fees for fixed standards, it did require a study of the possible effectiveness of fees in reducing nitrogen oxide emissions from stationary sources. Moreover, both the offset policy and the noncompliance charge (the Connecticut Plan) incorporated aspects of the economic incentives approach; the former established a "market" for allocating emissions units while the latter attempted to remove any economic gains from delay or noncompliance.[60]

In sum, despite the substantial changes in relevant socioeconomic conditions since 1970 and the enormous conflicts involved in amending the Clean Air Act over a three-year period, the 1977 amendments really continued the policy established in the 1970 act. While the deadlines for achieving the automobile emissions and general air quality standards were postponed, the standards themselves—except nitrogen oxide emissions from automobiles—were not relaxed, and the fundamental priority of protection of public health was retained. Moreover, controls on stationary sources and on trucks were actually increased. In the process, the 1977 amendments addressed many of the specific problems encountered in implementation of the 1970 act, e.g., the need for better impact analyses and more coordination with transportation officials in the development of transportation control plans, the critical role of stationary sources and trucks in hydrocarbon and nitrogen oxide emissions, and the need for better warranties on new automobiles.

The 1977 amendments also reaffirmed Congress' traditional reluctance to impose direct constraints on urban motorists by restricting the use of the automobile or (except in areas seeking extensions to 1987) forcing motorists to maintain properly their pollution control system. Congress thus seemed to be saying, "The improvement of air quality in order to protect public health is a fundamental priority as long as it does not seriously constrain the transportation habits of urban Americans or their preferences for dispersed housing patterns." The 1977 amendments clarified a value choice that was, at most, only implicit in the 1970 act. But that choice will substantially impede any effort to reduce vehicle miles traveled and thus place a considerable obstacle in the attainment of the primary air quality standards for carbon monoxide and oxidant in Los Angeles and several other areas by 1982 (or 1987).

Implications of this case for the conceptual framework of the implementation process

There is no doubt that the 1970 Clean Air Act sought a major change in the behavior of automobile manufacturers, stationary sources of carbon monoxide, hydrocarbons, and nitrogen oxides, and—at least by implication—urban motorists if it were to achieve its major goal of attaining the primary air quality standards in all areas of the country by mid-1977 and its subsidiary objective of a 90 percent reduction in new car emissions by the 1975–76 models. In fact, very few statutes have ever sought to achieve such substantial behavioral change in so short a period of time.

If we use the implementation of this case to evaluate the conceptual framework presented in chapter 2, we should ask at least three questions. First, does the framework help provide a post-hoc explanation of the extent to which statutory objectives were actually attained, both overall and across different programmatic or geographical areas? Second, and highly related, does the framework focus on the most important causal factors? For example, were some of the framework variables trivial in this case? Conversely, were important variables in the case ignored in the framework? Finally, does this analysis of the implementation of the automotive-related provisions of the 1970 Clean Air Act suggest certain modifications—e.g., clarification of important terms, addition or deletion of variables, specific hypotheses— which need to be made in the framework?

In Table 4.6 we assess the extent to which the six summary conditions of the framework were met—first in the overall implementation of the 1970 Clean

Table 4.6
Extent to Which the Implementation of the 1970 Clean Air Amendments Met the Six Conditions of Effective Implementation, 1970–77

		Extent to Which Conditions Were Met		
			Specific Programs	
Condition	Overall Program (and stationary sources)	Reducing emissions from new cars	Reducing emissions from in-use cars	Reducing VMT through transportation controls
1. Statute contains clear and consistent policy directives.	MODERATE/HIGH. Clear priority to protecting public health. Economic welfare of the regulated clearly secondary, though ambiguous with respect to urban motorists.	HIGH. 90 percent reduction in emissions by 1975–76; little mention of cost or other constraints.	MODERATE/HIGH. Clear implication that new car standards should last 50,000 miles.	LOW/MODERATE. Implication that reduction of VMT should fill gap left by phase-in of new car standards, but not explicit and constraints not addressed.
2. Statute incorporates sound causal theory identifying and providing jurisdiction over sufficient factors to have the potential to attain objectives.	MODERATE/LOW. General relationships between emission sources and public health and welfare understood, but not with the precision required by numerical standards. Real problem with lack of fit in deadlines for 1975–76 auto emission standards and 1977 ambient air quality standards due to slow turnover in auto fleet.	MODERATE/UNCERTAIN. Meeting standards required development of new technology. EPA had jurisdiction over auto companies but little ability to develop new technology and no authority to market low-emission vehicles.	UNCERTAIN/LOW. Uncertain whether emission systems lasting 50,000 miles could be developed. Unclear whether EPA given sufficient jurisdiction over motorists. Uncertain availability of quick emissions test required for I&M program.	LOW. EPA had poor understanding of effects of various transportation controls on VMT. Moreover, Congress soon withdrew its ability to require most effective controls, e.g., gas rationing and parking controls.

3. Statute structures implementation to maximize probability of compliance from implementing officials and target groups.	MODERATE overall.	MODERATE overall.	MODERATE/LOW overall.	LOW overall.
a. assignment to sympathetic agency	MODERATE/VARIABLE. Lead agency (EPA) could be expected to be sympathetic, but views of state and local pollution control agencies highly variable.	HIGH. EPA expected to be sympathetic.	MODERATE/LOW. EPA sympathetic, but local and state officials needed for I&M program often hostile.	LOW/MODERATE. EPA supportive, but transportation agencies and local governments generally hostile.
b. hierarchically integrated system with few veto points and adequate incentives for compliance	MODERATE/LOW. EPA had legal authority to promulgate and enforce SIPs, but often lacked necessary funds or personnel for enforcement. Moreover, attorney general a significant obstacle in enforcement actions.	MODERATE/LOW. Few veto points but ultimately no effective sanctions against auto companies given their critical role in the economy.	LOW. Many veto points in I&M programs. EPA without effective sanctions against state and local governments.	LOW. Enormous number of veto points in implementing TCPs, and EPA without effective sanctions.
c. supportive decision rules	MODERATE/LOW. Burden of proof generally on EPA. Not an important factor.	MODERATE. Specified findings necessary for granting auto emission waivers.	SAME as for overall program.	SAME as for overall program.

d. financial resources	MODERATE/LOW. Might have been adequate had state and local agencies been supportive. But not at all adequate to replace hostile agencies.	MODERATE/LOW. EPA funds probably adequate to monitor auto companies but inadequate to develop low-emission vehicles.	LOW. EPA did not have funds (or perhaps even legal authority) to establish I&M programs given states' reluctance to do so.	LOW. Inadequate funds to (1) research into effects of transportation control measures; (2) provide EPA personnel to gain entry to transportation subsystems; (3) actually implement TCPs.
e. formal access to supporters	MODERATE/HIGH. Citizen suit provisions gave legal standing over nondiscretionary decisions, limited in enforcement actions. Requirements for public hearings about SIP. Independent studies by National Academy of Sciences.	SAME as for overall program.	SAME as for overall program.	SAME as for overall program.
4. Commitment and skill of top implementing officials.	MODERATE/VARIABLE. Probably fairly high for EPA, but quite variable for state pollution control officials.	MODERATE/HIGH. Probably fairly high for EPA officials.	MODERATE/LOW. Probably quite high for EPA, but low for state officials of I&M programs.	MODERATE/LOW. Probably fairly high for EPA (at least on commitment) but quite variable for federal and state transportation officials.

5. Continuing support from constituency groups and sovereigns.	MODERATE/VARI-ABLE. Environmental groups active at national level, though variable at state and local levels. Congressional support waned, but slippage minimized by Sen. Muskie. White House in 1975–76 unsupportive. Courts varied.	MODERATE. Same as for overall program except President Ford quite hostile.	MODERATE/VARI-ABLE. Same as for overall program although environmental group support at state and local levels critical for I&M programs varied.	LOW. Critical here was Congressional hostility to parking controls, as well as variable environmental group activity at state and local levels.
6. Changing socioeconomic conditions over time.	LOW/MODERATE. Energy crisis, recession (especially in auto industry), and inflation dealt a major blow to the program.	LOW. Fuel crisis and unemployment hit auto industry very hard; critical in UAW's change of position.	LOW/MODERATE. Not a major factor, although perception of catalysts' fuel penalty did not help I&M programs.	MODERATE. Concern with fuel economy helped EPA's support of mass transit systems.

Legend: HIGH   = Very conducive to attaining statutory objective(s).
           MODERATE = Condition met fairly well, but some problems.
           LOW   = Condition not met; a serious obstacle to attaining statutory objectives.

Air Act (including its application to stationary sources), and then in the three programs specifically dealing with automotive-related pollutants: (*a*) new car emissions, (*b*) emissions from in-use cars, and (*c*) reductions in vehicle miles traveled through transportation controls. Given the stringency—i.e., the amount of behavioral change required—of the act's objectives, we believe that each of the conditions would have to receive at least a moderate to high rating in order for the objective to be attained.

The table indicates that neither the overall program nor any of the automotive-related programs received the requisite rating on all six conditions. The overall program (particularly as it affected stationary sources) came closest, receiving at least moderately favorable ratings on all variables except the last—changing socioeconomic conditions over time. In many cases, however, the rating was moderate to variable, indicating a moderately favorable rating at the national level but great variation in state or local programs (e.g., with respect to the policy predispositions or the skill of agency officials and the continuing support from constituency groups). From these ratings, we would expect, first of all, that the act's air quality objectives would not have been achieved nationwide but that they may well have been met, at least with respect to stationary sources, in those areas where the goals had strong support from state and local pollution control officials and constituency groups. Although the data presented in this chapter do not enable us to test the geographical variation hypothesis, Table 4.5 clearly indicated that the objectives regarding air quality were not met nationwide. In addition, the lack of congruence between the 1975-76 emissions from new cars deadlines and the 1977 timetable for the achievement of air quality standards afflicted the entire program. Because of the slow turnover in the auto fleet, attainment of the ambient objectives was contingent upon probably unrealistic reductions in emissions from stationary sources and in vehicle miles traveled.

As for variation among the three automobile-related programs, Table 4.6 suggests that the transportation controls would be the least successful (receiving low ratings on virtually all of the conditions), followed by emissions reductions from in-use cars, and the program to reduce emissions from new cars (as they left the assembly line) would be the most successful of the three. The data in this chapter generally confirm this ranking. Transportation controls were clearly the least successful measures. Reducing emissions from in-use vehicles was somewhat more successful, at least beginning with the 1975 models. Virtually all the improvements were, however, attributable to the efforts of EPA and the automobile companies rather than the result of inspection and maintenance programs or other efforts of state and local authorities or individual motorists; this is exactly what the framework would predict, given the much lower number of veto points involved in the EPA/manufacturer interface. Finally, the most successful of the three automotive-related programs concerned the ability to reduce emissions from new cars, particularly after introduction of the 1975 interim standards and

EPA's efforts to improve quality control on the assembly line. In short, the framework did a good job of anticipating program outcomes, but it should be remembered that the judgments involved were admittedly subjective.

It is worth noting, however, that even the new car emissions program—with generally moderate or high ratings on the independent (framework) variables—was only moderately successful (roughly 50 to 60 percent reductions in emissions rather than 90 percent) because of a few critical deficiencies: the problem in developing any new technology (i.e., uncertain causal theory); the lack of effective sanctions against the automobile companies, particularly after the energy crisis and the recession; and the inability of EPA (because of inadequate funding and, ultimately, the lack of legal authority) to develop and market a low-emission, fuel-efficient automobile—in effect, to serve as an alternative to the private manufacturers.

This bring us to the second function of the framework, namely, its ability to identify the important causal factors affecting the degree of attainment of statutory objectives. In effect, what is the degree of fit between the problems identified in the study of the implementation of the 1970 Clean Air Act and the variables identified in the conceptual framework? We find that it is really quite good. For example, as noted in the discussion of the new car emissions program, the major problems were the uncertain causal theory inherent in the development of any new technology, the inadequate research and development funds provided EPA, the fact that EPA did not have authority to market automobiles itself (thereby increasing the importance of the private companies' veto), and the lack of adequate sanctions against the automobile companies—at least in a period of economic difficulty. In the case of the in-use emissions programs, insofar as program failure lay with the domestic manufacturers, the variables would be the same as above; insofar as it lay with motorists, the dominant problem was the unwillingness of state and local governments to institute inspection and maintenance programs. This, in turn, can be traced to what the framework terms "inadequate hierarchical integration," i.e., the lack of incentives available to EPA to bring potential veto points into compliance. The failure of the transportation controls to reduce vehicle miles traveled could be traced to (a) inadequate knowledge (causal theory) concerning the effects of vehicle miles traveled on air quality and other social goals, (b) a very poorly integrated system with numerous veto points and practically no efffective sanctions in the hands of EPA, and (c) Congressional refusal to give EPA legal authority to impose some of the more potentially effective measures. Finally, the problems with the overall program established by the 1970 Clean Air Act (particularly with respect to stationary sources) could be traced to an imperfect understanding of the relationship between emissions, air quality levels, and public health; added to the only modestly (hierarchically) integrated administrative process given EPA's inability to actually replace hostile state and local agencies (except in isolated instances), as well as the attorney general's potential veto over any enforcement actions; and to the incongruence between achievement of air quality standards and auto emissions deadlines.

This analysis, however, does not explain why the automobile companies and urban motorists proved to be such difficult target groups (the strong opposition of the latter was certainly one of the principal reasons for the reluctance of state and local officials to approve transportation controls or inspection and maintenance programs). To understand this problem, recall our discussion in chapter 2 of what was termed "the tractability of the problem." We argued there that tractability was a function of, among other things, (a) the *availability* of a valid causal theory, (b) the percentage of the population represented by the target group, and (c) the extent of behavioral change required of target groups. The first variable was clearly behind many of the problems with causal theory in this case; it was not that the 1970 Clean Air Act did not incorporate the best theory available but rather that, in many critical areas, there was simply no sufficiently precise valid theory to be incorporated in 1970 and many of these problems remained during the very tight deadlines established by the act.

But perhaps this case's greatest contribution to the refinement of the framework is its ability to give some indication of which target groups are likely to be most intractable. In the case of both the automobile companies and urban motorists, part of the difficulty lay in the magnitude of the behavioral change required. For automobile companies, reducing new car emissions by 90 percent within a four- to five-year period would require changes in production techniques, research and development costs, development of new sources of supply, etc., by major corporations accustomed to considerable autonomy in such matters. For motorists, substantially reducing vehicle miles traveled would require not only major modifications in transportation habits (the substitution of mass transit and car pools for the private automobile) but probably also the acceptance of more concentrated housing patterns—in short, a reversal of two of the major trends in American society since 1945.

In addition to the magnitude of the change required, two aspects of these target groups compounded the tractability problem. For example, urban motorists (1) involved a very substantial percentage (roughly 50 percent) of the American population which was (2) dispersed among a substantial percentage of legislative (congressional) districts.[61] Given the amount of behavioral change required, one could therefore expect citizens in a great many congressional districts to raise a substantial protest against transportation controls (or even inspection and maintenance programs). And, of course, the situation was even worse for local elected officials, for whom the target group constituted virtually their entire electorate.

The situation was similar in the case of the automobile industry, which (1) constituted a significant percentage (16 to 18 percent) of the nation's gross national product and employment and (2) whose factories were dispersed among thirty-six states. If one adds the automobile dealers and the portions of the steel, rubber, and other industries dependent upon the welfare of the domestic automobile manufacturers, the potential political clout of the industry as a whole is truly staggering. Among other things, it means that any sanctions which would risk substantially endangering the welfare of the industry are simply unthinkable. Sensitivity to such risks is, as we have seen, substantially increased when the industry is in a period of economic difficulty.

This discussion suggests, in sum, that the tractability of the problem being addressed is, in part, a function of the target group (1) as a percentage of the total population or economy in the relevant political jurisdiction and (2) its dispersion among the legislative districts in that jurisdiction. If only the percentage is high, substantial behavioral change (in the face of target group opposition) is difficult to accomplish, as the struggle to desegregate southern schools certainly illustrates. If the percentage is high and dispersion is wide, behavioral change is almost impossible, as indicated by the failure to desegregate northern schools.

This analysis—and the evidence presented in this case study of the implementation of the 1970 Clean Air Act—also suggest that changes in socioeconomic conditions over the course of implementation are particularly critical insofar as they affect the economic welfare of target groups, especially if those groups constitute a significant portion of the economy and are widely dispersed among legislative districts in the relevant political jurisdiction. If conditions have adverse effects, then attempts at behavioral change are likely to be delayed or relaxed—as happened in this case—or subsidies will be employed to soften the effects of regulatory controls.

In closing, we make one final point. Throughout this case study we have implicitly assumed that each of the American automobile manufacturers constitutes a single veto point. This is, however, probably simplistic on two grounds. First, it assumes that each company is a hierarchically integrated organization with respect to decisions about emissions control systems. This supposition conflicts with much of organization theory. Second, viewing the four domestic manufacturers as four veto points assumes—again, probably erroneously—that, in the development of emissions technology, each company was in control of the necessary sources of supply.[62] These comments do not, of course, deny the importance of veto points, but they should remind us that enumeration of veto points is often more complicated than it first appears.

For further reflection

1. In the introduction to their book, *Innovation and Implementation in Public Organizations* (Lexington, Mass.: D. C. Heath & Co., 1978), Richard Nelson and Douglas Yates contend that the politics of successful legislative innovation almost directly contradicts the logic of successful

innovation. They state that successful policy formulation requires both ambitious and ambiguous description of goals and benefits in order to appeal to the broadest possible audience. In contrast, implementation requires clarity of goals and precision in the scope of change desired and the distribution of benefits and costs. What evidence for or against this thesis is suggested by the enactment and implementation of the 1970 Clean Air Act? (See the sources cited in note 13 of this chapter).

2.   What seems to have made Senator Muskie such an effective "fixer" in protecting the 1970 Clean Air Act? See Bernard Asbell, *The Senate Nobody Knows* (Garden City, N. Y.: Doubleday, 1978).

3.   The Swedish government's strategy for reducing air pollution emissions, according to Lennart Lundqvist in *The Hare and the Tortoise: Clean Air Policies in the United States and Sweden* (Ann Arbor: University of Michigan Press, 1980), was to require only technologically feasible solutions in contrast to the "technology-forcing" strategy adopted in the United States. Yet the results in terms of emissions reductions are comparable between the two nations. If, in 1970, Congress had adopted the more modest goals of the Swedish plan, what is the prospect that emission reductions in the United States would have been comparable to those achieved under the "technology-forcing" 1970 Clean Air Act?

4.   A standard position taken by economists is that effluent taxes (or fees) are the most efficient and effective method of inducing new technological and organizational innovation, in contrast to the mandated standards approach adopted in the 1970 Clean Air Act. See, for example, Charles Schultz, *The Public Use of Private Interest* (Washington, D.C.: Brookings Institution, 1977); Edwin Mills and Lawrence White, "Government Policies Toward Automotive Emissions Control," *Approaches to Controlling Air Pollution,* ed by Ann Friedlaender (Cambridge, Mass.: MIT Press, 1978), pp. 349-52; Giandomenico Majone, "Choice Among Policy Instruments for Pollution Control," *Policy Analysis* 2 (Fall 1976): 589-613. Yet Majone suggests that effluent taxes are subject to many of the same political and other constraints. You have examined the implementation problems that occurred under the mandated standards approach of the 1970 Clean Air Act. Critically analyze Mills and White's detailed proposal for an automotive emissions tax. See Mills and White, "Government Policies Toward Automotive Emissions Control."

5.   Because of the wide dispersion of the principal beneficiaries of air pollution control—all persons in most major metropolitan areas of the country—Mancur Olson believes that they are quite unlikely to organize effectively. See *The Logic of Collective Action* (Cambridge, Mass.: Harvard University Press, 1965). Can this viewpoint be reconciled with the fact that the Clean Air Act was passed in 1970 and was actively defended through the 1974–77 revisions by the National Clean Air Coalition? What does this suggest about Olson's thesis? Would his thesis be of greater or lesser relevance in considering the long-term viability of

the act's stringent provisions? For a critique of the Olson thesis, see Robert Mitchell, "National Environmental Lobbies and the Apparent Illogic of Collective Action," in *Collective Decision Making*, ed. Clifford Russell (Baltimore, Md.: The Johns Hopkins University Press, 1979.

Notes

1. "Special Report: America Faces Turning Point in its Long Love Affair with the Automobile," *National Journal* 8 (January 3, 1976): 1–23. See especially pp. 2, 13.
2. Ibid., pp. 2–4, 19–23.
3. The relative contribution highway vehicles made to atmospheric pollutants remained quite stable throughout the 1970–77 period (with the exception of carbon monoxide, which rose from 69 percent in 1970 to 76 percent in 1977). Passenger cars account for about 70 percent of emissions from highway vehicles, the remainder coming mainly from gasoline-powered trucks. See U.S., Environmental Protection Agency, *National Air Pollutant Emission Estimates, 1970–78* (Research Triangle Park, N.C.: EPA January 1980).
4. For a history of control efforts, see James Krier and Edmund Ursin, *Pollution and Policy* (Berkeley: University of California Press, 1977).
5. Aaron Wildavsky, *Speaking Truth to Power* (Boston: Little, Brown, 1979), chapter 2.
6. The national air quality standards promulgated by EPA in April 1971 (*Federal Register*, Vol. 36, no. 84) were based upon the Air Quality Criteria documents for each of the major pollutants previously published by the National Air Pollution Control Administration (NAPCA) in 1969–70. For reviews of the health and property effects of various pollutants as of the mid-1970s, see Frank Grad et al., *The Automobile and the Regulation of Its Impact on the Environment* (Norman: University of Oklahoma Press, 1975), pp. 41–61; and U.S. Congress, Senate, Committee on Public Works, *Air Quality and Automobile Emissions Control*, A Report by the National Academy of Sciences, 93rd Cong., 2d sess., September 1974, Vol. 2 [hereafter cited as 1973–74 NAS Study]. For a more recent assessment of some of the problems with the SO_2 standards, see Richard Tobin, *The Social Gamble* (Lexington, Mass.: D. C. Heath, 1979).
7. On the revision of the oxidant standard from .08 ppm to .12 ppm (not to be exceeded more than one hour per year), see Barbara Finamore and Elizabeth Simpson, "Ambient Air Standards for Lead and Ozone: Scientific Problems and Economic Pressures," *Harvard Environmental Law Review* 3 (1979): 261–74.
8. Arthur Davidson, Margaret Hoggan, and Mike Nazemi, *Air Quality Trends in the South Coast Basin* (El Monte, Calif.: South Coast Air Quality Management District, June 1979), p. 58.
9. According to Los Angeles County air pollution officials, the background ozone concentration in the basin is .05–.06 ppm. Even EPA officials admitted in 1974 that meeting the .08 ppm ozone standards would require such drastic measures as reducing gasoline consumption (and vehicle miles traveled) by 80 percent. Even meeting the more lenient .12 ppm standards by 1987 would probably require eliminating all refineries along the coast, allowing no new population growth, removing power plants and polluting industries from the basin, and finding a substitute for the gasoline-power internal combustion engine. See Eli Chernow, "Implementing the Clean Air Act in Los Angeles: The Duty to Achieve the Impossible," *Ecology Law Quarterly* 4 (1975); 537–81; Sandra Blakeslee, "Outlook Dim in Smog Battle," *Los Angeles Times*, September 21, 1979.
10. Edwin Mills and Lawrence White, "Government Policies Toward Automotive Emissions Control," in *Approaches to Controlling Air Pollution*, ed. Ann Friedlaender (Cambridge, Mass.: MIT Press, 1978), pp. 349–52.
11. Ibid.; Krier and Ursin, *Pollution and Policy*, chapters 2–11.
12. Henry Jacoby and John Steinbruner, *Clearing the Air* (Cambridge, Mass.: Ballinger, 1973), pp. 10–11; Council on Environmental Quality, *Public Opinion on Environmental Issues* (Washington, D.C.: Government Printing Office, 1980), p. 7; James McEvoy, "The American Concern with Environment," in *Social Behavior, Natural Resources, and the Environment*, ed. William Burch et al. (New York: Harper & Row, 1972), pp. 214–36; Paul Sabatier, "Social Movements and Regulatory Agencies," *Policy Sciences* 6 (Fall 1975): 301–42.

13. The two best overall accounts of the passage of the 1970 Clean Air Amendments are Helen Ingram, "The Political Rationality of Innovation," in *Approaches to Controlling Air Pollution,* ed. Ann Friedlaender, pp. 12–56, and Charles Jones, *Clean Air* (Pittsburgh: Pittsburgh University Press, 1975), chapter 7.

14. The Clean Air Amendments of 1970, PL 91–604, Sec. 101(b) (1), 42 USC sec. 1857 et seq.

15. Ibid., Sections 110–113.

16. The sections dealing with mobile source control are found in Title II of the 1970 amendments. The Barth Report (upon which the 90 percent reductions were based) has been criticized because of (1) its linear roll-back technique and (2) its worst-case assumptions. For example, its estimates were based upon attainment of the prescribed air quality standards in the worst cities—Chicago for CO, Los Angeles for oxidants. The report assumed that mobile sources were totally responsible for these two pollutants and used the highest published estimate on automobile growth rate. On the other hand, it completely neglected deterioration in pollution control equipment over time. The decision of the Muskie subcommittee to advance the auto emission deadline from 1980 to 1975–76 was based in part upon a study by the Batelle Institute and several prototype vehicles being developed by NAPCA. For the origins of Title II, see Grad et al., *Automobile,* pp. 332–34; U.S. Congress, Senate, Committee on Public Works, *The Impact of Auto Emission Standards,* A Staff Report, no. 93–11, 93d Cong., 1st sess., October 1973 [hereafter cited as *1973 Senate Staff Report*]; and the symposium on the Barth Report found in the July 1970 issue of the *Journal of the Air Pollution Control Association.*

17. The only mention of land use and transportation controls is in 1970 Clean Air Amendments, Sec. 110(a) (2) (b). For the committee report, see U.S. Congress, Senate, Committee on Public Works, *Report on the National Air Quality Standards Act of 1970,* Report 91–1196, 91st Cong., 2d sess. (1970), p. 2; it acknowledged that, "as much as 75% of the traffic may have to be restricted in certain large metropolitan areas if health standards are to be achieved within the time required by this bill."

18. 1970 Clean Air Amendments, Sections 113, 205, and 304.

19. This strategy was reasonable given (a) the agency's much greater experience with stationary sources and automobiles, (b) the Barth analysis, and (c) the agency's understandable desire to avoid antagonizing urban motorists as long as possible. See Alfred Marcus, *Promise and Performance* (Westport, Conn.: Greenwood Press, 1981), p. 168. For an excellent discussion of the suspension decision, see Grad et al., *Automobile,* pp. 339–60.

20. Paul Downing and Gordon Brady, "Implementing the Clean Air Act: A Case Study of Oxidant Control in Los Angeles," *Natural Resources Journal* 18 (April 1978): 225–61; Chernow, "Implementing the Clean Air Act in Los Angeles," pp. 537–81; Krier and Ursin, *Pollution and Policy,* pp. 213–34; and "Pollution: Cleaning the Air While Keeping the Car," *National Journal* 8 (January 3, 1976): 8–12.

21. Grad et al., *Automobile,* pp. 345–64; John Quarles, *Cleaning Up America* (Boston: Houghton Mifflin, 1976), pp. 178–90; Joseph O'Connor, "The Automobile Controversy— Federal Control of Vehicular Emissions," *Ecology Law Quarterly* 4 (1975): 664–69; Raphael Kasper, "Automobile Emission Standards Suspension," in National Research Council, *Decision-Making in EPA,* vol. 2a: *Case Studies* (Washington, D.C.: National Academy of Sciences, 1977).

22. Downing and Brady, "Implementing the Clean Air Act," pp. 262–70; "Pollution: Cleaning the Air While Keeping the Car," pp. 9–11.

23. The use of retarded spark timing to control carbon monoxide and hydrocarbons emissions in the early 1970s had decreased fuel economy very slightly in compacts and about 10 to 15 percent in standard-sized cars; Grad et al., *Automobile,* pp. 132–35, 283–95; Marcus, *Promise and Performance,* pp. 163–64; Bernard Asbell, *The Senate Nobody Knows* (Garden City, N.Y.: Doubleday, 1978), pp. 101–2.

24. For example, there were about 150,000 fewer employees in the domestic auto industry in late 1975 than during the peak year of 1973; see "Economic Impact: Timing May be Key to Future," *National Journal* 8 (January 3, 1976): 21–22. This was the result of the increase in sales of foreign cars and the fact that manufacture of domestic compacts provides fewer jobs than manufacture of standard-sized cars. For the political repercussions, see Quarles, *Cleaning Up America,* pp. 192–93, 205–8.

25. Norman Ornstein and Shirley Elder, *Interest Groups, Lobbying, and Policymaking* (Washington, D.C.: Congressional Quarterly, 1978), pp. 171–72; see also Asbell, *The Senate Nobody Knows,* pp. 37–38, 173–77, 430.

26. Downing and Brady, "Implementing the Clean Air Act," pp. 245–53; Council on Environmental Quality (CEQ), *Environmental Quality—1978* (Washington, D.C.: U.S. Government Printing Office, 1979), pp. 2–3; Finamore and Simpson, "Ambient Air Standards for Lead and Ozone," pp. 269–74. It should be noted, however, that reinterpretation of the original studies was only one of several factors leading to the revision of the oxidant standard.

27. Downing and Brady, "Implementing the Clean Air Act," pp. 259–61.

28. For example, whereas forty-seven air quality regions had originally been found in violation of the nitrogen oxides standards, after the June 8, 1973, revision by EPA only four remained in violation. Grad et al., *Automobile*, pp. 285–86; 368; *1973 Senate Staff Report*, pp. 101–23.

29. For discussions of the sulfate controversy, see Marcus, *Promise and Performance*, pp. 165–67; John Burby, "Environment Report: Sulfates Present Major New Problem in Growing Debate Over Clean Air Act," *National Journal Reports*, September 22, 1973, pp. 1412–17; Arthur Magida, "Environment Report: EPA Study May Bring Reprieve for Catalytic Converter," *National Journal Reports*, April 12, 1975, pp. 552–58; W. B. Rood, "EPA Admits It Erred on Sulfate Buildup Estimates," *Los Angeles Times*, April 15, 1976; and David Chock, "An Overview of the General Motors Sulfate Dispersion Experiment," *Transportation Research Record*, no. 670 (1978), pp. 36-43.

30. Downing and Brady, "Implementing the Clean Air Act," pp. 245–53; Asbell, *The Senate Nobody Knows*, pp. 349, 359.

31. This section on the constraints facing the auto manufacturers is taken largely from the following sources: Jacoby and Steinbruner, *Clearing the Air*, chapters 2 and 3; Asbell, *The Senate Nobody Knows*, pp. 34–35, 188–89, 319–30, 365–67; Grad et al., *Automobiles*, pp. 115–35, 279–309.

32. *1973 Senate Staff Report*, foreword and introduction; Mills and White, "Government Policies Toward Automotive Emissions Control," pp. 380–82; Asbell, *The Senate Nobody Knows*, passim.

33. Jacoby and Steinbruner, *Clearing the Air*, chapter 3; Asbell, *The Senate Nobody Knows*, pp. 322–24; O'Connor, "The Automobile Controversy," pp. 679–87.

34. For excellent reviews of the results of the tests of in-use cars, see Mills and White, "Government Politics," pp. 369–78 (especially Tables 8-6 and 8-9); Comptroller General of the U.S., *Better Enforcement of Car Emission Standards* (Washington, D.C.: General Accounting Office, January 23, 1979), pp. 4–8; and Jack Appelman, "Testing and Maintenance of In-Use Vehicles," in *Clearing the Air*, ed. Jacoby and Steinbruner, pp. 113–33.

35. Comptroller General, *Better Enforcement of Car Emission Standards*, pp. 29–31; Milton Weinstein and Ian Clark, "Emissions Measurement and the Testing of New Vehicles," in *Clearing the Air*, ed. Jacoby and Steinbruner, pp. 63–112.

36. Comptroller General, *Better Enforcement of Car Emission Standards*, pp. 7–8.

37. Inspection and maintenance costs are difficult to estimate, but one study found them to be about $27 to $37, exclusive of major repairs (Mills and White, "Government Policies," p. 395); see also Paul Downing, "An Economic Analysis of Periodic Vehicle Inspection Programs," *Atmospheric Environment* 7 (1973): 1237–46, and the articles by Horowitz and by Schwartz in the April 1973 issue of the *Journal of the Air Pollution Control Association*.

38. EPA's list of transportation controls also included the previously discussed efforts (such as inspection and maintenance programs and retrofit programs) to reduce emissions from in-use vehicles. For inventories of transportation and land use controls, see Elizabeth Bennett, Greig Harvey, Ann Rappaport, and Mabelle Bessey, *Air Quality Considerations in Transportation Planning*, Phase II Report to the EPA (Cambridge, Mass.: MIT Center for Transportation Studies, December 30, 1975), pp. 77–78.

39. Bennett et al., *Air Quality Considerations*, p. 54; "Pollution: Cleaning the Air While Keeping the Car," p. 9.

40. Bennett et al., *Air Quality Considerations*, pp. 41–42, 49, 64; Elizabeth Bennett, Greig Harvey, Marvin Manheim, John Shurbier, Mabelle Bessey, and Joseph Bain, *The Transportation Control Planning Process: Findings and Recommendations for Improved Decision-Making*, Phase I Report to EPA (Cambridge, Mass.: MIT Center for Transportation Studies, March 27, 1975), pp. 9–15, 27–28.

41. Bennett et al., *Air Quality Considerations*, pp. 34, 99, 124, 130–37; Shirley Angrist and Shelby Stewman, *Controlling Automotive Pollution* (Boston: Intercollegiate Case Clearing House, 1977). For more technical analyses, see the articles in *Transportation Research*

Record on ride sharing [no. 673 (1978): 7–15], car pooling [no. 599 (1976): 35–40], automobile restricted zones [no. 634 (1977): 7–13], and the entire issue of no. 670 (1978).

42. O'Connor, "The Automobile Controversy," p. 678.
43. Bennett et al., *Air Quality Considerations,* pp. 54, 92–94, 101–22, 136–38; see also Marcus, *Promise and Performance,* pp. 167–72. For the Portland case, see Council on Environmental Quality (CEQ), *1978 Annual Report* (Washington, D.C.: U.S. Government Printing Office, 1979), p. 19.
44. Gasoline consumption is a frequently used indicator for vehicle miles traveled, as the latter is obviously extremely difficult to measure directly. This measurement assumes that gasoline consumption per mile remains relatively constant over time, which was true for motor vehicles (including trucks) during this period as average miles/gallon increased slightly from 12.14 in 1970 to 12.18 in 1976 (cf. U.S., Dept. of Commerce, *Statistical Abstract of the United States 1978,* Table 1101). Moreover, one might argue that gasoline consumption is an even better indicator than vehicle miles traveled of what one is actually interested in, namely, the amount of fuel combustion by motor vehicles.
45. Lawrence White, "Automobile Emissions Control Policy: Success Story or Wrongheaded Regulation?" in *Government, Technology, and the Future of the Automobile,* ed. Douglas Ginsburg and William Abernathy (New York: McGraw-Hill, 1980), pp. 411–13.
46. For example, 32 percent of the 1589 stations with adequate data for analysis exceeded the annual primary standard for TSP in 1972 (EPA, *Monitoring the Air Quality Trends Report, 1972,* Table 3-6).
47. Most stations which violate the oxidant standard probably do so only for a few days per year. For oxidant trends, see EPA, *National Air Quality, Monitoring, and Emissions Trends Report, 1977,* chapter 3, pp. 7–10 and chapter 2, pp. 11–15; CEQ, *Environmental Quality— 1978,* pp. 19–25.
48. EPA, *National Air Quality, Monitoring and Emissions Trends Report, 1977,* p. 3: 6; also, CEQ, *Environmental Quality, 1978,* pp. 14–19, and EPA, *Air Quality Trends in the Nation's Largest Urbanized Areas,* pp. 10–11.
49. EPA, *National Air Quality, Monitoring, and Emissions Trends Report, 1977,* pp. 3: 10–11, and CEQ, *Environmental Quality, 1978,* pp. 22–27.
50. It should be noted, however, that during the 1970s there was increasing evidence of the need for a short-term (one- to three-hour) nitrogen dioxide standard and the need to examine the effect of nitrogen oxides emissions on the production of a class of carcinogenic chemicals termed nitrosamines (cf. U.S. Congress, Senate, Committee on Environment and Public Works, *Report on the Clean Air Amendments of 1977,* No. 95-127, 95th Cong., 1st sess., May 10, 1977, pp. 118–19).
51. On the contribution to inflation of pollution control regulations, see Chase Econometrics, *The Macroeconomic Impacts of Federal Pollution Control Programs,* Report to CEQ and EPA, January 1975; U.S., Congress, Joint Economic Committee, *Achieving Price Stability Through Economic Growth,* 93d Cong., 2d sess., December 1974, pp. 36–42.
52. Recall that the 1970 Clean Air Act was passed with very little organized group support at the *national* level. The most active organizations in the National Clean Air Coalition were the American Lung Association, the Sierra Club, Friends of the Earth, the League of Women Voters, the National Resources Defense Council, the Environmental Defense Fund, and the Ralph Nader-sponsored Center for Automobile Safety. (Based on personal interviews and documents in NCAC files, as well as Ornstein and Elder, "Clean Air Legislation," pp. 165–68).

The 1973 emergency energy legislation, which made rather drastic changes in the Clean Air Act concerning automobile emission standards and coal conversion, passed Congress in the wake of the Arab oil embargo but was vetoed by President Nixon because of its gasoline-rationing provisions. By the time the Energy Supply and Coordination Act was approved in June 1974, Senator Muskie and others had considerably softened the legislation's impact on the Clean Air Act.
53. President Ford, a former Republican Congressman from Michigan, had excellent contacts with automobile company executives (Asbell, *The Senate Nobody Knows,* p. 175).
54. Asbell, *The Senate Nobody Knows,* pp. 440–47. For a discussion of the 1975–76 session, see Asbell (*passim*) and Ornstein and Elder, "Clean Air Legislation," pp. 174–77.
55. Quoted in Ornstein and Elder, "Clean Air Legislation," p. 177.

56. For a discussion of the 1977 session, see Ornstein and Elder, "Clean Air Legislation," pp. 177–84; Asbell, *The Senate Nobody Knows*, p. 451.

57. The principal justification given for the delay was to give the automobile companies additional time to perfect the dual catalyst and the attendant engine adjustments (U.S., Congress, Senate, Committee on the Environment, *Report on the Clean Air Amendments of 1977*, pp. 4–7, 12–14, 67–75).

58. The central feature of the so-called Connecticut Plan is to assess a monetary penalty for noncompliance (or delayed compliance) which is equal to the amount of money the firm is saving by not being in compliance, e.g., via saving on delayed capital investment for pollution control equipment, avoided operations and maintenance costs, etc. (cf. comments by Edwin Clark and William Drayton in *Approaches to Controlling Air Pollution*, ed. Ann Friedlaender, pp. 227–33). Following are the relevant portions of the House conference report which discuss the specific topics: offsets, p. 157; hydrocarbon vapor recovery, pp. 181–82; civil and criminal penalties, p. 132; the noncompliance penalty based on the Connecticut Plan, pp. 138–40; the expanded citizen suit provision, p. 173; and the requirements concerning Justice Department and EPA, pp. 173–77 (see U.S., Congress, House, *Conference Report on the Clean Air Act Amendments of 1977*, Report 95-564, 95th Cong., 1st sess., August 3, 1977).

59. Although EPA estimated that I&M programs were needed in twenty-six air quality regions, as of December 1977 programs had been established in only six of them (GAO, *Better Enforcement of Car Emission Standards*, pp. 10–11, 33–35); by August 1979, however, twenty states—but not the critical one of California—had at least given cities the legal authority to establish I&M programs (EPA press release, August 24, 1979).

60. For general discussions of the debate between the relative merits of emissions fees and the classical regulatory approach, see Giandomenico Majone, "Choice Among Policy Instruments for Pollution Control," *Policy Analysis* 2 (Fall 1976): 589–613; Charles Schultze, *The Public Use of Private Interest* (Washington, D.C.: The Brookings Institution, 1977).

61. This is the rough percentage of the population in the thirty SMSAs which EPA indicated needed transportation control plans.

62. For example, the entire catalyst technology was dependent upon (a) secure sources of platinum and (b) the wide availability of unleaded gasoline. The major sources of platinum are Zimbabwe/Rhodesia and South Africa—hardly the most stable regimes in the world—and the whole unleaded gasoline program was clouded by a court suit throughout much of the mid-1970s (Asbell, *The Senate Nobody Knows*, pp. 366–67).

Chapter 5
One principle, two programs: desegregation of the nation's schools, south and north

In 1954 and 1955, the Supreme Court handed down decisions in *Brown* v. *Board of Education of Topeka, Kansas,* that had an enormous impact on race relations and public education in the United States. In its 1954 ruling, the Court overturned the *Plessy* v. *Ferguson* decision of 1896 and declared unconstitutional the "separate but equal" doctrine on the grounds that any segregation sanctioned by the state, whether equal facilities are provided or not, stigmatizes one race with a brand of inferiority and consequently denies that race its constitutional guarantee of equal protection under the Fourteenth Amendment. In the 1955 ruling, the Court went on to say that merely preventing segregation was not enough; the historic pattern of state sanctioned segregation was to be abolished "with all deliberate speed."

Reaction to the decisions varied from violent opposition in the South to tentative hopefulness among civil rights leaders. While the *Brown* decision resulted in the dismantling of many dual school systems in the six border states and the District of Columbia, it had virtually no impact on *de jure* segregation (that created by government action) in the eleven states of the old Confederacy for the next ten years, until both Congress and the president used their authority to force implementation of the desegregation order. The attempt of the federal government to desegregate northern school districts, where segregation was either *de facto,* that is, not caused by government action per se but by "natural" housing and other settlement patterns, or far more subtle than the dual systems of the South, has been far less determined and effective.

The results of the desegregation order are shown in Table 5.1 in terms of the proportion of black pupils attending schools with whites in the South, the border states, and the North. Probably the most telling statistic is the proportion of "blacks in schools 99–100% black;" in effect, all-black schools. In the South, as late as 1964, virtually all (97.7 percent) black pupils were still isolated in all-black schools. The figure dropped an impressive fifteen percentage points by 1966, then fell off even more dramatically during the 1966–70 period, with modest reductions thereafter, reaching 17.9 percent by 1976. Meanwhile, by the early 1960s, the border states had already reduced the percentage of black pupils in all-black schools to less than 50 percent. However, while the formally sanctioned dual school systems of the border states were rapidly dismantled after *Brown,* by the end of the 1960s, the South had reduced racial isolation to a far greater degree (17.9 percent compared to the border states' 38.1 percent).

Table 5.1 also shows how desegregation progressed in the North from the late 1960s (the first point at which systematic statistics were gathered for the region) through 1976, to the point at which the percentage of black pupils in all-black schools reached 14.4 percent. However, as we shall see, the reduction in the North did not come about as the result of a concerted implementation effort by the federal government with a backing of Congress and the president. Rather, strides toward desegregation have been made at the insistence of the courts in the face of congressional and executive opposition.

As a study in implementation, the desegregation of public schools in both the South and the North highlights the tug-of-war between the judicial, executive, and legislative branches of government that can take place in the implementation of any important and controversial social program. It also reveals the importance of the tractability variables of a problem, especially the percentage of the population affected, the uniformity of the behavior in question, and the extent of behavioral change required. These considerations, in turn, affect the ability of implementors to clearly define acceptable and unacceptable target group behavior, as well as to establish standard remedies and accurately estimate their probable impacts. The dramatic difference between the federal government's ability to desegregate schools in the South versus those in the North is in large part attributable to tractability factors. Finally, the case of school desegregation illustrates the limited ability of an elected government, faced with entrenched public opposition, to provide fundamental human and constitutional rights to ethnic and racial minorities. In a democratic system, the inability of the government to resort to the degree of coercion that would be required to accomplish even the most praiseworthy objectives in the face of widespread opposition is, of course, a function of electoral and constitutional checks on public officials. This inability also shows that, without substantial public support, no democratic government is likely to orchestrate a social revolution of the scope sought by the advocates of nationwide school desegregation—at least not for long. The ultimate measure for judging the degree of effective implementation of the federal government's desegregation policy must therefore be, in view of circumstances, how great a change has been accomplished.

Table 5.1
Percent of Black Students in Desegregated Public Schools, by Region, 1962–76

	1962	1964	1966	1968	1970	1972	1974	1976
South								
Blacks attending schools with whites	0.5	2.3	16.8	—	—	—	—	—
Blacks in schools 0–49% black				23.4	34.0	37.9	39.2	40.0
Blacks in schools 50–98.9% black				36.9	41.8	41.6	41.3	42.1
Blacks in schools 99–100% black	99.5[a]	97.7[a]	83.2[a]	39.7	24.2	20.5	19.5	17.9
Border States and District of Columbia								
Blacks attending schools with whites	51.8	58.3	71.7	—	—	—	—	—
Blacks in schools 0–49.9% black				28.4	21.8	25.7	30.1	29.8
Blacks in schools 50–98.9% black				46.4	28.6	27.7	27.4	32.1
Blacks in schools 99–100% black	48.2[a]	41.7[a]	28.3[a]	25.2	49.6	46.6	42.5	38.1
North								
Blacks in schools 0–49.9% black				27.6	37.2	41.5	42.4	42.5
Blacks in schools 50–98.9% black				41.5	30.2	41.3	41.8	43.1
Blacks in schools 99–100% black				30.9	22.6	17.2	15.8	14.4
National								
Blacks in schools 0–49.9% black				23.4	34.0	37.9	39.2	40.0
Blacks in schools 50–98.9% black				46.9	41.8	41.6	41.3	42.1
Blacks in schools 99–100% black				39.7	24.2	20.5	19.5	17.9

Source: Charles S. Bullock, III, "Implementation of Selected Equal Education Opportunity Programs." (Paper presented at the annual meeting of the American Political Science Association, Washington, D.C., August 28–31, 1980). Tables 1 and 3. Blacks in schools 50–98.9% black is computed from the data provided.

[a] Approximate figure, calculated by subtracting "Blacks attending schools with whites" from 100 percent.

This leads to a series of more pointed questions: Exactly what constitutes desegregation in public schools and does it differ from North to South? What specifically is the policy of the federal government in this area? What was the public reaction to articulation of the policy? What was the reaction of those affected most directly, and what sanctions were required to bring target groups into compliance? How did responses feed back into the legislative, executive, and judicial arenas? Finally, how effective has been the effort?

The Court's *Brown* decision

The *Brown* decision was the final product of a lengthy legal struggle by the National Association for the Advancement of Colored People (NAACP) and other civil rights groups to dismantle the dual and racially segregated school systems that had prevailed in the South and border states for more than fifty years. In the *Brown* case, the plaintiffs were attempting to undermine the entire moral and legal rationale for state-sanctioned separate but equal schooling by arguing that separation, by law, is inherently unequal.[1] Their attempt was successful. In its unanimous opinion, written by Chief Justice Earl Warren, the Court found segregation in public schools an anachronism that had to be abolished. The Court argued:

> *To separate children from others of similar age and qualification solely because of their race generates a feeling of inferiority as to their status in the community that may affect their hearts and minds in a way unlikely ever to be undone . . . .*

The opinion adopted the reasoning spelled out most clearly in the opinion of the lower court that originally heard the case, that

> *Segregation of white and colored children in public schools has a detrimental effect upon the colored children. The impact is greater when it has the sanction of the law; for the policy of separating the races is usually interpreted as denoting the inferiority of the Negro group. A sense of inferiority affects the motivation of a child to learn. Segregation with the sanction of law, therefore, has a tendency to retard the educational and mental development of Negro children and to deprive them of some of the benefits they would receive in a racially integrated school system.*[2]

However, the Court did not subscribe to the NAACP's recommendation for immediate desegregation. In its 1955 *Brown* ruling, the Court announced its implementation scheme which reflected a very cautious attitude toward correcting what the Court acknowledged was a blatantly unconstitutional practice of many of the nation's school districts. The Court said that "full implementation may require solution of varied local school problems. School authorities have the primary responsibility for . . . solving these problems:

courts will have to consider whether the actions of school authorities constitute good faith implementation." Thus, local authorities were only required to make a "prompt and reasonable start toward full compliance" and once this start had been made, nothing further was needed. Delays were legally authorized if "necessary in the public interest and . . . consistent with good faith compliance . . . ."[3] The lower courts, which were delegated responsibility to oversee implementation of *Brown,* were urged to take into consideration problems peculiar to individual districts when defining "good faith."

Thus, the authoritative directive that set the wheels of government in motion was a profound and sweeping Supreme Court decision directed specifically at the dual school systems of the South and border states, but with implications for segregated schools nationwide. Yet the Court's prescribed criteria for implementation, in its attempt to accommodate local problems, provided numerous loopholes that were skillfully exploited by segregationists for a decade to come.

Before turning to details of more than ten years of resistance to *Brown,* then rather swift compliance in the South, but continued evasion in the North, we should examine the capacity of the Court to make and implement policy. The Supreme Court was reluctant to prescribe a strict and narrow remedy for segregation through an insistence on immediate action for several reasons. First, its professed concern was legitimate; the desegregation decision attacked traditional racist attitudes and deeply embedded social norms. The Court, while condemning these norms, acknowledged their influence and tried to soften the blow of its decision. After all, local schools are the most sacred public institutions and any attempt to alter the status quo would surely meet stiff local opposition. Second, the judiciary is in many ways the least powerful branch of government; its authority ultimately rests on such intangible factors as "respect for the law." The desegregation decision was widely perceived in the South as an illegitimate incursion by the federal government into the domain of states' rights; indeed, some states even tried to interpose state authority and nullify federal authority within the state.[4] Surely, the Court anticipated this resistance and, understandably, feared total defiance of its authority. Consequently, the Court provided loopholes as a sort of safety valve; the South could delay and obstruct implementation yet not violate the law outright. Third, the judiciary, because of its institutional weakness in administration and enforcement, is poorly equipped to devise a narrow and specific blueprint for effective implementation.[5] Judicial administration is difficult since the courts have no direct control over executive agencies and no means of gathering information other than through the adversary process, which will necessarily reveal only the details of an individual case. Except for expensive and time-consuming follow-up litigation, the courts have no feedback mechanism to ascertain whether decisions are actually being carried out. The courts cannot offer inducements to comply as can the legislative and executive branches; thus, the judiciary is a very "reactive" political institution. All these factors impeded the Supreme Court's construction of a specific and demanding implementation program. In 1955, without strong congressional and presidential support for the school desegregation plan, the Court opted for prudence by articulating a principled decision but leaving significant opportunities for evasion and delay.

From "all deliberate speed" to compliance in the South

The South took full advantage of the loopholes left by the Court. Many districts took no action toward the formulation of desegregation plans until confronted with a lower court injunction. The courts could not initiate such action, of course, and had to await the filing of a suit before becoming involved. This placed a heavy burden on blacks, whose legal and political resources were scarce. The NAACP was virtually the only organization equipped to press the claims of black parents during this period, and since it, too, had limited resources, it would usually only take on cases that had the potential to set broad legal precedents. Consequently, most blacks were unable to bring suit against recalcitrant school districts and those that did were often subjected to physical and economic harassment. In the event that a suit was finally brought to court and decided in the plaintiff's favor, the school district would usually appeal, citing "local" difficulties in implementation. This would set off another round of litigation and delay. If and when an injunction was finally handed down, the district might make token motions to desegregate while making numerous appeals for postponement, and when finally forced into action would desegregate as little as possible. Since *Brown* established no numerical definition of acceptable levels of black enrollment, blacks dissatisfied with school districts' efforts also had to go through the courts to determine what constituted "all deliberate speed" in achieving desegregation for each district.

The most effective strategies southern districts used to frustrate desegregation efforts were local pupil placement procedures. If absolutely forced to adopt a desegregation plan, districts would typically opt for a "freedom of choice" plan. Under these plans, students were allowed to choose their preferred school prior to the fall term; if no "problems" arose, students were assigned to the school of their choice. In adopting this approach, school boards were confident that black parents usually would not place their children in what would likely be a hostile and intimidating setting of a white school. Black students who did choose white schools were frequently turned away on the basis of "overcrowding." Yet as long as the dual school system had been terminated formally and the denial of transfer could not be traced explicitly to discriminatory motives, this type of plan was not illegal. Consequently, as shown in Table 5.1, by 1964, only slightly more than 2 percent of black schoolchildren in the eleven southern states attended desegregated schools. Only 604 of the 2220 districts covered by the *Brown* decision had acted on the desegregation order by 1964, and even these had complied in merely a token fashion.[6]

Federal indifference

Part of the problem in enforcing desegregation was that there was no formal implementation mechanism other than the courts. Up to this point Congress had failed to establish an executive office responsible for monitoring desegregation progress and enforcing court-ordered civil rights actions. Presidents were also opposed to taking the initiative. President Dwight D. Eisenhower, in office when *Brown* was handed down, was unwilling to commit himself to school desegregation for both political and ideological reasons. As a Republican, he depended on the conservative Republican-Dixiecrat alliance in Congress and relied little on black votes. And philo-sophically he was reluctant to use the powers of the federal government to bring about changes in entrenched social institutions and attitudes. This reluctance was exemplified by his administration's refusal to back legislation proposed by Harlem Congressman Adam Clayton Powell (Dem.-N.Y.) that would deny federal money for school construction to any school district that was "in absolute defiance of the Supreme Court."[7] However, at the insistence of then Vice-President Richard Nixon, the administration did support the modest Civil Rights Act of 1957 that created the United States Commission on Civil Rights and a civil rights unit within the Justice Department. The administration's general indifference to vigorous enforcement of *Brown,* nevertheless, encouraged segregationists by further undermining the legiti-macy of the Court's decision.

With the election of President John Kennedy in 1960, the executive branch commitment to civil rights in general and the enforcement of *Brown* in particular became slightly more vigorous, at least in rhetoric. Kennedy, as a Democrat, had been elected with the support of black voters. Yet even under Kennedy, progress was slow. When civil rights activists pressed Abraham Ribicoff, Kennedy's Secretary of Health, Education and Welfare (HEW), to withhold federal impact aid (money to local schools heavily impacted by children from U.S. military bases) from segregated southern school districts, action to terminate funds was initiated. But Ribicoff backed off and the effort collapsed when the school district of Columbus, Mississippi, retaliated by closing the affected school.[8] Furthermore, Kennedy did not introduce a major civil rights bill into Congress until 1963. Even then the bill was proposed only in response to civil rights activists who had taken to the streets because they had lost patience with the strategy of winning civil rights through the slow process of case-by-case litigation.

As the country watched nightly news broadcasts showing civil rights activists attacked and beaten across the South, legislators were forced into action. The march of 200,000 activists on Washington, D.C., in 1963, and the extensive media coverage of black leaders such as Martin Luther King, Jr., demonstrated how important the issue of civil rights had become since the days of the Eisenhower administration. Desegregation was no longer of concern to only a handful of blacks and their white sympathizers. Polls showed that in 1965 a substantial majority of northern whites favored a greater degree of integration, with 65 percent saying that they did not object to educating their children in a school that was 50 percent black.[9] Within a few short years civil rights had become a crusade for northern whites and blacks against deplorable race relations practiced in the South. It was an issue ideally suited to cutting across traditional political bonds because of its moral tone. It could draw both Democratic and Republican support. Even though desegregation was one of the most salient and visible national issues of his term, Kennedy was cautious. The Republican-Dixiecrat alliance remained a powerful force in Congress and made the passage of a strong civil rights bill unlikely. Yet until such a bill was passed, segregated schools were likely to remain untouched by the federal government despite the *Brown* decision.

The 1964 Civil Rights Act

Kennedy's assassination in November 1963 marked a watershed in the federal government's stance on civil rights. Three elements combined to make Congress more receptive to bold civil rights efforts. First, in 1963, immediately upon assuming office after Kennedy's assassination, President Lyndon Johnson adopted civil rights legislation as a major order of business for his administration. Second, the clamor for federal action and the attendant media coverage highlighted the importance of the issue throughout the nation. Finally, working behind the scenes, the Leadership Conference on Civil Rights, "nearly 80 organizations, crossing racial, economic, and religious lines, put together one of the most disciplined and effective lobbying efforts congressional observers have recalled"[10] to win passage of a strong civil rights bill. Thus, with substantial support from President Johnson and the civil rights lobbyists, liberal members of Congress successfully fought back the many attempts to thwart passage of the 1964 Civil Rights Act, the strongest civil rights bill passed by Congress in the twentieth century. Despite filibusters led by southern Democrats, the act was swiftly passed and signed into law by Johnson, who was committed to its enforcement.

The 1964 Civil Rights Act provided two mechanisms for effecting school desegregation. Though the act was usually considered as applying to the South, in principle at least it was applicable nationwide. Title IV empowered the Justice Department to file suits on behalf of black plaintiffs against uncooperative school districts. This power had the potential to alleviate the burdens carried by the NAACP and other civil rights groups, which had assumed major responsibility for filing such suits since 1954. However, the

Justice Department was still handicapped by loopholes in *Brown,* and segregationists could still use litigation as an effective means of delaying implementation. Title IV also called for HEW to provide technical support and resources for school districts attempting to comply with the law.

Title VI, however, was the section of the law that provided the critical administrative leverage in the drive toward desegregation. Its broad purpose was sweeping and to the point. Section 601 of Title VI states:

No person in the United States shall, on the ground of race, color, or national origin, be excluded from participating in, be denied the benefits of, or be subjected to discrimination under any program or activity receiving Federal financial assistance.

Enforcement of this provision was to be an integral responsibility of the entire federal bureaucracy. Section 602 continues:

Each Federal Department and agency which is empowered to extend Federal financial assistance to any program or activity . . . is authorized and directed to effectuate the provisions of section 601 with respect to such program or activity by issuing rules, regulations or orders of general applicability which shall be consistent with achievement of the objectives of the statute authorizing the financial assistance in connection with which the action is taken.

In a single stroke the federal government moved from extreme reluctance and caution to a firm commitment to eliminate segregation in all activities touched by federal programs and monies.[11] Congress mandated HEW to pursue the effort that was begun by the Court in 1954. Furthermore, the all-important powers of federal financial assistance were to be tied to compliance. Passage of Title VI clearly opened a second major chapter in the federal school desegregation effort.

While its general intent was obvious, neither Title VI nor any other provision of the Civil Rights Act gave HEW much direction to define precisely what activities constituted discrimination in public school. Nor did it specify within what time limits discriminatory activities would have to be terminated to ensure the continued flow of federal dollars. Also, it failed to state how HEW was to administer Title VI: Was a new oversight bureau to be created within HEW? Was each program office in HEW to create its own administration and monitoring capacity? Or, was an entirely new agency to be established to oversee civil rights enforcement throughout all federal departments?

What followed, in brief, was that no serious attempt was made to coordinate Title VI activities throughout the government and Congress provided no funds to HEW for the specific purpose of carrying out its responsibilities under Title VI. As a result, implementation of the provision was slow to get off the ground. On the other hand, in 1965 Congress appropriated funds for the semiautonomous United States Office of Education (USOE) within HEW to provide federal assistance to schools that were in some way attempting to desegregate as ordered in Title IV. USOE was also the bureau responsible for distributing the $1 billion in federal aid to schools provided by the Elementary and Secondary Education Act of 1965. Therefore, USOE was the logical bureau to be assigned Title IV responsibilities by the secretary of HEW.[12] In a sense, implementation of Title VI was being piggybacked on Title IV. Moreover, USOE, as the bureau with the best working knowledge of the nation's thousands of school districts, had the capacity to implement the two titles most effectively. Among the arguments against entrusting Title VI to USOE were its traditional mission as a source of technical assistance and as a representative of local school districts in the nation's capital; the fact that its staff generally supported the ideology of local control of schools; it had operated independent of the secretary of HEW; and, it had no experience in regulating and policing local school districts to ensure enforcement of what local districts viewed as onerous national objectives. Thus, it was not long before Secretary of HEW John Gardner created an Office of Civil Rights (OCR) within the office of the secretary to coordinate and oversee all civil rights activities within HEW, in effect, checking the authority delegated to USOE. The lack of statutory guidance, the failure to provide funding, and the problems of competition between HEW and USOE virtually assured a shaky beginning for Title VI enforcement.

OCR guidelines and enforcement strategy

HEW's task was made somewhat simpler in the South by the fact that the problem to be remedied could be readily identified. Thanks to the *Brown* decision, the existence of a *de jure* school system presented a prima facie case of discrimination and thus violation of Title VI. Even so, progress was slow. One of OCR's first official actions was to formulate guidelines against which to measure southern progress. These guidelines originally received much criticism, first from civil rights groups who said they were too lenient, and then from southern officials who argued that they were too vague. Indeed, the guidelines promulgated in 1965 were both weak and confusing. For example, OCR would not examine any district that was under court order to desegregate. Since the courts usually accepted weaker plans than those allowed by OCR, and since the courts could not enforce compliance with the plans they accepted anyway, school districts often chose to go through the courts in formulating their plans. Moreover, the OCR guidelines were originally worded as loosely as the *Brown* decision, stating only that school systems must "begin" desegregation and provide a "substantial good faith start" toward that end. Freedom of choice plans, although demonstrably ineffective, were also permitted; thus desegregation need never take place as long as no blacks requested transfers.[13] Openly defying the law, many southern school districts evaded compliance during 1965 by completing HEW Form 441, which was simple declaration by the district that it was fully desegregated.

Nevertheless, the formulation of a standard against which to measure desegregation was an important milestone in policy enforcement. Guidelines formulated in 1966 included a more easily gauged measure of compliance; the stipulation was that "percentages would be used to measure compliance—i.e., whether a school district had achieved 15% integration by the time the (1966–67) school year had opened."[14] While the guidelines were intended to provide a positive goal toward which school officials could work to desegregate, the experience in the South showed that hostility toward the general policy was so great that, almost without exception, compliance would have to be coerced. It was at this point that HEW made receipt of the Elementary and Secondary Education Act of 1965 (ESEA) funds contingent upon progress toward compliance. By the end of 1966, 126 fund cutoff cases were pending.[15] While it could be argued that this decision hurt poor (i.e., black) districts the most since they depended most heavily on federal money, it is clear in retrospect that the strategy was the first effective mechanism placed in the hands of OCR.

The procedure worked as follows: OCR would first threaten noncooperative districts with cutoff of funds and attempt to negotiate a satisfactory plan; if this failed, OCR would deny the district access to additional federal school (mainly ESEA) funds while initiating aid termination procedures. If OCR decided to cut off funds, the decision had to be approved by HEW and by Congress. A school district could request a hearing from an examiner and if termination was still found to be justified, the district could appeal to the secretary of HEW. If the appeal was rejected, Congress was notified of the intended fund termination and the district's money was impounded. In spite of these several veto points, fund termination was generally carried out without much problem. Within an administration that openly supported desegregation policy, these several steps of approval were usually mere formalities and generally free from outside pressure to impede the cutoff procedure. It is worth noting that since final approval of fund termination is statutorily left to the secretary of HEW and, in effect to the president, OCR's actions would be much more constrained under an administration that did not support desegregation.

Under Johnson, however, OCR achieved positive results in many southern districts. According to Bullock, 53 percent of southern districts negotiated plans in anticipation of HEW action even before OCR began fund cutoff procedures; 7.5 percent agreed to plans before resolution of the procedures; and 18 percent refused to negotiate, thus losing their federal funds and prompting referral of their cases to the Justice Department. Thus, despite the initially weak guidelines promulgated in 1965, by the 1966–67 school year 16.8

percent of all black students in the southern states were attending school with whites—a sevenfold increase from three years earlier.

In sum, the main flaws in the 1965 guidelines were the acceptance of freedom of choice plans, the absence of any particular desegregation performance standards, and mere signed assurances that race was not a criteria in denying transfers to black students. If blacks were not convinced by these assurances, the burden was on them to initiate change; this, of course, left black parents and children susceptible to extensive harassment from the local community. Ironically, the ambiguity of the guidelines had a perverse effect on those school boards trying to cooperate with OCR; strict standards were often desired by local elected officials who believed that desegregation was inevitable but who, for political reasons, needed to cloak their desegregation efforts under the guise of compulsion. The guidelines promulgated in 1966 established a numerical standard for percentages of blacks to be enrolled in schools with a majority of whites. Although these guidelines were more specific than those of 1965, they caused further confusion as they required certain goals for those districts that had made some progress toward desegregation in 1965, but only gently criticized districts that had remained completely segregated, stating that "a very substantial effort would normally be expected to enable such a school system to catch up as quickly as possible." Moreover, the 1966 guidelines did not change the emphasis on freedom of choice; the success of these plans continued to be a function of community racial tolerance, a consideration that did not bode well for the prospects of widespread desegregation.

The 1968 Supreme Court decision in *Green* v. *New Kent County, Virginia* permanently altered the enforcement picture. In recognizing the dangers of freedom of choice, the Court concluded that freedom of choice plans were constitutionally insufficient unless they led to significant desegregation. The Court thus insisted that school districts adopt a plan that promptly produced schools that were not "identifiable by race." This decision coincided with stricter guidelines promulgated by OCR in 1968 and ensured that the agency would take a more rigorous approach to southern desegregation. No longer would OCR simply judge a district's compliance by its intent to desegregate, as indicated by a submission of plans or an agreement not to discriminate. Compliance was now to be determined by an adherence to numerical standards that would be strictly enforced. Meanwhile, heavier reliance was placed on OCR's regional monitoring offices, which were statutorily authorized to conduct surveys and on-site inspections to determine racial composition. Under the 1968 guidelines, and paralleling *Green,* school systems were expected to achieve unitary status by the fall of 1968. The deadline was later extended to 1969 and school systems with black majorities were given an additional year. Districts that failed to negotiate plans were subject to cutoff of funds, and by fall of 1969 more than 200 southern districts had lost federal aid.[16]

The blindside of an implementing agency

As enforcement evolved from 1965 onward it became evident that OCR's implementation ability, as an executive agency, was clearly superior to that of the courts. However, in considering the sanctions ultimately required to bring about compliance in the large number of districts still segregated in 1968, Rodgers and Bullock have questioned the effectiveness of placing implementation and evaluation responsibilities within the same agency. In those school districts that required some measure of coercion, they classified compliance as the result of five increasingly severe coercive methods.[17] First, compliance could be won through Justice Department enforcement of Title VI, which would involve a suit for breach of contract as an alternative to fund termination. Second, districts could be forced to desegregate through private litigation. Third, districts could be threatened with a loss of federal funding through the OCR's administrative procedure; this method provided a much stronger threat than the prospect of a Justice Department suit. Fourth, the Justice Department could sue under Title IV to have *state* funds withheld from segregated districts. Fifth, as a result of Justice Department suits and OCR administrative procedures, districts could be threatened with a loss of both state and federal funds. Of these methods, the last two proved the most successful in eliciting cooperation from hostile districts.

Unlike most nonsouthern states, school districts in the South have traditionally been dependent on state rather than local financing and could not easily forego these funds. In Georgia, for example, the state provided funds to every district on the basis of average daily attendance. This money was sufficient to meet minimum school expenses, while local property taxes paid for additional expenditures above the state minimum. In 1968, 55.3 percent of the educational funds came from the state, 32.3 percent from local taxes, and 12.5 percent from federal programs.[18] Clearly, the threatened withholding of state monies would be a much more serious sanction than the withholding of federal funds. In view of this, one might have expected OCR to attempt to bring about compliance by applying increasingly severe sanctions to noncompliant behavior. Yet this did not occur, in large part because many of the HEW staff felt that termination of funds would place a greater burden on black schools than on white ones. Moreover, the new Nixon administration that came into office in 1969 removed the power to terminate funds from OCR. Thereafter, if OCR could not negotiate an acceptable plan, a district would not automatically lose federal money but would be referred to the Department of Justice for suit.[19]

While this move was viewed by many as a weakening of the Title VI enforcement effort, it actually resulted in the final push for southern desegregation. Within a month of the shift of enforcement powers to the Justice Department, that department filed suit against eighty-one Georgia school districts and the Georgia Department of Education *(U.S. v. Georgia)*, threatening to cut off state funds from the districts which failed to prepare plans for eliminating all-black schools by the fall of 1970. Rodgers and Bullock relate that

> *Thirty of the defendant districts had already lost federal funds. The threat to impound state money was too severe to be ignored since on the average, fifty-five percent of local school districts' money came from the state. Consequently, all the defendants, including those which had operated for months without federal assistance, quickly honored the terms of the decision. The success of the Georgia suit prompted Justice to use statewide litigation in several other states in 1970 to bring the last recalcitrant districts into compliance.[20]*

They go on to argue that far from being a logical and internal response to the failure of less coercive methods used by OCR, the use of this ultimate sanction had to be initiated outside the agency. OCR, which should have recognized the flaws of the federal funds cutoff method in districts that depended relatively little on those funds, was unable to see that threatening cutoff of state funds might be a more effective method of forcing compliance. OCR held steadfast to the contention that federal funds cutoffs were the best tool for desegregation enforcement. Ironically, it was a pair of Georgia state elected officials who, convinced that desegregation would ultimately be good for their state's image, suggested to the Justice Department the strategy of state funds cutoffs.[21]

Rodgers and Bullock conclude by noting that "the availability of quantitative measures of program success, a quantitative measure of the policy objective, an enforcement agency, and support of program goals from above make the elimination of southern dual schools particularly conducive to internal assessment."[22] In spite of this, OCR never recommended what proved to be the most useful desegregation technique—threatened termination of state funds—nor did it acknowledge the success of this procedure. As an agency empowered to withhold federal funds, its bureaucratic goal apparently biased its approach to desegregation in favor of this technique alone. If OCR, which had a clear policy goal and fairly comprehensive impact data, failed to evaluate effectively its own strategy, one must wonder about the ability of agencies with less explicit policy objectives to evaluate their own performance.

The shortcomings of OCR's internal feedback mechanism illustrate the importance of monitoring by outside groups, particularly in areas where coercion is such a critical factor. We have seen the important role played by private parties in changing the law in the area of school desegregation. Private organizations have also been valuable in providing independent assessments of progress of the desegregation effort. In addition to the continued monitoring by the NAACP, particularly in the South, the American Civil Liberties Union has taken an active role in collecting data on school districts in order to launch numerous desegregation cases in the North and West. More systematic evaluations have been provided by the Center for National Policy Review in Washington, D.C., a private, foundation-supported organization established to monitor civil rights enforcement. The Center, for example, prepared the report on HEW's failure to enforce the 1964 Civil Rights Act in the North and participated in the 1973 litigation aimed at forcing HEW to implement the law. Similar research and monitoring has been conducted, mainly in the North, by the Harvard Center for Law and Education.[23]

Regardless of OCR's monitoring difficulties and internal weaknesses, once freedom of choice plans were eliminated under OCR's 1968 guidelines and the *Green* decision, southern desegregation progressed at a fairly rapid pace. Greater desegregation was achieved from 1968 to 1970 than in the preceding fourteen years since the *Brown* decision; see Table 5.1. And "of the 28 large school districts selected by the Senate Select Committee on Equal Opportunity as having 'significantly reduced black-student isolation' between 1968 and 1971, 26 were in the South and one was in a border state." Moreover, an analysis of the 135 largest school districts in the nation "shows that southern urban districts not only made much more rapid progress between 1967 and 1972 toward achieving racial balance; by the latter year the mean score for fifty-eight southern districts showed less racial isolation than in eighty-five northern districts."[24]

Nixon's attempt to turn back the clock

The final push for desegregation in the South did not come, however, from an activist OCR supported by the president. As it had been in 1964, civil rights was a major issue in the 1968 presidential campaign, but this time desegregation was to suffer for it. Republican candidate Richard Nixon, conscious of George Wallace's potential for drawing off votes, devised a "southern strategy" with which he hoped to carry the South. Opposition to busing and the sanctity of neighborhood schools became recurrent themes in Nixon's southern addresses. He also emphasized his feeling that federal judges were unqualified to dictate solutions to local problems, and how, under his administration, the Supreme Court would become more "strict construction-ist." In general, Nixon portrayed himself as a defender of the long-neglected South against an unreasonable and insensitive federal bureaucracy. It would have been impolitic for Nixon to condemn desegregation outright; opposition to desegregation was thus redefined as opposition to busing, an issue much less racist in tone.[25] Transporting students by bus was not, however, a major problem in the South, particularly in the rural South where busing actually decreased as a result of desegregation. Nevertheless, Nixon's approach had a substantial impact on the southern enforcement effort even before the election, since districts believed that if they could only procrastinate until after the election, desegregation would be virtually abandoned under Nixon. Nor was Congress impervious to Nixon's campaign strategy and the changing mood of the country. During 1968 southern congressmen were able to attach two amendments to HEW appropriations bills, both of which gave OCR new responsibilities without allocating any additional resources for the agency. The intention, at least in part, was to divert OCR's attention from school desegregation in the South. These amendments were the first steps of a rather successful long-term campaign to dilute HEW's power in civil rights, and the strategy had two tactical advantages: appropriations bills are passed yearly, thus change could be incremental; appropriations bills are relegated to behind-the-scenes and often conservative conference committees, thus a procedural bias in favor of opponents of desegregation was established.

Once elected, Nixon was prepared to act on his campaign promises. Yet the administration was placed in the difficult constitutional position of being obliged to enforce the Court's interpretation of the law, which differed substantially from its own. Nevertheless, Nixon directed both HEW and the Justice Department to play down their civil rights activities. OCR was specifically instructed to delay fund cutoffs for districts that had already been found in violation of the guidelines, while districts still within the administrative termination process were frozen there without financial penalty. Under Attorney General John Mitchell, the Justice Department was initiating almost no new suits to force desegregation and was, in fact, verbally undermining the OCR-imposed deadline to achieve total southern desegregation by 1970. Jerris Leonard, head of the Justice Department's Civil Rights Division, declared six months before the deadline that "it is wrong to set arbitrary deadlines we cannot meet";[26] at the time of this statement, HEW had already negotiated plans acceptable to most of the districts in the South.

This switch in presidential posture at first had a tremendous impact on southern and border districts in the midst of negotiating plans acceptable to OCR. The fate of the desegregation effort in Prince Georges County, Maryland, is one example. Prince Georges had undergone virtually no desegregation since the *Brown* decision. As part of its strategy of leaving the most difficult districts till last, OCR had not pressured the district before 1967. However, in the summer of 1968, the district was told to devise a desegregation plan by December 31. Prince Georges stood to lose approximately $12 million if OCR withheld federal funds; consequently, OCR was asked by local authorities to help draft an acceptable plan. After encouragement from some members of the Nixon administration, however, the day after Nixon's election the school board publicly announced its opposition to the proposed plan.[27] Under Nixon, HEW retreated from the December 31 deadline, stating that its own plan was ill-conceived and needed further study. Enforcement action was never taken against Prince Georges, in spite of its clear and flagrant violation of the guidelines. Eventually the district was desegregated by a court injunction, but with absolutely no assistance from either the Justice Department or OCR.

In short, after 1969 HEW ceased to enforce the funds cutoff provisions of the 1964 Civil Rights Act. And although by congressional mandate OCR was now supposed to concentrate equally on all sections of the country, only a handful of northern districts were ever reviewed by OCR.[28]

As noted earlier, the number of veto points in OCR's termination procedure was not overwhelming, but did include a number of political appointees clearances. For example, all fund terminations had to be approved by the Secretary of HEW, a consideration which, under the Johnson administration, proved to be no problem. However, Nixon's HEW secretary, Robert Finch, stopped approving terminations. Before Nixon's election federal money had been withheld from 600 districts, but after the inauguration no new districts were deprived of funds.[29]

In stark contrast to the general tenor of Nixon appointees, Leon Panetta, Nixon's first Director of OCR, was highly committed to achieving the objectives of the 1964 Civil Rights Act. He was initially able to maintain at least some credibility by insisting that those terminations held up by administration request in early 1969 be acted upon, even in the face of substantial opposition from Congress and the Justice Department. Panetta was soon fired, however, and with its funds termination powers already removed by Congress, OCR was left without the will or authority to vigorously enforce school desegregation.

A new civil rights policy statement issued by the White House in the summer of 1969 declared that funds terminations would no longer be used by the administration to compel compliance; instead, OCR would become an "advisory body" to districts needing assistance in formulating desegregation plans, while the Justice Department would be primarily responsible for seeing that those plans were enforced. The vigor of that enforcement under Attorney General Mitchell, who publicly favored an amendment to the 1964 Act that would allow reinstatement of the freedom of choice plans even though the Supreme Court had declared such plans unconstitutional, was highly questionable.

The stance taken by the Nixon administration with regard to desegregation in Mississippi further discouraged advocates of desegregation. OCR had long attempted to negotiate plans in Mississippi with little success; however, as a result of OCR's continued pressure, the state agreed to work with plans submitted by the Office of Education. The Nixon administration, in response to appeals from Mississippi Senator John Stennis, subsequently forced HEW to reject those plans and to recommend a delay in implementation. When the NAACP sued Mississippi in *Alexander* v. *Holmes* (1969), the Justice Department found itself in the awkward position of siding with the segregationists, a move which shattered whatever credibility the government had been able to maintain in the civil rights area.

While the White House undermined the bureaucracy from within, the Supreme Court rejuvenated it from without. First, it mitigated somewhat the disastrous effect of the administration's actions by ruling in *Alexander* that delays would no longer be tolerated and that desegregation must be effected immediately. In Orfield's view, only this unanimous decision by a Supreme Court under Chief Justice Burger, a Nixon appointee, prevented a total collapse of southern desegregation.[30] In spite of the ruling neither HEW nor the Justice Department was inclined to act aggressively toward desegregation. Nevertheless, under *Alexander* all the southern districts that had entered into agreement with HEW were compelled by the courts to follow through with their desegregation plans, all of which had 1969 and 1970 completion dates.

The *Alexander* decision was followed in 1971 by *Swann* v. *Charlotte-Mecklenburg Board of Education,* in which the Court ruled that in cities which had historically been segregated, schools were to be desegregated no matter what the inconvenience and extra transportation entailed. Finally, in *Adams* v. *Richardson* (1973), the Court took the highly unusual step of granting standing to a private organization (a Washington, D.C., law firm representing several civil rights groups) to sue a federal agency. The Court found HEW guilty of "subverting the law" through its failure to enforce desegregation policy, stating that HEW had illegally ignored the Court's "presumption against schools that are substantially disproportionate in their racial composition."[31] The Court declared that the 1964 Civil Rights Act gave HEW only "limited discretion" in implementation and that the abandonment of OCR's enforcement machinery violated the law. This decision prompted HEW to accelerate its enforcement procedures, but little real change resulted. As Orfield notes, "the Court had been able to act so forcefully not because the agency had made the wrong enforcement decisions, but because it had done no enforcement at all."[32] In its opinion in *Adams,* the Court noted a number of procedural failings in the enforcement mechanism; HEW responded by rectifying its procedures while making little change in its new policy of nonenforcement.

Factors conducive to implementation in the South

Desegregation policy, defined as the elimination of *de jure* systems and racially identifiable schools, has been implemented fairly well in the South. No dual school systems remained after 1970 and the percent of black pupils attending racially mixed schools in the South rose continuously during the entire period under review. Implementation of desegregation has certainly not been without pitfalls or contradictions, and it has not been complete, but a number of factors worked together to facilitate the policy's relative degree of effectiveness. First, the political environment during the early and mid-1960s was conducive to the civil rights movement and its efforts to promote school desegregation. Black activism in the South helped focus attention on civil rights issues. Congress was sympathetic to civil rights activity during this period because of its fairly liberal composition under President Johnson. Johnson himself provided valuable executive support for the movement; he frequently voiced his personal endorsement of its aims. The issue of civil rights applied to the South alone enjoyed a great deal of popular support throughout the rest of the country. Northern voters were appalled at the injustices and violence perpetrated against southern blacks as a result of black activism; this moral outrage helped the civil rights lobby to form political coalitions against this "backwater" region of the country. These political conditions made it much easier for Congress to pass the strong civil rights bill in 1964. Titles IV and VI of the 1964 Civil Rights Act were used effectively in ending in southern schools most of the segregation outlawed under *Brown*. The act also allowed the Justice Department to assist in private enforcement suits. OCR was established to force compliance, allocate resources, and invoke sanctions. Between 1964 and 1968 OCR evolved numerical and stringent standards with which to gauge desegregation and was generally persistent in its enforcement effort. A staff strongly committed to the agency's policy goals assisted this enforcement effort. Moreover, OCR had a feedback apparatus, albeit not a perfect one, with which it could monitor progress. The courts supported OCR's efforts and, in fact, proved a valuable catalyst in helping to increase the stringency of OCR guidelines, particularly through the *Green* and *Swann* decisions. Several fundamental characteristics of school systems in the South also played a significant role in facilitating implementation. Because southern school districts encompassed large areas, often entire counties, and because nearly every district had a heterogeneous population, desegregation was not a major logistical problem. Furthermore, once desegregation was begun it seemed to have some positive effect on southern racial attitudes and continued progress became easier. Finally, the nature of *de jure* segregation had a great deal to do with the success of dismantling segregated school systems. Segregation in the South had been blatant and legally mandated. It was therefore easily identified and, at least theoretically, easily remedied; one had only to seek dual systems and then "racially identifiable" schools to determine which districts were segregated. Consequently, resistance was easy to detect and address.

Federal impotence in the North

Up until the 1960s school districts outside the South and border states had also enjoyed a long history of racial separation in their schools, but with at least three major distinctions. First, districts did not maintain a formal system of dual schools, one for whites and one for blacks. Therefore, if patterns of racial isolation developed, school officials would contend, often with justification, that the separation was not the product of their willful action but the result of other social forces, such as the availability of housing. Never mind that housing patterns themselves were often the result of racial attitudes and class barriers. Furthermore, where neighborhoods were naturally integrated, school districts did not act to prevent integration of the schools. Second, segregated schools in a district did not fall into a checkerboard pattern—one white, one black—as in the South. In most urban centers vast tracts of predominantly black or other minority schools were grouped in one area and predominantly white schools in another. This pattern would inevitably compound the logistical problem of desegregation. Third, if the federal government was going to extend its efforts outside the South, it would face not an isolatable region of the nation that willfully violated the constitutional rights of blacks, but a majority population that believed it was acting within the law and, moreover, one that would vociferously oppose the methods proposed to remedy the problem.

The first factor presented HEW with a formidable problem. While the language of the 1964 Civil Rights Act clearly called for elimination of all vestiges of segregation, HEW had no *Brown* decision to identify precisely what that meant for the *de facto* segregation of the North. Furthermore, the Supreme Court has been extremely cautious in all its pronouncement on this score. Congress, in turn, failed to define discrimination in specific terms in the 1964 Civil Rights Act. Yet under Title VI of the Act, HEW's Office of Education was to oversee elimination of discrimination in *all* public schools, South and North, and sought to take its mission seriously. Unfortunately, despite continuing discussion, the USOE staff, HEW's legal council, and the Justice Department could not agree on a standard and acceptable criterion for identifying racial discrimination in northern schools. Eager to establish a nationwide program, USOE acted without first establishing its own internal guidelines.

The Chicago debacle

USOE moved in response to a complaint filed in early 1965 by a local civil rights group that Chicago schools were grossly segregated and that the city was intending to use new federal money to reinforce its pattern of segregation. Invoking Title VI, HEW Commissioner Frank Keppel deferred $32 million in federal funds allocated to the district under the just enacted 1965 Elementary and Secondary Education Act. Through this first case, USOE hoped a workable definition of discrimination in non-*de jure* school districts would evolve, and with it a strategy for winning Title VI compliance in the North. An important procedural matter was that USOE was only "deferring" funds in Chicago, not terminating them, until it could complete its investigation. Chicago officials nevertheless immediately labeled the action arbitrary and capricious and turned it into the test case of northern resolve and noncompliance with Title VI. Mayor Richard Daley, the powerful kingpin of Democratic politics in Illinois and valuable ally to President Johnson, simply bypassed USOE and HEW and went straight to Johnson (who had not been informed in advance of the deferral). Within a week the deferral was rescinded, ESEA funds released, and USOE severely smitten, Leon Panetta would later recall that the Chicago debacle

taught that no law enforcement program can get by on a bluff. Without firm proof of discrimination and accepted standards to hold up to public scrutiny, a politically powerful man like Daley and a raving demagogue like Pucinski [Chicago congressman] can call the bluff and win out every time.[33]

The lesson was not lost on USOE, which for several years thereafter focused its attention exclusively on the South, nor on Secretary of HEW John Gardner, who took a first step toward centralizing all civil rights activities in HEW by establishing the Office for Civil Rights (OCR) directly under the secretary. It was not until mid-1969, late in the Johnson administration, under Attorney General Ramsey Clark that the federal government again initiated desegregation suits in the North; against the localities of South Holland, a suburb of Chicago; Pasadena, California; and Indianapolis. While South Holland adopted a desegregation plan fairly readily, the Pasadena and Indianapolis cases carried over into the next administration, with the latter dragging on for nearly an entire decade.

Enforcement under Nixon

The attitude of the Nixon administration toward integration explains in large part the demise of the federal government's desegregation effort in the North. Just as OCR began to focus attention on *de facto* segregation in the North in 1968 and 1969, the Nixon administration stepped in and curtailed OCR's authority to terminate funds to school districts and shifted authority for all litigation to the Justice Department. These steps effectively turned executive-level caution into paralysis. The Justice Department pressed few court cases, and of those that were, the department urged that court rulings be interpreted as narrowly as possible.

Despite several local cases brought against northern school districts in lower courts, it was not until 1973 that the Supreme Court addressed the problems of school segregation in the North. In *Keyes* v. *School District No. 1 of Denver,* a landmark case brought by the NAACP's Legal Defense Fund, the Court shifted its focus from the effect of existing segregation to a district's intent to segregate. If intent was proven, local authorities were required to offer a remedy that would desegregate the entire district, not just the portion of the district in question. By placing the burden of proof on the district, the Court made demonstration of discriminatory intent much easier for civil rights groups, particularly since this meant that a district-wide remedy did not have to be the result of proven segregation in each school. However, the Court still had not articulated a standard by which to determine the constitutionality of *de facto* segregation. The *Green* decision of 1968 had established that schools were not to be "racially identifiable"; however, this criterion applied only to explicitly *de jure* segregation and no attempt had been made to apply the *Green* principles in northern schools. The Justice Department was predictably unenthusiastic about testing a broader application of *Keyes;* even after this decision the Court continued to document northern segregation on a school-by-school basis. Thus, as one scholar has noted, "the *Keyes* decision, rather than establishing a new standard for the North, as *Green* had in the South, may, in retrospect, have only been a high-water point, not to be reached again soon."[34]

After *Keyes,* the Court continued to focus on intent rather than on the consequences of official action but appeared to narrow the scope of the *Keyes* decision where remedies were concerned. In *Dayton* v. *Brinkman* (1977), the Court ruled that a remedy was necessary only where an intent to segregate could be shown, but in fashioning a remedy the lower courts could only require actions necessary to compensate for earlier discrimination. This ruling effectively shifted the burden of proof back to the plaintiff and still did not clarify exactly what constituted official discrimination.

Clearly, the lack of a coherent set of administrative standards and guidelines like the ones OCR promulgated for the *de jure* segregated school system of the South has made progress in the North difficult.[35] The logistical considerations of northern desegregation compound the problem. To integrate effectively, most northern districts require extensive busing programs at a time when busing is extremely unpopular. Even if busing is undertaken, white flight into the suburbs severely limits the impact of any desegregation effort. Gary Orfield persuasively argues that the most reasonable solution to the problem of inner-city racial isolation is a busing program that crosses school district lines between city and suburb in order to eliminate the suburb as a haven for white parents fleeing from integration.[36] Political opposition to such a plan may be great, yet without a "metropolitan plan," he argues, inner-city desegregation is meaningless. However, in the Detroit case of *Milliken* v. *Bradley* (1974), the Supreme Court reaffirmed its decision that the Court could not impose interdistrict busing but offered no other way of integrating northern cities.

More recently, in what many busing proponents consider a victory, the Supreme Court let stand fairly massive busing schemes in Columbus and Dayton, Ohio; Louisville; Minneapolis; and Austin, Texas, that have resulted mainly from NAACP and other private suits. In deciding the Ohio cases in July 1979, the Court ruled that *Brown* imposed on school boards both North and South a "continuing duty" to eradicate the effects of all official segregation.[37] Yet with the continuing decline in the number of white children in most large northern cities since 1960, school desegregation restricted to the inner city has only accelerated white flight while providing little meaningful racial mixing. Parenthetically, in the South and in a few isolated instances in the North where metropolitan plans have been required (mainly where school districts are organized along county rather than city lines), districts have experienced "less than average loss of white enrollment."[38] However, it is unlikely that local courts in large urban centers will sanction interdistrict plans. For example, in Los Angeles Judge Paul Egly went to great lengths in 1979 to devise a plan for the Los Angeles school district to mix a student population that was roughly 24 percent black, 42 percent hispanic, and only 21 percent white, without incorporating white students who attend the numerous suburban school districts encircling the city.[39]

Finally, HEW's busing plans have been severely limited by the antibusing measures passed by the House of Representatives since the late 1960s and the all-important Byrd amendment adopted by the Senate in 1976, requiring HEW to follow a neighborhood school policy only. It is not surprising that during this period OCR underwent a rather dramatic internal transformation. The transfer of the bulk of the enforcement responsibility from HEW to the Justice Department has been discussed; Panetta's departure from the administration marked a change in OCR's role from activist to fact finder. When performance of even this minor function resulted in staff frustration because of the administration's inaction, OCR largely abandoned its school desegregation responsibilities and turned to other aspects of civil rights enforcement. Congress had meanwhile assigned OCR the task of monitoring sexual discrimination, bilingual education, and other less controversial policy areas. OCR officials estimated that by 1974, only one tenth of their time was being spent on school desegregation, a figure that seems to reflect fairly accurately the pace of federal desegregation efforts since 1970.[40] Thus OCR survived the Nixon administration's effort to eviscerate it as a bureaucratic entity basically through a redefinition of its role.

By the time Democrat Jimmy Carter took over the presidency in 1977, HEW was so hemmed in by Congressional prohibitions against the use of federal funds for busing and HEW enforcement mechanisms for Title VI that little action was possible. When early in the Carter administration Secretary of HEW Joseph Califano attempted to strengthen HEW guidelines, Congress reacted by disallowing even his modest efforts. Lacking the aggressive backing of the president and facing substantial congressional opposition, by 1978 Califano had largely conceded the struggle, claiming that enforcement was "in the hands of the federal courts."[41]

Comparison of North and South

It is important to realize that the collapse of a concerted federal push to desegregate schools in the North was due to more than just loss of executive and congressional leadership. To begin with, northern segregation is primarily an urban phenomenon. Unlike many southern school districts which often include a large rural area, northern districts are small and divide an urban area into several racially identifiable sections, usually along center-city and suburban lines. Effective desegregation thus requires extensive transportation of children from one part of the region to another. Furthermore, local authorities consistently deny responsibility for regional racial concentrations, arguing that blacks and other minorities are not legally compelled to live anywhere and the fact that such minorities are completely unrepresented in schools in some sections is not the school board's responsibility.

Northern resistance efforts have also been far more subtle than those of the South. Northern authorities can argue that neither the Supreme Court nor HEW has established clear standards by which to identify *de facto* segregation and thus a determination of segregation in a northern district is purely arbitrary. Moreover, since most school districts in the North never established dual school systems per se, it is more difficult to determine discrimination by the local school authorities. Hence, while attendance zones may have been drawn with discriminatory intentions, any number of plausible explanations for the boundaries can be offered.

A third difference between school desegregation in the North and the South is the uncertain state of the law as applied to *de facto* segregation. A definition of *de jure* segregation was self-evident, but OCR was uncertain how to fashion a constitutionally acceptable definition of *de facto* segregation. Moreover, throughout the 1960s the Supreme Court failed to hear a *de facto* case; lower courts had ruled inconsistently and did not provide any clear standard OCR could use to bolster its guidelines. *Green* declared freedom of choice plans unconstitutional and insisted that racially identifiable schools be abolished. And *Swann* later declared the constitutionality of busing in urban districts but only as a remedy to officially sanctioned segregation.

Fourth, complicating the enforcement issue, were the changing attitudes of both whites and blacks in the North toward race relations and school desegregation. The urban riots of the late 1960s appreciably dampened the enthusiasm of northern whites for an aggressive civil rights effort by the federal government and particularly for compulsory school desegregation. This change is reflected in a series of national surveys, which by 1975 showed that 56 percent of the nation's adult population favored desegregation in principle, but 74 percent opposed busing to achieve desegregation of public schools.[42] Meanwhile, the unity among blacks as represented by the NAACP in the 1950s and early 1960s in favor of a legalistic, nonviolent approach to integration was undermined by the increasing number of black radical militants, who not only frightened whites in the North but often opposed the diluting of black culture and strength they felt resulted from filtering black students into predominantly white schools.

In short, target group behavior in the North was more complex than in the South. Northern racial isolation has not necessarily resulted from explicit segregation laws but has been caused by a variety of housing and other practices. In 1964, the Supreme Court ruled that northern segregation was not related to illegal state action and therefore had no legal remedy.[43] OCR was understandably reluctant to press too hard in the North. The experience in Chicago had demonstrated the difficulty of enforcing desegregation and showed that congressional support for desegregation by the northern majority in Congress could evaporate quickly once it became clear that desegregation orders would apply to the North. And OCR was reluctant to push for integration in the North without the full support of the courts.

In 1967, OCR began to create a capacity for attacking northern cases but showed little disposition to act. It studied northern cities for "patterns of overcrowded classrooms and less qualified teachers in largely Negro schools, inadequate and inferior equipment, gerrymandering of school attendance zones, and racial discrimination in teaching assignments."[44] However, HEW made it clear that it was not condemning segregation that arose from fair neighborhood attendance zoning applied to segregated housing patterns. As a result of southern pressure, rather vague guidelines were developed to apply to the North. Yet the guidelines were applied quite gently and only in smaller cities. Orfield notes that "investigations in the late 1960s focused on either little-known, smaller districts or on moderately sized cities. Investigators spent a great deal of time, for example, studying segregation in the suburbs of Ferndale, Michigan,"[45] a case which affected only 800 minority students. Had OCR acted more forcefully during this period, the action might have been a catalyst for new law. It seems clear that OCR badly needed a *Brown* decision aimed at the North that would clearly define what constituted segregation. Unfortunately, the judiciary failed to provide such definition.

The failure of the executive branch and Congress to enforce the Civil Rights Act of 1964 in the North and of the Supreme Court to provide the kind of sweeping mandate in the North as it did with *Brown* in the South does not mean desegregation has failed to move forward. As shown in Table 5.1, the proportion of black students in majority white schools rose fifteen percentage points between 1968 and 1976. HEW, however, merits little credit for this progress. The totality of HEW efforts to desegregate schools in the North in the first eight years after passage of the Civil Rights Act, before it terminated virtually all effort, occurred in thirteen small local school systems, of which Wichita, Kansas, was the largest. Throughout the Nixon and Ford administrations OCR field staff often sent evidence of segregation in northern schools to Washington, only to have the materials reviewed, considered, or simply set aside on someone's desk until, much later, the materials would be sent back with the explanation that the data were either insufficient or now out-of-date.

Orfield reports that, in contrast to HEW's poor performance, "private civil rights groups, whose resources were minuscule compared to HEW's large staff, had filed federal law suits [in the North] affecting more than twice as many black children. Private litigation had desegregated systems enrolling more than 400,000 minority children."[46] Some of the major cases resulted in desegregation plans for Minneapolis, St. Paul, Indianapolis, Fort Wayne, Dayton, Cleveland, Cincinnati, San Francisco, Sacramento, Detroit, and St. Louis. Even with these case-by-case court victories, however, the change in the

North plaintiffs have gone to great lengths to prove that school boards have progress there has been, little credit is due either Congress, which originally passed the Civil Rights Act of 1964, or the enforcement efforts of HEW and the executive branch.

Implications of this case for the conceptual framework of the implementation process

Desegregation of the nation's schools obviously required a substantial departure from the status quo. The Supreme Court's attempt to commit the resources of the federal government to the task was both bold, and, as the record since *Brown* has shown, has often been very problematic. Why the federal government's effort was so much more effective in the South than the North is described in Table 5.2, in terms of the six conditions of effective policy implementation. Implicit in discussing this issue by region, of course, is that the court actually launched two or, more accurately, one and one-half programs for school desegregation; a full-scale effort in the South and an ambivalent effort in the North. Despite its universal language, the Civil Rights Act of 1964—as subsequently interpreted by Congress—never really changed this fact.

The core of the difference, North and South, it appears, relates to Condition 1 (the clarity of objectives), Condition 5 (the degree of interest group and sovereign support), and Condition 2 (the adequacy of the causal theory), of which little has been mentioned up to this point. In the South the problem was defined primarily as a constitutional one; state-ordered separa-tion of schoolchildren by race is inherently unequal under the Fourteenth Amendment. Correcting this injustice was given precedent by many Court decisions and by Congress (through Title VI) over virtually all other educational goals. Indeed, maximum coercion was eventually applied through the threat to terminate all state and federal school funds. In contrast, desegregation of northern schools has been pursued not to dismantle what were perceived as state-sanctioned dual school systems with their connotation of racial inferiority. Rather, the intention has been to undo the inequalities in education that occur when racial minorities are grouped together in urban, often ghetto, schools and to attain the positive social benefits to both white and black students believed to accompany integrated classrooms. Thus, in the North plantiffs have gone to great lengths to prove that school boards have intentionally separated races through the drawing of school boundaries, pupil assignments, and so forth, in the hopes that the *de jure* redress sought would accomplish their primary goal of meaningful racial integration.

This has proven to be an awkward strategy. First, proof of state-sanctioned racial separation is difficult; evidence that will withstand courtroom scrutiny is seldom available. The federal government, moreover, has not provided

Table 5.2
Extent to Which the Implementation of *Brown* **and Subsequent Mandates**
Were Met, South and North, 1954–80

Condition	Extent to Which Condition Was Met	
	South	North
1. Authoritative directives contain clear and consistent objectives.	i. Elimination of *de jure* segregation: from MODERATE to HIGH over time. Moderate under *Brown*, made more explicit under 1964 Civil Rights Act, quite clear under *Green* and 1968 OCR guidelines with elimination of "freedom of choice" plans and racially identifiable schools.	i. Elimination of *de jure* segregation: from LOW to MODERATE over time. *De jure* not recognized in North until *Keyes* decision of 1973. Since *Keyes*, *de jure* has been acknowledged when demonstrated case-by-case.
	ii. Create environment conductive to achievement and self-worth of black pupils, elimination of all racial barriers in public schools: MODERATE. Clear intention of Court in *Brown* and implied by 1964 Civil Rights Act.	ii. Create environment conducive to achievement and sense of equality of black pupils, elimination of all racial barriers in public schools: LOW to MODERATE over time. Nonexistent under *Brown* until *Keyes*. Implied by Congress under 1964 Civil Rights Act, which provided basis for attacking *de facto* segregation.
2. Authoritative directives incorporate sound causal theory identifiying and providing jurisdiction over sufficient factors	i. *De jure:* HIGH. Separate was unequal by definition under the Fourteenth Amendment. Lower courts and HEW were given	i. *De jure:* LOW. Courts shied away until *Keyes*. Congress opposed primary means of desegregation—busing. Courts

Condition	Extent to Which Condition was Met	
	South	**North**
to have the potential to attain objectives.	authority to oversee desegregation of dual school systems.	and Congress prohibited interdistrict desegregation and busing plans. In effect, minimum jurisdiction provided.
	ii. Achievement and self-worth of black pupils: LOW. *Brown's* assumption that racial mixing would improve minority performance and self-worth appears to be problematic. In any event, no authority given to lower courts or HEW to focus on these factors, and this criterion never used by the government in evaluating desegration plans.	ii. Achievement and self-worth of black pupils: LOW. No authority given to lower courts or HEW to consider these factors in desegregation plans and not considered in government evaluations.
		iii. *De facto* segregation: LOW. Despite Civil Rights Act, Congress refused to grant HEW jurisdiction in *de facto* situations; Courts did not act.
3. Authoritative directives structure implementation to maximize probability of compliance from implementing officials and target groups.	From MODERATE to HIGH over time.	From LOW to MODERATE over time.

Condition	Extent to Which Condition was Met	
	South	**North**
a. assignment to a sympathetic agency	MODERATE but variable. Lower courts varied in sympathy but Supreme Court persistent, even with Nixon appointees. Strong support from HEW 1964–69, moderate to low support from HEW and Justice departments 1970–80.	LOW. Courts refused to intervene until 1970s. HEW and Justice departments moved cautiously.
b. hierarchically integrated system with few veto points and adequate incentives for compliance	MODERATE. Moderate number of veto points, but White House clearance of funds cutoffs had devastating effect under Nixon/Ford. Sanctions quite inadequate until 1965, only modest until 1969 *Georgia* decision.	LOW. As effort moved North, Nixon removed OCR funds cutoff authority; Congress prohibited HEW from using federal funds for busing. Little incentive for compliance.
c. supportive decision rules	HIGH. *De jure* system prima facie evidence of violation of law. Funding tied to desegregation plan approval.	LOW. Chicago debacle. HEW and Justice departments never applied Title VI. Courts created rules (e.g., *Keyes)* but never applied universally.
d. formal access to supporters	HIGH in courts, standing easily established. Usual political channels in Congress, HEW and Justice departments.	HIGH in courts, standing easily established. Usual political channels in Congress, HEW and Justice departments.

Condition	Extent to Which Condition was Met	
	South	**North**
4. Commitment and skill of top implementing officials.	HIGH commitment; MODERATE skill. Under first OE then OCR, HEW staff was usually quite committed. However, staff often naive about political barriers and public opposition.	MODERATE commitment; LOW skill. With few exceptions, HEW staff rarely had the will or know-how to circumvent the restrictions set by Congress, keeping them off backs of northern school boards.
5. Continuing support from constituency groups and sovereigns.	HIGH through 1969, MODERATE thereafter. Sufficient support was sustained in the courts, the executive branch, and/or Congress to win compliance from most southern school districts by the time the federal effort slowed down after election of Nixon though Congress was never generous with funds.	Generally LOW, to some MODERATE over time. The focus on northern schools came after the civil rights movement had peaked. Only the courts have maintained the struggle in the 1970s with aid from a much weakened and divided civil rights constituency. Congress severely restricted HEW through funding cuts and Presidents Nixon and Ford hostile.
6. Changing socioeconomic conditions over time.	NEUTRAL. The communities affected by desegregation remained fairly stable throughout the period of implementation.	LOW. The changing demographics of northern urban cities with whites moving to suburbs seriously threatened desegregation in inner-city school systems.

Legend: HIGH   = A strong asset in effective implementation of legal objectives.
        MODERATE   = Conducive to effective implementation, although some problems.
        LOW   = Notable obstacle to effective implementation.
        NEUTRAL   = Insignificant; factor played little or no role in implementation effort.

much support for these cases despite the powers of the Justice Department and HEW to do so. Also, each district must be challenged case-by-case. Even when a *de jure* violation can be found, since the objective of desegregation in the North is ambiguous, the court's remedy is never obvious; it is one thing to require elimination of dual school systems, but how does one eliminate discriminatory school boundaries or compensate students for past violations? Recall, neither the federal courts nor Congress has ever required affirmative integration—as opposed to desegregation—of public schools. If they had, a generally applicable solution to northern segregation might be easier to find. Under severe public pressure in the North, the courts have not required, and Congress has flatly stated its opposition to, the interdistrict racial mixing of students as a solution to civil rights violations in northern school districts. In short, civil rights activists in the North have been frustrated by the lack of a statutory or constitutional directive to promote integration. Without such a mandate, desegregation plans that have been approved for the North have resulted in little meaningful integration, nor does it seem likely that future plans will be any more successful.

This is not to say that, had an affirmative mandate to integrate public schools in the North existed, all would have run smoothly, or even that such a program could ever be as effective as elimination of *de jure* school systems in the South. When considering the differences between the northern and southern programs, we must keep in mind several other important distinctions between the North and South, which will ultimately affect any future program.

As we have stated earlier, school desegregation since *Brown* has been most successful in the South largely because of the nature of *de jure* segregation itself. *De jure* segregation could be identified as a regional phenomenon and was easily seen as a function of blatant racial policy. Moreover, it presented a clear target group of offenders; obviously, an all-black school was a product of discriminatory state action because there were state laws making such schools mandatory. The behavior to be modified by policy was thus easy to detect and fairly uniform. Although efforts to desegregate met strong resistance, this resistance usually took the form of outright defiance and could be punished accordingly. Black activism during the early 1960s brought southern racial practices to the attention of northern voters, and the civil rights movement took on the flavor of a moral crusade. Southern school desegregation received top presidential priority when Lyndon Johnson assumed office in 1963. An intense lobbying effort by a coalition of black and white civil rights leaders posed the issue as one, not of racial rights, but of fundamental constitutionally protected civil rights. In general, the courts strongly supported the desegregation effort during this period, working in conjunction with the federal enforcement apparatus to tighten the numerous loopholes left by the *Brown* decision. The *Green* decision marked an end to the main southern resistance strategy of "freedom of choice," while *Alexander* served notice that further delay in implementation was legally intolerable.

However, the courts, while capable of making new policy, are unable to enforce it effectively in the face of hostility from Congress and the president. Had the 1964 Civil Rights Act not made federal agencies responsible for its implementation, southern segregation may have gone on indefinitely in spite of its clear violation of the law. Congress intended the dismantling of *de jure* segregation by HEW and, toward that end, allowed the use of federal funds as a lever to measure progress. Also, although bureaucratic actions were initially inconsistent with court-ordered plans, the two were eventually brought into alignment. The funds cutoff procedure had relatively few veto points and functioned well under the Johnson administration which allowed OCR considerable autonomy. This autonomy bolstered the agency's reputation for credibility and persistent enforcement. The sense of inevitability generated by OCR's actions by 1968 largely convinced school districts that they had nothing to gain and much to lose by noncompliance.

In contrast, nearly all these preconditions of effective implementation in the South were lacking in the North. *De facto* segregation, the kind most prevalent in the North, has not been clearly defined by the courts and no positive goal, e.g., integration, was ever formally articulated. The changing political character of the late 1960s divested the civil rights issue of much of its popular appeal as it moved north. Race riots across the nation generated fear and suspicion among northern whites and made them less willing to endorse desegregation in their neighborhoods. Rodgers and Bullock point out that to some extent this shift in attitude was a function of "whose ox was being gored." Whereas southern discrimination could be easily condemned as immoral and inhumane, northern segregation was rationalized as a product of complex "natural" causes and therefore required far more complex and delicate solutions. Clearly, the northern majority was more willing to support change in someone else's behavior, i.e., southerners, than in its own.

De facto segregation is much harder to attribute to government action than *de jure,* and consequently resistance to desegregation in the North has been more effective; if plaintiffs cannot show an intent to segregate in official actions, there is no violation of the Fourteenth Amendment's equal protection clause and thus the court cannot impose a remedy. Compounding the problem of northern enforcement is the actual pattern of segregation, with the size and distribution of white and minority pupils in northern school districts presenting formidable logistical problems to desegregation. Busing has long been cited as the only feasible means of accomplishing a significant racial mix in northern urban areas, but in *Milliken* the Supreme Court declared that it does not have the authority to require metropolitan interdistrict plans. The busing issue has proven so unpopular politically that even those strongly committed to northern desegregation have been unwilling to advocate busing too forcefully. In the early 1970s, OCR, faced with continued inertia in policy enforcement and stripped of much political authority, redefined its goals and functions in order to survive. Northern school desegregation became a low priority within OCR as it apparently had become nationwide.

There are two important points to add to this assessment, both relating to the comprehensiveness of the "causal theory" underlying the Supreme Court's *Brown* decision. First, the decision relied heavily on limited psychological and sociological data presented by the plaintiffs that *de jure* segregation has a strong, negative affect on the learning ability of minority children. In the words of the Court, "Segregation with the sanction of law . . . has a tendency to retard the educational and mental development of Negro children . . ." The remedy provided by the Court and eventually HEW, however, focused on elimination of dual school systems as an end in itself rather than on the impact of desegregation on the learning atmosphere of black children.

In examining the actual effects on learning of desegregation plans that have been adopted, both Armor and Jencks and his colleagues present rather startling findings that school desegregation does not appear to eliminate the

Table 5.3
Chronology of the Implementation of Desegration

Event	Comment
1954–55. *Brown* v. *Board of Education of Topeka,* Kansas.	Supreme Court declares unconstitutional separate but equal schools in the South and border states under the Fourteenth Amendment. Little desegregation followed.
1963. Lyndon Johnson assumes presidency after assassination of Kennedy in November.	Johnson became outspoken proponent of school desegregation. Provided executive leadership and support.
1964. Civil Rights Act prohibiting discrimination in all activities receiving federal monies enacted.	Authorized HEW to act against segregated school systems; initial steps taken against South and border states.
1965. Elementary and Secondary Education Act enacted.	ESEA provided a substantial boost in federal funding to local school districts' funds that would eventually be used by HEW to coerce many districts into compliance with desegregation orders.
1968. *Green* v. *New Kent County School Board,* Virginia.	Clarified that dual school systems must be promptly eliminated; plans must produce schools not identifiable by race. Greatly strengthened HEW's enforcement efforts.
1968. First of many Congressional amendments to HEW authorization bill prohibiting use of federal funds for busing.	
1969. Richard Nixon elected president of United States.	Abrupt about-face on desegregation policy. HEW efforts in South greatly inhibited; no movement North.

gap in academic achievement between the two races.[47] Indeed, Jencks and associates conclude that performance of both whites and blacks is virtually unaffected. These results were widely circulated in the early 1970s and used by opponents to further undermine desegregation. Several years later, however, in a comprehensive survey of all available studies, Orfield found the picture much more mixed. At a minimum, the data suggest that desegregation does not adversely affect white children's performance scores in any noticeable manner. And, under some circumstances, black students' achievement scores after desegregation show notable improvement. At least in the South, for example, tests conducted between 1969 and 1973 showed gains by black pupils in science achievement and revealed that blacks performed best in schools with large white majorities.[48]

Overall, however, Orfield contends that *Brown* is based on a fundamentally

Event	Comment
1969. *United States* v. *Georgia..*	Justice Department filed suit against Georgia school districts to adopt desegregation plans or lose *both* federal and state funding. Compliance quickly followed. Federal authority over state funds established.
1971. *Swann* v. *Charlotte-Mecklenburg Board of Education.*	Busing and other "awkward" remedies could be required of school districts that had been segregated by law.
1973. *Keyes* v. *School District No. 1 of Denver.*	First major case in which the court ruled that a northern school district had violated the Constitution and was therefore subject to the same desegregation requirements as the South.
1974. *Milliken* v. *Bradley.*	Court ruled that a desegregation plan for Detroit could not be imposed on surrounding school districts, irrespective of Detroit's racial composition. Effectively precluded metropolitan desegregation in the North.
1976. Byrd Amendment to 1964 Civil Rights Act.	The amendment required HEW to follow a neighborhood school policy. Had little immediate impact since HEW was not pursuing a contrary course. However, after fending off numerous attempts to water down the 1964 act, the Senate finally gave up. Symbolized end of federal desegregation effort.

faulty theory of academic achievement. Poor performance is not so much a problem of racial isolation, though that may contribute, as one of class isolation. Thus, to the extent that desegregation results only in the mixing of less-well-off or lower-class blacks and whites, it is unlikely that the academic performance of blacks (or whites) will improve. Rather, the mixing of lower-class blacks or whites with middle-class blacks or whites appears to lead to a general improvement in the academic performance of the pupils from lower-class backgrounds. Desegregation by race, of course, can affect this situation only indirectly.

A second shortcoming in the causal theory underlying *Brown,* and all subsequent court- and HEW-desegregation plans, is the failure to prevent white families from evading participation in a plan either by moving to another, typically suburban white, school district or by withdrawing their children from public and enrolling them in private schools. During the period of rapid desegregation in the South, for example, approximately 10 percent of the white children population did switch to private "academies."[49] Although it may be unconstitutional to attempt to prevent switching to private schools, metropolitan desegregation plans, if they were adopted, would effectively remove the option of moving outside a center-city school district to avoid desegregation. Indeed, it is probably true that without the escape route to the suburbs, the white exodus from center-city areas would have been far less extensive during the past decade. James S. Coleman, author of the initial mid-1960s study documenting the positive effects of integration on black children, concluded by 1975 that white flight caused by desegregation plans restricted to center-cities has rendered school desegregation futile if not counterproductive to the broader goal of racial integration.[50] In short, in devising an implementation strategy, if the courts and HEW had relied more on the substantive goal of providing black children a truly integrated educational experience as suggested by the *Brown* decision and the 1964 Civil Rights Act, rather than on the procedural goal of eliminating segregation within the politically important but constitutionally (and pedagogically) irrelevant existing school district boundaries, more meaningful desegregation presumably could have been achieved. As it now stands, however, many experts believe that the degree of racial segregation within the metropolitan areas of the North is increasing as a result of present desegregation policy.

For further reflection

1. As the key domestic policy advisor for a liberal Democratic presidential candidate, you are asked to formulate a program for achieving school desegregation in the North. Using your political know-how, draw up an accurate outline of the principal causal factors that explain the segregation that does exist and propose a series of remedies to the candidate.

2. To what extent does the case of school desegregation illustrate the Court's ability to initiate and oversee implementation of major policy changes? Consult, if you wish, Lawrence Baum, "Comparing the Implementation of Legislative and Judicial Policies," in *Effective Policy Implementation,* ed. Daniel Mazmanian and Paul Sabatier (Lexington, Mass.: D. C. Heath and Company, 1981), pp. 39–62; Donald Horowitz, *The Courts and Social Policy* (Washington, D.C.: The Brookings Institution, 1977); Kenneth Dolbeare and Phillip Hammond, *The School Prayer Decisions: From Court Policy to Local Practice* (Chicago: University of Chicago Press, 1971).

3. Acknowledging the limits of the judiciary as policy implementor, under what conditions might the courts nevertheless be the appropriate instrument of action to turn to in order to bring about major policy changes?

4. To what extent has school desegregation been achieved in your community and what factors account for its presence or absence?

5. The presidential vote between Richard Nixon and Hubert Humphrey in 1968 was extremely close. Had Humphrey won, what might have been the effect on the course of school desegregation in the North and in the South, and why?

Notes

1. The evidence clearly indicates that the education and facilities provided black students under the dual school system did not approach those for whites. Richard Kluger, *Simple Justice* (New York: Alfred A. Knopf, 1976).
2. *Brown* v. *Board of Education of Topeka,* 374 U.S. 483, 74 S.Ct. 686, 98 L.Ed. 873 (1954).
3. *Brown* v. *Board of Education of Topeka,* 394 U.S. 294, 75 S.Ct. 753, 93 L.Ed. 1083 (1955).
4. Thomas R. Dye, *The Politics of Equality* (Indianapolis, Ind.: Bobbs-Merrill Co., 1971), p. 39.
5. Lawrence Baum, "The Influence of Legislatures and Appellate Courts Over the Policy Implementation Process," *Policy Studies Journal* 8, special issue no. 2 (1980): 560–74.
6. Dye, *Politics of Equality,* p. 38.
7. Leon Panetta and Peter Gall, *Bring Us Together* (Philadelphia, Pa.: J. B. Lippincott Co., 1971), p. 26.
8. Panetta and Gall, *Bring Us Together,* pp. 28–29.
9. Charles Bullock, "Implementation of Equal Education Opportunity Programs: A Comparative Analysis," in *Effective Policy Implementation,* ed. Daniel Mazmanian and Paul Sabatier (Lexington, Mass.: Lexington Books, 1981), pp. 97–98.
10. Beryl Radin, *Implementation, Charge, and the Federal Bureaucracy: School Desegregation Policy in HEW, 1964–1968* (New York: Teachers College Press, 1977), p. 143.
11. Beryl Radin argues that, in fact, the executive branch did not really intend to go as far as Title VI suggests. Title VI was included in the Civil Rights Bill by Kennedy aides in 1963 as a bargaining chip—something to be traded away. However, following the Kennedy assassination, election of a more liberal Congress, push by President Johnson, and heightened public awareness, the strongly worded Title VI remained intact. (*Implementation,* pp. 56–57.)
12. Panetta and Gall report that within the entire HEW staff, only twenty-three people were assigned full- or part-time to Title VI enforcement, and only a handful of these were in OE. (*Bring Us Together,* p. 33.)
13. Dye, *Politics of Equality,* p. 43.
14. Radin, *Implementation,* p. 110.
15. Radin, *Implementation,* p. 124.
16. Harrell Rodgers and Charles Bullock, *Coercion to Compliance* (Lexington, Mass.: Lexington Books, 1976), p. 19.

17. Rodgers and Bullock, *Compliance*, pp. 48–51.
18. Rodgers and Bullock, *Compliance*, p. 51.
19. Rodgers and Bullock, *Compliance*, p. 20.
20. Rodgers and Bullock, *Compliance*, p. 21.
21. As a rather fascinating insight into what turned out to be a critical juncture in the desegregation effort, the story behind *U.S.* v. *Georgia* bears repeating. As told by Rodgers and Bullock, "the statewide Georgia suit resulted not from line attorney's recommendations, but from two prominent Georgia state officeholders. These officials were concerned about disparities in the amount of desegregation found in Georgia districts. In a remarkable shift from the uniform opposition to desegregation found among Georgia officials only a few years earlier, they asked Jerris Leonard, then Assistant Attorney General for Civil Rights, to sue the state's Department of Education and all Georgia districts not having terminal plans. Acknowledging the need to complete the desegregation process, these officials were understandably unwilling to commit political suicide by acting unless directed to do so by court order" (*Compliance*, p. 92).
22. Rodgers and Bullock, *Compliance*, p. 93.
23. Gary Orfield, *Must We Bus? Segregated Schools and National Policy* (Washington, D.C.: The Brookings Institution, 1978), pp. 371–72.
24. Bullock, "Implementation of Equal Education Opportunity Programs," p. 91.
25. Daniel Mazmanian, *Third Parties in Presidential Elections* (Washington, D.C.: The Brookings Institution, 1974), chapter 1.
26. Orfield, *Must We Bus?*, p. 286.
27. *Washington Post*, November 7, 1968.
28. Orfield, *Must We Bus?*, pp. 267, 310–11.
29. Orfield, *Must We Bus?*, p. 289.
30. Orfield, *Must We Bus?*, p. 244.
31. *Adams* v. *Richardson*, 480 F .2d 1159 at 1162 (1973).
32. Orfield, *Must We Bus?*, p. 294.
33. Panetta and Gall, *Bring Us Together*, pp. 35–36.
34. Bullock, "Equal Education," p. 101.
35. Orfield concludes that, "The fundamental problem in the northern and western investigations was that HEW had developed no administrative standards. The advantage of administrative enforcement as opposed to litigation should come from the capacity of bureaucratic specialists to apply relatively simple standards to large numbers of cases. Without any workable definition of what constituted a violation of the law, the staff gathered vast amounts of data only to be told that whatever they uncovered was not quite enough"(*Must We Bus?*, p. 310).
36. Orfield, *Must We Bus?*, Part 3.
37. Jim Mann, "High Court Upholds Massive Busing," *Los Angeles Times*, July 3, 1979.
38. Orfield, *Must We Bus?*, pp. 411–12.
39. *Los Angeles Times*, June 29, 1979.
40. Orfield, *Must We Bus?*, p. 315.
41. Orfield, *Must We Bus?*, p. 318.
42. Bullock, "Equal Education," p. 103.
43. Between 1963 and 1966 the NAACP lost several major cases in lower courts in its attempt to have the *Brown* decision's condemnation of the harm to black students extended to the North (Orfield, *Must We Bus?*, p. 363).
44. *Washington Post*, September 15, 1967.
45. Orfield, *Must We Bus?*, p. 283.
46. Orfield, *Must We Bus?*, p. 311.
47. David Armor, "The Evidence on Busing," *Public Interest* (Summer 1972), pp. 90–126; Christopher Jencks et al. *Inequality: A Reassessment of the Effect of Family and Schooling in America* (New York: Basic Books, 1972).
48. Orfield, *Must We Bus?*, p. 126.
49. Bullock, "Equal Education," p. 97.
50. James S. Coleman, "Liberty and Equality in School Desegregation," *Social Policy* 6 (January-February, 1976), pp. 9–13.

Chapter 6
The delayed takeoff of compensatory education: implementing Title I of ESEA, 1965–78

Millions of young Americans are denied their full right to develop their minds. This bill [the 1965 ESEA] represents a national determination that this shall no longer be true. Poverty will no longer be a bar to learning, and learning shall offer an escape from poverty.—President Lyndon Johnson, April 1965[1]

I would have to say at the present stage, after 7 years of Title I, . . . the bottom line does not show very much. In other words, the measurable conditions . . . do not make a strong case yet for saying the $8 or $9 billion which have gone broadly to the disadvantaged have yet made a sweeping difference.—Sidney Marland, Asst. Sec. of Education, HEW, in testimony before the House Appropriations Committee, March 1973[2]

The [1977] NIE study indicates that compensatory services can be extremely effective in enhancing the [educational] achievement of participating students . . . In Newark, N.J., the number of first grade pupils reading at or above the national norm has increased from 31% in 1973 to 60% in 1977, an achievement which [local] witnesses attributed to experience with the Title I program.—House Education and Labor Committee, Report on the 1978 Education Amendments, May 1978, pp. 6-7.

During the late 1950s and early 1960s, the nation's schools were confronting a major crisis. Part of the problem was fiscal. The postwar population boom led to a vast increase in the number of school students—for example, a doubling of the number of high-school graduates between 1954 and 1964—which placed a severe strain on state and local education systems. This was exacerbated by the effects of the Depression and World War II in deferring

Table 6.1
Combined Per Pupil Expenditures by State and Local Agencies,
Selected States, 1967

State	Per Pupil Expenditure from State and Local Funds*
California	
Central cities	$ 645
Suburbs	777
Nonmetropolitan areas	587
New York	
Central cities	808
Suburbs	1006
Nonmetropolitan areas	892
Texas	
Central cities	441
Suburbs	449
Nonmetropolitan areas	472
Michigan	
Central cities	654
Suburbs	649
Nonmetropolitan areas	599

Source: Adapted from Berke and Kirst, *Federal Aid to Education*, Table 1–10.
aExcludes federal funds, which constituted about 7 percent of total revenues.

capital outlays for new buildings and equipment, thus leaving the nation with a large number of antiquated buildings in 1946.

Although state and local governments increased their expenditures for education from $2 billion in 1939–40 to $7.5 billion in 1953–54 and $11.7 billion in 1957–58, there still remained wide disparities among states and among school districts within the same state. Particularly hard-pressed were rural districts in poor Southern states and urban districts in the North and East which were trying to meet the social service needs of poor immigrants from the South and Puerto Rico and yet were consistently shortchanged in the allocation of state revenues.[3] Table 6.1 reveals that 1967 combined state and local per pupil expenditures for education in central cities in selected states varied from a mean of $808 in New York State to $441 in Texas—and expenditures in Texas were probably considerably greater than in the poorer states of the South. Moreover, within two of the four states (New York and California) suburban districts spent over $100 per pupil more than districts in the central cities or rural areas.

In addition to these apparent fiscal inequities, there were serious doubts about the educational performance of students in American schools. In 1963, for example, 22 percent of the entrants to the armed services were rejected because they could not read or write at an eighth-grade level. The launching of the Russian satellite Sputnik in 1957 and several critical pieces published in the late 1950s and early 1960s contributed to the debate over the fundamental adequacy of the American educational system.[4]

There was increasing evidence indicating that the schools were doing an especially poor job of educating the poor. For example, the selective service rejection rates for draftees from the ten states with the lowest per capita income ranged from 25 percent to 48 percent (against the national mean of 22 percent). And in the late 1950s some urban school superintendents were realizing that traditional educational methods were inadequate to meet the learning problems of several groups, particularly blacks and Puerto Ricans in urban ghettos. As a result, by 1963 there were at least forty-two experimental projects (concentrated in a few states) for disadvantaged children.[5]

Given the economic and political constraints on school districts and state legislatures to meet demands for increased school funding, educators looked to the federal government to provide financial assistance in what had traditionally been a state and local domain. A number of limited efforts were approved by Congress. These included aid to school districts impacted by heavy concentrations of federal employers (approved in 1950); expanded assistance for vocational education programs; and, as a direct response to the Sputnik launching, passage of the National Defense Education Act of 1958, which provided support to secondary and higher education in the training of scientists, engineers, and foreign language specialists.

But efforts to provide more general and substantial assistance to the nation's schools floundered on what Bailey and Mosher termed the three "Rs" of Race, Religion, and Reds (federal control). Northern liberals, led by Congressman Adam Clayton Powell of New York, insisted that federal funds be withheld from Southern school districts resisting judicial desegregation orders; this, of course, meant that the legislation no longer had the support of Southern members of Congress. In addition, most Republicans and Southern Democrats were adamantly opposed to any efforts to provide aid to parochial schools, and this placed legislators from districts with substantial concentrations of Catholics in a politically untenable position. Finally, conservatives, led by President Eisenhower, were afraid that federal funding of schools would ultimately lead to federal control of school curricula, textbooks, and other school materials. Even the election of John Kennedy, a strong proponent of federal aid, did not substantially change the situation. Bills proposed by the Kennedy administration in 1961, 1962, and 1963 sought to provide aid for school construction and teachers' salaries—excluding private schools—but were defeated because of the active opposition of the National Catholic Welfare Conference and the fears of conservatives in both parties.[6]

In 1965 changes in the political situation and a new strategy adopted by reformers broke the impasse. The Democratic landslide in the 1964 elections resulted in a liberal Democratic majority in both houses of Congress and meant that federal aid would have the vigorous and very skillful support of President Johnson. In addition, the Elementary and Secondary Education

Act of 1965 that became the cornerstone of federal funding focused not on financial assistance to schools per se but rather on aid to educationally disadvantaged children. This strategy placed the program in the context of the Johnson's then-popular War on Poverty as supporters hoped to avoid the constitutional prohibition against governmental aid to religion while still helping children in parochial as well as public schools.

In this chapter we will examine the implementation of Title I of ESEA, by far the act's most important provision. It authorized almost $1 billion in fiscal year 1966—representing a doubling of federal aid to schools—"to provide financial assistance . . . to local educational agencies serving areas with concentrations of children from low-income families . . . which contribute particularly to meeting the special educational needs of educationally deprived children" (Sec. 201). In the first section we will discuss the passage and content of ESEA, giving particular attention to the compromises and ambiguities that were required to obtain congressional approval. Throughout the rest of the chapter we will analyze the implementation and reformulation process, focusing on (a) the gradual clarification of the legislation's intent; (b) the increasing role played by the federal government in targeting funds and in monitoring the performance of state and local education agencies, particularly after 1969; and (c) the continuing problems in funding and in the legislation's causal theory, i.e., in schools' knowledge of how to improve the educational performance of target groups. As we shall see, there has been substantial increase over time in the amount of federal funds spent on educationally disadvantaged children. Moreover, in the late 1970s evidence began to accumulate that Title I programs could actually improve the educational performance of children from low-income families. Nevertheless, the ability of compensatory education programs to improve the performance of such children *over the long term*—i.e., to overcome problems in innate ability and/or social environment—is still open to question.

Passage and content of the 1965 Elementary and Secondary Education Act

In the 1970s and 1980s—times dominated by inflation, unemployment, disillusionment with government, and personal introspection—it is sometimes difficult to remember the social protests begun in the late 1950s, the economic prosperity of the early and mid-1960s, and the rhetorical and political skills of Presidents Kennedy and Johnson that produced an era of reform in the mid-1960s characterized by a widespread belief in the duty of government to redress a wide array of social injustices. For example, Congress in 1964 approved President Johnson's War on Poverty with the passage of the Economic Opportunity Act that created a number of programs directed at disadvantaged youths and community action programs designed to serve as umbrella agencies for fighting poverty. A decade of social protests also culminated in 1964 with the passage of the landmark Civil Rights Act outlawing discrimination in all federally aided programs (see chapter 5). This legislation played a critical role in the subsequent approval of ESEA, as Title VI of the Civil Rights Act essentially incorporated the Powell Amendment that prohibited federal aid to schools resisting desegregation and thus removed the race issue as an obstacle to Southern Democratic support for federal aid to education. Finally, the landslide victory of President Johnson in 1964 indicated voter approval of Johnson's Great Society program, and substantial Democratic gains in both the House and the Senate marked the decline of the Republican-Dixiecrat coalition which generally opposed federal involvement in education.

Legislative history

Despite the favorable conditions and President Johnson's strong commitment to federal aid to local schools, the legacy of previous failures to win congressional approval for bills providing federal funding of schools made supporters cautious about the prospects for success. Thus, the president and congressional leaders basically agreed to go along with any compromise that key negotiators, most notably Commissioner of Education Francis Keppel, could reach with the principal interest groups, particularly the National Education Association (representing the public schools) and the National Catholic Welfare Conference. The intention then was to speed the measure through Congress with only minor amendments in the House in order to minimize the risks that the delicate compromise on aid to parochial schools would be destroyed.[7]

The bill drafted by Keppel and the White House staff was, by all accounts, a political masterpiece. Its general strategy incorporated four main features:

1.   to get around the church-state impasse by explicitly prohibiting the use of funds for religious instruction and using the child benefit strategy as a means of providing financial aid to parochial school students without violating the constitutional ban against aid to establishments of religion;[8]
2.   to focus on aiding "educationally disadvantaged children" who were understood to be primarily, but not exclusively, the poor, while at the same time distributing funds to more than 90 percent of the nation's school districts;
3.   to allay fears of federal control through (a) establishing a complicated procedure for administering Title I funds which apparently left principal responsibility in the hands of state and local education authorities, (b) allocating funds for the upgrading of state departments of education, and (c) clearly prohibiting federal involvement in the selection of curricula, personnel, or instructional materials;
4.   to appeal to education reformers by earmarking funds for educational research, innovative projects, and libraries.

Table 6.2
Major Provisions of the 1965 Elementary and Secondary Education Act,
(Public Law 89-10, 79 Stat. 27)

Title I   Financial Assistance to Local Education Agencies to Educate Children of Low Income Families
Authorized grants totaling $1071 million to local schools in areas with concentrations of children from low-income families in order to contribute particularly to meeting the special educational needs of educationally deprived children (Sec. 201).

Title II   School Library Resources, Textbooks, and Other Instructional Materials
Authorized $100 million in FY 1966 for grants to state education agencies who are to submit proposals for disbursing the funds on an equitable basis to public and private elementary and secondary schools for the acquisition of library resources, textbooks, and other instructional materials.

Title III   Supplementary Educational Centers and Services
Authorized $100 million in FY 1966 to stimulate and assist in the development of exemplary elementary and secondary programs to serve as models for regular school programs (Sec. 301).

Title IV   Educational Research and Training
Authorized $70 million in FY 1966 for the U.S. Office of Education to provide grants for educational research and for the establishment of a number of new university-connected R&D centers and autonomous regional educational laboratories.

Title V   Strengthening State Departments of Education
Authorized $25 million in FY 1966 to assist state education agencies in providing leadership in identifying and meeting the educational needs of their states.

Title VI   General Provisions
Prohibited any federal control over curriculum, personnel, or educational materials (Sec. 604).

In short, the bill provided something for nearly everyone and was, in fact, supported by the NEA, the Catholic Welfare Conference, and their allied groups which had previously thwarted attempts to pass a major education bill.

The proponents intended to introduce the bill in the House (the traditional graveyard for education legislation) and then to rush the bill as approved by the House Subcommittee on Education through both the House and the Senate without further amendment. This is precisely what happened. Identical bills, sponsored by the chairmen of the House and Senate education subcommittees, Congressman Carl Perkins of Kentucky (H.R. 2362) and Senator Wayne Morse of Oregon (S. 370), were introduced on January 12, 1965. After about ten days of hearings before each subcommittee in late January, the bill was approved by the House subcommittee on February 5 on a 6–3 party-line vote with only a few amendments, the most important of which were the requirement for evaluation of the effectiveness of Title I projects and the provision to include AFDC children from families receiving more than the $2000 poverty ceiling in welfare benefits in the allocation of Title I funds. The bill was then approved in full committee (23–8) and on the floor (263–153) after withstanding amendments proposed by Congresswoman Edith Green (Dem., Oreg.) to facilitate judicial review and to alter the Title I allocation formula to provide greater benefits to districts west of the Mississippi and in New England rather than to the traditionally Democratic strongholds of northern industrial cities and the rural South. The House bill was then approved without formal amendment by the Senate committee and on the floor (73–18), after changes similar to those proposed by Congresswoman Green were rejected. Both the speed of passage and the willingness of the Senate to accept the House version attest to proponents' awareness of the fragility of the compromise, as numerous senators voted against amendments which would have increased the allocations to their states. The Elementary and Secondary Education Act of 1965, Public Law 89-10, was signed by President Johnson on April 11, 1965, barely three months after it had been introduced. Its major provisions are summarized in Table 6.2.

Legacy of the formulation stage

Of the five major provisions of ESEA, Title I was by far the most important. It involved over 80 percent of all funds and sought the greatest change in the nation's educational system. In fact, the remaining titles can be viewed partly as either concessions to particular groups to win support for the bill as a whole (e.g., Title II directed primarily at parochial schools and Title V at state education agencies) or as means of accomplishing Title I objectives. It was hoped, for example, that Titles III and IV would stimulate the educational research and innovation necessary if schools were to meet the educational needs of the poor. Similarly, strengthening of the state education agencies was required if they were to fulfill their Title I responsibilities. Our discussion of ESEA will thus focus primarily on Title I.

In discussing the legacy of the policy formulation stage on the implementation process, we must begin with the content of the statute itself. But in the case of Title I, perhaps more so than in most laws, we must also consider different actors' perceptions of what Congress "really" intended, as these various interpretations were to have a powerful effect during at least the first four to five years of implementation.

Clarity and consistency of objectives	The principal congressional documents—the statute itself and the House and Senate committee reports—stated rather clearly that the major objective of Title I was, as indicated in Sec. 201 of the act, "to provide financial assistance . . . to local educational agencies serving areas with concentrations of children from low-income families to expand and improve their educational programs . . . to meet the special educational needs of educationally deprived children." This formula was repeated in Sec. 205 requiring "that payment under this title will be used for programs . . . which are designed to meet the special educational needs of educationally deprived children in school attendance areas having high concentrations of children from low-income families and which are of sufficient size, scope, and quality to give reasonable promise of substantial progress towards meeting those needs." In short, while the allocation formula (based on the number of students from low-income families in the district) distributed funds to more than 90 percent of the nation's school districts,[9] the statute clearly indicated that these funds were to be used to meet the needs of "educationally deprived children."

There were, however, several ambiguities. First, the statute nowhere defined "educationally deprived children," although the law itself and the committee reports clearly implied that these would be predominately children from low-income families and would also include physically handicapped children.[10] Second, Congress was not always clear about the extent to which the funds were to be targeted exclusively for programs involving "educationally deprived children." For example, both committee reports listed forty-nine possible programs for such children; while many were clearly directed at the disadvantaged (e.g., teachers' aides, remedial programs, special audiovisuals for disadvantaged children), others were of a more general nature (e.g., in-service training for teachers, school plant improvements, audiovisual aids), and a few ("classes for talented elementary students" and "college coaching classes") seemed to have no plausible relationship to "educationally disadvantaged children."[11] Perhaps the best summary of congressional intent is found in the Senate committee report discussing "uses of funds by school districts":

> *A local public school district may use funds granted to it for the broad purpose of programs and projects which will meet the educational needs of educationally deprived-children in those school attendance areas in the district having high concentrations of children from low-income families. [The selection of projects] is left to the discretion and judgment of the local public educational agencies since educational needs and requirements for strengthening educational opportunities for educationally deprived elementary and secondary school pupils will vary from district to district . . . There may be circumstances where a whole school system is basically a low-income area and the best approach in meeting the needs of educationally deprived children would be to upgrade the regular program. On the other hand, in many areas the needs of educationally deprived children will not be satisfied by such an approach.*[12]

This summary suggests that, despite some ambiguities and uncertainties, the goal was clearly to meet the needs of "educationally deprived children."

Complicating matters, however, was the perception by many people that what Congress "really" intended was general aid—particularly to hard-pressed urban districts—but that Congress disguised this intention in order to realize the constitutional advantages of the child benefit strategy and to place the program under the umbrella of the popular War on Poverty. After all, general aid was what the vast majority of local, state, and federal educational officials really wanted. All previous federal school aid bills had been very general in scope. The focus on the poor in the 1965 bill was primarily the brain child of a few reformers in the executive branch rather than the result of strong interest group or congressional support. Finally, the House minority report explicitly charged that "this bill is a thinly veiled attempt to launch a general federal aid to education program by means of a spurious appeal to purposes which it would not adequately serve."[13]

In sum, although the statutory language rather clearly targeted aid for the educationally disadvantaged in poverty neighborhoods, confusion about whether the law really intended to direct funds to the poor and other educationally deprived students or to be general aid to local school districts was to complicate and weaken administration of the law for years.[14]

Intergovernmental division of authority   Although Title VI of the 1964 Civil Rights Law had supposedly taken care of the race issue and the framers of ESEA had overcome the obstacle of aid to parochial schools by resorting to the child benefit strategy, there remained the very sensitive issue of federal oversight of local schools. On the one hand, the vast majority of public school officials, administrators in the U.S. Office of Education (USOE), and (probably) members of Congress were concerned that federal funding would gradually lead to strong federal influence over local educational policy— thereby undermining local diversity and the autonomy of local and state officials, as well as arousing conservatives' fears of Big Brother in Washington. On the other hand, reformers in the executive branch and in Congress felt that most local school officials were not that interested in, or that knowledgeable about, aiding the poor and other disadvantaged children. In their view, strong federal controls on the use of Title I funds by local educational agencies (LEAs) would assure that the funds were targeted on disadvantaged children and would stimulate greater involvement of low-income parents in local school decisions.[15]

The legislation passed to implement Title I involved a complicated sharing of responsibility among federal, state, and local officials. Funds were to be distributed to local school districts on the basis of a formula involving the number of children of low-income families and the state per pupil expenditures. Once the overall appropriation was determined by Congress, LEAs were virtually entitled to a given level of funding. Since there was no local competition for federal funds, federal and state agencies had little authority. On the other hand, funds could not actually be spent by LEAs until the state education agency (SEA) approved local proposals concerning eligible children and program design. The SEA's decisions were to be guided by Sec. 205 of ESEA which required:

1. that payments be used to meet the special educational needs of educationally disadvantaged children in areas with high concentrations of

low-income families and be "of sufficient size, scope, and quality to give reasonable promise of substantial progress toward meeting those needs;"
2. that provision be made for developing programs (e.g., dual enrollment and educational television) involving educationally disadvantaged children enrolled in private elementary and secondary schools, provided that the control of funds and the property derived therefrom be vested in a public agency;
3. that the LEA annually submit a report to the SEA regarding the expenditure of funds and containing "objective measurements of . . . the effectiveness of the programs in meeting the special educational needs of educationally deprived children" [Sec. 205(a)(5)];
4. that the combined state and local per pupil expenditure for the previous fiscal year not be less than for FY 1964 [Sec. 207(c)(2)]; this was an obvious attempt to assure that federal funds did not supplant state and local ones.

These statutory provisions were to be elaborated by regulations ("basic criteria") promulgated by the U.S. Commissioner of Education.[16] Finally, Secs. 206 and 210 of ESEA gave the commissioner authority to withhold funds from the SEA if it failed to comply substantially with the provisions in the state's application for federal funds (which specified the criteria for evaluating local projects and required adequate fiscal control and reporting). In short, federal officials could exercise only an *indirect* influence over local projects, i.e., through review of the SEA's annual program application.

On its face, then, the statute appeared to give state and (perhaps) federal officials adequate authority to review local programs and to require that such programs targeted toward meeting the special educational needs of educationally disadvantaged children in areas with high concentrations of low-income families. But this intention would be realized only if state and federal officials attempted to exercise their legal authority. This was unlikely as both the USOE and most SEAs had traditionally viewed their role as one of providing technical services to their professional peers rather than as exercising any supervisory control.[17] Moreover, neither the USOE nor SEAs had the staff or technical capability to carefully monitor LEAs' behavior, although Title V of ESEA and the 1966 HEW appropriations bill attempted to rectify this situation. Members of the Senate, especially Republican senators, had made it quite clear to USOE officials that they expected the agency to be circumspect in the exercise of its authority to establish "basic criteria."[18] Finally, Title I funds were to constitute only a very small proportion (5 to 10 percent) of LEAs' total budgets.

In sum, while the formulation process resulted in a statute which gave rather considerable formal review authority to state and (possibly) federal authorities, these officials had traditionally been very deferential to LEAs and the legislative history of ESEA suggested that federal officials should be cautious in exercising their new legal authority. As a result, local school officials—most of whom were more interested in using Title I funds as general aid than in targeting them for disadvantaged children—remained in the dominant position, at least in the short run.[19]

Requirements for program evaluation   One of the most innovative and potentially important features of Title I was an explicit requirement for program evaluation:

> *that effective procedures, including provision for appropriate objective measurements of educational achievement, will be adopted [by LEAs] for evaluating at least annually the effectiveness of the programs in meeting the special educational needs of educationally deprived children [Sec. 205(a) (5)].*

This provision was added to the bill in House subcommittee at the insistence of Senator Robert Kennedy (Dem., N.Y.), who felt that most schools were doing a poor job of educating children from low-income families and intended the provision to be a means of increasing the schools' accountability to local parents and (probably secondarily) to federal reformers.[20] If test scores (or some other objective measurement) indicated that School A was doing a much better job of educating disadvantaged children than School B, presumably parents in School District A would demand that school officials improve the program.

Not surprisingly, Kennedy's proposal upset many educators. Most had had very little experience with program evaluation, and many others questioned the validity of standardized tests. In addition, they feared that interschool comparisons would produce precisely the sort of pressures from local parents and federal officials that Kennedy sought. Finally, there was a concern that focusing on objective performance measures would stifle local creativity and result in less attention to the multiple needs of poor pupils. As a result, state and local educators brought pressure on Commissioner Keppel to make the evaluation mandate as ambiguous as possible in order to allow them greater discretion.[21]

Another related indication of reformers' apprehensions about the manner in which local officials would implement Title I was the requirement for the establishment of a National Advisory Council on the Education of Disadvantaged Children. This council was charged with reviewing the implementation process, "including its effectiveness in improving the educational attainment of educationally deprived children." Unfortunately, the legislation left the selection of Council members entirely to the president's discretion rather than requiring, for example, that a majority of members be unaffiliated with LEAs or SEAs or that representatives from organizations representing the poor or minority groups be included.

Underlying causal assumptions   Even assuming that local education authorities spend Title I funds on targeted pupils, the ability of the legislation to achieve its ultimate objective of improving the educational performance of disadvantaged children was contingent upon two assumptions:

1. that the schools knew how to teach such children;
2. that good school programs could compensate for an adverse social environment (e.g., poor nutrition, parental disinterest, inadequate time or environment for studying) and/or inherited limitations in intelligence or physical ability.

Although Commissioner Keppel assured Congress that successful compensatory programs existed in 1965, this was an extremely debatable assessment of the situation. As McLaughlin noted:

In 1965 only three states had compensatory education legislation on the books and only a handful of school districts had ongoing compensatory education programs. Although many schoolmen may have had ideas they wanted to try, there was little certainty in 1965 about educational strategies that would "work" for disadvantaged pupils. Title I was targeted at the very group of children that the schools had traditionally seemed least able to help.[22]

As we shall see, it was still not clear ten years after passage of Title I that there existed compensatory strategies which could help close the gap in basic educational skills between disadvantaged and statistically average students.

In fact, the Republican minority on the House Education and Labor Committee challenged the basic strategy of Title I which focused on elementary and secondary school students between the ages of five and seventeen. Citing evidence that a poverty environment has its most debilitating effects in the first few years of life and that normal schooling may be unable to make up for a preschool deficiency, these opponents went on to argue that Title I should "be making a very large effort . . . to provide nursery school and kindergarten experience for educationally deprived children as a part of our regular school system."[23] In their view, ESEA virtually ignored probably the best strategy of aiding culturally disadvantaged children, namely, early childhood education.

While we cannot definitively assess the adequacy of compensatory education programs in 1965 nor attest to the validity of the opponents' criticism, we can view the evaluation requirement of Title I and the rather extensive R&D programs in Titles III and IV as implicit acknowledgement by ESEA's framers that perhaps the legislation's underlying causal assumptions were more problematic than they admitted in public.

Program funding: process and amount   The policy formulation process in 1965 brought to light several problems concerning funding which were to plague the subsequent implementation of Title I. First, congressional action on the HEW appropriations bill involving Title I was not completed until September 23, 1965. This was more than three months into the new fiscal year and several weeks after the commencement of the school year. In fact, local school districts did not learn of their allocations until a month or so later; thus, they faced enormous difficulties in program planning and the hiring of new personnel.[24] This lack of synchronization between the congressional appropriations process and the school calendar (in which programs are planned and personnel hired the previous spring and summer) was not resolved for several years. Second, there was some question whether the funds appropriated were sufficient. For example, USOE planners originally estimated that Title I projects would involve approximately 5.4 million children at a cost of about $200 each. This figure represented a rough professional judgment (based on the results of earlier compensatory programs) of the level of spending necessary to make a substantial improvement in the educational achievement of most disadvantaged children.[25] But this assumed, first, that the pilot programs were successful and widely applicable and, second, that the funds would be spent exclusively on disadvantaged children. The former assumption was dubious and the latter proved to be invalid for almost a decade.

Conclusion

Passage of the 1965 ESEA followed a lengthy battle over the proper role of the federal government in providing aid to education. While the committee reports were subject to multiple interpretations, the legislation itself was reasonably clear that its principal objective was to provide financial aid to school districts to improve the educational performance of educationally deprived children, understood to be primarily students from low-income families and handicapped children. The statute also made some effort to structure the implementation process to bring about this objective. State educational authorities and, indirectly, USOE were to review local schools' proposals to make sure that they were targeted for disadvantaged children and were properly designed. In order to promote local compliance, the bill required the filing of periodic reports, including evaluations of the projects' effectiveness in improving academic performance. It also gave federal (and state) officials authority to withhold funds from LEAs with inadequate programs. Finally, the statute authorized what planners considered adequate funds to accomplish its principal objective. On the other hand, there was some doubt in 1965 that the schools knew how to educate disadvantaged children and that they were capable of overcoming deficiencies in the children's background.

In addition to the problematic causal theory incorporated in ESEA, the formulation process left implementing officials with a number of other problems. First, the objective of focusing on disadvantaged children probably had little committed support among relevant elites, implementing officials, and organized interest groups. Most local, state, and federal educational officials would have preferred general aid, had there been a way to get around the church-state issue. Many members of Congress probably felt the same way. In fact, the act's committed supporters were probably limited to a few reformers in the executive branch, several members of Congress (notably Senators Kennedy and Morse), and presumably President Johnson. Second, given the traditional deference of state and federal education officials to local school districts, there was no assurance that state and federal officials would effectively exercise their new legal authority. Reformers could only hope to gradually change the policy orientation of the USOE and SEAs, as it was politically infeasible to circumvent these agencies. Finally, delays in the congressional authorization of program funds created substantial problems for state and local educational agencies in implementing compensatory education programs.

Implementing Title I of ESEA: an overview

If Title I of ESEA were to achieve its principal objective of improving the educational performance of disadvantaged children in low-income areas, a number of conditions would have to be fulfilled:

1.   Program objectives would have to be clarified, first to allay the suspicion that Congress intended Title I to be little more than general aid to the nation's schools and, second, to delineate more precisely the program's educational goals and target population(s);
2.   Title I funds would have to be sufficient to attain the objective and would have to be applied to the designated target groups;
3.   Schools would have to learn how to teach educationally disadvantaged children and to overcome deficiencies in the children's background;
4.   Once successful educational techniques were developed, they would have to be widely applied in the nation's schools.

The first two conditions deal with the decade-long struggle to establish a nation-wide program of compensatory education which would use Title I funds to provide supplemental educational programs for disadvantaged children. The third concerns fundamental issues of causal theory: once sufficient funds are targeted on disadvantaged children, do the schools actually have the means of substantially improving the children's educational performance? The last concerns the variety of educational innovations: once successful compensatory techniques are developed, can school teachers and administrators throughout the nation be induced to use them?

Establishing a nationwide program of compensatory education

The administration of Title I can probably best be understood as a struggle between traditionalists and reformers within the education establishment.[26] Traditionalists have been preoccupied with the fiscal crisis confronting the nation's schools and believe that LEAs should be allowed wide discretion in the use of Title I funds. It is, after all, local administrators and teachers— rather than state or federal bureaucrats—who supposedly have the best knowledge of the needs of children within their districts and the most experience in meeting those needs within widely varying local conditions. Implicit in this view is a respect for the professional judgment of local officials, sympathy for the political context in which many of them operate, and a reluctance to admit that the schools have any special obligation to the educationally disadvantaged, particularly children from low-income minority groups. The reformers, on the other hand, perceive Title I as a program that should be focused on the educational needs of disadvantaged children who have traditionally been neglected by the vast majority of middle-class professionals running local schools. In their view, the program will fail without the active involvement of USOE and—at least in the eyes of the more sophisticated—the support of a politically active constituency in favor of compensatory education. While the fundamental positions of both groups have remained constant since 1965, their relative strength within the educational policy subsystem and the specific policies at issue have changed considerably.

Reformers vs. traditionalists

Initially, the traditionalists were clearly predominate, not only among state and local educators but also within the USOE. In 1965 large numbers of new personnel joined USOE and Commissioner Keppel and his chief assistant tried to reorganize the agency in order to place some of these new people in key positions in order to disrupt the close ties between traditionalists and their state and local colleagues. Despite these conditions, traditionalists controlled the first year of Title I's implementation. This reflected both their initial position of dominance within the educational establishment and the preoccupation with spending as much of the congressional appropriation as possible and with distributing the money to the districts. It was also a result of USOE's humiliating defeat in early October 1965 at the hands of Mayor Richard Daley and Superintendent Benjamin Willis of Chicago over the federal agency's efforts to withhold Title I funds because of alleged racial discrimination in that city's schools (see chapter 5, pp. 150–51). While the case in Chicago concerned more directly the administration of Title VI of the Civil Rights Act than Title I of ESEA, the outcome of the incident apparently left USOE officials much more sensitive to the issue of federal control.

The supremacy of the traditionalists during 1965 and early 1966 is reflected in the initial regulations concerning the targeting of funds on disadvantaged children.[27] As originally proposed in September 1965, the regulations and guidelines would have required LEAs to rank school attendance areas on the basis of the number of children from low-income families and then to select project areas according to this ranking. The number of children served by the Title I projects was not to exceed the number of low-income children used to compute the LEA's eligibility for funds. These proposed guidelines were protested by state and local educational officials—both directly and through their representatives in Congress—who argued that, once Title I funds had been allocated to school districts on a poverty basis, local officials should have considerable discretion in determining spending priorities (as long as funds generally went to the educationally disadvantaged). Stung by the recent confrontation with Chicago officials and philosophically opposed to the degree of federal direction incorporated in the original draft, Commissioner Keppel insisted on the elimination of the requirements that LEAs relate the number of Title I participants to the number of children upon which LEA eligibility had been based. Furthermore, he assured state officials that the final regulations (issued in March 1966) would be much more permissive concerning selection of beneficiaries and concentration of funds. As a result, whereas USOE officials in the summer of 1965 had estimated that Title I projects would involve 5.4 million children at a cost of about $200 each, the number of children actually participating in Title I in FY 1966 reached 8.3 million—at a per capita expenditure of $120. In short, during ESEA's first year, Title I funds resembled general aid to school districts distributed roughly on the basis of their number of children from low-income families.

After the first year, reformers gradually gained strength. USOE during the 1970s was the scene of a continuous battle between reformers in the Division of Compensatory Education and their traditionally oriented superiors in the Bureau of Elementary and Secondary Education, with the commissioners of education arbitrating the disputes.[28] On the whole, however, support from auditors in HEW, from allies in several SEAs and LEAs, and from various exposés—most notably, the 1969 Martin-McClure Report (see p. 194)—gave reformers sufficient leverage to establish a nationwide program of compensatory education. As we shall see, by the end of the 1970s Title I funds were being effectively targeted on educationally disadvantaged children, although there were still problems in convincing some schools not to reduce the services provided by *state and local funds* to such pupils.

This increasing compliance with Title I's objective of providing services to educationally disadvantaged children over the years from 1969 to 1978 can be attributed to three interrelated factors: (1) the clarification and reaffirmation of congressional intent in favor of compensatory education rather than general aid; (2) the gradual emergence of a compensatory education constituency both within the education establishment and in external interest groups; and (3) repeated evidence that, in the absence of strong federal controls, many state and local officials would be lax in using Title I as supplementary funds focused exclusively on educationally disadvantaged children.

Clarification of congressional intent   Despite substantial Republican gains in the 1966 elections, whereby they increased their House seats from 140 to 187, the Ninetieth Congress actually clarified and reaffirmed Title I's focus on the poor. While making some minor adjustments to the allocation formula, Congress in 1966 explicitly included migrant workers, Indians, handicapped children, and delinquent and neglected children in institutions within the definition of educationally disadvantaged.[29] The 1967 amendments to ESEA provided that appropriations under the act could be made a fiscal year in advance, thereby permitting LEAs to know their allocation prior to the beginning of the school year.[30] Finally, and most importantly, in 1967 Congress defeated a proposal by Congressman Albert Quie (Rep., Minn.) to substitute block grants to the states for the categorical aid of Title I. Because it would expand the SEA's authority while greatly reducing that of the USOE, the Quie Amendment was supported by most state educational officials, many Republican governors, the U.S. Chamber of Commerce, and, in principle, the National Education Association. It was, however, vigorously opposed by officials from urban and parochial schools and by civil rights and labor groups, largely out of fear that their interests would be shortchanged by the SEAs. Moreover, the substitution of block grants for the child-benefit strategy of ESEA raised the possibility that funds to parochial schools—and possibly all of Title I—would be invalidated by state courts as violating state constitutions. At any rate, rejection of the Quie Amendment in the House on a 168–197 vote marked a crucial defeat for the proponents of general aid and an important victory for supporters of a program of compensatory education with active federal involvement.[31]

Support for compensatory education was reaffirmed in 1970 and again in 1973 and 1974. After disclosures in 1969 of widespread abuses of Title I funds in many southern and other states (see p. 186), the Senate committee report regarding the 1970 reauthorization of ESEA admonished USOE to "exercise [its] full authority and responsibility under the law to see that state agencies abide by assurances they have given in agreeing to adminster the Title I funds in keeping with the intent of the law."[32] Moreover, the 1970 amendments explicitly stipulated that Title I funds could not be used to substitute for funds from nonfederal sources and that, within school districts, state and local funds in schools served by Title I projects must be at least comparable to amounts available in schools where no Title I projects existed.[33] The amendments also required that funds "be used solely for programs and projects designed to meet the special educational needs of educationally deprived children . . . serving areas with the highest concentration of children from low-income families" (Sec. 415).

In its 1973–74 session, Congress rejected the Nixon administration's proposal to substitute educational revenue sharing, which would have greatly weakened the role of USOE, for the categorical grant approach of Title I. This defeat was particularly significant because the same Congress accepted President Nixon's proposals for block grants to replace a variety of categorical programs in two other areas, manpower training and community development (see chapter 3). In addition, the 1974 extension of ESEA retained the act's principle of allocating funds on the basis of the number of low-income children in a district (while changing the specific criterion employed); required each school receiving Title I funds to establish a parent advisory council, a majority of whose members were to be the parents of children served by the program; required USOE to develop more detailed regulations concerning program evaluations; and strengthened USOE's authority to provide services to educationally disadvantaged students in nonpublic schools in the event of resistance by local public school authorities.[34]

In short, by the end of 1974 Congress had clarified its intention that Title I was a program of compensatory education serving low-income and other educationally disadvantaged children from public and parochial schools; that the federal funds were to be used to *supplement* normal state and local per pupil expenditures; and that the active participation of both USOE and the parents of Title I children was essential if the program were to overcome the opposition of many state and local educational officials. These basic principles were reaffirmed—and even strengthened slightly—in the 1978 extension of ESEA.[35] On the other hand, while Congress has established increasingly tight restrictions on the use of Title I funds, it has been much less willing to agree to the withholding of funds or the imposition of financial penalties in actual cases of noncompliance.[36]

Emergence of a compensatory education constituency   In 1965 there existed very little active support for compensatory education, specifically, for reformers' argument that Title I should be used to provide supplemental services to poor and other educationally disadvantaged children. Most school officials and organized interest groups concerned with education would have preferred some form of general aid but went along with Title I for strategic reasons. There were a few states—California, for example—and a few school districts in which key officials actively supported compensatory education programs, but these were definitely the exception.[37]

This situation changed rather substantially over the next half-dozen years, as constituencies actively supporting compensatory education emerged both within the school system and among outside interest groups. Without this change in the education subsystem, it is highly unlikely that Title I would ever have been transformed from the thinly disguised general aid program of 1965–66 to the reasonably effective program of supplemental assistance to designated target groups of the mid-1970s.

Turning first to changes within the education establishment, we find some evidence that reformers within USOE actively sought to develop groups of supporters within SEAs and LEAs. In order to circumvent the chief state school officers, for example, reformers tried to identify liaison persons within the SEAs who could be trusted to carry out the legislative mandate. These liaisons were designated (by USOE) as "State Title I Coordinators" and the SEAs were strongly encouraged to use Title I administrative funds (1 percent of the state's allocation) to provide them with staff. Liaisons were also bombarded with interpretive guidelines and invited to regional meetings in the hope that they would support the reformists' views. In the same fashion, LEAs were encouraged to designate "Title I Coordinators" who would at least be familiar with USOE guidelines and requirements. There is some evidence that this tactic of creating subunits of support within SEAs and LEAs has been at least reasonably successful. According to Kirst and Jung, the billions of dollars spent on Title I have produced an extensive group of educational administrators whose careers depend on providing special services to disadvantaged children and whose members are linked in a national network through regular regional meetings, yearly gatherings in Washington, and frequent newsletters and special bulletins.[38]

A second compensatory education constituency within the schools consists of the thousands of teachers and particularly teachers' aides involved in Title I programs. The technique of using aides—usually parents—from the poverty community was borrowed from the Head Start programs established during the early years of the War on Poverty. After some initial resistance from the schools, such aides were accepted as valuable, low-cost assistants within the classroom and as ambassadors to the poverty communities. By the third year of the Title I program, there were 64,000 aides employed in local projects and 180,000 volunteers (mostly parents) who were serving the target population children in regular and summer sessions.[39] As some of the principal beneficiaries of the program, either as employees or as parents committed to improving their children's education, these aides and volunteers became important advocates of compensatory education within the schools.

A third mechanism for developing support for compensatory education within the schools has been the creation of parent advisory councils.[40] These also can be traced to the War on Poverty and to the general demand for greater citizen participation. Although USOE sought from the beginning to involve parents in local Title I programs, these efforts were resisted by most state and local educators jealous of their professional prerogatives. Early USOE guidelines only required "appropriate parental participation," thereby allowing LEAs enormous discretion, and proposals by the federal agency in June 1968 to require the establishment of local advisory committees were withdrawn after protests by educational officials and members of Congress. Thus in 1969 only about 40 percent of LEAs receiving Title I funds had parent advisory councils. But USOE reformers persisted, and in 1970 Congress, led by Senator Walter Mondale (Dem., Minn.) explicitly gave USOE authority to establish regulations concerning parental participation. This authority was strengthened under the 1974 amendments, which required each school receiving Title I funds to establish a parent advisory council, a majority of whose members must be parents of children served by the program. Nevertheless, the 1978 Final Report on Compensatory Education of the National Institute of Education (NIE) revealed enormous variation in the operation and influence of parent advisory committees, with no more than half—more nearly only a third—of them playing an informed and active role in the development and evaluation of their school's compensatory education program.[41]

Thus far we have been discussing the emergence of compensatory education constituencies *within* the nation's schools. At least as important, however, was the emergence of a constituency external to the school system. Given the decline since the mid-1960s in public support for antipoverty programs, the growth of this group of supporters has been a rather impressive accomplishment.[42]

Civil rights and anitpoverty groups did, however, manage two rather important victories before their gradual decline in the late 1960s and early 1970s. First, they were able to defeat the first serious effort to destroy Title I, i.e., the Quie Amendment of 1967. Second, the 1968 Poor People's Campaign organized by Ralph Abernathy of the Southern Christian Leadership Conference (SCLC) was instrumental in convincing Harold Howe, commissioner of USOE from 1966 to 1968, to create a method for the poor and professionals working on their behalf to gain access to local school files concerning Title I expenditures and then bring complaints directly to USOE rather than have to work through LEAs and SEAs.[43]

The information obtained through this procedure—together with data which had been uncovered by the previously unused program audits carried out by HEW—revealed widespread irregularities in state and local administration of Title I funds, particularly in the South. Leading the investigation into Title I expenditures was the Legal Defense and Educational Fund of the NAACP. Not only did its formal complaints in December 1968 prompt USOE investigation of statewide violations in Mississippi, but its report—the Martin-McClure Report—issued in the fall of 1969 documented widespread violation of federal regulations, including the use of federal funds to replace local monies in the target schools, the excessive use of federal funds for capital outlay, the use of Title I funds to maintain segregated schools, and the use of Title I funds to serve nontarget schools and children. The Martin-McClure Report further revealed that USOE had made practically no efforts to recover misspent funds or to withhold subsequent grants to the offending states—even in the case of flagrant abuses such as the use of Title I funds to purchase two swimming pools in Louisiana.[44]

Seldom has an investigative campaign led by an outside interest group had such significant impacts.[45] In Mississippi, the complaints filed by the NAACP's Legal Defense and Educational Fund resulted in a decision by USOE in July 1969 to withhold future funds from the state until it had agreed to correct the glaring inadequacies in its program—a decision which was to have ripple effects in Texas and much of the South. On a more general level, the revelations of widespread irregularities resulted in the formation of a Title I task force strongly supported by the new Commissioner of Education James Allen and by HEW Secretary Robert Finch. The task force instituted a number of reforms, including a substantial increase in the number of USOE personnel monitoring compliance by SEAs and LEAs and a partial overhaul of conflicting regulations and guidelines to clarify the requirement for targeting funds on poor children and to prohibit the use of Title I funds as substitutions for state and local expenditures. Congress approved these steps through passage of the 1970 ESEA amendments, which required that Title I funds be used to supplement normal state and local per pupil expenditures, specified that Title I funds be used solely for the purposes of meeting the special educational needs of educationally deprived children, and called on USOE to make sure that state and local agencies complied with federal law and regulations. Finally, the Martin-McClure Report helped mobilize a Title I constituency ranging from establishment groups, such as the League of Women Voters and the National Catholic Welfare Conference, to radical organizations, such as the National Welfare Rights Organization, to a number of local antipoverty groups, such as the Harvard Center for Law and Education. These organizations, in turn, gave USOE reformers the political support necessary to tighten regulations, e.g., with respect to parent advisory councils, during 1970 and 1971.

As often happens, the initial flurry of activity among external constituency groups had receded somewhat by 1972. Throughout the middle and late 1970s, the critical task of monitoring the performance of USOE and the state and local agencies has fallen primarily on a few individuals in the NAACP Legal Defense and Educational Fund, the Lawyers' Committee for Civil Rights Under the Law (LCCRUL), the National Advisory Council for the Education of Disadvantaged Children, and several local organizations. While these are primarily small law firms rather than membership-based interest groups, they apparently have been quite influential in convincing USOE and Congress to tighten and enforce the categorical requirements of Title I. For example, Robert Silverstein of LCCRUL did the analysis of the Title I regulatory framework for the NIE's report on compensatory education, and the 1978 Title I amendments bore a striking resemblance to the draft statute prepared by LCCRUL.[46] Unfortunately, there is very little information on the existence of any compensatory education constituencies outside the schools at the state and local levels.

In contrast, then, to the situation in 1965 when traditionalists dominated the implementing agencies and the interest groups in the education subsystem, by the mid-1970s there was an equal number of reformers within USOE and reformers represented a significant minority within state and local educational agencies. The change within USOE was probably the product of the clarification of congressional intent in 1967, 1970, and 1973–74; the active support for the reformers from HEW secretaries and commissioners of education between 1966 and 1972; the skill and determination of Dick Fairley, director of the Division of Compensatory Education during most of the 1970s; and the gradual discrediting of the traditionalists' position by the Martin-McClure Report and other studies. These factors were likely also important in altering the perspectives of many state and local educators, although that was also the product of concerted efforts by USOE reformers to create subunits of supporters within SEAs and LEAs and of the demands for greater accountability and community participation in the schools (and, indeed, in government as a whole). While the grass-roots support for compensatory education has certainly increased over time—as seen, for example, in the quadrupling of *state* compensatory programs from three in 1965 to fourteen a decade later—there is still enormous variation in support among states and school districts. Given the preference of many local school officials for maximum discretion in the use of Title I funds and their seeming indifference to compensatory education, we remain skeptical that tightened federal regulations and monitoring will be able to bring about a fundamental change in local policy in the absence of a strong and active compensatory education constituency—e.g., the parent advisory committee or outside interest groups—at the local level.[47]

Repeated evidence of disinterest and/or malfeasance by SEAs and LEAs   As indicated in the discussion of the passage of ESEA, in 1965 the vast majority of state and local school officials would have preferred a program of general aid to financially troubled schools rather than Title I, which focused on helping educationally disadvantaged students in areas with concentrations of poor families. Many school officials probably disagreed with the program's goal of concentrating additional resources on such children. And even those who may have been personally sympathetic to this objective still preferred to have maximum discretion in the disbursement of funds to enable them to balance the needs of disadvantaged students against those of other groups such as teachers' unions and middle-class parents who have traditionally dominated local and state educational politics. Finally, local school officials were understandably unenthusiastic about the reporting and evaluating requirements built into Title I when such funds would constitute only 3 to 10 percent of their total revenues and when the mismatch between congressional and educational fiscal years would enormously complicate program planning.[48]

Thus, many state and local school officials continued to operate on the basis of their antecedent preferences even after the passage of Title I (a finding consistent with the findings from much of the implementation literature).[49] There was, to be sure, considerable variation as some officials openly supported compensatory education (particularly officials in states and districts which had their own programs), while others soon accepted the basic objectives of the program though they argued over the details. Yet a substantial majority of state and local school officials continued to try to use Title I funds as general aid.[50] This was particularly true during the late 1960s, when congressional intent was still ambiguous. The pattern persisted even after Congress in 1970 and again in 1973–74 clarified its intention that Title I was to provide supplemental services to educationally deprived children from poverty areas.

Resistance from SEAs and LEAs centered on two critical requirements of Title I: (1) targeting, or the use of federal funds to serve only "the special educational needs of disadvantaged children in school attendance areas having high concentrations of low-income children," and (2) the comparability and supplement-not-supplant provisions which sought to assure that services provided by state and local funds were to be comparable in Title I and non-Title I schools and that Title I funds were to be added to, rather than replace state and local funds.[51] While the fiscal crisis confronting most schools prevented them from refusing to apply for Title I funds, many state and local officials found it very difficult to resist the temptation to use Title I funds to serve the general student population or to decrease service to Title I students provided by state and local funds in order to meet more general needs.

Evidence of rather widespread noncompliance with Title I arose early and was periodically reaffirmed during the first decade of implementation, although the extent of noncompliance—particularly with the targeting requirements—declined rather substantially after the late 1960s. Listed here are some of the more important examples.

1. Audits and program reviews conducted in 1966–67 in Chicago, New York, and Detroit revealed glaring misuses of Title I funds in noneligible schools, in merely funding existing programs on the assumption that these were consistent with the Title I mandate, and in using Title I funds for "overhead" in clear defiance of federal regulations.[52]

2. A 1967 study that examined supposedly exemplary programs in eleven school districts concluded that it was virtually impossible to identify a Title I program—let alone improvements in achievement test scores—because of the byzantine accounting methods and poor reporting by LEAs.[53]

3. The 1968 and 1969 surveys of compensatory education programs sponsored by USOE were again plagued by poor reporting by LEAs and revealed such widespread use of Title I funds as general aid and such little improvement in student achievement that the reports were essentially suppressed by the agency.[54]

4. A 1969 HEW audit of four Massachusetts cities revealed inadequate documentation of the procedures used in choosing eligible Title I schools and widespread use of federal funds as general aid in Boston.[55]

5. The 1969 Martin-McClure report based primarily on HEW audits revealed widespread noncompliance with both the targeting and anti-supplanting regulations, particularly in the South.

6. Decisions in 1964 and in the 1969 ruling in the case of *Hobson* v. *Hanson* revealed disparities of 30 percent in median per pupil expenditures among schools in the District of Columbia and no reduction in such disparities before and after Title I.[56]

7. A 1972 survey of 5900 school districts by USOE's Division of Compensatory Education indicated that 44 percent of the districts failed to offer

comparable services with state and local funds for Title I and non-Title I schools.[57]

8. As of April 1975, HEW auditors recommended that a total of $242,000,000—or 1.6 percent of all Title I funds—be repaid to the federal treasury because of malfeasance by LEAs and SEAs. While the auditors may sometimes have been in error, it is also true that only a small percentage of total expenditures were ever subjected to a federal audit.[58]

9. Finally, while virtually all observers agreed in 1977 hearings that the gross abuses prevalent during the late 1960s had been eliminated, the NIE's 1977 compensatory education study nevertheless concluded that "because LEAs have strong incentives to use their grants for general aid or to defer tax increases, explicit funds allocation requirements [e.g., targeting, comparability, antisupplanting] are necessary."[59]

As we can see from these examples, the preferences of many state and local officials diverged substantially enough from Title I's objectives to require careful monitoring and enforcement if the federal programs were to have any chance of attaining Title I goals. This review also points to the importance of outside monitoring of an agency's behavior. In fact, the creation of the National Institute of Education in 1970 was stimulated in part by the recognized need for a research and assessment agency independent of the schools and USOE, and much of the most influential work in improving compliance with Title I, e.g., the Martin-McClure Report and a 1972 report on comparability violations by the LCCRUL, was done by private groups.[60]

Repeated evidence that many LEAs and SEAs could not be trusted to comply with Title I regulations has certainly contributed to the strengthening of the Title I legal mandate and program administration over time. The Martin-McClure Report and other accounts of widespread noncompliance which surfaced in 1969 led directly to a substantial increase in USOE monitoring, the 1970 ESEA amendments, and a clarification and tightening of USOE regulations regarding supplanting. In addition, such evidence may well have strengthened the determination of reformers within USOE and elsewhere and convinced school officials and members of Congress sympathetic to Title I's objective but nervous about "federal control" that active federal involvement was nevertheless necessary if Title I objectives were to be attained.[61]

Results: the allocation of compensatory education funds, 1965–78

By 1978, or thirteen years after the passage of ESEA, to what extent were Title I funds allocated consistent with the proximate statutory objective of providing supplemental services to educationally disadvantaged children in areas with high concentrations of low-income families? (The legislation's ability to meet the ultimate objective of significantly improving the educational achievement of such children will be discussed in the next section.) The extent to which adequate funds were allocated in such a way as to establish a nationwide program of compensatory education was, in turn, a function of the degree to which:

1. Title I funds were correctly targeted, i.e., used to provide services to educationally deprived students in areas with concentrations of low-income families;
2. Title I funds were sufficient to provide services for all such students;
3. The increase in federal funds was not counterbalanced by a decrease in state and local monies. That is, did the SEAs and LEAs comply with the comparability and antisupplanting regulations and/or provide additional funds from their own compensatory education programs?

The basic data on the first two points have been compiled by Kirst and Jung and are listed in Table 6.3. The data show, for selected years between 1966 and 1978, the number and percentage of eligible children who actually participated in the program, as well as the total Title I appropriations and the per pupil expenditures over time.

The data indicate, first of all, that there have been very substantial improvements in targeting over time. Assuming that the children counted in LEA entitlements correspond to the population of eligible students, the figures confirm our previous conclusion that Title I in FY 1966 represented *de facto* general aid. While 5.5 million children were supposedly eligible, 8.2 million actually participated in Title I programs. The ratio of participants to eligible children declined substantially thereafter, reaching parity by 1974. By 1978, the population figures used to establish local entitlements substantially exceeded the number of students actually participating in the program. By that time average per pupil expenditures from Title I funds had reached the $200 figure (corrected for inflation) which USOE officials in 1965 had deemed the minimum necessary to provide adequate compensatory services. This does not imply that the targeting regulations were being perfectly administered, i.e., that only the most educationally disadvantaged students within each school were being served by the program. We have already examined evidence of noncompliance with the regulations, although in many instances noncompliance could be attributed to disagreements about the most effective means of utilizing limited funds.[62] Beyond a doubt, however, the program has made enormous strides in the area of targeting, and the gross abuses of the middle and late 1960s have been eliminated.

Our second conclusion is far less optimistic. If the 1965 USOE estimate of needed per pupil expenditures was correct—as implied by the efforts since that time to restrict the number of participating students in order to attain the $200 figure (corrected for inflation) which USOE officials in 1965 had deemed commensurate with needs in 1966, has become increasingly inadequate over time. As can be seen by comparing Rows 1, 4, and 7 of Table 6.3, while the number of eligible children almost doubled between 1966 and 1978, Title I appropriations (controlling for inflation) remained constant, with the net result that only about half of eligible students could be accommodated in Title I programs in 1978 if an adequate per pupil expenditure were to be maintained.

Shortages of funds have forced schools to make some very difficult choices. In Cleveland, for example, during the initial years of Title I funds were spread thinly over 55,000 children in elementary and secondary schools. But pressures from state and federal officials to concentrate funds, combined with evidence that the diluted services were having virtually no effect, led local school officials to restrict the program by the fifth year to reading and math training for only 20,000 elementary school children. Because there were only enough funds to provide reading services to about half of the children in the target schools who needed them, Cleveland officials chose to randomly select the half to receive the services and used the remainder as a "natural" control group.[63] The choices made in Cleveland—the focus on reading and math services for a subset of needy elementary school pupils to the virtual exclusion of secondary school students—are typical of most Title I programs.[64] While this strategy is apparently capable of bringing targeted students up to grade level *while* they are in the program, it is not clear whether these gains can be sustained once students are no longer receiving compensatory services.[65]

The origins of the funding dilemma reside principally in the 64 percent increase in the number of poor children between 1966 and 1978, which in turn can be attributed to the deterioration of the nation's economy and to changes in the poverty indicators employed.[66] The reluctance of Congress to appropriate additional (noninflated) funds for Title I probably reflected the decline in public and organized political support for antipoverty programs, declining federal revenues, and the lack of evidence until the late 1970s that the program was having demonstrable effects on student achievement (see next section). As all of these factors except the last seem likely to continue and as significant improvements in the cost-effectiveness of compensatory services are unlikely, it appears that LEAs will continue to have sufficient funds to provide such services to only a fraction of the children who need them.

Of course, the efficacy of a nationwide compensatory education program is also contingent upon the degree of funding from state and local sources for disadvantaged children. We find no studies comparable to the work of Kirst and Jung on targeting in this very complicated area. Nevertheless, a few tentative judgments are possible. First, we have seen that during the 1960s and early 1970s there were serious problems with reductions by LEAs in services provided from state and local sources to Title I students. Recall, for example, the 1972 survey of 5900 LEAs which revealed that 44 percent were not providing comparable services to Title I and non-Title I schools.[67] Implementation of the 1970 and 1974 ESEA amendments concerning comparability and nonsupplanting likely improved the situation, yet there is also evidence that disputes within USOE between reformers in the Division of Compensa-

Table 6.3
Targeting Figures for Title I from 1966 to 1978

Children	1966	1970	1974	1978
1. Counted for LEA Entitlements (in thousands)[a]	5531	6952	6247	9045
2. Participating (in thousands)[a]	8235	7526	6100	5155
3. Percent Participating of Counted	149	108	98	57
4. Per-pupil Expenditure (unadjusted)	$116	$162	$248	$379
5. Per-pupil Expenditure (adjusted for inflation)[b]	$120	$140	$168	$194
6. Total Title I Appropriation (in millions)	$1193	$1339	$1653	$2247
7. Total Title I Appropriation (in millions, adjusted for inflation)	$1217	$1151	$1232	$1162

Source: Kirst and Jung, "A Thirteen-Year View of Title I of ESEA," Table 1.

Note: Figures derived from tables provided by Department of HEW, Office of Education.

[a]Figures for Rows 1 and 2 include only "educationally disadvantaged" children but do not include handicapped children, juvenile delinquents, migrants, or children in agencies for the neglected.

[b]All adjusted figures are derived from the Bureau of Labor Statistics, "Consumer Price Index for All Urban Consumers U.S. City Average" with 1967 as base year.

tory Education and their traditionalist superiors in the Bureau of Elementary and Secondary Education hampered the implementation of nonsupplanting regulations during the mid-1970s.[68] Second, the number of state and compensatory education programs increased from three in 1965 to seventeen in 1976, with expenditures of $364 million (or about 40 percent of Title I allocations to those states).[69] Even larger sums were allocated to disadvantaged children by SEAs and LEAs through more indirect instruments, such as staff allocation formulas which allow lower teacher-pupil ratios in schools with large concentrations of disadvantaged children.[70] While definite data are lacking and exceptions certainly exist, it is probably reasonable to conclude that overall state and local funding for disadvantaged children did not diminish (in real terms) during the 1970s.

Problems in causal theory: can schools substantially improve the educational performance of disadvantaged children?

While it has sometimes been argued that one of the goals of Title I was to provide special services to educationally disadvantaged children in areas having high concentrations of low-income families, it seems reasonably clear to us that the statute's ultimate objective was to improve the educational performance of such children by, for example, bringing them up to grade level (i.e., mean test scores) in such basic educational skills as reading and mathematics.[71] In order to accomplish this goal, the schools would not only have to provide supplementary services to such children but would also have to (1) control sufficient levers affecting educational achievement to be able to overcome the factors contributing to low achievement and (2) know *how* to teach such children. This brings us to what we have termed, respectively, the jurisdictional and cognitive components of the causal theory (see chapter 2) incorporated in Title I. Definitive conclusions are still premature, but evidence of improvements in educational achievements of Title I students— particularly for studies conducted starting with the 1976–77 school year— suggests that, after a decade, educators may finally have begun developing a more adequate understanding of the cognitive component and perhaps marginally sufficient leverage over the jurisdictional.

With respect to most Title I children, the jurisdictional component deals with the schools' ability to overcome a variety of environmental (and perhaps genetic) factors summarized under the rubric of "the culture of poverty."[72] Children from low-income families generally start schooling with a number of disadvantages (relative to their middle-class classmates) which can affect educational performance: poorer nutrition; fewer reading materials in the home; less encouragement from parents (and perhaps peers) to do well in school; and lower expectations that doing well in school will bring future benefits in terms of income, social status, and satisfactory careers. Moreover, family financial difficulties—particularly if combined with unemployment— can produce a stressful home environment, unconducive to study and to a positive self-image. Finally, there is some evidence that poverty may be associated with genetic factors such as lower cognitive capacity and chemically induced psychological disorders.

While many educators had been vaguely aware of these considerations, their potential effect on educational achievement was dramatically illustrated in the Coleman Report published in the summer of 1966.[73] Based upon an exhaustive analysis of over 600,000 students in 4000 schools by some of the country's most respected social scientists, *Equality of Educational Opportunity* concluded that minority-group students attended schools with poorer-trained teachers, larger classes, and lower-quality educational materials. Not surprisingly, minority-group students (with the exception of Orientals) scored lower than whites on achievement tests at every grade level, and the gap increased with the number of years in school. Using regression analysis, Coleman et al. found that "school factors" were much less important than family background and socioeconomic factors in explaining variation in student achievement. But the report also indicated that the single most important factor in explaining achievement differences was the extent to which an individual felt some degree of control over his or her destiny.

Although such influence is impossible to determine with any precision, the Coleman Report and other research on the culture of poverty probably alerted educators to the importance of environmental factors on educational performance. This, in turn, may have increased their receptivity to the demands of many low-income parents that a portion of Title I funds be used for lunches, clothing, transportation, and other support services, as well as educators' awareness of the importance of increasing parental involvement in the program through parent advisory councils, teacher's aides, etc.

But the work of scholars like Coleman and Jencks also pointed to the potentially limited impacts of any compensatory education program—no matter how well designed it is—on the educational performance of disadvantaged children. Do the schools have enough control over the multiple factors affecting educational achievement to have any long-term effects on student performance? The difficulty of demonstrating improvements in achievement scores for children in compensatory education programs and in sustaining such improvements after children have left the programs suggests that the school's ability to overcome unfavorable environments may be quite limited.[74]

We turn now to the cognitive component of the causal theory implicit in Title I, namely, that professional educators in public (and private) schools knew how to teach disadvantaged children. While Commissioner Keppel and other witnesses assured Congress in 1965 that successful techniques were available and needed only the funds to be implemented, American public schools had, in fact, had very little experience with compensatory education. And virtually none of the existing programs had demonstrated any proven effectiveness in significantly improving educational performance.[75]

In fact, for a decade after the passage of Title I there was very little evidence that compensatory education programs could even halt the tendency of disadvantaged children to fall further and further behind grade level in such basic skills as reading and mathematics. The 1967 study of supposedly exemplary programs and USOE's 1967–68 nationwide compensatory education surveys indicated practically no effects on educational achievement, in part because of difficulties in identifying the presence of any Title I program.[76] A 1975 GAO study of compensatory education programs in fifteen LEAs in fourteen states during the 1972–73 school year reported discouraging findings. Only 34 percent of the students in the programs were beginning to close the gap between their reading test scores and the national mean; 49 percent of program participants made *less* improvement over a school year while in the program than they had previously made outside it; and a majority of students regressed after leaving the program.[77]

The picture began to change, however, as data accumulated from studies conducted after the 1975–76 school year. For example, Title I fifth- and sixth-grade students in Cleveland progressed about fourteen months in reading and math during the 1976–77 school year, compared with a progression of seven months for the Cleveland control group and ten months for all students nationwide.[78] A more comprehensive NIE study during the same school year of 100 schools in 14 LEAs throughout the country found that first-grade students in stable compensatory programs made rather sizable gains in closing the gap between themselves and "average" students in both reading and mathematics; third-grade students also significantly improved relative to their peers in math, although less so in reading.[79] The NIE study also examined the effects of selected program characteristics on student achievement in order to provide guidance to local officials. Among its findings were that improvements were related to the intensity and direct relevance of instruction; that individualized instruction is effective but not uniquely so; and that programs which provide supplemental instruction within the regular classroom generally are more effective than those which provide it in a "pullout" situation.[80]

In response to previous studies which had found that a significant proportion of gains made during the school year often disappeared during the summer, NIE retested in fall 1977 a subsample of 3000 of the 1976–77 tested students from 27 schools in 7 LEAs.[81] The study found that there was no *absolute* loss in achievement (i.e., a decline in test scores between spring 1976 and fall 1977). On the other hand, there were practically no summer gains and, consequently, Title I students tended to lose ground over the summer *relative* to students whose test scores were at or above the national norm, although the differences were not very great and varied by grade level and subject matter. Finally, the study found no statistically valid differences between Title I students who participated in summer programs and those who did not, although the small numbers of students involved and ambiguous selection criteria called for caution in interpreting the results.

In sum, by 1977 there was reasonably good evidence that Title I programs in many schools were at least beginning to close the gap in reading and math skills between disadvantaged children and the national norm. It also appeared that these gains were, for the most part, sustained over summer breaks. Of course, shortages in funding for compensatory education programs and federal regulations assigning priority to the lowest achievers meant that many of the students who progressed during the year were subsequently dropped from the program before they reached the school (or national) mean. There was still, however, very little evidence about the ability of Title I students to sustain their gains several years after they had left the program. In short, the ability of compensatory education programs to overcome unfavorable environmental (and perhaps genetic) factors in children's backgrounds was, and still is, an unanswered question.

Can schools be induced to adopt or develop effective compensatory education programs?

Given evidence from the NIE studies that, by the 1976–77 school year, a substantial number of elementary schools had developed reasonably effective compensatory education programs—i.e., ones that succeeded in bringing disadvantaged students closer to the national average in reading and math— what is the likelihood that other schools would soon develop similarly successful programs?

In 1965 it might have been assumed that, once successful techniques were known, they would gradually be extended throughout the educational system. But extensive studies by the Rand Corporation of USOE's efforts in the mid- 1970s to encourage wide use of a variety of educational innovations— including a reading improvement program for disadvantaged students— revealed the naiveté of this view. The researchers found instead that the development of different educational practices at the local level involved a process of mutual adaptation in which any externally developed innovation was modified according to conditions in the schools and to teachers and students' characteristics. At the same time, the schools' standard operating procedures and classroom practices were changed to accommodate the innovation.[82] The reasons for this pattern of mutual adaptation were traced to the variety in local settings, the lack of federal (and often state) incentives or sanctions sufficient to bring about behavioral change by local school officials, and the critical importance of real commitment by local teachers and principals to the new program. The Rand researchers found that the most effective new reading programs involved a heavy measure of participatory planning, staff training keyed to the local situation, and development of local materials. On the importance of the last item, Berman and McLaughlin concluded:

> *The value of producing one's own project materials may not lie principally in the merits of the final product, but in the activity of development itself. The exercise of "reinventing the wheel" can provide an important opportunity for staff to work through and understand project precepts and to develop a sense of "ownership" in the project methods and goals.*[83]

The fact that successful implementation was so contingent upon teacher commitment meant that there were many more veto points involved in the implementation of a new teaching practice than in the allocation of Title I funds within a school system (which was basically the province of school boards, superintendents, and principals). There were also some teachers who were uninterested in helping disadvantaged children or unwilling to change their current practices. On the other hand, it is natural to assume that, once the funds had been allocated for a compensatory program, the professionalism of many teachers would lead them to try to improve their performance, as long as they were heavily involved in determining program details and as long as the practice did not impose significant new costs on them. In fact, insofar as compensatory education programs usually involved the hiring of aides and reductions in class size, they provided some real benefits to teachers.[84] But the professional autonomy of classroom teachers and school principals significantly limits the ability of outside actors to change teachers' behavior against their wishes. In fact, Richard Elmore has suggested that a compliance strategy may be quite inappropriate in such situations; the focus instead should be on somehow convincing teachers to invest their professional identity in helping disadvantaged children.[85]

Finally, it should be noted that, while USOE had long encouraged the dissemination of innovative techniques, prior to 1972 its procedures for evaluating the effectiveness of supposedly exemplary programs left something to be desired.[86] Since that time, USOE and NIE have developed a more effective screening process and have also sought to hire contractors to go back to the project originator to bring together all of the curricular and training materials in order to aid potential users. But USOE has left LEAs complete autonomy in the adoption of any innovations, in part because of statutory restrictions concerning federal involvement in curricula and in part because of the findings of the Rand study.

Conclusions

This review of the implementation of Title I of ESEA from its passage in 1965 through the 1978 amendments has at least two implications for a general analysis of policy implementation.

First, it points to the importance of program evaluation by actors external to the implementing agencies particularly when, as in this case, neither the USOE nor most SEAs and LEAs were initially very supportive of the reform. At the insistence of Senator Robert Kennedy, the 1965 ESEA sought to promote such review by requiring LEAs to submit annual program evaluations, including "objective measures of educational achievement." But, as McLaughlin and others have clearly shown, this requirement had little effect during the 1960s, in part because many LEAs and SEAs chose to ignore it, in part because USOE was so preoccupied with protecting state and local officials and with protecting its budgetary allocation during a time of appropriation reductions that it went to considerable efforts to mask evidence of program ineffectiveness.[87]

That situation might have persisted had it not been for (1) the audits of fund allocations by LEAs and SEAs carried out by the HEW auditors and (2) the publicity given the auditors' findings—as well as those from the NAACP's investigations—by the Martin-McClure Report and other studies in late 1969.

The Martin-McClure Report was a watershed in the implementation of Title I, as it led rather directly not only to the 1970 amendments but also to the appointment of the Title I task force within HEW and thus to the clarification of Title I regulations and to a substantial increase in the number of reformers in USOE's Division of Compensatory Education. Subsequent investigations of funds allocations, program effectiveness, and evaluation procedures by GAO, NIE, LCCRUL, and other groups have undoubtedly strengthened the hands of reformers within USOE and Congress and thus contributed to the 1974 and 1978 amendments as well as to the tightening of USOE regulations.

The implementation of Title I thus provides an excellent illustration of not only the reluctance of organizations to critically evaluate their own performance but also of the potential effects that competent external evaluations can have in altering agency behavior. Without external review Title I would probably still be a program of *de facto* general aid to schools with concentrations of low-income families rather than a reasonably effective program of compensatory education.

The second implication of the Title I experience is the need to take a fairly long-term perspective—as long as a decade or more—to evaluate the effectiveness of any ambitious social program. This is not really very surprising when we consider that Title I sought to change the behavior of approximately 13,000 LEAs involving thousands of individual schools and probably over a million teachers and other school officials—many of them against their will. Moreover, Title I was to involve the redistribution of scarce funds and operate through a federal system in an area with a very strong tradition of local autonomy. To have expected success after only four or five years in even the limited area of funds allocation was, in retrospect, quite naive. And the decade or so it took to develop reasonably effective programs capable of significantly narrowing the gap between the most disadvantaged children and the national mean in large numbers of schools is probably not unreasonable given the behavioral changes required in school officials and parents and children, the lack of previous experience with such programs, and the difficulties in reallocating scarce funds to the disadvantaged.

Our review of the history of Title I distinguishes two different periods of Title I implementation: 1965–69 and 1970–78. Other recent analyses also follow this approach.[88] During the first period, Title I was little more than a thinly disguised program of general aid and, not surprisingly, had virtually no success in raising the achievement scores of disadvantaged students. The statutory and administrative reforms of 1970 began an eight-year period during which the targeting, comparability, and antisupplanting restrictions were greatly tightened; parent advisory councils became legally mandated; reformers gained control of at least the Division of Compensatory Education within USOE; Congress (in 1973–74) resolved any lingering suspicions that Title I was "really" general aid; and an influential Title I constituency developed in Washington and in many states (as revealed by increased state funding for compensatory education programs). Moreover, by 1976–77

Table 6.4
Extent to Which the Implementation of Title I of ESEA Met the Six
Conditions of Effective Implementation: (1) 1965–69 and (2) 1970–78

	Extent to Which Conditions Were Met	
Condition	1965–69	1970–78
1. Statute contains clear and consistent policy directives.	MODERATE/LOW. Statutory language was fairly clear that principal objective was to aid disadvantaged in poor areas, but widespread perception that Congress "really" intended general aid sowed considerable uncertainty.	MODERATE in early 1970s, HIGH after 1974. The 1970, and especially the 1974, ESEA amendments with respect to supplanting, comparability, parent advisory councils, etc., made it clear that Congress intended a compensatory education program.
2. Statute incorporates sound causal theory identifying and providing jurisdiction over sufficient factors to have the potential to attain objectives.	LOW/UNCERTAIN. Dismal results in student performance and Coleman report raised serious doubts about (a) whether schools knew how to teach the disadvantaged and (b) whether they controlled sufficient levers to overcome the culture of poverty.	MODERATE but still UNCERTAIN. By 1976–77 it was clear that schools knew how to (temporarily) raise student performance. But whether these gains remain several years after students leave the program is still uncertain.
3. Statute structures implementation to maximize probability of compliance from implementing officials and target groups.	LOW/MODERATE overall.	MODERATE overall.
a. assignment to sympathetic agencies	VARIED, but generally LOW. Most federal, state, and local educational officials in 1965 were known to prefer	MODERATE but VARIED. Same agencies in charge, but officials became more sympathetic to CE be-

	Extent to Which Conditions were Met	
Condition	1965–69	1979–78
	general aid rather than compensatory education (CE). Strong norms of deference to local educators.	cause of other statutory changes and development of CE constituencies.
b. hierarchically integrated system with few veto points and adequate incentives for compliance	LOW/MODERATE. USOE had only indirect authority to review LEAs' funds allocation and virtually no control over educational services.	MODERATE. 1970 and 1974 amendments gave USOE clearer authority to cut off funds and clarified comparability and antisupplanting restrictions. But still little control over classroom practices.
c. supportive decision rules	NEUTRAL. Burden of proof on feds to prove noncompliance. But not an important factor.	NEUTRAL. Same as in previous period.
d. financial resources	HIGH in 1965, MODERATE thereafter. Vietnam War, declining economy, and increases in eligible children eroded initial adequate appropriations.	MODERATE/LOW. Constant appropriations and substantial increases in eligible children created real problems by mid-1970s (see Table 6.3).
e. formal access to supporters	LOW/MODERATE. Evaluation requirements potentially important, but weakened by LEAs' reluctance to meet them and by general hostility to outsiders.	MODERATE. 1970 and 1974 amendments strengthened evaluation requirements and potential role of parent advisory committees. But still problems with LEAs and parental indifference.

	Extent to Which Conditions were Met	
Condition	1965–69	1979–78
4. Commitment and skill of top implementing officials.	MODERATE at top, LOW elsewhere. Keppel and Howe supportive and skillful, but USOE indifferent and most state school officials were indifferent if not hostile.	MODERATE but VARIED. Top-ranking USOE officials were often indifferent, but Division of Compensatory Education personnel became quite dedicated to CE; received strong support from HEW auditors. SEAs varied, but certainly more supportive than in previous period.
5. Continuing support from constituency groups and sovereigns.	LOW/MODERATE. Little support initially except for President Johnson, but that soon waned because of Vietnam. Big turning point in late 1969 with NAACP's revelations of widespread abuses.	MODERATE/HIGH. Congress strengthened funds allocation and evaluation requirements, though reluctant to actually impose sanctions. CE constituency groups strong in Washington, varied elsewhere.
6. Changing socio-economic conditions over time.	LOW/MODERATE. Vietnam War and declining public support for antipoverty programs hurt Title I funding and perhaps willingness to tighten regulations.	LOW/MODERATE. Declining economy of the 1970s certainly contributed to funding difficulties as did public disinterest in antipoverty programs. Conversely, increasing public concern with school performance perhaps helped.

Legend: HIGH = A strong asset in effective implementation of legal objectives.
MODERATE = Conducive to effective implementation, although some problems.
LOW = Notable obstacle to effective implementation.
NEUTRAL = Insignificant; factor played little or no role in implementation effort.

improvements in the funds allocation process and continued research resulted in significant increases in achievement test scores by disadvantaged children in many schools.

Table 6.4 compares the extent to which the six conditions of effective implementation were met during the two periods. It reveals that virtually all the variables were more conducive to compensatory education during the latter period, with the greatest changes occurring in the clarity and consistency of statutory directives, the increased support from sovereigns and constituency groups, and the degree of commitment (or, more precisely, the decline in hostility) from implementing officials. In addition, the table suggests that program improvements over time have occurred despite unfavorable socioeconomic conditions (first Vietnam, then increasing economic difficulties) which have eroded public and legislative support for funding compensatory education programs. Finally, the table illustrates the continuing problems with Title I—namely, inadequate funding and continued uncertainty about whether the schools have the knowledge or jurisdiction over sufficient factors to raise achievement levels permanently.

But the fact that almost all the variables were rated during the 1970s as MODERATE, i.e., conducive to effective implementation but with some problems, suggests that significant social change may be possible if virtually all elements of a system are moderately conducive to it over a decade or so. As Kirst and Jung have argued, Title I is probably an excellent example of cumulative incrementalism: "When aggregated across time, the incremental changes have resulted in substantial modifications in implementation policies and practices."[89]

This process of cumulative incrementalism contrasts with the pattern described in chapter 7 when a very supportive legal and political environment (i.e., many HIGH ratings) was able to bring about substantial changes in coastal land use policy in California over a much shorter time period. Evidentally, there are at least two roads to the moderate attainment of statutory objectives. In the concluding chapter, we shall offer some tentative suggestions about which of these is more likely to have permanent effects.

For further reflection

1. One of the most important factors in the implementation of Title I has been the statutory requirement for periodic evaluation of student performance. What has been the experience with Title I evaluations in your local school system? What have been the test results? How sophisticated has been the testing procedure? What has been the attitude of teachers and school administrators to the evaluation requirements? What is the status of Title I implementation today versus five years ago?

2. Under Title I a fairly extensive internal support constituency grew up

among program administrators and teacher aides. But parent support has varied widely among communities. In contrast, it appears that the federal aid to the handicapped program has developed less of an internal constituency, but far more vocal and organized support among parents. [On the latter, see Erwin Levine and Elizabeth Wexler, *PL 94-142: An Act of Congress* (New York: Macmillan Publishing Co: 1981).] Which type of support would you expect to be more effective in fending off severe budget cutbacks a president might propose for the program?

(A hint: One method of comparing the relative strength of the support constituencies between the two programs is to compare budget allocations to both, pre- and post-1981, at both the federal and local levels.)

3. It could be argued that a voucher system could be used as an alternative means of providing the kinds of specialized services Title I was intended to provide. This is a system whereby the parents of affected children would receive supplementary public funds in the form of a "special services" voucher. In turn, the parents could "cash in" the voucher at the school of their choosing. Thus, the market mechanism would be used to ensure optimum delivery of special services. [For a discussion of vouchers, see David Cohen and Eleanor Farrar, "Power to the Parents?— The Story of Educational Vouchers," *The Public Interest,* no. 48 (Summer 1977): 72-97.]

    What might a member of Congress, a public school superintendent, a classroom teacher, and an affected parent see as the advantages and disadvantages in the implementation of a voucher system to aid educationally disadvantaged students? Compare these to what already exists with respect to Title I.

4. Given that the quality of Title I services is critically dependent upon the quality and commitment of individual classroom teachers, how would you design an implementation process that maximizes teachers' commitment to the program—without undermining the other functions of the school system?

5. Compare the number and importance of veto points in the implementation of Title I versus implementation of the southern school desegregation program.

Notes

1. Taken from U.S., Congress, Senate, Committee on Labor and Public Welfare, *Elementary and Secondary Education Act of 1965, Report No. 146,* 89th Cong., 1st sess., 1965, p. 4 [hereafter 1965 Senate Committee Report].
2. Quoted in U.S., General Accounting Office, *Assessment of Reading Activities Funded Under the Federal Program of Aid for Educationally Deprived Children* (Washington, D.C.: Government Printing Office, December 1975), p. 10.
3. See Stephen K. Bailey and Edith K. Mosher, *ESEA: The Office of Education Administers a Law* (Syracuse: Syracuse University Press, 1968), pp. 4-14; also Joel S. Berke and Michael W. Kirst, *Federal Aid to Education: Who Benefits? Who Governs?* (Lexington, Mass.: D. C. Heath, 1972), chapter 1.
4. Bailey and Mosher, *ESEA,* pp. 5-6.
5. *1965 Senate Committee Report,* pp. 3-5; Bailey and Mosher, *ESEA,* pp. 8-9.

6. Bailey and Mosher, *ESEA*, pp. 21–23; Eugene Eidenberg and Roy D. Morey, *An Act of Congress* (New York: W. W. Norton, 1969), chapter 2.
7. Unless otherwise noted, the following discussion of the legislative history of the 1965 ESEA is based on Bailey and Mosher, *ESEA*, chapter 2; and Eidenberg and Morey, *An Act of Congress*, chapters 4–6. You may also wish to consult Philip Meranto, *The Politics of Federal Aid to Education in 1965* (Syracuse: Syracuse University Press, 1967).

   Although many Republicans and other supporters resented the no-amendment strategy, some of their concerns—such as including physically disabled children in the definition of "educationally disadvantaged" and placing restrictions on the scope of U.S Office of Education regulations—were incorporated through the strategem of placing letters from the Commissioner of Education in the Senate Committee Report indicating that the commissioner accepted their interpretation of legislative language. The no-amendment strategy was ultimately saved by the willingness of numerous senators—including Jennings Randolph in committee and over twenty members on the floor—to vote against their states' short-term interests in voting down amendments to revise the Title I allocation formula (Eidenberg and Morey, *An Act of Congress*, pp. 158, 165). Of course, the senators knew that such adjustments could be made in the future—once the law establishing federal aid to education was securely on the books.
8. The First Amendment to the U.S. Constitution declares that "Congress shall make no law respecting an establishment of religion or prohibiting the free exercise thereof . . ." While both the establishment clause and the free exercise clause have been the subject of extensive litigation, the U.S. Supreme Court in *Everson* v. *Board of Education*, 330 U.S. 1 (1947), upheld a New Jersey statute authorizing local school boards to provide transportation for children to and from public and parochial schools on the grounds that the law was aiding students rather than the schools per se. It was this "child benefit" theory on which the framers of ESEA based their hopes for surviving any constitutional challenge. Moreover, several federal laws, including the G.I. Bill, the National Defense Education Act, and the National School Lunch Act, had provided federal assistance to various secular aspects of sectarian institutions (Bailey and Mosher, *ESEA*, pp. 33–34). On the other hand, several state courts have ruled that *state* constitutions prohibit the use of public funds to provide bus rides for parochial school students; see, for example, *Board of Education* v. *Antone*, 384 Pac. 2nd. 911 (Oklahoma, 1963).
9. Sec. 203 allocated funds to local education agencies based on the number of school age children from low-income families (those earning less than $2000 a year or those on Aid to Families with Dependent Children) multiplied by half of the state average per pupil expenditure. All local education agencies with at least 3 percent of their pupils from poverty families and/or 100 such children—or about 95 percent of all school districts—were eligible for funds.
10. *1965 Senate Committee Report*, pp. 3–5, 15–16; also U.S., Congress, House of Representatives, *Elementary Secondary Education Act of 1965, Report No. 143*, 89th Cong., 1st sess., p. 2 [hereafter, *1965 House Committee Report*].
11. *1965 House Committee Report*, pp. 6–7; also *1965 Senate Committee Report*, pp. 10–11.
12. *1965 Senate Committee Report*, p. 9; see also *1965 House Committee Report*, p. 5.
13. *1965 House Committee Report*, p. 66.
14. For an excellent discussion of this topic, see Jerome T. Murphy, "The Education Bureaucracies Implement Novel Policy: The Politics of Title I of ESEA, 1965-72," in *Policy and Politics in America: Six Case Studies*, ed. Allan Sindler (Boston: Little, Brown, 1973), pp. 168–69. For slightly different view that places greater emphasis on the congressional desire for general aid, see Floyd E. Stoner, "Federal Auditors as Regulators: The Case of Title I of ESEA," in *The Policy Cycle*, ed. Judith V. May and Aaron B. Wildavsky, Sage Yearbooks in Politics and Public Policy, vol. 5 (Beverly Hills: Sage, 1978), pp. 202–3.
15. Bailey and Mosher, *ESEA*, pp. 46–47; Murphy, "Politics of Title I of ESEA," pp. 169–70: Milbrey W. McLaughlin, *Evaluation and Reform: ESEA, Title I* (Cambridge: Ballinger, 1975), pp. 1–4.
16. ESEA, Sec. 205(a). The same section also required (5) that the Title I programs be developed in cooperation with the local antipoverty agency (CAP); and (6) that effective procedures be developed for disseminating educational research to local teachers and administrators. But these requirements played only a minor role in the implementation process, in part because the *1965 Senate Committee Report* (pp. 14–16, 83–84) clearly stated that the local CAP agency had no veto over Title I programs.

17. Bailey and Mosher, *ESEA*, pp. 17–19, 72–75; Berke and Kirst, *Federal Aid to Education*, pp. 63–72 and passim.
18. *1965 Senate Committee Report*, pp. 8–9; Murphy, "The Politics of Title I of ESEA," pp. 171–72.
19. Murphy, "The Politics of Title I of ESEA," pp. 169–72. For example, a 1966 survey of nearly a thousand school superintendents by the Bureau of Social Science Research (BSSR) revealed that 70 percent of respondents felt that Title I funds should not be allocated on a poverty basis and this pattern did *not* vary according to the district's income level; for example, about 69 percent of the superintendents in districts with median family incomes of less than $5000 disagreed with the statute (Bailey and Mosher, *ESEA*, p. 306).
20. McLaughlin, *Evaluation and Reform*, pp. 1–4; Bailey and Mosher, *ESEA*, pp. 162–63.
21. McLaughlin, *Evaluation and Reform*, pp. 8–11, 17–18.
22. Ibid., pp. 9–10; also *1965 House Committee Report*, p. 5.
23. *1965 House Committee Report*, pp. 71–72. While ESEA certainly did not focus on early childhood education, Sec. 201 of ESEA did indicate that Title I funds could be spent for preschool programs.
24. Bailey and Mosher, *ESEA*, pp. 67–70, 100–103.
25. Ibid., p. 117.
26. This interpretation is most clearly articulated by John Hughes, Title I program director from 1965 to 1969; see John F. Hughes and Anne O. Hughes, *Equal Education* (Bloomington: Indiana University Press, 1972), pp. 32–39.
27. Hughes and Hughes, *Equal Education*, pp. 45–48; Bailey and Mosher, *ESEA*, pp. 116–19.
28. Systematic data on this topic are lacking, but an excellent case study involving administration of the supplement-not-supplant regulations during the middle 1970s can be found in National Institute of Education, *Administration of Compensatory Education* (Washington, D.C.: Author, September 1977), chapter 3. Moreover, interviews conducted in December 1980 with several very knowledgeable observers indicate that this was part of a more general conflict which has permeated the agency since the late 1960s. They also suggested that different recruitment patterns were partially responsible, with the Division of Compensatory Education staffed largely by reformist civil servants recruited in the early 1970s while their supervisors in the Bureau of Elementary and Secondary Education were largely political appointees recruited from LEAs and SEAs.
29. Eidenberg and Morey, *An Act of Congress*, pp. 192, 201.
30. It was not, however, until the 1971 school year that this plan was actually realized. And despite further improvements made in Sec. 403 of the 1970 and 1974 ESEA amendments, the appropriations process apparently still lagged behind schools' planning calendars, in which, for example, teachers are normally hired three to six months before the beginning of the school year. See U.S., Congress, House, Committee on Education and Labor, Subcommittee on Education, *Hearings, Part 18: Administration of Title I of ESEA*, 95th Cong., 1st sess., October 1977, p. 85.
31. Eidenberg and Morey, *An Act of Congress*, pp. 203–12; "Two-Year Elementary School Aid Bill Enacted," pp. 611–18.
32. Quoted in Hughes and Hughes, *Equal Education*, p. 20.
33. ESEA, Title I, Sec. 141(a)(3)(B-C) [1971]. Enforcement of this provision was, however, delayed by Congress until FY 1973 at the insistence of Chicago Congressman Roman Pucinski (Dem., Ill.) because it would make it more difficult for the city's schools to continue to assign its highest paid teachers to middle-class schools.
34. The principal reason for the revision in the low-income criterion was that the pre-1974 formula based on the number of families below a given income level or on Aid to Families with Dependent Children (AFDC) was resulting in rapidly increasing allocations to wealthy industrial states (e.g. New York and California) with growing AFDC populations. Congress decided to switch to another formula based largely on the Orshansky Poverty Index which was both more sophisticated and gave greater allocations to states with large numbers of rural low-income families. For discussions of the passage and content of the 1974 amendments, see "President Signs $25.2 Billion Education Bill," *1974 Congressional Quarterly Almanac*, vol. 30 (Washington, D.C.: Congressional Quarterly, 1975), pp. 441–74; David Bresnick, "The Federal Educational Policy System: Enacting and Revising Title I," *Western Political Quarterly* 32 (June 1979): 189–202.
35. The 1978 extension of ESEA again revised the allocation formula slightly, this time to benefit northern industrial states; required school districts to rank schools on the basis of the number

of poor children, while requiring that funds be allocated on either this basis or, in exceptional circumstances, on the basis of the number of students failing standard achievement tests; tightened program requirements regarding parent advisory councils, record keeping, and supplanting; explicitly gave USOE authority to withhold funds from school districts violating regulations under the act; and instituted a new program of grants to SEAs and LEAs seeking to improve instruction in the basic skills of reading, writing, and mathematics. In addition, on a 79-290 vote, the House rejected an amendment by Congressman John Ashbrook (Rep., Ohio) to substitute a program of block grants based solely on school enrollments (i.e., pure general aid) for the Title I program. See "Massive Aid to Education Programs Extended," *1978 Congressional Quarterly Almanac*, vol. 34 (Washington, D.C.: Congressional Quarterly, 1979), pp. 557–68. Although Congress in 1978 considered using achievement test scores—rather than poverty indices—as the criterion for allocating Title I funds to LEAs, a study the same year by the National Institute of Education (NIE) concluded that the sources of achievement data were inadequate to use for basing allocations of funds to the state or within states to school districts, NIE, *Compensatory Education Study: Final Report to Congress* (Washington, D.C.: U.S. Dept. of HEW, September 1978), pp. 3–4.

36. Stephen M. Barro, "Federal Education Goals and Policy Instruments: An Assessment of the 'Strings' Attached to Categorical Grants in Education," in *The Federal Interest in Financing Schooling*, ed. Michael Timpane (Cambridge: Ballinger, 1978), p. 274. Of course, the 1980 election of President Reagan and the Republican majority in the Senate may result in relaxation of the federal controls established during the 1970s.

37. Berke and Kirst, *Federal Aid to Education*, chapters 2–8; Hughes and Hughes, *Equal Education*, chapters 4–5.

38. Michael Kirst and Richard Jung, "The Utility of a Longitudinal Approach in Assessing Implementation: A Thirteen-Year View of Title I, ESEA," Program Report No. 80-B18, School of Education, Stanford University, June 1980, p. 21. For a similarly optimistic view of the ability of USOE to create supportive subunits within SEAs and LEAs, see Hughes and Hughes, *Equal Education*, pp. 41–43. This view, however, is not supported (through 1972) by Murphy's research in Massachusetts (Murphy, "The Politics of Title I of ESEA," pp. 179–84). For another example of efforts to change an agency's orientation through the creation of subunits supportive of the new policy, see Daniel Mazmanian and Jeanne Nienaber, *Can Organizations Change?* (Washington, D.C.: The Brookings Institution, 1979), chaper 3.

39. Hughes and Hughes, *Equal Education*, pp. 112–13.

40. This discussion of parent advisory councils is based primarily upon Hughes and Hughes, *Equal Education*, pp. 113–17.

41. NIE, *Compensatory Education Study*, pp. 93–105, especially pp. 101–6; see also Robert Goettel, "Federal Assistance to National Target Groups," in *The Federal Interest in Financing Schooling*, ed. Michael Timpane (Cambridge: Ballinger, 1978), pp. 197–98.

42. National polls show a modest decline in public support for antipoverty programs, especially welfare, in the period from 1965 to 1980, but no decline in public spending for education. See Council on Environmental Quality et al., *Public Opinion on Environmental Quality* (Washington, D.C.: Author, 1980), pp. 7, 10.

43. Hughes and Hughes, *Equal Education*, pp. 125–27.

44. Stoner, "Federal Auditors as Regulators," pp. 208–9; Ruby Martin and Phyllis McClure, *Title I of ESEA: Is It Helping Poor Children?* Washington, D.C.: Southern Center for Studies in Public Policy and the NAACP Legal Defense and Educational Fund, December 1969.

45. Hughes and Hughes, *Equal Education*, pp. 55–56, 103–4, 127–30; Murphy, "The Politics of Title I of ESEA," pp. 184–88; and Timothy Wirth, "Incrementalism in Education Policy Making: Title I of ESEA" Ph.D. diss., Stanford School of Education, May 1973), pp. 37–41, 75–85.

46. Kirst and Jung, "A Thirteen-Year View of Title I of ESEA," pp. 21–22. Compare this view, however, with a more pessimistic assessment from the early 1970s in Murphy, "The Politics of Title I of ESEA," pp. 191–92.

47. For an excellent review of the evidence concerning the reluctance of school officials in many areas to support compensatory education, see Barro, "Federal Education Goals and Policy Instruments," pp. 237–40, 274.

48. Berke and Kirst, *Federal Aid to Education*, pp. 42–46, chapter 9. In the 1975–76 school year, Title I represented 3 percent of all expenditures for elementary and secondary education and

34 percent of federal educational expenditures [National Institute of Education, *Evaluating Compensatory Education: An Interim Report* (Washington, D.C.: Author, December 1976), p. 3–13].

49. See, for example, Harrell Rodgers and Charles Bullock, *Coercion to Compliance* (Lexington, Mass.: D. C. Heath, 1976); Daniel Mazmanian and Paul Sabatier, "The Role of Attitudes and Perceptions in Policy Evaluation by Attentive Elites," in *Why Policies Succeed or Fail*, ed. Helen Ingram and Dean Mann (Beverly Hills, Calif.: Sage, 1980), pp. 107–33.

50. For the general picture, see Barro, "Federal Education Goals and Policy Instruments," pp. 237–40.

51. For a discussion of the legal framework and these terms, see NIE, *Administration of Compensatory Education*, pp. 8–11.

52. Hughes and Hughes, *Equal Education*, pp. 63–69.

53. McLaughlin, *Evaluation and Reform*, pp. 33–40.

54. Ibid., pp. 51–61.

55. Murphy, "The Politics of Title I of ESEA," pp. 180–81.

56. Hughes and Hughes, *Equal Education*, pp. 105–6. For discussions of fiscal inequalities within school districts, see Barro, "Federal Education Goals and Policy Instruments," pp. 238, 278–79, and Christopher Jencks et al., *Inequality: A Reassessment of the Effect of Family and Schooling in America* (New York: Basic Books, 1972), chapter 2.

57. House Subcommittee on Education, *1977 Hearings, Part 18: Administration of Title I of ESEA*, p. 23. Even more damaging evidence was presented in a 1972 LCCRUL study of compliance with comparability regulations which revealed that seventy-nine of the eighty school districts examined had one or more noncomparable schools (Murphy, "The Politics of Title I of ESEA," pp. 192–93).

58. U.S., Congress, House, Committee on Education and Labor, Subcommittee on Education, *1977 Hearings, Part 19: Title I Funds Allocation*, 95th Cong., 1st sess., November 1977, pp. 504–5.

59. NIE, *Administration of Compensatory Education*, p. vi.

60. McLaughlin, *Evaluation and Reform*, pp. 64–65.

61. This is probably an excellent example of what Carol Weiss has termed "the enlightment function of social research," i.e., the effect of research not on specific short-term decisions but rather on gradual alteration of the world view or assumptions of decision-makers ["Research for Policy's Sake: The Enlightment Function of Social Research," *Policy Analysis* 3 (Fall 1977): 531–45].

62. Comptroller General of the U.S., *Assessment of Reading Activities Funded Under the Federal Program of Aid for Educationally Deprived Children* (Washington, D.C.: General Accounting Office, Fall 1975), pp. 22–27.

63. Hughes and Hughes, *Equal Education*, pp. 86–89; House Subcommittee on Education, *1977 Hearings, Part 19: Title I Funds Allocation*, pp. 445–89.

64. The 1977 NIE *Compensatory Education Study* (pp. 5–6) found that only about two thirds of students in need of services in Title I eligible *elementary* schools were being served and that only about 1 percent of Title I funds were going to high-school students. The study also found that instructional services emphasized basic reading and math skills and that about half of LEAs used some funds for noninstructional (e.g., health) services.

65. See the testimony of Sol Pelavin of the Stanford Research Institute in House Subcommittee on Education, *1977 Hearings, Part 19: Title I Funds Allocation*, pp. 491, 500–501.

66. While the substantial increase in students from low-income families during the late 1960s was originally attributed to the increase in AFDC children, the shift in the 1974 ESEA Amendments to a system based largely on the Orshansky poverty index resulted in even greater increases in eligible children (see Table 6.3); for discussion of this issue, see the sources cited in note 35 as well as NIE, *Evaluating Compensatory Education*, chapter 2, and House Subcommittee on Education, *1977 Hearings, Part 19: Title I Funds Allocation*, passim.

67. House Subcommittee on Education, *1977 Hearings, Part 18: Administration of Title I of ESEA*, p. 23.

68. In brief, the dispute centered on reformers' contention that schools should be required to provide comparable *services within* a given school to Title I and non-Title I schools while traditionalists argued that USOE should look only at the *aggregated level of funding between* Title I and non-Title I schools. The net result was not only confusion among SEAs and LEAs but also an increasing unwillingness among HEW auditors (who supported the reformers) to investigate the issue. The 1978 ESEA amendments do not appear to have resolved the

dispute. For discussions of this issue, see NIE, *Administration of Compensatory Education,* chapter 3.

69. NIE, *Administration of Compensatory Education,* chapter 5, especially p. 58.

70. Barro, "Federal Education Goals and Policy Instruments," p. 239–40.

71. See, for example, National Institute of Education, *The Effects of Services on Student Development* (Washington, D.C.: Author, September 1977), pp. x–xi.

72. Although Title I was originally designed to serve the physically handicapped, migrants, and children in institutions, as well as low-achievers from poverty areas, the physically and mentally handicapped were subsequently given their own program. In FY 1976, about 90 percent of Title I funds went to LEAs on the basis of the poverty formula (House Subcommittee on Education, *1977 Hearings, Part 18: Administration of Title I,* p. 128).

73. James S. Coleman et al., *Equality of Education Opportunity* (Washington, D.C.: Government Printing Office, 1966); Bailey and Mosher, *ESEA,* pp. 177–78, 220.

74. Jencks et al. were quite explicit about the inherent limitations of schooling on long-term educational performance or social mobility (*Inequality,* pp. 255–56). For more recent analyses of postprogram drop-offs in achievement gains, see Charles Kenoyer et al., *Sustaining Effects Study, Report No. 11* (Santa Monica: System Development Corporation, November 1979).

75. McLaughlin, *Evaluation and Reform,* pp. 8–9.

76. Ibid., pp. 33–60.

77. Comptroller General, *Assessment of Reading Activities,* pp. 6–9.

78. House Subcommittee on Education, *1977 Hearings, Part 19: Title I Funds Allocation,* pp. 464–68.

79. Because the NIE sampling methodology was designed to evaluate the effects of different program characteristics rather than to provide a nationwide assessment of Title I programs and because the study was restricted to stable programs, the findings should *not* be generalized to all Title I programs. The most important findings were that first-graders made average gains of twelve months in reading and eleven months in math in the seven-month period between fall and spring testing. Third-graders gained eight months in reading and twelve months in math (NIE, *The Effects of Services on Student Development,* chapters 3 and 4).

80. Ibid., pp. 22–23. The last finding is particularly important, as pullout instruction is frequently utilized at least in the early grades.

81. For a review of earlier studies, see House Subcommittee on Education, *1977 Hearings, Part 19: Title I Funds Allocation,* pp. 486–502.

82. Paul Berman, "The Study of Macro- and Micro-Implementation," *Public Policy* 26 (Spring 1978): 173–74. The best summary of the Rand Studies is found in Paul Berman and Mibrey W. McLaughlin, "Implementation of Educational Innovation," *The Educational Forum* 40 (March 1976): 345–70.

83. Berman and McLaughlin, "Implementation of Educational Innovation," p. 361. For an excellent discussion of the limited ability of USOE officials to influence local schools, see David K. Cohen and Eleanor Farrar, "Power to the Parents? The Story of Education Vouchers," *Public Interest,* no. 48 (Summer 1977): 72–97.

84. NIE, *Evaluating Compensatory Education,* chapter 3, pp. 20–22, 37–67.

85. Personal communication; see also Richard Elmore, *Complexity and Control: What Legislators and Administrators Can Do About Implementing Public Policy* (Washington, D.C.: National Institute of Education, August 1980).

86. This discussion of USOE's diffusion efforts is taken from U.S., Congress, House, Committee on Education and Labor, Subcommittee on Education, *Hearings, Part 10: Administrative Issues,* 95th Cong., 1st sess., July-August 1977, pp. 81–111.

87. McLaughlin, *Evaluation and Reform;* see also Louis K. Comfort, "Evaluation as an Instrument for Educational Change," in *Why Policies Succeed or Fail,* ed. Helen Ingram and Dean Mann (Beverly Hills: Sage, 1980), pp. 35–57.

88. Kirst and Jung, "The Utility of a Longitudinal Approach," pp. 12–24.

89. Kirst and Jung, "The Utility of a Longitudinal Approach," abstract.

Chapter 7
An initial success in the quiet revolution: the California Coastal Commissions, 1972–77

The "quiet revolution" it was called.[1] It began during the late 1960s and early 1970s when, from hundreds of points across the fifty states, came calls for more land use planning and control. The calls originated not at the traditional local level, but at the federal, and even more often, at the state level of government. Land use is not the stuff revolutionary movements, quiet or otherwise, are typically made of. In fact, since the founding of the nation, land use management has usually been left to local businesses, property owners, and governments to suit local needs. At least in theory, the rule has been the less government control, the better. Yet the allocation of land resources has an enormous effect not only on natural habitat and wilderness, but also on congestion, pollution of streams and waterways, urban sprawl, air pollution, and the entire environment. During the early 1970s environmentalists and planners seized upon land use regulation and management as one of the best leverage points for dealing with the interrelated issues of environmental destruction, resource scarcity, and urban decay facing the nation.

Most environmentalists rejected the idea of working through existing land use regulatory bodies such as city and county zoning and planning boards as a means of implementing their programs. Rather, critics of the existing system turned to developing state-level capacity for environmentally sensitive land use programs. The critics believed that local bodies were, and would continue to be, unsympathetic to land use programs. More importantly, local regulatory bodies were considered structurally incapable of dealing with many environmental problems; for instance, they could not address critical adverse spillover effects of air and water pollution that went beyond their own political boundaries. Second, certain natural resources that required protection, such as coastal wetlands and beaches and agricultural lands, were considered statewide resources which had not been given adequate attention by local governments. Third, during the post-World War II era there had been many cases in which small local jurisdictions had been overpowered by large commercial or subdivision developers. Thus, it was believed that only the state could protect the public interest in these cases.

Some effort was given to passage of national land use standards in 1971 and 1972—as seen by passage of the Coastal Zone Management Act of 1972 and numerous changes in the environmental guidelines for managing land owned by the Bureau of Land Management, the Forest Service and the National Park Service. Most attention, however, was directed at the states. State governments were both near enough to the scene to be sensitive to local needs and appreciate local variations, yet sufficiently distant from local projects to exercise authority in the "collective" (meaning environmental protection) interest.

Within only a few years environmentalists and their allies among professional planners and a variety of civic groups succeeded in establishing some meaningful state regulatory powers over land use in half of the fifty states.[2] The effectiveness of the various state land use programs is difficult to assess. While several case studies and some comparative analyses have been undertaken, the picture is still rather sketchy.[3]

However, the experience in California of establishing state land use control over the state's entire 1100-mile coastline between 1972 and 1976 has been studied fairly extensively and provides an excellent case of an effective implementation effort. Furthermore, as "the most powerful state land-use regulatory body and the most powerful coastal management agency in the United States,"[4] the experience of California is worthy of study. Coastal zone protection in California is also interesting for several analytical reasons: (a) the guiding statute provided a clear mandate for public access and environmental protection without the normal balancing language, thereby representing a dramatic break from policies pursued by most local governments; (b) this is one of the few cases which comes reasonably close to meeting our hypothesized six conditions of effective implementation; and (c) the case provides a good illustration of the formulation-implementation-reformulation cycle.

The historical and legal background of the coastal commissions

The California coast stretches approximately 1100 miles from the Mexican border to Oregon.[5] The southernmost 300 miles, from San Diego to Santa Barbara, are marked, on the one hand, by an almost unbroken string of excellent swimming and surfing beaches and, on the other, by the rapidly

Figure 7.1
The California Coast

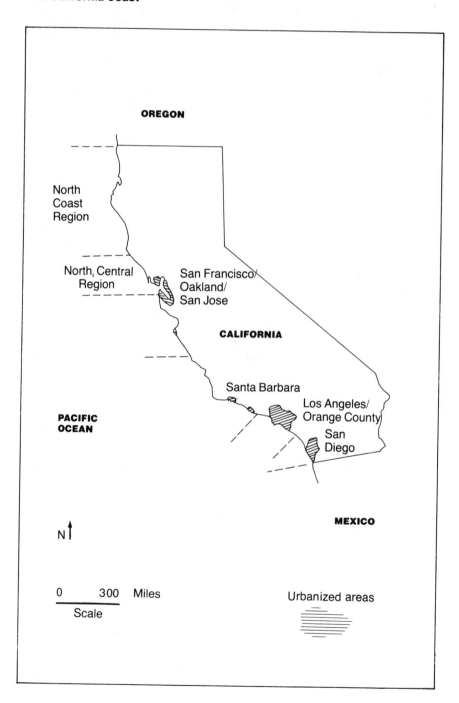

expanding urban development along most of the coastline. North of Santa Barbara, the coast is quite rural except for urban concentrations around Monterey Bay (Monterey), San Francisco Bay (the San Francisco metropolis), and Humboldt Bay (Eureka). This region also offers some of the nation's most spectacular scenery, including hundreds of miles of magnificent coastal bluffs south of Monterey (Big Sur) and north of San Francisco, as well as beautiful forests of redwoods and Douglas fir in the region around Humboldt Bay.

Because the California coast is such a magnificent aesthetic, recreational, and commercial resource, it is often subject to enormous demands for often-conflicting uses. Should wetlands be left in their natural state to serve as wildlife habitat or should they be turned into boat harbors, ports, and residential areas? Should the coastal bluffs and beaches of Malibu in northern Los Angeles County become the exclusive preserve of the very wealthy or should this area be available as a recreational resource to the remaining seven million residents of the county? Should the magnificent coast of northern California (exclusive of San Francisco) retain its wild character with majestic vistas where mountain meets ocean or should it be dotted periodically with second-home subdivisions? Should power plants be placed along the coast where water is plentiful and adverse impacts on air quality are minimal—even though the effects on water habitat and on aesthetic resources are often considerable—or should they be placed on inland waterways, where competition for air and water resources is considerably greater? Should the extensive oil and gas reserves on the continental shelf off southern California be developed, even at the increased risk of oil spills and pumping platforms visible from crowded beaches?

Conflicts over the proper utilization and allocation of coastal resources were rooted ultimately in the large and rapidly growing population along the coast. In 1970 California's fifteen coastal counties had a population of 12.8 million people, an increase of 31 percent since 1960. Within these counties, the population ultimately included in the planning jurisdiction of the coastal commission (from the coast to roughly five miles inland) was 4.2 million, located mainly in the southern portion of the state.

The demands on coastal resources created by the enormous and growing population in the coastal counties created considerable unease among environmental groups, planners, civic associations such as the League of Women Voters, legislators, and many other people, both among political elites and the general public. There were, however, limits to what could be done. Population growth could not easily be reversed. Housing starts, commercial developments, and the accompanying infrastructure might be restricted in the immediate coastal area and the building out of existing urban areas might be emphasized to preserve some open space, but it was unlikely that the basic pattern of intensive urban development could fundamentally be altered, at least not in the southern portion of the state and the urbanized areas of the north. Nevertheless, there were a number of specific substantive and institutional problems over which there was widespread dissatisfaction and which could feasibly be addressed. It was these issues which lead eventually to the formation of the coastal commissions.

First, probably the most widespread concern among the general public was a general fear that the beauty of the coast was being eroded by the rate and type of development. A 1972 poll of the state's electorate revealed that by far the most widespread perceived benefit of stopping or slowing coastal development was the preservation of the natural beauty of the coast—an opinion volunteered by 44 percent of the respondents.[6]

A second major concern was public access to the coast. By California law, all land seaward of the mean high tide line is in the public domain, subject to disposition by the legislature. As residential and commercial development along the coast increased, however, the public's ability to reach the wet sand beaches diminished. In the Los Angeles area, this was graphically illustrated by Malibu—an extremely exclusive 26-mile string of houses between the coastal highway and the ocean—in which both lateral and vertical access to the wet sand had been severely restricted by residents. In the north, essentially the same issue was illustrated by the Sea Ranch, an enormous second-home subdivision occupying 10 miles of the rugged Sonoma coast 100 miles north of San Francisco. Another aspect of public access involved the shortage of public beaches and campgrounds. Although about 25 percent of the mainland coast, or 263 miles, was legally available for public access, the demand for coastal recreation was fast outgrowing the supply and there was a basic mismatch between the largest population and greater demand for facilities in the south and the concentration of coastal parks in the north.[7]

A third source of dissatisfaction with the prevailing pattern of coastal land use during this period was the effect on wildlife habitats, particularly wetlands. While this was apparently a minor issue in the eyes of the general public, it was an important motivating factor for many environmental activists. A 1971 report by an official of the California Department of Fish and Game estimated that construction of commercial and pleasure craft harbors and general commercial and residential development had resulted in a 67 percent reduction in coastal wetland habitat statewide and a more than 75 percent reduction in southern California since the beginning of the twentieth century.

In addition to these three substantive issues, there were two institutional problems which were widely perceived (at least among political elites) to be at the root of the dissatisfaction with coastal land use policy. The first was the generally laissez-faire and prodevelopment bias of most local governments, arising from their dependence upon property and sales taxes for most of their revenue, as well as the prominent role of the construction industry and building trade unions in financing local political campaigns. The other perceived deficiency of existing governmental institutions was the lack of coordination among the multiplicity of local, state, and federal agencies which affected the coast. Although estimates of the precise number of institutions varied, several writers during this period cited approximately fifteen counties, forty-five cities, forty-two state agencies, and seventy federal agencies with jurisdiction over some aspect of coastal resources and called for a more coordinated approach which would deal in an integrated fashion with the coast as a special resource. There was also considerable concern with spillover effects in which the actions of one jurisdiction affected the citizens of another.

Moreover, critics of the existing practices could point to a number of alternative institutional arrangements. By far the most important of these was the San Francisco Bay Conservation and Development Commission (BCDC), established by the legislature in 1965 after extensive grass-roots opposition to the gradual erosion of the San Francisco Bay shoreline through dredging and filling. The agency was widely regarded as a success,[8] and many of its features—including the mix of local government representatives and state-appointed officials on the governing board, its permit authority over developments in the near-shore area, and its creation for a limited period sufficient to prepare a general plan with continuation dependent upon legislative approval—were incorporated into the 1972 Coastal Initiative.

Enactment of coastal legislation

Beginning in 1970 environmentalists and their allies among planners and civic groups made serious efforts to convince the California legislature to pass a variety of bills transferring some authority for planning and permit review along the coast from local to state institutions. Although the environmentalists were successful in obtaining approval from the California Assembly in 1970, 1971, and 1972, their efforts were continually thwarted by the more conservative state senate (even after the Democrats obtained a majority of seats following the 1970 elections).

However, the initiative provision of Article IV of the California Constitution provided an alternative to the multiple vetoes of the legislative process. This process, however, requires several steps. First, a bill has to be drafted; then the necessary signatures have to be obtained to place the bill on the ballot as a statutory initiative. Finally, the initiative proposition has to obtain the approval of a majority of the electorate in November.

The first task was easily accomplished. The 1972 Sieroty-Grunsky Coastal Protection Bill, which had been approved overwhelmingly by the assembly but defeated in senate committee, was used as the initiative vehicle. The second task was considerably more difficult. Although supporters had only about a month's time after the May 15 senate committee vote to obtain the 325,000 signatures necessary to qualify the proposition for the November 1972 ballot, the two-and-a-half-year campaign to pass coastal legislation had resulted in fairly widespread public awareness of the issue. Furthermore, there was a rather substantial number of organizations within the Coastal Alliance, as well as thousands of Sierra Club members in local chapters throughout the state, who were able to obtain 418,000 valid signatures before the deadline.

Proposition 20, the Coastal Initiative, was approved by 55 percent of the state's voters in November 1972 after an extremely hard-fought campaign. Although opponents—composed largely of land development firms, the building trades unions, oil companies, utilities, and many local government officials appointed by city, county, and regional governments and "public" three to one, their media-oriented campaign was unable to overcome the initial reservoir of public support which Proposition 20 had from local civic and environmental groups and many state legislators and other elected officials (with the exception of Governor Reagan).

Provisions of the California Coastal Zone Conservation Act of 1972

The Coastal Initiative as passed by the voters established a state coastal commission and six regional commissions charged with the dual task of preparing a comprehensive coastal plan to be presented to the 1976 legislature and of regulating all development in the interim from the seaward boundary of the state's jurisdiction to 1000 yards landward of the mean high tide. The fate of the commissions after 1976 would be determined by the legislature. Each regional commission was composed of equal numbers of local elected officials appointed by city, county, and regional governments and "public" members appointed by state officials (the governor, the assembly speaker, and the senate rules committee), while composition of the state commission was divided equally between public members and one delegate from each regional commission. Each commission was assisted by a full-time staff of from six to fifteen professionals, while the commissions' activities were funded by a $5 million guaranteed appropriation.[9]

The Coastal Initiative contained a relatively clear mandate to protect the environmental and scenic resources of the coast and to maximize public access to the wet sand beaches; it declared "that it is the policy of the state to preserve, protect, and, where possible, to restore the resources of the coastal zone for the enjoyment of current and succeeding generations."[10] While these objectives were stated in fairly general terms and no attempt was made to reconcile minor conflicts between, for example, access to the beaches and the protection of tide pools, the statute contained no requirements that public access and environmental protection be balanced against such things as additional housing or energy facilities. It thus had a reasonably clear and consistent general orientation.

Also, the Initiative assumed that its goals could be realized (at least during the 1972–76 period) by giving the commissions absolute jurisdiction over all development within 1000 yards off the shore. This development review authority was certainly adequate to protect the scenic resources of the coast and most coastal wetlands, although the absence of authority to acquire and manage land would create some difficulties in actually providing public access to the coast. And the commissions' decision rules were strongly biased toward the achievement of statutory objectives: The burden of proof was placed on applicants to substantiate that their proposed development would be consistent with statutory objectives; almost all important developments required a two-thirds affirmative vote of the commission membership; and the statute clearly indicated that regional permit decisions could be appealed to the state commission and that the state commission would have final authority over the coastal plan presented to the 1975 legislature. Furthermore, the statute provided very liberal rules allowing interested parties to participate in agency decisions and to appeal those decisions to the courts.

Most studies of policy implementation—especially in social programs such as job training, education, and health—have focused on relationships within and among large bureaucracies in which the dominant theme has often been the subtle distortion of program intent through delay and resistance by officials defending their traditional programs or responding to local resistance. From our perspective, however, many of these problems arose because the statutory framers were unable or unwilling to minimize the number of veto/clearance points involved and to assign implementation to sympathetic agencies that would give the new program high priority.

The framers of the Coastal Initiative managed to avoid, or at least to minimize, most of these difficulties. To begin with, they placed almost the entire responsibility for implementation of the initiative in the hands of a new agency. They thereby assured that the new program would be given the highest priority; that there would be no need to integrate it into existing bureaucratic routines; and that all positions in the new agency would be open at a time when the supporters of coastal protection were at their greatest strength. The last point is very important, particularly in the recruitment of commission staff, as there is some evidence that officials in newly created regulatory agencies come disproportionately from among strong advocates of regulation, particularly if the agency is established after a controversial and highly visible political campaign.[11]

The framers also took a number of steps to increase the probability that a majority of formal policymakers—the commissioners—would support the statutory objectives. Not only were the public members to be appointed by state officials—and thus presumably more likely to reflect state and regional interests rather than purely local concerns—but there were also some loose statutory requirements that public members be trained in the environmental sciences or planning, backgrounds which presumably would enhance their sensitivity to statutory objectives. Moreover, since a majority of voters in twelve of the fifteen coastal counties had voted in favor of the Coastal Initiative, there was some expectation that several of the local officials selected for the commissions would mirror those preferences and thus that a majority of the overall membership of most regional commissions would also support the act's objectives.

Finally, the framers provided that ultimate decisions on the coastal plan and most important permit cases would be made by the state commission, whose membership was to be equally divided between public members and representatives from each of the regional commissions. Thus, there was no direct representation of local governments on the state commission. Moreover, since statutory supporters would probably control most of the regional commissions and since most local government officials probably would not have the time to serve on both the regional commission and as the regional representative to the state commission, it was highly likely—though by no means certain—that a majority of the members of the state commission would be supporters of the act. Despite these efforts to increase the probability that a majority of regional and state commissioners would support statutory objectives, the appointment criteria were still sufficiently vague that the general policy orientation of the regional commissions was heavily dependent on the appointment process.

Subsequent surveys of commission officials indicated that the vast majority of state commissioners and staff supported Proposition 20, as did most regional staff. Among regional commissioners, however, the record was more varied. In general, public members were more supportive than local commissioners, with the latter being opposed except in cases where their constituents had voted for Proposition 20 by a large plurality. As a result, supporters of Proposition 20 clearly dominated only two of the six regional commissions, with two others dominated by opponents, and the remaining two rather evenly balanced.

Finally, the 1972 Coastal Conservation Act sought to avoid the indeterminateness (and even secrecy) characteristic of most bureaucratic decision-making by establishing clear decision points within specified time limits on both planning and permit decisions. The act also required that all important decisions be made in public following extensive notification and ample opportunities for public testimony. These explicit decision points and provisions for public participation were intended to encourage monitoring and participation by outside actors.

General factors affecting the coastal commissions, 1972–76

No new government agency, not even one created through a direct vote of the electorate, can expect to operate fully independent of the established bases of power within government. The real issue becomes the degree of autonomy that can be maintained in the face of these external bases of power. Also, the commissions could not expect to be free from internal divisions that would result from the decentralized and somewhat independent nature of the six regional commissions.

External actors

The Coastal Initiative was especially designed to insulate the coastal commissions from the kinds of political pressures that usually flowed from the governor and the legislature as a result of their ability to set and change the agency's goals, monitor its activities, and determine its level of funding. For example, with the exception of gubernatorial appointment powers, neither the governor nor the state resources agency had formal authority over the commissions. Nevertheless, some degree of cooperation was required and was generally forthcoming, even during the Reagan Administration (probably out of the governor's respect for the popular vote of November 1972).

The state legislature, which exercises control over agencies through oversight hearings, the annual budget review process, and statutory revisions, was also denied much of its usual prerogative because of the automatic $5 million appropriation provided by Proposition 20 from the Bagley Conservation Fund for funding of the commissions, and the two-third vote requirement for weakening of an initiative statute. Although the Commissions requested sizable supplemental funding (more than $1.6 million between 1974 and 1975), the legislature did not take the occasion to influence commission activities. Even the legislative appointing authorities—the speaker and the senate rules committee—seldom attempted to influence permit and planning decisions.

The United States Office of Coastal Zone Management (OCZM), which through its funding of state coastal programs could have exercised considerable influence, followed the same pattern of noninterference. However, OCZM was itself just getting off the ground in 1973, and viewed the California commissions as the prototype aggressive state coastal resource protection agency that OCZM wanted to encourage. With little more than pro forma review, OCZM made fairly generous special projects awards to the commissions from 1974 on; $720,000 in 1974, $900,000 in 1975, and $1,200,000 in 1976.[12]

The initiative could not, however, insulate the commissioners from the judiciary. Thus, opponents (and proponents) of the act immediately turned to the courts. By the time the commissions had completed the Coastal Plan, the Attorney General's office had been involved in nearly 240 cases dealing with implementation of the act. Although state superior (district) courts occasionally sided with property owners, the state appellate courts ruled in favor of the commissions in all but one of the twenty-seven cases decided by the spring of 1977. The most important of these cases was *CEEED* v. *The California Coastal Conservation Commission,* in which the California Supreme Court rejected property owners' contentions that the 1972 Coastal Act constituted an unlawful taking of private property for public purposes without just compensation and failed to assure procedural due process to permit applicants.[13]

Although the governor, OCZM, the legislature, and the courts gave the commissions a rather free hand, the commissions could not perform their mission without becoming a part of the web of federal, state, and local agencies that held planning and resource development responsibilities affecting the coastline. Although the commissions had the authority to review the proposals of other agencies and to veto development proposals which would have an adverse effect on the coastal environment, they did not have the authority or resources actually to provide management services. For example, while the commissions could veto a proposed private development because of the property's potential value for public recreation, they could not purchase the land and develop a recreation facility. Such action required the cooperation of the state Parks and Recreation Department and the Public Works Board.

Furthermore, it proved difficult to halt a private project that had been undertaken prior to the enactment of the Coastal Act and which had already won the active support of other government agencies. This was well illustrated in the commission' confrontation with the Aliso Water Management Agency. Aliso was actually a conglomeration of water districts and local governments in southern Orange County, created in 1972 to construct and operate an areawide sewage treatment facility. The facility would bring sewage discharge in the area up to state standards and accommodate the rapidly expanding population in the southern part of the county, which at the time had reached a little more than 50,000 residents. The plant itself would not be located in the coastal permit zone, but the outfall pipe would traverse it. To deny the Aliso permit would clearly accomplish the objective of the more staunch environmentalists to restrict further urbanization in the southern part of Orange County, inland and along the coast, or at least place a moratorium on further urbanization until completion of the Coastal Plan. But under pressure from Aliso and its tight deadlines schedule (a schedule imposed by federal funding sources), the South Coast Regional Commission granted the permit. In doing so, it added two important conditions; the diameter of the outfall pipe was to be decreased from fifty-four to forty-eight inches, reducing the projected growth in the area by the year 2000 from 220,000 persons to 174,000, and the water quality standards for discharge were to be more stringent than those required by the State Water Resources Control Board (SWRCB). These conditions not only created substantial difficulties for Aliso in retaining its funding support from SWRCB and the federal government, but infuriated state water pollution control officials—an affront which was to have serious consequences when the commission faced the 1976 legislature.

While this conflict with the water quality agency represented perhaps the dominant pattern of interagency relations—reflecting the commissions' genesis in the widespread perception that existing state and local agencies had not adequately protected coastal resources—there were certainly instances of more cooperative behavior. The best example concerns the symbiotic relationship between the coastal commissions and the California Department of Fish and Game in the protection of wetlands. What evolved, in effect, is that the commissions allowed the Fish and Game Department surrogate regulatory authority and the department provided the commissions with expertise and monitoring capability. Rather than having to rely entirely on public acquisitions, as had been the case in the past, the Department of Fish and Game could now intervene on both permit and planning matters, knowing that it would receive a sympathetic hearing from the coastal commissions, who generally supported wetlands protection but lacked any detailed knowledge of which areas merited protection.

Internal dynamics of the commissions

The Coastal Initiative made very little direct effort to structure the internal dynamics of the state and regional commissions. The provision in Section 272743 that each commission elect its own chairman and appoint its own executive director, however, made each commission relatively autonomous. Moreover, the tight deadlines imposed by the statute—ninety days for each permit application and essentially two and a half years for development of a plan for the entire 1100-mile coast—may have created some incentive to submerge internal disagreements in the interests of meeting those deadlines, at least through the final decisions on the Coastal Plan in the summer of 1975. The relative insulation of the commissions from the governor, the state legislature, and from partisan politics in general may also have reduced the incentives for political grandstanding and for ensnarling the commissions in the political ambitions of state officials. On the whole, however, statutory drafters could only hope that the mix of public members and local elected officials, the pressure of tight deadlines, and the general insulation from partisan politics would produce a harmonious and hard-working agency which was able to meet its deadlines and generally to act in a manner consistent with statutory directives.

　　This expectation was most clearly achieved in the state commission. Part of the effective interaction could be attributed to the general homogeneity of basic viewpoints, as the vast majority of commissioners and staff had supported the Coastal Initiative and were deeply committed to seeing it work. Part could also be attributed to the remarkable leadership skills of Mel Lane, who was unanimously elected chairman at the initial meeting and was universally respected for his judgment, his integrity, and his ability to run meetings fairly and expeditiously. Similarly, Joe Bodovitz, the executive director, was highly respected by the commissioners, continued his excellent working relationship with Lane (as both had held similar positions at BCDC), and was able to elicit an enormous amount of work from the staff.

　　Although the 1972 Coastal Initiative clearly gave the coastal commissions a great deal of review authority over the actions of state and local agencies within the coastal zone (and particularly the 1000-yard permit area), it was much less explicit about allocating authority between the state and the regional coastal commissions. While this general independence was tempered by the strong role of the state commission in planning and permit review, the net result was a somewhat ambiguous degree of hierarchical control within the commissions. In practice, however, a rather high degree of cooperation eventually evolved—albeit with a great deal of effort and some notable exceptions. Even regions like the North Coast, which were dominated by commissioners who did not support Proposition 20, had to consider seriously the general guidelines on planning and permit review developed by the state commission if they were to have any influence on the decisions ultimately adopted. Moreover, while there was some tendency in the North Coast region to ignore state decisions on permit appeals, most commissioners ultimately realized that such an attitude created a real hardship for applicants and thus there was some effort to work within state guidelines and at least to inform applicants of the likely consequences of appeal.

Commission decisions: the review of proposed developments

Recall that the coastal commissions' permit review process began only *after* a project had obtained approval of the relevant local governments and other state agencies and that it was a *de novo* review. Thus, an analysis of the commissions' decisions represents a magnificent opportunity to examine the ability of a state government agency to alter the allocation of critical resources from what probably would have taken place in the normal system of control by the economic market and local governments. At the very least, every condition imposed or application denied by the commissions represented a clear effect of their superimposition on the antecedent process of local review.

Moreover, there is some evidence that a simple comparison of developments as approved by local governments and as approved (or denied) by the commissions underestimates the commissions' impact on the overall magnitude and quality of coastal development. A longitudinal study of housing construction in Los Angeles and Ventura counties indicates that the number of building permits in the permit zone declined during the 1972–76 period (compared with pre–1972 figures) while in the area just beyond the permit zone the number increased, thereby suggesting a displacement of some development from the permit zone. In addition, virtually all observers agreed that the quality of proposed developments in the coastal area increased noticeably during the 1973–76 period—again probably an anticipatory response of applicants to the commissions' policies and to the other recently enacted environmental protection laws. Finally, there were a few communities in southern California which changed their development review criteria—for example, off-street parking and bluff setback requirements—in response to coastal commission permit decisions.

One must also understand the role of permit review within the overall implementation of the Coastal Initiative. Unlike most state land use statutes, the initiative combined the dual function of permit review and planning by utilizing the former both to preserve planning options and to stimulate the formulation of planning policies in the context of concrete controversies. Moreover, the permit process provided a base of three years' experience by which the 1976 legislature could evaluate the commissions' performance in deciding whether to renew or alter the commissions' statutory mandate.

The permit review process and consistency with statutory objectives

The permit process began once an applicant had obtained all other local and state permits. He or she then submitted a form to the relevant regional commission describing the nature and location of the proposed project (and, in the South Coast region, its cost) and its probable effects on habitat, water quality, public access, and a number of other areas; for large projects an environmental impact report was also required by California law. After a preliminary analysis, the regional staff assigned the application to either an administrative calendar involving small developments (less than $10,000) or repairs (less than $25,000), a consent calendar for those projects staff felt did not involve any significant issues, or the public hearing calendar reserved for potentially significant or controversial projects. The application was then assigned to the staff person familiar with that area or type of project for more detailed analysis. This normally involved discussion with the applicant and the applicant's staff, personnel from the relevant state and local agencies, and a site visit. The staff then prepared a report and recommendation for the regional commission.

At the commission meeting, the administrative and consent items were voted on together. Discussion of items on the hearing calendar normally involved presentations by the staff and the applicant, as well as testimony from neighbors, environmental and other interest groups, or government officials who wished to speak. In most cases, the permit was voted on at the same meeting. Approval required a simple majority of the total commission membership (not simply those members present) and a two-thirds majority in projects involving dredging and filling, restrictions on physical or scenic access to the coast, or effects on water quality, fisheries, or agricultural land.

Normally, this was the end of the process. About 4 percent of all regional permit decisions were, however, appealed to the state commission by the applicant and/or "any aggrieved party" (meaning anyone who had testified in person or in writing at the regional hearing). This very liberal interpretation of legal standing provided ready access to opponents of development and, in fact, about two thirds of the appeals were brought by environmental groups or neighborhood associations. The decision process at the state level involved two distinct stages. First, the state staff contacted regional staff, the applicant and appellants, personnel in the relevant state and local agencies, and occasionally other actors in preparing its report and recommendation concerning whether the appeal posed "a substantial issue." The public hearing involved rather brief presentations by state staff, the applicant and appellants, and other interested parties. As at the regional level, the hearing was rather informal. If the commission decided that the appeal raised no substantial issue, the decision of the regional commission was final. In the approximately 50 percent of all appeals which the commission decided a substantial issue had been raised—thereby triggering the second stage of the process—additional testimony was taken, and a final vote was deferred until the subsequent meeting to enable the staff to conduct additional analyses and to make a substantive recommendation. At the second meeting, discussion was normally dominated by staff and commissioners. The commission then voted, following the same rules as at the regional level.

About 25 percent of state commission decisions (or about 1 percent of all applications) were subsequently appealed to the courts by the applicant or other "aggrieved party."[14] However, the courts (at least at the appellate level) seldom overturned the commissions' decisions, although appellants sometimes achieved part of their objective through a negotiated settlement.

A general—though, as will be noted, somewhat misleading—overview of the commissions' permit review activity suggests that of the many thousands of permits considered only 3 to 4 percent were ever denied by the regional commissions. In contrast to this miniscule percentage of denials at the regional level, the state commission denied about 40 percent of the cases deemed to have raised a substantial issue. On the basis of these figures, which were essentially the only type of aggregate permit data published by the commissions, one would probably conclude (a) that the regional commissions had very little effect on the pattern of coastal development and (b) that there was an enormous gulf in policy orientation between the state commission and even the most environmentalist regional commissions (for example, the North Central).

The figures are, however, misleading for at least three reasons. First, as indicated previously, they do not include the effect of the commissions on the number and quality of developments *proposed* within the permit zone. While very difficult to quantify, these anticipatory effects were certainly significant. Second, the regional data do not distinguish among the three permit calendars. They thus lump projects having an insignificant effect on coastal resources—for example, the addition of a few rooms to a single family residence, the repair of a highway culvert, or the construction of a small apartment house a half-mile from the coast in highly urbanized Los Angeles— with those projects on the regional hearing calendars which had potentially significant effects on statutory objectives. Given the very broad scope of the commissions' authority (all proposed developments from the seaward boundary of the state's jurisdiction to 1000 yards, or 0.57 miles, inland of the mean high tide line), a large percentage of the proposed developments did not affect coastal resources and thus had no reason to be denied. Third, the figures on both regional and state commission decisions fail to indicate that "permit approvals" covered a wide spectrum from permits approved as submitted by the applicant, to those approved with minor conditions, to those approved with major conditions (normally over the strong objections of the applicant). In fact, permits approved with major conditions were sometimes perceived by the applicant as *de facto* denials.

A more detailed and accurate view of the permit review activities suggests that only a little more than one fifth of the permit applications were considered sufficiently important to require public hearings. Of these applications, the commissioners in the South Coast Region, which handled almost half of all applications, imposed conditions on 20 percent of the permits. This figure rose to 70 percent in the North Central Region (San Francisco and environs).

A more useful gauge of the commissions' record in permit review can be found by looking at the consistency of the decisions with the Coastal Act's major statutory objectives. This has been done on a sample of 166 permit applications appealed to the state commission in the 1973–75 period, a figure which comes close to representing the subset of the most significant and controversial cases that came before the coastal commissions.

The data presented in Table 7.1 show that—with the exception of habitat protection and preserving planning options—the commissions either denied the permit or imposed relevant conditions about 75 percent of the time that any of the seven key statutorily related issues was a major consideration in the permit hearings. Note, however, that the manner in which the relevant issue was addressed varied. If public access or the conversion of agricultural land was the issue, the permit was likely to be denied, while the protection of scenic resources and water quality impacts were often dealt with by approving the project with relevant conditions, for example, landscaping and placing of utility lines underground for the former and better septic systems for the latter. Even the issues where this analysis suggests that the commissions had a comparatively poor record—habitat protection (37 percent), the preservation of planning options (54 percent), and, to a lesser extent, public access (66 percent)—can be partially attributed to methodological difficulties in developing categories of "relevant" conditions. For example, transportation conditions were not coded as relevant to the issue of public access because it could not be ascertained whether this was generally the case; nevertheless, there were certainly instances in the South Coast and other regions where parking restrictions were definitely imposed to improve public access to the beach. Moreover, as we shall see, the commissions did an excellent job of

Table 7.1
Percentage of Permit Appeals in Which Final Decision of Coastal
Commissions "Addressed" Issues Relating to Various Statutory
Objectives (sample of 166 permit applications)

	When Issue Raised, Final Commission Decision			
Issue	Appeals on Which Issue Raised	Relevant Condition(s) + Imposed	Permit = Denied	Total (Percentage of Cases in Which Issue "Addressed")
A. Issues Directly Related to Statutory Objectives				
1. Public access to beach	21	8	58	66
2. Effects on scenic resources or view corridors	24	43	48	91
3. Wildlife habitat	9	n.c.[a]	37	37
4. Effects on water quality	11	51	26	77
5. Geologic hazards /erosion	11	36	44	80
6. Conversion of agricultural land	11	11	59	70
7. Preservation of planning options	19	n.c.[a]	54	54
B. Other issues				
1. Transportation, e.g., parking	20	16	61	77
2. Cumulative impacts on land use	23	12	60	72
3. Consistency with existing development	20	12	72	84

[a]n.c. = not coded because could not identify conditions relevant primarily and exclusively to this issue.

protecting wildlife habitat in and around Humboldt Bay. In short, on these three issues the percentage appeals in which the issue was raised and extent to which relevant conditions were imposed is almost certainly underestimated.

Table 7.1 also presents a similar analysis for three other issues which were probably indirectly related to statutory objectives: transportation, cumulative impacts on land use, and consistency with existing development. This was clearly the case, for example, in the parking restrictions just mentioned. Similarly, cumulative impacts on land use and consistency with existing development were related to the commissions' efforts to restrict development as much as possible to existing urban areas, thereby protecting the scenic resources of the rural coast (among other things). But these issues—all of which were similarly "addressed" by the commissions about 75 percent of the time they were raised—are also traditional preoccupations of planners. This suggests that the professional norms of commission staff may well have supplemented statutory directives in serving as decision guides to the commissions.

In sum, the data in Table 7.1 indicate that, at least for those permit applications which were important or controversial enough to be appealed to the state commission, the commissions either imposed relevant conditions or simply denied the permit application in about 75 percent of the cases in which issues relating to statutory objectives were raised in the staff reports or at the public hearings.

While this analysis of aggregate data provides an indication of the general consistency of permit decisions with statutory objectives, it does not give a sense of how the commissions handled specific cases and their effects on specific areas of the coast. For this we turn to two important examples: wetlands protection around Humboldt Bay and provision of public access at Malibu (Los Angeles County).

The protection of wetlands and agricultural land around Humboldt Bay (North Coast region)

Humboldt Bay was the largest and most productive wetland under the jurisdiction of the coastal commissions, second in the state only to the enormous expanse of San Francisco Bay/Suisun Marsh. Like most wetlands in the state, Humboldt Bay had shrunk in size—from about 27,000 acres a century ago to 16,000 acres by 1973—because of siltation and the reclamation of salt marshes and intertidal flats. The bay and its surrounding agricultural land provided an important link for migratory waterfowl (particularly the Pacific black brant), as well as major nesting areas for egrets, herons, cormorants, and numerous other species. In addition, the bay was a major fisheries resource, providing nursery areas for English sole and several crab species, rearing areas for herring and anchovy, lifelong habitat for large numbers of oysters, mussels, and clams, and transportation routes for salmon and steelhead trout on their way to spawning areas on the Eel River and other tributaries. In fact, the bay and its tributaries annually provided waterfowl hunting for about 25,000 hunter-days, sports-fishing for about 35,000 angler days (exclusive of marine fishing), by far the largest oyster fishery in the entire state, and the largest commercial fishery north of Los Angeles.

But the area around Humboldt Bay was also the largest urban and industrial center on the California coast north of San Francisco. Eureka, with a 1970 population of 24,000, was the administrative and commercial hub of Humboldt County, as well as the major port and mill center for the North Coast lumber industry. On the northern shore of the bay, Arcata (1970 population of 9000) was the home of Humboldt State University. Although the area had historically grown at a very slow rate, a modest (5 percent) population increase during the 1970–74 period subjected the eight miles of marshes and marginal agricultural lands between Eureka and Arcata on the east side of the bay to rather considerable pressures for development between 1972 and 1976. For a map of the area and the location of the major projects during this period, see Figure 7.2.

Although some of the most valuable habitat area in the region was part of a National Wildlife Refuge in 1973—particularly the heron-egret rookery on Indian Island—much of the rest was either privately owned or under the jurisdiction of a variety of public agencies. Virtually all of the undeveloped portions of the bottomland around the bay, particularly those portions subjected to seasonal flooding, provided important foraging and protective habitat during at least part of the year. Thus, one of the responsibilities of the coastal commissions was to protect as much of this habitat as possible while avoiding the inverse condemnation of private property and also permitting needed development in this economically depressed region.

An analysis of the twelve permit cases affecting the Humboldt Bay region (listed in Figure 7.2) indicates, first and foremost, that the coastal commissions did a very good job of protecting wetlands and agricultural land in and around Humboldt Bay during the 1973–76 period.[15] Of the twelve permit applications, six were either denied or withdrawn. Even those which were approved involved very little *net* loss in wildlife habitat, in part because of restrictions on the development process (for example, the prohibition against using dredging soil on the Arcata Freeway), in part because the commissions generally required applicants to purchase off-site habitat comparable in size to what had been destroyed and then return the site to tidal action. In addition, the commissions brought a considerable amount of habitat owned by private parties or development-oriented public agencies under the legal protection of fish and game agencies. This was most notable, of course, in the Woodley Island case, where the entire northern half of the island was transferred from the Harbor Department to the U.S. Fish and Wildlife Service. As a result, both local fish and game officials and environmental group leaders felt there was no appreciable loss in wildlife habitat around Humboldt Bay during the 1973–76 period.

Figure 7.2
Humboldt Bay and Vicinity

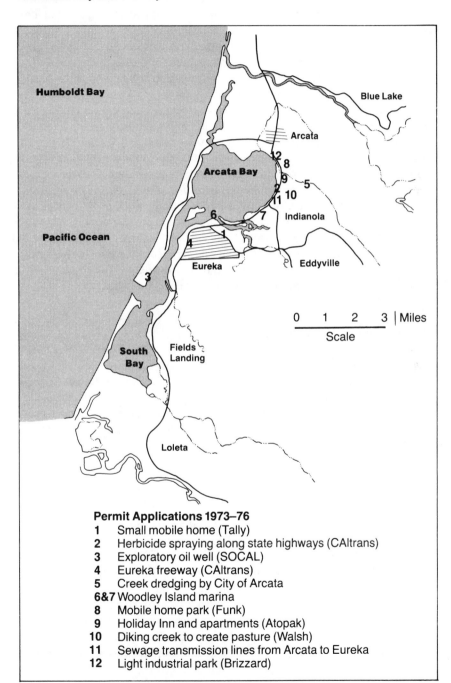

Permit Applications 1973–76
1 Small mobile home (Tally)
2 Herbicide spraying along state highways (CAltrans)
3 Exploratory oil well (SOCAL)
4 Eureka freeway (CAltrans)
5 Creek dredging by City of Arcata
6&7 Woodley Island marina
8 Mobile home park (Funk)
9 Holiday Inn and apartments (Atopak)
10 Diking creek to create pasture (Walsh)
11 Sewage transmission lines from Arcata to Eureka
12 Light industrial park (Brizzard)

This success would not, however, have been possible without the strong appellate process built into the 1972 Coastal Act. In fact, in eight of the twelve cases the state commission imposed more stringent review criteria than the North Coast Regional Commission, denying six permits which had been approved by the region and imposing additional conditions on two others. Moreover, it is quite likely that the threat of appeal forced the Harbor Department finally to accept conditions on the Woodley Island marina which it (and probably the regional commission) deemed unnecessary and/or undesirable. The appellate process would not have worked, however, without the active participation of the Sierra Club, local environmental groups, and, to a lesser extent, the California Department of Fish and Game, for it was they who formally brought the appeals and who presented a counterweight to applicants before the state commission. It is also possible that the appeals process would not have worked as well without the willingness of the regional staff to make the case for wetlands protection and to recommend specific measures to achieve that objective. In fact, there were four cases (Funk, Atopak, Woodley Island, and the Arcata-Eureka interceptor) in which the recommendation of the regional staff was overturned by the regional commission but then largely upheld by the state commission. In these cases, the regional staff essentially provided much of the detailed knowledge of the local situation which was then utilized by their state colleagues.

Providing beach access at Malibu

Probably no single issue was as important in the passage of the 1972 Coastal Initiative as the need to provide greater access to the beaches for the 7 million residents of Los Angeles and the 1.5 million residents of Orange County. While almost half of the 116 miles of coast in this region was under public ownership, recreational demand was enormous—with estimates of as many as 2 million people at the beaches on peak summer weekends.

There were at least four components to "the access problem" in the South Coast region: The first was limited access to the beach and tidelands. This was particularly severe in the twenty-six-mile stretch of Malibu coast in northern Los Angeles County. Second was the limited parking facilities both at public beaches and adjacent neighborhoods. Third was the unavailability of visitor facilities, which again was acute in Malibu. Finally, new high-rise developments and walled-off housing units were dramatically reducing the view corridors from coastal roads and the coastal highway to the beach.

These several issues came to a head in Malibu. Although beaches in the southern third of Malibu were too narrow to provide recreation for large numbers of people, the area nevertheless was the site of one of the most important disputes over access in the entire South Coast region, if not the entire state, in part because it occupied so much of the coast, in part because it raised the issue so clearly of whether wealthy residents should be able to block public access to the state-owned wet sand beaches. In the period between February 1973 and June 1975, the state commission took action on fourteen appeals involving proposed developments between the coastal highway and the ocean (all but one involving single family residences). Of these fourteen, the commission either denied or imposed vertical access conditions on ten and imposed lateral access conditions on two more projects.[16] Since most of the denials explicitly involved attempts to preserve options for public acquisition, the commissions would seem to have been doing a good job of using their permit review authority to protect public access to the coast. In addition, two other Malibu projects involved visitor facilities: In the case of a proposed 200-unit private recreational vehicle park, the state commission reversed the regional commission denial on the grounds that the land would best be used for such a facility rather than for housing, although it also imposed conditions to improve the design of the project and to replace seventy-five recreational vehicle sites with tent campsites. In another case, the state commission approved the conversion of apartments to retail shops on the conditions that the shops be oriented toward beach users and the owner provide additional parking and dedicate a portion of the land for a park.

But the apparent success of the commissions in providing public access requires an important caveat. It must be remembered that through the permit process the commissions could only deny permits in order to preserve acquisition options or require access easements as a condition of development. The effective provision of public access was in turn contingent upon future actions of other agencies and/or the legislature concerning the maintenance of accessways and the provision of funds for public purchase. As we shall see, while some lots were subsequently designated for purchase as part of the 1976 Coastal Parks Bond Act, few, if any, of the accessways have yet been opened to the public because of the unwillingness and/or inability of local and state agencies to assume maintenance and liability responsibilities.

Impacts of the development review process

We now turn to an assessment of the overall impacts of the commissions in three major areas: (1) the provision of greater recreational opportunities through opening accessways and expanding coastal parks and recreation facilities; (2) the protection of wetlands; and (3) the potentially adverse effects of the commissions on the housing market through increases in the cost of land, new construction, and the purchase price of existing units. Each of the three impacts was chosen either because it was a major objective under the act or it was identified by a large sample of public officials and active citizens concerned with implementation of the act.

Access and acquistions   Article X Section 4 of the California Constitution states unequivocally that access to the state's shoreline and adjacent waters shall be provided the public:

No individual, partnership, or corporation, claiming or possessing the frontage or tidal lands of a harbor, bay, inlet, estuary, or other navigable water in this state, shall be permitted to exclude the right of way to such water whenever it is required for public purpose . . . and the Legislature shall enact such laws as will give the most liberal construction to this provision so that access to the navigable waters of this state shall always be attainable for the people thereof.

Despite the many public parks along the coast and the numerous accessways maintained by coastal cities and counties, the need for even greater access, especially in the urban areas, was a major impetus to the passage of the 1972 Coastal Initiative. The combined pressures of an ever increasing population, the mismatch between substantial access in the northern counties and the population in the south, the rapidly diminishing open spaces and available sandy beaches, and the walling off of large stretches of the coast made the provision of access a central concern of the commissions.

To begin with, the commissions exercised their permit authority to win a fair number of dedications of lateral accessways across beachfronts and a more limited number of vertical accessways from the nearest public road to the beach from individual permit applicants, although a good deal of regional variation existed; from 1973 to 1976 the number of dedications that were incorporated into approved permits varied from 2 in the North Coast to 9 individual and 5 subdivisions in the North Central to 123 in the South Coast regions. The varying interest by commissions appears to have paralleled need. In Los Angeles and Orange counties much of the coastline was developed and, short of acquiring the remaining undeveloped parcels of land, one of the few existing ways of creating more access to the beach was through permit conditions. In contrast, in the rural counties of the North Coast where access is far less of a problem, the issue was seldom raised.

Beyond the point of requiring access dedications, the causal theory underlying the act fell short. A dedication of access could be required, but the commissions could not guarantee that the accessway would be opened. For lateral accessways this was not too serious a problem at least under the 1972 act. The property owner, in effect, agreed not to cordon off or develop the strip of land covered by the dedication (usually from three to twenty-five feet from the mean high tide) but promised little more. The accessway was simply left in its natural state and questions of improvements, maintenance, and liability costs were rarely considered. For the all-important vertical accessways, however, paths, walkways, and roadways from Coastal Highway 1 or the nearest public road to the beach were involved. These typically required improvements and always involved maintenance and liability costs. Therefore, most vertical access dedications stipulated that the accessway would be made available for public use contingent upon a public or private agency assuming the expenses and legal responsibilities involved.

The coastal commissions did not have the legal or financial authority to assume such responsibilities themselves, nor could they require others to do so. When they turned to other agencies, their requests generally fell on deaf ears. They received much sympathy but no financial aid from the state legislature. And with only a couple of exceptions, neither other state agencies, such as the California Department of Parks and Recreation, nor local governments were willing to accept the responsibility and the costs for opening and maintaining commission-won accessways. The end result, of course, was that little access actually materialized in the 1973–76 period. For example, in the very congested Malibu area, only three vertical accessways had actually been dedicated between 1973 and 1976, and of these, only one had been improved, clearly marked, and open for use.[17]

The only other instances in which vertical accessways were opened as a result of permit conditions imposed by the commissions were those incorporated into larger commercial or residential developments not requiring action by a local or state agency. For instance, the Hotel del Coronado (along the San Diego coastline) opened a well-marked accessway across the hotel property in an area of the coast where the public would otherwise have been denied entrance to the beach. Though similar accessways have been promised in developments such as the Westport Beach Club in Playa del Rey in Los Angeles, they have yet to materialize.

It may seem unfair to fault the Coastal Act for failing to include adequate mechanisms for connecting permits to the actual opening of accessways. After all, the act basically established a four-year planning and permit review process pending definitive decisions by the 1976 legislature. Preserving options by denying some permits outright and placing access conditions on others obviously preserved options for future action. Yet the proponents of the act promised access; the voters of the state surely expected access; and the commissions demonstrated their awareness of such expectations by trying hard within their limited capacity to encourage property owners, other government agencies, or anyone else to assume the dedications the commissions had won. This suggests that both the public and the commission viewed their responsibility as more than simply wringing easements and promises of dedication from coastal property owners. The fact that so few of the critical vertical accessways were opened by 1976 (or since) points to a serious misconception by the act's framers that it was a simple step between permit conditions and actual impacts.

A related problem surfaced with respect to the access to be provided through acquisitions for coastal parks, recreation, and wetlands protection. The commissions could deny development as a means of preserving options and did so on numerous occasions. But they did not have the funds to actually purchase and manage additional parks. In this instance, however, the issue was resolved in a more positive manner.

As part of their planning function, the commissioners devoted a good deal of effort to generating publicity about the need for greater acquisitions, to developing criteria for setting priorities among acquisitions, and to ranking 154 prime acquisition sites. Priority was assigned to (1) lands best suited to serve the recreational needs of urban populations, (2) lands of significant environmental importance, such as wetlands, and (3) of highest priority, lands in either of the above categories proposed for development or use incompatible with their basic resource and recreational value. The development of specific criteria and the emphasis on urban sites was contrary to the traditional approach to acquisition followed by the state legislature and the Department of Parks and Recreation. The legislature had often previously treated park acquisition as another pork-barrel issue, while recommendations from the Parks Department had traditionally emphasized the purchase of large tracts in rural areas rather than much more expensive (per unit area) urban acquisitions.

It followed from the commissions' focus on urban area acquisitions and sites of imminent development that the region of greatest need was the South Coast. In Malibu, for example, the commissions recommended the acquisition of approximately 420 acres of prime beach, bluff, and wetlands properties, at an average cost of $26,000 per acre (in 1975 dollars) for a total cost of more than $10 million. Likewise, in Orange County, an incredibly expensive 1050 acres of the Irvine coast (estimated cost, $20 million) was targeted for acquisition.

Overall, the acquisitions on the commissions' list ranged from extremely large sites, such as 2500 acres at Fort Ross (estimated cost, $855,930) all the way down to additions of a few acres to existing parks and wetlands. The estimated purchase cost of 131 of the 154 sites was $200 million. Realistically, of course, due to inflation, the conservative nature of the original estimates, and the time lag between the time the list was developed and when acquisition could actually take place, the cost of the 131 sites (as well as the 23 sites without costs estimates) would likely be much higher than suggested by the commissions. While there was sentiment in the legislature favoring park acquisitions, it was not exclusively for coastal parks and wetlands, nor for the specific sites identified by the commissions. Consequently, after extensive negotiations among key legislators, the commissions, the governor, local governments, and environmental and development groups, the Nejedly-Hart State, Urban and Coastal Bond Act of 1976 was passed and placed on the November ballot. The Bond Act was for a total of $280 million, but included only $120 million for coastal acquisitions (approximately two fifths of the amount proposed by coastal commissions), $85 million for all cities and counties for local recreation projects, $34 million for improvement of existing state parks, $15 million for wildlife management, and $26 million for inland water sports and camping areas. Yet, a major coastal acquisitions package was before the voters. At a time when most all other government spending measures were going down to defeat at the polls in California and across the nation, the Bond Act was approved by 51 percent of the state's voters in November 1976.

Actual acquisitions for the 1978 fiscal year were subsequently spelled out by the 1977 legislature in AB 924. Of the 25 sites in the bill, 16 were from the commissions' March 1976 list of 154 sites—although only about a third were from the highest priority category. Clearly, the commissions' grand acquisition design was not being carried out in a comprehensive manner (and probably would not be in the foreseeable future). Yet an important step had been taken. Thus, for example, of the 420 acres designed by the commissions for purchase in the Malibu area, 104 acres, at Malibu bluff, were included in the AB 294 acquisitions.

The proportion of the commissions' impact on acquisitions is impossible to determine exactly. But the commissions' highlighting of the issue, assaying of the entire coastline, setting of priorities among acquisitions based on the principles of the Coastal Act and Coastal Plan, and concerted effort on behalf of subsequent acquisitions suggests that their contribution was substantial.

Wetlands protection   Wetlands, made up of the tidal marshes and mudflats and related freshwater marshes where the land meets the sea, are a crucial component of the marine food chain and the coastal water system. Yet, coastal estuaries and wetlands have been dredged for ports and marinas, subjected to sedimentation from upland erosion, filled in for development, used as sumps for urban sewage and industrial waste, and denied needed freshwater inflow through water diversions. The result has been a two-thirds reduction in the coastal wetland acreage since 1900, with two thirds of the remaining acreage located in the San Francisco Bay. In the southern half of the state (from Morrow Bay to the Mexican border), coastal wetlands acreage has been reduced to one fourth the 1900 level. Remaining wetlands in southern California total an estimated 31,700 acres, of which 18,600 are open water.

Of all the goals of the 1972 Coastal Act, wetlands protection was the one adhered to most closely. Through the permit process the commissions imposed a virtual moratorium on all building in the wetlands and placed conditions on development along feeder streams and floodways. Though the actual number of permit applications involved were relatively few in number, the consistent denials or strict conditioning by the commissions clearly signaled their position. The commissions' attitude was further illustrated by their decisions on the proposals for development at Humboldt Bay, where either at the regional level or on appeal to the state commission, no major encroachments were allowed.

A similar example is the case of the Los Penasquitos Lagoon in San Diego County. This case (although it goes somewhat beyond our focus here on the

1972 Coastal Act) also illustrates how the commission effectively used their expanded permit authority in wetlands areas under the 1976 act. The salt-marsh area of Los Penasquitos Lagoon had already been under the management of the Department of Parks and Recreation for some time but the upland freshwater marsh and surrounding buffer zone were not. Under the 1972 act the commissions allowed no new development in or around the lagoon, to the extent of its 1000-yard authority. Yet they had no authority over the inland area of the lagoon or its three feeder streams. Thus they could not curtail the expanding industrial park along Soledad Creek which was pushing into the creek's floodway and which would ultimately have an adverse effect on the lagoon. Under the 1976 act the regional commission imposed conditions on most new developments in the industrial park to protect the creek's floodway and issued one outright denial. Of equal significance, AB 924 provided for purchase of the inland freshwater marsh portion of the lagoon along with a buffer zone. The combination of the acquisitions program in and about the lagoon and restriction of development along the feeder streams through the permit process has been a major step in assuring the long-term protection of the lagoon.

The importance accorded wetlands protection by the commissions was also reflected in other acquisition efforts. Of the commissions' 154 recommended purchases in 1976, 46 were for wetlands habitats. And of the 16 acquisitions on the commissions' list included in AB 924, 5 were from the wetlands category.

Housing costs   One of the most controversial impacts of the commissions has been their effects on the cost of housing. It is controversial mainly because opponents of the commissions have contended that prices for coastal residential sites have risen dramatically because of the commissions' restric-tive policies. Moreover, opponents have argued that the commissions had little regard for the desires of many moderate- or lower-income families to live along the coast.

The rebuttal by commission defenders has been, first, that the commis-sions' mandate calls only for environmental protection and provision of greater coastal access, without consideration of economic implications. Second, commissions' proponents have argued that the commissions have been instrumental in protecting existing neighborhoods of moderately priced homes and preventing the conversion of rental apartments to condominiums (for example, in Venice and Santa Monica in Los Angeles County) in instances where local governments have failed. Third, supporters have also noted that the commissions have generally required that at least some moderately priced homes and rental units must be included before large multiple-family developments or subdivisions can be approved.

For all the outcry over rising housing costs, there is an amazing lack of good empirical evidence. Nevertheless, the logic behind the criticism of the commissions is a fairly straightforward application of market economics. If the commissions impose new restrictions on and/or prevent development of sites in the coastal zone while demand for coastal sites continues to rise, several results should follow.

First, the value of undeveloped land, especially larger holdings, that have come under the regulation of the commissions should decrease in market value. Indeed, some evidence indicates that the assessed value of undeveloped parcels in the coastal permit zone were revised downward as a result of the uncertainties over their prospects for development under the commissions. In Los Angeles County, for example, owners of undeveloped land in the permit zone were granted a 10 percent reduction in assessed valuation.[18] A comparison of the rise in value of undeveloped land in the permit area in the city of Ventura and inland several miles between 1971 and 1975 showed the rise inland was 15 percent higher than along the coast. This suggests that, all else being equal, the commissions' presence "depressed" the market value, as reflected in assessed value, of undeveloped land in the permit area.

Second, the price of developed sites, of which sites for housing constitute the majority, should rise in value. Prices should rise because as demand continues to grow (presumably people are still eager to live along the coast), the supply of new houses is artificially depressed (because of the commissions' regulatory policies) and the resale price of existing units is increased by buyers competing for the limited number of resale units. Stories of drastic escalations in resale value of homes along the coast abound. But during the commissions' existence a substantial (though lesser) rise also occurred inland, thus leading to the suspicion that something other than the commissions was responsible for the rise in prices on (and off) the coast. The appropriate question, then, is what proportion of the rise is due to the commissions and what proportion to other factors?

The most sophisticated study of the effects of the commissions on housing costs is that recently conducted by Kneisel.[19] He analyzed all actual resale housing prices for single-family dwellings in the 1000-yard coastal permit zone, resale prices in a border zone approximately 800 to 900 yards wide just landward of the permit zone, and a sample of resales several miles inland from the coast in Los Angeles County. His study shows that throughout the entire period (1972–76) the average sale price of housing in the coastal permit zone was higher by several thousand dollars than in either the border area or inland. More important, in light of the debate over the commissions' effect on housing costs, although there was a precipitous increase in prices that coincided with the starting of the commissions in January 1973, prices were rising in all three areas, presumably due to more systematic factors such as inflation.

Nevertheless, it is important to gauge the precise contribution of the commissions to the rise in prices in the permit zone. To estimate the size of this impact, Kneisel first adjusted all prices for a variety of housing characteristics that would otherwise affect differences in the prices of houses in the three areas (e.g., number of rooms, floor area). Using several different regression models, he then examined the unique contribution of construction costs, mortgage rates, unemployment, population growth, density, and the presence of the coastal commissions on the adjusted resale prices in each area. The analysis shows that after allowing for the impact of construction costs and other factors on prices, a net increase in the permit zone of approximately $4000 per house remains to be accounted for. While some of this increase may be caused by factors such as local down-zoning, which are not figured into the analysis, the $4000 appears the best estimate available of the maximum dollar impact on the sale price of homes in the permit zone of Los Angeles County that resulted from the various restrictions on development (real and perceived) imposed by the coastal commissions. The $4000 figure represents 7 percent of the mean sale price of houses in the permit zone from 1973 through 1975.

The third result that should follow from placing restrictions on development along the coast is an increase in the value of unregulated sites immediately adjacent to the permit zone. This should occur because some people wishing to reside close to the coast but deterred from buying higher priced homes in the permit zone will choose to buy in the next closest location. This in turn may cause a slight rise in the price of houses in these adjacent areas, but prices should not be as great as in the regulated area. Kneisel's results suggest that this is what happened. Repeating the regression analysis, this time for the border zone, he figured an estimated maximum impact of slightly more than $1000 on the average sale prices of homes.

These results provide the best indication available that at least in Los Angeles County the commissions had a discernible impact on housing costs. It is not an impact that the commissions welcomed nor one called for in their statute. Yet it is not the massive transfer of wealth from the "poor to the rich" nor the kind of added cost that generates "class conflict" that the commissions have been accused of. More accurately, the transfer is between the moderate to wealthy residents on the coast before 1973 and the wealthy ones who are gradually replacing them.

Summary of impacts

Given the extraordinary difficulty most public agencies face in achieving any significant positive impact, overall the coastal commissions must be judged fairly successful in achieving several of the key objectives of the Coastal Act. Of the three principal statutory objectives—wetlands protection, the protection of scenic views of the ocean, and the provision of public access to the coast—the coastal commissions were quite successful on the first two. In both cases, the policy directives of the act were quite clear; the commissions' permit authority was generally adequate; the agency leaders were committed to the goals; and, finally, changes in public opinion, socioeconomic conditions, and other factors during the 1973–76 period did not undermine the pursuit of these objectives. Moreover, the high priority accorded wetlands in subsequent acquisitions programs augurs well for permanent wetlands protection. The record on public access was not nearly so successful. The 1972 Coastal Act did not provide the coastal commissions (or any other state or local agencies) sufficient authority to manage accessways or to purchase coastal parcels for recreational purposes. The commissions did achieve some success in this area, nevertheless, through maintaining interest in and developing a program of acquisitions that was partially realized through the Nejedly-Hart Bond Act. On the whole, then, the commissions were quite successful in achieving two of the three principal statutory objectives.

Finally, the moderately adverse impact that the commissions appear to have had on the cost of housing was not intended under the Coastal Initiative, though it may have been inevitable. It is hard to imagine that any statute which restricts certain types of development, lowers the density of development, and requires additional checkpoints in the development process would not contribute to the rising costs of both developed and the remaining developable sites.

The development of the Coastal Plan

Up to now we have focused on the adjudicatory function of the coastal commissions, namely, the review of applications for development within the 1000-yard permit area. We have examined the general stringency of permit decisions, their consistency with statutory objectives, and the impacts of the permit process on public access, wetlands, and housing costs.

We now turn to the other principal task of the commissions—the preparation of a Coastal Plan to be presented to the 1976 legislature. The two processes were, of course, interrelated. Permit decisions were to protect planning options. And, as a practical matter, the permit review experience would provide guidance in developing plan policies, particularly in areas such as the location and intensity of permissible development. Likewise, as the plan policies evolved they provided guidance in permit review, particularly starting in late 1975 after the adoption of the Coastal Plan by the commissions.

Nevertheless, the principal function of the Coastal Plan was not to guide the commissions' adjudicatory decisions during the 1973-76 interim period but rather to serve as a proposal to the 1976 legislature—consistent with the objectives of Proposition 20—outlining the detailed policies needed to guide the long-term utilization of coastal resources and the institutions necessary to administer those policies. The planning process was to be an open one, with extensive public participation on the first round of planning to take place separately in each of the six regions, and then again when the state commission synthesized proposals from the six regions.

The 1972 Coastal Initiative did far less to structure the planning process than it did to guide interim permit review. The initiative required the plan to be consistent with a set of general objectives, all of which had a strong environmental "tilt" but provided little meaningful guidance. It also required the plan to incorporate a number of components, only a few of which provided much substantive direction. Finally, the statute said very little about the manner in which the plan was to be developed—only that the regional commissions were to present their recommendations, after public hearings in each county, to the state commission by April 1, 1975, and that the state commission was to adopt the plan by December 1, 1975. In short, the only explicit requirements in the Coastal Initiative for the plan and the planning process were that public access and environmental protection be accorded high priority, the plan be completed within definite deadlines, and that the state commission be ultimately responsible for the content of the plan.

Given this minimal guidance and the enormous conflicts involved in proposing policies for the very large and diverse expanse of the coastal planning zone—an area 1100 miles long and approximately 5 miles wide—it was no mean achievement that the commissions managed to prepare on time a Coastal Plan generally consistent with statutory objectives and to build sufficient political support to shepherd a reasonable facsimile of the plan through the 1976 legislature. This achievement was the result of an enormous amount of work by staff and commissioners and of a general strategy which emphasized building public understanding and support and developing a cooperative relationship between the state and the regional commissions.

Instead of attempting to anticipate preferences of the state's legislators, state commissioners and staff decided to develop a plan consistent with their preferences and the act's objectives. In the process they hoped to garner sufficient public support to convince the legislature to go along with their plan. This approach was based on perceptions about the legislature, including uncertainty about who the key members would be in 1976, doubts that even key legislative committees were sufficiently interested to devote large periods of time to plan formulation, and past experience which indicated that development interests and local governments were sufficiently strong that a plan consistent with the act's objectives would not emerge without a long campaign to mobilize public support. The strategy was also based on the belief that the success of the Coastal Initiative had given the commissions a strong popular mandate which was at least implicitly critical of the previous performance of the legislature and state and local agencies. Finally, it was based on the knowledge that a similar strategy of using the preparation of a plan as a means of mobilizing political support for a stronger legislative mandate had been successfully utilized by BCDC and was worth trying to repeat even in the far more complex and politically controversial case of protection of the state's entire 1100-mile coastline.

The strong emphasis on "participatory planning" involved a number of tactics. First, in order to facilitate public participation and understanding, the plan was broken into nine elements—marine resources, geology, coastal land resources, energy, recreation, appearance and design, transportation, intensity of development, and government powers and funding—and attention was focused on the development of fairly general policies by the regional and state commissions after extensive public hearings. The separate elements were then integrated into a preliminary plan, which was subjected to additional hearings before it was revised and adopted as the final plan by the state commission. The second basic component of the planning process was the development of a cooperative arrangement between the state and the regional commissions. Because coastal issues were more easily comprehended at the local and regional levels, the state staff clearly recognized that the participatory strategy would have to be implemented primarily by the regional commissions, which were more accessible to people. Nevertheless, state-level officials retained final authority. It was the state staff who integrated the (often-conflicting) proposals from the six regions which after further hearings, were adopted and/or revised by the state commission.

The Coastal Plan adopted by the state commission in September 1975 consisted of 162 policies plus an additional 200 pages of maps and notes applying those policies in a very general way to different areas along the coast. For example, in order to protect scenic views, the plan prohibited development on beaches, dunes, and coastal bluffs and required new developments in scenic areas to be subordinate to natural landforms and views of the ocean from the coastal road not to be obstructed. In order to expand public access to the ocean, the plan recommended that new development between the coastal road and the ocean be required to provide public accessways; that water-related recreational facilities to serve visitors be accorded priority over other types of development along the coast; but that recreational use of the coast be limited where necessary to prevent damage to valuable habitat areas. In order to protect wetlands, the commissions recommended that developments near wetlands provide suitable buffer areas; that developments within wetlands be required to restore to tidal action other areas equal in value to those damaged; and that dredging or filling of wetlands to provide recreational boating facilities be prohibited. With respect to general controls on coastal development, the plan recommended that new development be concentrated in or adjacent to existing urbanized areas; that priority be given to coastal-dependent development, for example, ports and water-related recreational facilities, over general housing and commercial projects; and that energy facilities be permitted only under stringent environmental safeguards.

Probably the most important and controversial section of the plan concerned the institutional arrangements deemed necessary to carry out these substantive policies. In this regard, the commissions first recommended that the jurisdiction of the successor coastal agency by expanded from the 1000-yard inland boundary under the 1972 act to cover all significant coastal resources, or an area 5 to 8 miles wide along the northern and central coasts and 1 to 2 miles wide from Los Angeles to the Mexican border. Within this broadened jurisdiction, local governments were to be given four years to bring their land use plans and zoning ordinances into conformity with Coastal Plan policies—as certified by the successor coastal agency. Local governments would thereafter exercise principal development review authority, although most important decisions were subject to appeal to the successor coastal agency. Finally, the plan recommended that a new agency, the Coastal Conservancy, be created to acquire and manage public accessways and habitat areas and to provide some land-banking and redevelopment functions —in short to provide some of the management functions necessary to supplement the regulatory activities of the successor coastal agency.

On the whole, the Coastal Plan was quite consistent with the objectives of the Coastal Initiative. This conformity is reflected in a survey of attentive elites who took interest in the work and effects of the commissions: 79 percent of those who had voted for Proposition 20 supported the plan while 81 percent of those who had opposed the initiative likewise opposed the plan.[20] By faithfully implementing the substantial changes in coastal resource utilization mandated by Proposition 20, the coastal commissions essentially assured that the Coastal Plan would arouse at least as much controversy in the 1976 legislature as had the coastal bills four years earlier.

Reformulation of the Coastal Act

Submission of the plan to the legislature marked the turning point of the Coastal Act of 1972 from implementation to the reformulation stage. Such change was a natural occurrence built into the act. What could not be foreseen by the act's framers four years earlier, however, were the changes in the broader social and political environment which occurred between 1972 and 1976.

California, like the rest of the nation, was emerging from a serious recession in 1974–75 which was particularly severe for the construction industry. In commissioning a study of the economic consequences of the coastal plan, the legislature indicated that it would be very sensitive to considerations of economic conditions. While polls indicated that public opinion generally supported the commissions in 1976, they also indicated a strong sentiment for returning some, and possibly even principal, authority for development review to local governments, as well as strong public support for the protection of property rights. A survey of the attentive public indicated widely different evaluations of the commissions' performance, with environmental groups and many community organizations strongly supportive, business groups and coastal property owners just as strongly opposed, and state and local agencies more or less evenly split. And the 1976 legislature itself was split between the generally supportive assembly and the very uncertain senate. Nevertheless, three developments since senate rejection of coastal legislation in 1972 promised a more even match this time: (1) awareness that another initiative was a possibility, although no one explicitly advocated such action; (2) several appointments to the Senate Natural Resources Committee which gave it a more even composition; and (3) the change from an opponent (Reagan) to a probable proponent (Brown) as governor.

The 1976 legislative session

In early 1976 major pieces of legislation incorporating the principal features of the Coastal Plan began to move through the legislature. The most important bill, introduced by Senator Beilenson (Dem., Los Angeles) sought to establish the basic policies to guide future utilization of coastal resources and to distribute authority for the implementation of those policies among the successor coastal agency, other state agencies, special districts (for example, ports), and local governments. While the bill did not include all the policies in the Coastal Plan, it contained substantial portions of most of them and, in many places, referred to specific plan policies.

The proponents of the Beilenson bill—the coastal commissions, environmental groups, a few state agencies, and the Democratic leadership within the legislature—sought to maintain the central thrust of the bill in its emphasis on environmental protection, public access, and a strong coastal agency, while at the same time accepting the compromises needed to obtain passage.

Opposition to the bill came from three basic groups. On the one hand were many state agencies which accepted the general outlines of the bill but sought rather limited and specific amendments, chiefly to reassert their functional authority within the coastal zone while at the same time acknowledging the need for some sort of concurrent jurisdiction by the successor coastal agency. At the other extreme were the building trades unions, property rights organizations, some business groups, and a few cities (notably Long Beach and Los Angeles) which essentially rejected any real role for a successor coastal agency and preferred a return to conditions as they existed before Proposition 20. In between these two groups were several critical groups— most notably moderate development interests, labor unions, and local government associations—which accepted the principle of a successor coastal agency but sought major revisions in the Beilenson bill in order to delegate more authority to local governments or to provide greater balance between economic development and environmental protection.

Between February 1976 when Senator Beilenson introduced the coastal bill and September, when Governor Brown signed it into law, the fate of coastal protection followed a roller-coaster path as the legislation was amended, defeated, resurrected, passed back and forth between assembly and senate, and finally saved by a last minute compromise with the AFL-CIO negotiated by Governor Brown. The resultant legislation included not only a coastal land use regulatory statute to carry forward the work of the coastal commissions— the Coastal Zone Act of 1976—but also companion legislation (the Nejedly-Hart Bond Act) to provide for parks and wetlands acquisitions subject to voter approval in November 1976. Also enacted was a bill establishing the

California Coastal Conservancy to provide grants to state and local agencies for the acquisition and management of accessways, buffer zones around parks, and wildlife habitat—powers not given to the coastal commissions by either the 1972 or the 1976 acts.

A comparison of the 1976 Coastal Act with the 1972 Initiative and the 1975 Plan

As has been emphasized throughout this discussion, the 1972 Coastal Initiative had a strong general tilt in favor of environmental protection rather than economic development. More specific objectives had to be inferred from those instances involving proposed developments affecting wetlands, public access, view sheds, agricultural land, and geological hazards in which a two-thirds vote was required and/or conditions (or denials) were specifically mandated. The 1975 Coastal Plan continued the strong environmental orientation of the initiative but "fleshed out" its implications by adding numerous policies designed to protect wetlands, to provide physical and scenic access to the coast, to concentrate new developments in existing urbanized areas, and to give priority to coastal-dependent development such as ports and water-oriented recreation. In addition, the plan added an entirely new set of policies relating to the protection of special coastal communities and moderately priced housing. The legislature's reaction to the plan was to retain the emphasis on wetlands protection, public access, priority for coastal-dependent development, and, to a lesser extent, concentration of development in urbanized areas (including strong protection for prime agricultural land). But it also increased the emphasis on meeting the housing and energy needs of the state, protecting the property rights of coastal residents, and involving local governments in the implementation process—as well as indicating in greater detail than did the plan the manner in which these objectives should be balanced against the statute's general goals of access and environmental protection.

The comparison of objectives among the three documents can perhaps best be seen by examining specific policies—for example, the requirements for public access in new developments. Proposition 20 simply required that "access to publicly owned or used beaches, recreation areas, and natural reserves be increased to the maximum extent possible by appropriate dedication" and made the granting of permits involving access contingent upon a two-thirds affirmative vote. Following are the relevant policies from the 1975 Coastal Plan and the 1976 Coastal Act.

1975 Coastal Plan (Policy 123)
New developments shall provide access to the shoreline except when

1976 Coastal Act (Sec. 30212)
Public access from the nearest public roadway to the shoreline

adequate access exists nearby, the development is too small to include an accessway, or access would endanger public or military safety, fragile natural resources, or agricultural land. When access dedications are infeasible, in lieu fees shall be required to help provide access elsewhere.

shall be provided except when adequate access exists nearby or would adversely affect public or military safety, fragile resources, or agricultural lands. A dedicated accessway shall not be opened to public use until a public agency or private association agrees to accept responsibility for maintenance and liability.

As can be seen, the principal changes made by the legislature were the deletion of the requirement for in-lieu fees and the addition of a requirement that accessways not be opened until maintenance and security could be provided. In effect, the 1976 Coastal Act retained the essential thrust of the plan policy, while it also met some of the concerns of property owners that they should not be responsible for providing access beyond the boundary of their property and that someone else should bear the maintenance costs.

For these objectives, the 1975 plan and the 1976 Coastal Act incorporated more sophisticated theories than the 1972 initiative about how the goals should be achieved. As indicated earlier, Proposition 20 implicitly assumed that its objectives of protecting habitat and access could be achieved through the commissions' total control over development for 3 miles seaward and 1000 yards landward of the mean high tide line. While such authority was adequate to protect view sheds from the coastal highway and to protect most wetlands, the absence of authority to purchase and to manage accessways and beachfront lots proved a serious impediment to actually providing access. In addition, the initiative gave the commissions no authority to affect the demand for coastal resources brought about, for example, by the inducements of property and estate taxes for more intensive uses of land.

The Coastal Plan addressed most of these deficiencies and many of its innovations were incorporated into the 1976 Coastal Act. The plan's recommendation for broadening the commissions' geographical jurisdiction (to five miles inland in most places) provided better authority to protect wetlands (by including upstream areas), recreational areas (such as the Santa Monica mountains) near the coast, and agriculture dependent upon a coastal climate. In addition, the recommendations for extensive acquisitions, a Coastal Conservancy, and the provision of public transportation and parking areas near the coast demonstrated a much more sophisticated understanding of what was required actually to provide beach access. Finally, the plan made some effort to address the demand for coastal resources through its suggestions concerning revisions in the property tax system as applied to agricultural land and timber, as well as its innovative recommendations for energy conservation (thereby reducing the need for petroleum drilling and energy facilities along the coast). The 1976 legislature shortened the proposed geographical jurisdiction to approximately 1000 yards landward plus extensive "bulges," in the process deleting protection of coastal-dependent agriculture (but not prime agricultural land which happened to be near the coast) as a statutory objective. It retained the Coastal Conservancy, but cut the proposed recreational and wetlands acquisition in half. It required tax assessors to take into account development restrictions imposed by the commissions in determining the taxable value of property; in addition, separate legislation completely revised the method of taxing timber. Finally, the legislature deleted the energy conservation recommendation as duplicative of authority previously assigned to the Energy Commission. In sum, the Coastal Plan and, to a slightly lesser extent, the 1976 Coastal Act addressed far more of the important causal factors affecting statutory objectives than had the 1972 Coastal Initiative.

While the plan and the 1976 Coastal Act provided clearer policy guidance to implementing officials and gave them more adequate jurisdiction than did the Coastal Initiative, Proposition 20 had assigned implementation to more sympathetic officials, that is, the coastal commissioners, whereas both the plan and particularly the 1976 act assigned principal responsibility to local governments after the certification of local coastal programs (LCPs). Proposition 20 also provided a much more hierarchically integrated system, with the state commission responsible for all important decisions within the 1000-yard permit zone. This was not greatly changed in the plan, as the coastal commissions were to retain primary jurisdiction over major public works and energy projects and to have extensive appellate review of local decisions, even after certification of LCPs. The 1976 Coastal Act, however, provided less appellate review following LCP certification and more liberal criteria for the exclusion of urban areas from any review by the commissions; as a result, in urban areas the commissions' review authority after certification would essentially be limited to major energy and public works projects and to developments within 300 feet of a beach or 100 feet of a wetland. In addition, the 1976 act went into considerable detail to clarify the substantive scope of the commissions' jurisdiction and to make sure the commissions deferred to other state agencies in the latter's area of expertise. With respect to sewage treatment plants, for example, the coastal commissions would have jurisdiction over the location, visual appearance, and scope of service area served by the facility, while decisions concerning the extent of treatment were expressly reserved to state water pollution control authorities.

Turning to other aspects of statutory structuring, the legislature decided to reject the requirement in Proposition 20 and the plan for a two-thirds vote on most major permits. But the 1976 act retained Proposition 20's provision to encourage citizen participation in agency proceedings and in judicial review, while rejecting the plan's suggestions for recovery of attorney's fees and civil penalties to litigants seeking to prevent violations of the act. Finally, while the 1976 act failed to renew the initiative's provisions insulating the commissions from annual legal and financial scrutiny by the legislature, it established the commissions as permanent agencies without any sunset clause.

In conclusion, if one assumes that Proposition 20 was instituted primarily to protect wetlands and other wildlife habitat and to provide physical and scenic access to the coast, it is clear that the Coastal Plan would have attained those objectives better than the Coastal Initiative because of the plan's clearer policy directives, more extensive geographical jurisdiction, and provisions for the acquisition and management of accessways and threatened wetlands. Just as clearly, the 1976 legislature rejected some provisions of the 1975 plan with respect to the coastal commissions' authority over state and local agencies throughout the five-mile wide coastal zone. In comparison to the plan, the 1976 Coastal Act restricted the commissions' authority to the protection of specific coastal resources (especially wetlands and access) and incorporated procedures designed to reduce the paperwork burden on permit applicants, increase the role of local elected officials in the implementation process, and balance access and environmental protection against the housing and energy needs of the state, particularly in urban areas.

It is not at all clear, however, whether the 1972 initiative or the 1976 Coastal Act did a better job of providing access and protecting wetlands. On the one hand, Proposition 20 did not worry about balancing environmental concerns with housing and energy needs; it provided a much more hierarchically integrated structure, with the state commission clearly able to override the decisions of other state and local agencies on development applications; and it insulated the commissions from annual legislative review and the attendant pressure legislators might exert on important permit cases. On the other hand, the 1976 Coastal Act provided clearer policy directives, with the balancing provisions probably having little effect on access and wetlands; the larger geographical jurisdiction and the provisions for acquisitions and the Coastal Conservancy provided for in the act have increased the ability to actually provide access and to manage wetlands; the act's revisions of tax assessment practices have probably had some dampening effect on pressures for more intensive utilization of coastal land. The most subtle but perhaps most important provision of the act was the creation of a "permanent" coastal agency and the (supposed) integration of coastal concerns into the decision structure of state and local agencies. These measures were intended to alter expectations of what constituted acceptable development along the coast and thereby reduce the enormous opposition the commissions aroused during the 1972–76 period by superimposing more stringent restrictions on projects which had already been approved by local (and state) agencies. On balance, we suggest that the 1976 act provided at least as much protection for wetlands and probably slightly greater public access to the coast than did the 1972 initiative.

Application of the implementation framework to coastal land use regulation in California

The California Coastal Initiative of 1972 mandated the commissions to "preserve, protect, and where possible, to restore the resources of the coastal zone for the enjoyment of current and succeeding generations." More specifically, the commissions were charged with maximizing public access to the beaches, preserving the scenic beauty of the coast and particularly views of the ocean from the coastal highway, and protecting wetlands and other wildlife habitats. They were to accomplish these objectives both during the interim (1973–76) permit review process and on a continuing basis by proposing, and then convincing the legislature to adopt, an enforceable Coastal Plan consistent with these goals.

This mandate was no mean task. While precise estimates are extremely difficult to obtain, changes in permit applications made by the commissions during the 1973–76 period indicate quite clearly that the principal target groups (that is, people wishing to develop property in the 1000-yard permit area) often had to change their behavior rather substantially to comply with statutory objectives. It was also quite clear from the beginning that there was an enormous variety of target group activities along the 1000-mile coast which were potentially inconsistent with statutory objectives. Consequently, no relatively simple set of regulations would suffice. Finally, repeated failures of the legislature to pass the precursors of Proposition 20 indicated that the commissions would face a very difficult task in convincing the 1976 legislature to approve an enforceable Coastal Plan consistent with the Coastal Initiative's objectives.

Nevertheless, there were two aspects of the problem which made it more tractable. First, the commissions were regulating only a small percentage of the population of the state (or even of coastal counties), while a much greater percentage of both populations were potential beneficiaries. Thus there was certainly an excellent opportunity—as demonstrated by the vote on Proposition 20—for obtaining a net balance of diffuse political support for regulatory objectives. Second, the knowledge base of the factors affecting—and of the means to obtain—access, scenic protection, and wetlands preservation was relatively well established (although not always incorporated into the statute). At any rate, the commissions lacked neither sufficient knowledge nor an adequate causal theory, substantial problems which have afflicted, for example, both the regulation of air pollution and nuclear power plants.

On the whole, then, one could conclude that the commissions faced a difficult task in bringing about target group compliance but one which was nevertheless potentially tractable from a political and scientific perspective. While the overall task was more difficult than that encountered by most land use regulatory agencies, it was nevertheless not as intractable as the one confronting, for example, the U.S. Environmental Protection Agency in achieving ambient air standards for automotive pollutants (see chapter 4).

Within this context, Table 7.2 summarizes the conclusions of our analysis concerning the extent to which the implementation of the 1972 Coastal Initiative met the six conditions of effective implementation. The table deals primarily with the conditions affecting the permit and planning decisions of the commissions during the 1973–76 period and the extent to which those decisions—and the attendant impacts—could be expected to conform to statutory objectives to protect wetlands, scenic views, and public access to the wet sand beaches.

The extent to which the 1972 Coastal Conservation Act met the hypothesized conditions of effective implementation may be summarized as follows:

1. The act gave clear priority to wetlands protection and to physical and scenic access over economic development, although these objectives were not stated in very precise terms.

2. In relying entirely on police power regulation during the interim period, the statute incorporated a causal theory which was quite adequate to protect scenic views (through controlling the size and location of development), but whose limited geographic jurisdiction would occasionally create problems in protecting wetlands from upstream developments beyond the 1000-yard permit boundary. More importantly, the commissions' lack of authority to acquire and manage accessways during the 1973–76 period promised substantial problems in actually *providing* access, as the commissions would be dependent upon other units of government over which they had absolutely no control for these services.

3. The statute generally did an excellent job of structuring the implementation process so as to maximize the probability that implementing officials and target groups would act consistently with statutory objectives. Of particular note were the largely successful efforts of statutory framers to assign implementation to a generally sympathetic agency (the coastal commissions) which was highly integrated, which had ultimate responsibility for plan development, and which placed responsibility for the most important permit decisions in the hands of the state commission. In addition, the statute contained penalties adequate to discourage noncompliance by target groups, incorporated highly supportive decision rules, and provided excellent access to statutory supporters while precluding weakening amendments by the legislature during the 1973–76 interim period. The only potential problem areas were funding, where the guaranteed appropriation contained in the initiative should have been sufficient but turned out to be only marginally so, and in enforcement, where defense of the statute in the courts depended upon the willingness of the commissions and the attorney general to devote scarce resources to this task.

4. Turning to the nonstatutory conditions, the combination of statutory structuring, popular support for Proposition 20, and the prestige of the commissions as an important innovation in environmental planning resulted in the selection of implementing officials who generally supported statutory objectives and were relatively skillful in using available resources. While this

Table 7.2
**Extent to Which the Implementation of the 1972 California Coastal Initiative
Met the Six Conditions of Effective Implementation**

Condition	Overall Assessment	Discussion
1. Statute contains clear and consistent policy directives.	MODERATE	Statute had a consistent tilt in favor of protecting wetlands and increasing public's scenic and physical access to the coast. No explicit need to balance with economic development.While priorities clear, objectives were not very precise, and no guidelines provided for resolving conflict among three major goals.
2. Statute incorporates sound causal theory identifying sufficient factors and target groups to attain statutory objectives.	MIXED: HIGH for scenic access, MODERATE for wetlands, LOW for public access	Factors affecting statutory objectives were fairly well understood, but adequate causal theory not always incorporated into statute. Commissions' authority to regulate all development within the permit zone sufficient to protect scenic access. Lack of control over upstream development a potential problem in protecting wetlands. Lack of management and acquisition authority a major problem in providing physical access.
3. Statute not only provides jurisdiction over target groups but also structures implementation to maximize probability of compliance from implementing officials and target groups.	HIGH/ MODERATE	Requirement for interim permit review and preparation of a plan in the context of considerable administrative discretion within a highly structured biased system a good way to deal with general uncertainty and extensive variation in target group behavior.
a. assignment to a sympathetic agency	MODERATE/ HIGH	Statute assigned implementation solely to newly created coastal commissions, thus guaranteeing high priority and— given their environmental mandate and

Conditions	Overall Assessment	Discussion
		genesis in initiative process—a highly supportive professional staff. Attempt to structure regional commissions through state vs. local appointees worked reasonably well, though dependent on local support for Proposition 20. Structuring of state commission quite successful.
b. hierarchically integrated implementing agencies with few veto points and adequate incentives for compliance	HIGH except for public access	Commissions had final control over all development during interim period with state commission making final decisions on Coastal Plan and most important permit decisions. *Provision* of physical access required cooperation of legislature and Parks Departments, i.e, loosely integrated. Adequate fines, although enforcement required cooperation of attorney general. Sunset clause meant, however, that fate of commissions and Coastal Plan ultimately dependent upon 1976 legislature.
c. supportive decision rules	HIGH	Burden of proof on permit applicants. Approval of most potentially harmful developments required two-thirds vote of commission membership.
d. financial resources	MODERATE to HIGH	Guaranteed appropriation in initiative should have been sufficient—especially when combined with federal grants—but inflation and commissions' initiatives in energy conservation and low-cost housing strained resources.
e. formal access to supporters	HIGH	Strong requirements for public hearings in permit review and planning vigorously implemented by commissions. Liber-

Conditions	Overall Assessment	Discussion
		al rules of standing to appeal permit decisions to state commission and to courts. Initiative specifically precluded weakening amendments by legislature prior to 1976 (although everything then subject to review).
4. Commitment and skill of top implementing officials.	MIXED, but generally HIGH	Although regional commissioners showed wide variation in support for statutory objectives (based largely on degree of local support for Proposition 20), regional staff were uniformly sympathetic. More importantly, state commissioners and staff were very supportive. Skill difficult to measure, but certainly high at the state level and moderate to high in the three regions studied (especially the North Central).
5. Continuing support from constituency groups and sovereigns.	Generally HIGH, although MIXED in 1976 legislature	Environmental groups and other supporters of Proposition 20 continued to participate actively in both planning and permit review, as well as in the 1976 legislative session. Courts and federal OCZM very supportive. Governor and legislature supportive during 1973–76 interim (e.g., supplemental appropriations), though eventually demanded compromise in Coastal Plan.
6. Changing socioeconomic conditions (and thus political support) over time.	LOW, but commissions insulated until 1976	Recession of 1974–75, which hit the construction industry particularly hard, affected public and elite support for Proposition 20, but statute essentially insulated commissions from political repercussions until 1976 legislative session. Effect at that point uncertain, although legislature clearly sensitive to economic impacts of regulation.

was not the case in regions such as the North Coast where local government representatives were strongly opposed to Proposition 20, it was certainly true for the state commission which, combined with the hierarchically integrated decision process, was expected to render final decisions on important planning and permit matters that were generally consistent with statutory objectives.

5. In addition, the implementation effort benefited from the continued participation of environmental and other constituency groups which had originally supported it and received strong support during the 1973–76 period from the state appellate courts, the federal OCZM, the state legislature, and the governor.

6. Finally, the implementation effort suffered from a substantial downturn in the state economy which hit one of the principal target groups (the construction industry) particularly hard, but the adverse effects of this change in socioeconomic conditions were minimized by the insulation which the initiative provided the commissions from weakening amendments by the legislature.

In sum, the implementation of the Coastal Initiative clearly met four of the six conditions of effective implementation at least moderately well during 1973–76: Condition 1 (relatively clear and consistent objectives); Condition 3 (a structured process to maximize agency and target group compliance); Condition 4 (supportive and skillful top implementing officials); and Condition 5 (continuing support from constituency groups and sovereigns). The only one which was not met (Condition 6—changing socioeconomic conditions) was essentially neutralized during the interim period by the statute. Finally, Condition 2 (incorporation of an adequate causal theory) was met much better for some objectives (protection of scenic resources and, to a lesser extent, wetlands) than for others, most notably, the maximization of public access to the wet sand beaches.

During the 1973–76 period, one would thus expect, first, that the permit and planning decisions of the commissions would generally be consistent with statutory objectives; second, that the commissions' ability actually to attain these objectives would vary according to the adequacy of the underlying causal theory (or jurisdiction); and, third, that the commissions would attempt to convince the 1976 legislature to correct deficiencies.

Table 7.3 summarizes our conclusions concerning the extent to which the three principal statutory objectives were met during the interim (1973–76) period and in the 1976 Coastal Act. It indicates, first, that the commissions' permit and planning decisions were in fact highly conducive to protecting scenic views, protecting wetlands, and increasing physical access to the coast. Second, while the commissions were quite successful in realizing the first two objectives during 1973–76, the third was plagued by problems in target group

Table 7.3
**Extent to Which the Principal Substantive Objectives of the 1972 Coastal
Initiative Were Met (1) During the Period of Interim Permit Review (1973–76)
and (2) in the Future Policies Governing the Utilization of Coastal Resources**

	Objective of Coastal Initiative		
	Protect the scenic resources especially views of the coast from the highway	Protect wetlands and other valuable habitat	Increase the physical access of the public to wet sand beaches
A: Interim Permit Review			
1. Consistency of commissions' final permit decisions with statutory objectives.	HIGH	HIGH	MODERATE/ HIGH
2. Compliance of target groups with those decisions.	HIGH	HIGH	MODERATE/ LOW
3. Incorporation of a valid causal theory in the Coastal Initiative.	HIGH	MODERATE	MODERATE/ LOW
4. End result—extent to which actual impacts were consistent with statutory objectives.	HIGH	Probably HIGH	Rather LOW
B: Future Policies Governing the Coast			
1. Consistency of Coastal Plan proposed by the commissions with objectives of Proposition 20.[a]	HIGH	HIGH	HIGH
2. Consistency of 1976 coastal legislation with objectives of Proposition 20.[b]	MODERATE/ HIGH	MODERATE/ HIGH	MODERATE

[a]Includes both the plan's substantive policies and its implementation proposals.

[b]Includes the 1976 Coastal Act (both policies and implementation scheme) as well as the Coastal Conservancy legislation and the Nejedly-Hart Bond act as approved and subsequently implemented by the legislature.

compliance and in the commissions' lack of authority to purchase or maintain accessways. Third, the commissions attempted to address these deficiencies in access authority by recommending (a) the passage of a bond act for the purchase of coastal parks (and wetlands) and (b) the creation of the Coastal Conservancy with authority to provide some of the management and acquisition functions needed to supplement the regulatory activities of the future coastal agency. In short, the data in the table generally conform to our expectations.

Finally, this case illustrates a couple of other features of policy implementation which were discussed in chapter 2. It clearly demonstrates the need to view implementation as a learning process in which more effective instruments are sought to meet legal objectives and in which those objectives may be revised in response to changing socioeconomic conditions or unforeseen costs. Given that the commissions were a new agency dominated by policy advocates and that they had a strong supportive constituency, it is not at all surprising that the commissions through the Coastal Plan not only sought to address the inadequacies in their authority to provide physical access but also to enhance their ability to protect coastal resources through very substantial expansions of their geographical jurisdiction. It is unlikely, for example, that anyone in 1972 thought that providing physical access to the beaches would entail jurisdiction over highway and subdivision projects several miles inland, but the commissions' experience clearly revealed that the public's ability to get to the beaches in heavily urbanized areas was strongly affected by the regional transportation system and by the density of development. Similarly, it is unlikely that many people in 1972 foresaw that assuring an adequate supply of coastal sand beaches would entail controls over dams many miles upstream. Of course, it is not surprising that the 1976 legislature decided that the protection of coastal resources had to be balanced against a number of other factors, for example, respect for property rights, as well as the jurisdictional autonomy of the Corps of Engineers and local governments inland from the coast.

What is perhaps slightly surprising is that even as aggressive a regulatory agency as the coastal commissions learned that the level of conflict they were imposing on the political system simply could not be sustained over the long run and thus that regulatory controls would have to be supplemented by a variety of measures to compensate hardship cases. This was, for example, one of the principal functions of the acquisitions program incorporated in the proposed bond act and the land-banking and redevelopment authority accorded the Coastal Conservancy. Both of these measures provided coastal officials with more supple means of balancing statutory objectives against property owners' expectations than had the rigid approach of simply denying or imposing major conditions (for example, for access easements) on proposed development projects.

For further reflection

1. Under the 1976 Coastal Conservation Act the coastal commissions were much more vulnerable to review, budget cutbacks, and restrictions on their authority by elected politicians (particularly the state legislature), and an organized support constituency was waning. At the same time, the 1976 act contained more specific policy directives to achieve coastal conservation than had the 1972 act. What would you expect to occur under the 1976 act in terms of the stringency of the commissions' permit decisions, the aggressiveness of its personnel, and any possible changes in its legal mandate? (Compare your estimates with the findings of Paul Sabatier and Daniel Mazmanian, *Can Regulation Work?* (New York: Plenum, 1982), chapter 9.)
2. In considering the broad social, economic, and cultural factors through which all public policies are filtered (see the opening discussion in chapter 2), why might it be that California has had a far more aggressive coastal land use protection program than virtually any other state in terms of both state review of local decisions and the degree of environmental protection sought?
3. Agency officials often attribute their agency's implementation failures as the result of insufficient staffing. Yet the coastal commissions were able to process thousands of permits and develop a detailed plan for the state's entire 1100-mile coastline with a very small staff (approximately seventy professionals at any given moment). What might account for the degree of staff accomplishments and to what extent might their experience be generalized to other programs?
4. Compare and contrast the goals and the adequacy of the causal theories of the New Communities program (chapter 3) and those of California's 1972 Coastal Act.

Notes

1. Fred Bosselman and David Callies, *The Quiet Revolution in Land Use Control* (Washington, D.C.: Government Printing Office, 1972).
2. Roberg G. Healy and John S. Rosenberg, *Land Use and the States,* 2nd ed. (Baltimore: Johns Hopkins University Press, 1979), p. 2.
3. Healy and Rosenberg, *Land Use;* Nelson Rosenbaum, *Land Use and the Legislatures: The Politics of State Innovation* (Washington, D.C.: The Urban Institute, 1976); Phyllis Myers, *Zoning Hawaii: An Analysis of the Passage and Implementation of Hawaii's Land Classification Law* (Washington, D.C.: The Conservation Foundation, 1976).
4. William K. Reilly, President, The Conservation Foundation, quoted in Robert G. Healy, *et al., Protecting the Golden Shore: Lessons from the California Coastal Commissions* (Washington, D.C.: The Conservation Foundation, 1978), p. 2.
5. The majority of the material presented in the remainder of this chapter comes from Paul Sabatier and Daniel Mazmanian, *Can Regulation Work? The Implementation of the 1972 California Coastal Initiative* (Final Report to NSF, December, 1979).
6. Opinion Research of California poll for Whitaker and Baxter, Inc., August 1972. The poll involved a stratified sample of 1247 voting-age adults.

7. Figures compiled from Security Pacific Bank, *California Coastal Zone Economic Study: An Area Profile* (Los Angeles: Security Pacific Bank, 1975), pp. 2–4.
8. Rice Odell, *The Saving of the San Francisco Bay* (Washington, D.C.: The Conservation Foundation, 1972).
9. For a brief introduction to the origins and consent of the 1972 Coastal Initiative see Peter Douglas, "Coastal Zone Management: A New Approach in California," *Coastal Zone Management Journal* 1 (Fall 1973): 1–25.
10. Section 27001, The California Coastal Zone Conservation Act of 1972 (also referred to as Proposition 20).
11. Marver Bernstein, *Regulating Business by Independent Commission* (Princeton, N.J.: Princeton University Press, 1955), chapter 3; Anthony Downs, *Inside Bureaucracy* (Boston: Little, Brown and Company, 1967), chapters 2, 8, and 9.
12. Letter from William J. Brah, Pacific Regional Program Assistant, Office of Coastal Zone Management, September 1, 1977.
13. *CEEED* v. *The California Coastal Conservation Commissions*, App., 118 Cal. Rptr. 315, decided by Court of Appeals, Fourth District, Nov. 19, 1974. CEEED is an acronym for Californians for an Environment of Excellence, full Employment and strong Economy through planned Development. The group was organized informally in early 1972 and incorporated in August of that year.
14. This approximation is based on periodic reports from the California Attorney General's Office concerning litigation involving the commissions.
15. Sabatier and Mazmanian, *Can Regulation Work?*, chapter 5.
16. Vertical access involves accessways from the coastal road to the beach, while lateral access involves the ability to go from one beachfront lot to another. (Lateral access might be guaranteed, for example, by prohibiting the erection of fences near the water.)
17. Joan Sweeney, "Beach Access: Slow Gains," *Los Angeles Times*, May 16, 1977. In reaction to this rather poor record, the state legislature created the "Coastal Access Program" in 1979 (AB 989), which placed greater pressure on the coastal commissions to accelerate and expand their access efforts and granted them additional powers and jurisdiction to do so.
18. Robert Healy, "Saving California's Coast: The Coastal Initiative and Its Aftermath," *Coastal Zone Management Journal* 1 (1974): 386.
19. Robert Kneisel, "The Impact of the California Coastal Zone Conservation Commission on the Local Housing Market: A Study of the South Coast Regional Commission" (Ph.D. diss., University of California, Riverside, 1979).
20. Sabatier and Mazmanian, *Can Regulation Work?*, chapter 9.

Chapter 8
The pathos of implementation, reconsidered

This . . . seems to parallel the way in which some social scientists have approached the study of organizational pathology. Instead of telling men how bureaucracy might be mitigated, they insist that it is inevitable. Instead of explaining how democratic patterns may, to some extent, be fortified and extended, they warn us that democracy cannot be perfect. Instead of controlling the disease, they suggest that we are deluded, or more politely, incurably romantic, for hoping to control it. Instead of assuming responsibilities as realistic clinicians, striving to further democratic potentialities wherever they can, many social scientists have become morticians, all too eager to bury men's hope.[1]

The policy implementation efforts examined in the preceding chapters can be viewed through two quite distinctive perspectives. On the one hand, the conclusion is inescapable that through the normal political processes in the United States, effective implementation of major programs designed to appreciably alter the status quo is exceedingly difficult. This is obviously cause for concern among proponents of change. Severe impediments to change are imposed by historical and cultural patterns, by current socio-economic conditions, by deeply held public preferences, and by long-standing government institutional arrangements of the sort identified by Hofferbert in his comprehensive model of policy formation (see chapter 2).

A list of specific impediments relevant to the United States includes the presence of a highly interdependent industrial society, wherein any given program (for example, clean air) can be undermined in whole or in part by events and activities in an entirely different policy sphere (for example, the

Arab oil boycott of 1973 and subsequent threats to America's oil supply). It includes the commitment of most citizens to the ideal of a market economy, with as little government intrusion as possible. Belief in the sanctity of individual liberties and property rights, again, implies great restraint on the part of government. Furthermore, implementation takes place within the boundaries of constitutionally prescribed checks and balances and faces a multiplicity of veto points without strong political parties or other extra-constitutional mechanisms for overcoming the maze of legislative, executive, judicial and intergovernmental clearance points.

Finally, the tasks undertaken by government today are often the most intractable, tasks the government often assumes by default. For example, *The* when the market economy fails to provide a national highway system, adequate financing for large-scale energy projects, care for the mentally or physically handicapped or generally disadvantaged, the government is called upon to assume these responsibilities. Even more troublesome from the standpoint of implementation is the fact that the government is asked to correct inequities in health care delivery, educational opportunities, job training, and related social needs that often result from shortcomings of the very market economy system that, in theory, is otherwise championed. Similarly, government is expected to intervene to preserve and protect highly prized coastal areas of the nation and other regions of extraordinary beauty and environmental sensitivity precisely because reliance on private ownership of land and the market have not provided the level of protection that a majority of Americans deem appropriate.

The often minimal successes in policy implementation experienced over the past two decades, especially in the provision of social services, have led to an increasing level of pessimism among practitioners and scholars. Berman, for example, after studying federal efforts to change service delivery at the local level, now argues that we must begin to consider different implementation strategies for different situations.[2] By this he means that a strategy that seeks to achieve effective implementation of statutorily prescribed goals, when this calls for substantial change, will work only when there is minimal goal conflict, an adequate causal theory, few agencies involved, and a stable socioeconomic and political environment. When these situational parameters are not satisfied, which is typically the case, a more "adaptive" implementation strategy involving bargaining and mutual adjustments among multiple participants is needed. In essence, in the large majority of cases program enactment must be viewed as merely the starting point of an evolutionary process of experimentation, goal definition, and search for the implementation strategy best suited to particular circumstances. Only rarely will the process of adjustment result in substantial change in the status quo along the lines statutorily prescribed. Berman also assumes that the behavior of recalcitrants probably will not be changed over time by clarification of goals, incorporation of more adequate sanctions, mobilization of additional political support, or other factors.

Aaron Wildavsky provides a similarly pessimistic view. Our recent history of implementing public programs, he contends, is a record of high aspiration but dismal failure to deliver. Rather than expect a slow and steady march forward, he argues that we must reconcile ourselves to far less ambitious goals for the public sector. Indeed, recognition of this fact, whether implicit or explicit, has led to a widespread "strategic retreat on objectives":

> *Constellations in the American public policy universe seem to be moving in remarkably similar directions, from concentrating on aggressive design (the war on X, the crusade against Y), through the current quagmire of implementation, and into the strategic retreat on objectives. The age of design is over; the era of implementation is passing; the time to modify objectives has come.*[3]

It is obvious that strategic retreats are made in many implementation efforts. There was at least a partial retreat, for example, in the implementation of the 1970 Clean Air Act Amendments when compliance timetables and some emission standards were delayed; though in this case there were also a number of steps taken over time to strengthen the act.

But are the prospects for effective implementation really as gloomy as these analysts suggest? In part, the answer depends on whether one views the cup as half full or half empty. Pessimists obviously see efforts of the past decades as leaving the cup half (if not more so) empty. Yet, it is clear from the work of Hofferbert and others who have placed the policy process in its broadest context that the weight of history and circumstance will usually result in far less than 100 percent effectiveness in engineering major social changes under the best of conditions. A more reasonable perspective, therefore, may be to consider the set of conditions under which we are most likely to attain a cup that is substantially full.[4]

Cumulative incrementalism

Based on the case material presented, we are persuaded that a more balanced and thus more optimistic perspective is warranted. We begin with the six conditions of effective implementation initially set forth in chapter 2.

1. The enabling legislation or other legal directive mandates policy objectives which are clear and consistent or at least provides substantive criteria for resolving goal conflicts.
2. The enabling legislation incorporates a sound theory identifying the principal factors and causal linkages affecting policy objectives and gives implementing officials sufficient jurisdiction over target groups and other points of leverage to attain, at least potentially, the desired goals.
3. The enabling legislation structures the implementation process so as to

maximize the probability that implementing officials and target groups will perform as desired. This involves assignment to sympathetic agencies with adequate hierarchical integration, supportive decision rules, sufficient financial resources, and adequate access to supporters.

4. The leaders of the implementing agency possess substantial managerial and political skill and are committed to statutory goals.

5. The program is actively supported by organized constituency groups and by a few key legislators (or chief executive) throughout the implementation process, with the courts being either neutral or supportive.

6. The relative priority of statutory objectives is not undermined over time by the emergence of conflicting public policies or by changes in relevant socioeconomic conditions which undermine the statute's causal theory or political support.

Experience has shown that in most cases not all six conditions, nor even a majority of them, will be adequately met in the early stages of implementation to produce instantaneous success, though the case of the California Coastal Zone Commissions indicates that notable early success is possible.

At the same time, it is not correct to conclude that initial shortcomings invariably degenerate into the downhill spiral of ever worsening implementation, followed in short order by a retreat on objectives as a means of concealing program failure. Nor does it appear to be true that the absence of the initial prerequisites for effectiveness are sure to result in accommodation to local pressures, and thus a necessary shift to an adaptive implementation strategy. Rather, it is just as plausible, based on the evidence of two of the cases presented, that implementation may evolve in a manner that strengthens the prospects of accomplishing statutory objectives. In the face of strong resistance, maintaining and building pressure for implementation is feasible if such key factors as a "fixer" to protect and oversee the program from above, an effective means of monitoring the performance of the implementation agency in light of the program's objectives, and organized constitutency support over time exist. This outcome is illustrated in the cases of Title I and school desegregation in the South. Though these two cases are not a random sample of all implementation efforts by any means, they do strongly suggest that an alternative view of the life cycle and prospects for (at least some) implementation efforts is in order.

The implementation of Title I is probably one of the more outstanding cases of cumulative incrementalism. Recall that the Elementary and Secondary Education Act of 1965 sought to provide compensatory education or, more specifically:

> *to provide financial assistance . . . to local educational agencies serving areas with concentrations of children from low-income families to expand and improve their education program . . . to meet the special educational needs of educationally deprived children.*[5]

However, taking advantage of somewhat ambiguous language in the act and responding to pressures from local school districts, legislators initially allocated Title I funds pretty much along the lines of general revenue aid to school districts with children from low-income families. Little accounting and monitoring followed, and the funds were often treated simply as a federal substitution for previously provided state and local monies.

Several developments over the next ten years began to bring Title I allocations in line with the initial statutory intent. These included the important monitoring and evaluation function provided by the NAACP—the Martin-McClure Report—and other constituency proponents of the act; the internal corrective measures taken in reaction to the in-house monitoring and compliance studies, which were required under the 1965 act at the insistence of Senator Robert Kennedy; the fixer role played by Congressman Carl Perkins (and selected others); the development of a supportive constituency within the United States Office of Education and across the nation's schools through creation of "State Title I Coordinators," hiring of thousands of Title I teachers and teacher aids, and establishment of parent advisory councils in each school district; and, finally, the series of strengthening amendments to the act in 1970, 1971, and 1978 which gradually shifted power away from the traditional centers of power in USOE and at the state and local districts to the reformist proponents of Title I. Though it took more than a decade of continual pushing, prodding, and cajoling, by the late 1970s there had been a substantial improvement in targeting funds to the children entitled. By 1978, while still providing no panacea for the disadvantaged, the program was far closer to its statutory objectives than had seemed possible in the late 1960s. This occurred, moreover, in the face of changing administrations in Washington, the onset of a more stringent fiscal climate, and the withering of a good number of other Great Society programs that were targeted at the neediest. As a result of improved targeting of funds and the fostering of educational innovation, recent evidence suggests that many Title I programs are able to overcome at least partially the declining relative performance of disadvantaged children as they proceed through the school system.

The evolution of school desegregation in the South followed a different path, yet also fits the model of cumulative incrementalism. Desegregation in southern schools moved from an initial minimal compliance to eventual successful elimination of dual school systems and a dramatic reduction in the proportion of racially isolated schools in the southern and border states. Begun by the Supreme Court in 1954 with its *Brown* decision, the push for desegregation went through a hiatus from 1954 to 1964 during which some school districts in the border states but very few in the deep South dismantled their system of dual schools. Evasion, resistance, and nonenforcement were the rule, and the Court had little meaningful implementation apparatus through which to enforce its decision. Concern with the broader issues of civil rights for blacks continued to grow, however, partly in response to the failure to implement *Brown*. In response Congress passed the 1964 Civil Rights Act.

This gave HEW the authority to intervene in the school desegregation effort and provided the important administrative apparatus necessary to oversee its implementation. Early monitoring, especially that done by civil rights organizations, vividly demonstrated the inadequacy of HEW's early implementation efforts and, in particular, the ruse of "freedom of choice" plans adopted by many school districts. Most important, under the Civil Rights Act (as interpreted by the courts) HEW was able to impose continually more stringent sanctions by cutting off funding, until by 1968 the cost of noncompliance was so great that it threatened to bankrupt school districts. The 1964 Civil Rights Act placed enormous power in the hands of a single agency. In short, extensive outside pressure and performance monitoring; development of numerical guidelines and deadlines for desegregation by HEW; tightened enforcement by HEW; constant intervention (in favor of of desegregation) on the part of the courts; and the imposition of severe financial sanctions led, by 1970, to total compliance with the order to dismantle dual school systems, and between 1962 and 1976, to a reduction of the proportion of all-black schools in the South from 99.9 percent to 17.9 percent, and in the border states from 48.2 percent to 38.1 percent.

These instances of rather notably improved implementation over time are exceedingly important to an overall understanding of the implementation process. Initial success is the critical first step in any implementation effort and obviously sets the tone of what is to follow. But all is not lost if the initial effort falls short of expectations either because of a failure of enforcement (for example, school desegregation), a lack of precision in targeting and directing of resources (for example, Title I), or any other shortcoming in the conditions critical to success. A retreat from objectives need not automatically follow from a failure to achieve initial success. These two cases also serve to highlight several factors in the implementation process that appear to be especially crucial to improving effectiveness over time. First is the need to refine and develop numerical measures of program performance (for example, the percentage of black pupils in a school, standardized testing of students in a compensatory education program). It is noteworthy that the push for numerical standards came from both the program administrators and outside support groups as a direct result of initial noncompliance by target groups. Both cases also indicate that sustained sovereign support is critical, whether it is the more typical legislative "fixer," the chief executive, or the courts. At the heart of the entire process, of course, lies constituency support for the program. Constituencies may be predominantly external to the implementing agency, such as the civil rights groups that provided continual monitoring and prodding to attain school desegregation, or they may be internal supporters, as were the Title I state coordinators, teachers, and aides who had a vested interest in the success and continuation of the Title I program.

The case of Title I implementation also highlights another relevant point. A reasonable degree of long-term success can be achieved even with only moderately high levels of achievement across our six conditions of effective implementation. The crucial factor appears to be that the effort be sustained and enhanced across virtually all dimensions so that the cumulative effect is a reasonable degree of performance.

The second way to view implementation is to view it within the boundaries set by social, cultural, technological, and historical considerations—the broad tractability factors. Within this context a great deal can be accomplished through the skillful structuring of the implementation effort over time and with adequate sovereign and constituency support. Although skillful structuring and the marshaling of support may not overcome entirely the barriers created by social, cultural, and other factors, nevertheless to the extent public intervention can make a difference, chances for success can be enhanced by understanding and structuring implementation. Naturally, the more intractable the problem (for example, guaranteeing meaningful integration of schools as opposed to dismantling dual public school systems), the more the structuring and orchestration necessary.

To look at implementation over time underscores the fact that the ratings we give our six conditions of effectiveness in any given case may vary from one point in the implementation process to the next. As policy directives become more clear and consistent, as in Title I, for example, our ratings on that variable change accordingly. This variation is evident in the thumbnail sketch of the cases examined in chapters 3 through 7 in Table 8.1.

One final word on the ratings: Though it is extremely useful to provide summary scores for an entire program as in Table 8.1, it may also be useful on occasion to evaluate subcomponents of the program, all of which may not be in line with the program as a whole. For example, the case of the California Coastal Act shows that while the coastal commissions achieved great success in wetlands protection, they were much less successful in implementing public access to the beaches as provided for in the act. Such distinctions are by necessity glossed over in the very process of attempting to arrive at an overall assessment of implementation success.

Implementation under suboptimal conditions

As the case studies presented have illustrated, it is rare indeed when all six conditions of effective implementation are met sufficiently (given a "high" rating), especially in the short run. Yet the failure to achieve initial success typically leads to frustration and disappointment with the level of accomplishments of statutory objectives. As noted above, the resultant pessimism has become the dominant theme in discussions of implementation of major public programs today. But, we have also seen that even if success does not reach an optimal level initially, the level of implementation can be enhanced over time until moderate to high levels of implementation are achieved. And this latter

Table 8.1
Conditions of Effective Implementation Across Five Policy Areas

	Policy Area		
Condition	New Towns, 1970–80	Title I, 1965–78	Clean Air Act 1970–77
1. Clear and consistent policy directives.	MODERATE	MODERATE to HIGH over time	MODERATE to HIGH over time
2. Valid causal theory and jurisdiction provided.	LOW to MODERATE over time	uncertain but probably MODERATE	MODERATE to LOW over time
3. Structures implementing process.			
a. assignment to sympathetic agency	MODERATE	LOW to MODERATE over time	MODERATE
b. hierarchical integration	LOW	LOW to MODERATE over time	LOW
c. supportive decision rules	NEUTRAL	NEUTRAL	NEUTRAL
d. financial resources	LOW	HIGH to MODERATE over time	LOW
e. formal access	LOW	LOW to MODERATE over time	HIGH
4. Commitment and skill of top implementing officials.	MODERATE to NEUTRAL over time	MODERATE	MODERATE
5. Continuing support from constituencies and sovereigns.	LOW	LOW to MODERATE over time	MODERATE
6. Changing socio-economic conditions.	LOW	LOW/ MODERATE	LOW
Overall Rating of Implementation Effectiveness	MINIMAL	MINIMAL to ADEQUATE over time	ADEQUATE

Legend:
HIGH = A strong asset in effective implementation of legal objectives.
MODERATE = Conducive to effective implementation, although some problems.
LOW = Notable obstacle to effective implementation.
NEUTRAL = Factor played little or no role in implementation effort.

Policy Area		
Desegregation, 1955–79		California Coastal Act 1972–76
South	North	
HIGH	LOW	HIGH
HIGH	LOW	HIGH
HIGH	HIGH	HIGH
MODERATE	MODERATE	MODERATE to HIGH over time
HIGH	LOW to MODERATE over time	HIGH
MODERATE	LOW	MODERATE
HIGH	MODERATE	HIGH
HIGH	LOW	HIGH
HIGH	MODERATE	HIGH
LOW	MODERATE	LOW
MINIMAL to SUBSTANTIAL over time	MINIMAL	ADEQUATE/ SUBSTAN-TIAL

pattern suggests a range of strategies that can be pursued when the six conditions are not initially met.

For example, valid causal theories may not be readily at hand. Less than complete information, conflicts over goals, and multiple vetoes in legislative bodies make it very difficult to pass legislation that incorporates unambiguous objectives and coherently structures the implementation process. Implementation must often be assigned to agencies that do not support policy objectives. Supportive interest groups and legislators with the resources to serve as fixers may not be available or may go on to other concerns over the long course of implementation. Nevertheless, even under such suboptimal conditions, several steps can be taken to increase the probability of effective implementation. We suggest the following:[6]

1.   If a valid causal theory linking target group behavior to policy objectives is not available or is clearly problematic, as, for example, was the case with Title I, then the proponents of the statute must make a conscious effort to incorporate in it a learning process through experimental projects, extensive research and development, evaluation studies, and an open decision process involving as many different inputs as possible.

2.   If the legislature insists on passing legislation with only the most ambiguous policy directives, then supporters can attempt to clarify the statute over time through the amendment process. This is by far the most common practice and was used skillfully in the implementation of Title I. As happened in the school desegregation case, of course, a legislature can also be called upon to elaborate on a position taken by the courts, that is, passage of the Civil Rights Act of 1964. Finally, supporters can initiate litigation to require the implementing agency to develop clearer objectives and procedures through rule making—a strategy which is receiving some support from federal courts.[7]

3.   If implementation cannot be assigned to strongly supportive agencies, then it is absolutely crucial to provide for intervention by outsiders through citizen suit provisions (for example, the Clean Air Act), periodic reporting to sovereigns, evaluation studies by prestigious and relatively independent outsiders (for example, Title I and school desegregation), and perhaps special legislative oversight committees.

4.   If there is no active supportive constituency with the necessary resources to monitor implementation carefully, then identification and mobilization of such a group within and/or outside the implementing agency must be a major priority of supportive legislators and implementing officials—as any program without such support is doomed in the long run. This strategy was, for example, successfully pursued in the case of Title I and, to a lesser extent, in the school desegregation and Clean Air Amendments cases. While it is occasionally possible to create new interest groups from scratch, a more feasible strategy is to convince an existing organization with the requisite resources to assume monitoring responsibilities, as was the case with the

Sierra Club monitoring the California Coastal Commissions and the NAACP monitoring the progress of school desegregation.[8]

5.   If a fixer is not readily available, then program supporters must make a major effort to find or nurture one. Efforts may involve convincing a competent new legislator (or, more realistically, his or her key staff people) to specialize in this area or convincing an existing legislator (and/or his or her staff) that constituents strongly support the program and thus require that it be given higher priority. If legislators in the relevant committees with jurisdiction over the implementing agencies are apathetic (or hostile) toward the new program, then efforts should be made to reorganize committee jurisdictions or perhaps to create a special oversight committee with a program supporter as chairperson. Alternatively, a surrogate fixer may be found in the form of an appellate court judge, a high civil servant, or even among specialized reporters in the media. Whatever the means, however, finding a fixer is of paramount importance to effective implementation.

6.   If systematic monitoring and oversight by which to gauge "performance gaps" are lacking, then the capacity must be created. Ideally, this might be accomplished by having sympathetic legislators amend the original statute to require both the collection of in-house performance data as well as commissioning periodic external reviews by prestigious and impartial organizations (for example, the National Science Foundation, the Rand Corporation). Should this approach fail, possibly a sympathetic court judge or an executive sovereign can be found who will require the necessary monitoring. A least desirable but still effective strategy, as shown in several cases, it to have external support groups themselves assume monitoring responsibilities. These groups, however, will rarely have the resources, expertise, and legitimacy to adequately carry out this function over an extended period since they are, after all, an interested party.

In short, individually or in tandem, significant steps can be taken to enhance prospects of successful implementation. While they are never a guarantee, the six strategies listed above have proved to be useful in moving toward effective implementation in several of the cases presented and are probably realistically available in any implementation setting. Thus, instead of acceding to Berman's perspective that most problems are intractable—and, thus, that mutual adjustment will usually prevail—or Wildavsky's view that the implementation process will inevitably bring a retreat on objectives, we need to think more about how to meet better the conditions of effective implementation over time.

Is it uphill all the way?

In a word, yes. Any implementation effort that goes against strongly held beliefs, long-standing practices, and potent political forces must be viewed as an uphill battle from start to finish. This is especially true given our rather fluid political system with its multiplicity of possible veto points.

Sometimes, of course, a new plateau is established in a policy arena which for all intent and purposes is irreversible. Future controversy begins at this point, not at the initial starting condition. As an example, now that open space and wetlands along the California coast are being purchased and set aside by the state, it is highly unlikely that even the abolition of the coastal commissions would lead to a reversal of these steps to protect the natural environment of the coast. Similarly, regardless of how heated the issue of racial mixing and integration in the South may become, it is extremely improbable that American society will ever revert formally to dual school systems.

Finally, the picture that emerges from even the short time-frames through which we have viewed the five implementation efforts is that *there seems to be no routine or "natural" progression to implementation.* It may begin slowly or quickly, pick up or lose momentum, or pass through several cycles. For instance, the implementation effort of the California Coastal Commissions from their inception to the late 1970s shows appreciable success: Development was curtailed where it was most offensive; a process of long-range planning and environmental regulation was set in motion; a permanent state agency was established; and a heightened sensitivity to the issues of coastal degradation was instilled throughout the state. But except for the plateau of protection achieved through the state's purchasing and dedications programs, the accomplishments of the commissions could conceivably be reversed by future policy. As analysts we have no foolproof way of forecasting whether this will occur. Based on what we know of the tenacity of development interests in American society, however, the successes of the commissions are likely to be eroded in the coming years. The point is that initial implementation effectiveness is no guarantee of long-term trends or outcomes. Yet another case examined here shows the opposite trend. Title I was initially judged by most supporters to be a dismal failure. However, implementation of this program continued to evolve until by the late 1970s the program had emerged as one of the few redistributive programs of the Great Society that was growing in effectiveness and showing promise of long-term success.

Moreover, the relative importance of factors in the implementation process changes in the long- versus short-term picture. As we have suggested, in the short term, effective implementation is especially dependent on the strength of the initial statute, particularly the clarity and consistency of policy directives, the assignment to a sympathetic agency, formal access for supportive constituency, the commitment of agency officials, the presence of a "fixer," and the resources of various constituency groups. In the long term, however, changing socioeconomic conditions and the ability of supportive constituency groups to maintain effectively their organized presence and to intervene when necessary are probably more important.

While there is no uniform pattern to the life cycle of an implementation effort, it is possible to identify several general patterns that suggest how changing circumstances can affect the effort. The first and possibly least problematic pattern is the **Effective Implementation Scenario,** depicted graphically in Figure 8.1. While characteristic of many public programs, this pattern is most applicable to programs which address a rather limited and well-defined set of problems and seek moderate changes in the status quo. Typically, the proponents of government action mobilize sufficient public and legislative support to pass a statute which establishes a new agency with substantial jurisdiction over the problem area. The agency is staffed initially by officials strongly committed to program objectives. Backed by public and constituency support, these officials quickly establish policies consistent with those objectives. Target group compliance is high, in part because noncompliance may be very visible and in part because agency staff are assisted by supportive constituency groups. After a few years, even though the original staff leave to go on to new jobs, the conformity of policy outputs and target group compliance with statutory objectives remain high because of the limited nature of the problem, the continued presence of strong public and constituency group support, no substantial decline in the local economy, and continued support from local legislators. Because target group compliance is directly related to the achievement of statutory objectives, the statute continues to have the desired impacts over time.

These are not the programs receiving major consideration today nor

Figure 8-1   The Effective Implementation Scenario

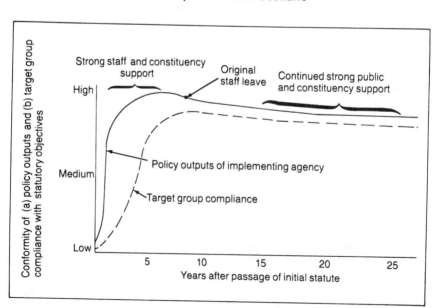

necessarily the ones selected for scrutiny in this book. Yet government does provide a wide range of services—from fire protection to income tax collection to coastal zone protection (at least to date in California)—that are implemented reasonably well, and we should not lose sight of this fact as we emphasize the more hotly debated and poorly implemented programs.

The second pattern of implementation is the **Gradual Erosion Scenario** (Figure 8.2) that pessimists suggest characterizes most public programs today and, which in some instances, for example, New Communities, may not be all that gradual.[9] In this pattern, the statute clearly mandates significant behavioral change. While the principal implementing agency is theoretically given extensive powers, it must work through other (state and local) governments and, moreover, is dependent on private citizens and businesses for development of the new technologies necessary to achieve statutory objectives or to actually carry out the policies of the act. This inevitably means that there are a rather large number of veto points in the process. Also, the lead agency is typically staffed initially by strong supporters of the statute, but their enthusiasm often leads them to cut corners in proposing rules and regulations, thereby undermining the agency's credibility. Moreover, the commitment of agency officials declines as enthusiastic staff wear out and leave, to be replaced by more professional-managerial types anxious to reduce conflict with target groups. Meanwhile, the agency's supportive constituency withers over time, while opposition is vociferous, well organized, and

Figure 8-2   The Gradual Erosion Scenario

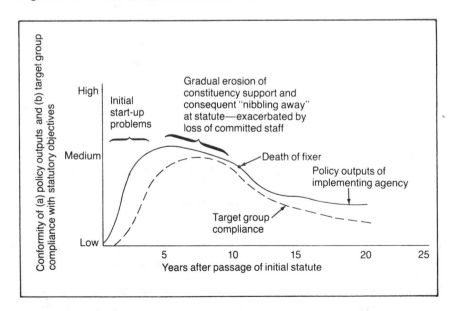

persistent. Opponents' efforts to weaken the statute may be thwarted in the short run by the able fixer. Eventually the fixer dies or his or her attention is diverted, and the statute suffers substantial revision, although rarely as much as sought by opponents. But conformity of the policy outputs with statutory objectives does decline over time—particularly after the demise of the fixer—and, thus, there is some erosion in impacts. This is the pattern, with one or another variation, that Berman and Wildavsky see as dominant in the public policy process today.

If we diverge slightly from the typical pattern depicted in Figure 8.2 and think of gradual erosion following from an even lower starting point than shown, this scenario can aptly fit the cases of New Communities and school desegregation in the North.

The **Cumulative Incrementalism Scenario** (Figure 8.3) represents a continual process of fine tuning, goal specification, constituency development, and enhanced administrative apparatus which gradually brings a program into greater accord with the law's intent. Programs in this category are distinguished from those in the Gradual Erosion Scenario, first, by the fact that their initial statutory authorization and six conditions of implementation are typically at lower thresholds (for example, the initially weak position of Title I). Second, if a continual and cumulative process is to evolve, the implementation effort usually must be directed primarily by a central authority (most often a central government) over subordinate units of the

---

Figure 8-3   The Cumulative Incrementalism Scenario

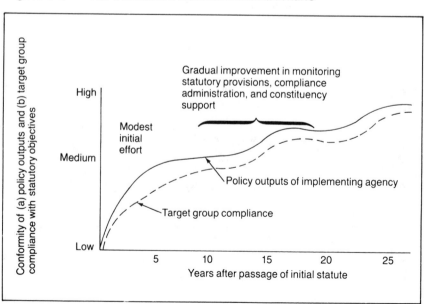

organization (for example, HEW over local public school systems). Despite the inevitable problems of hierarchical control and integration among superior and subordinate units such a pattern creates, with persistence the programs of subordinate units can be altered through ever stronger monitoring activities and sanctions. Greater compliance can be achieved than is the case when implementation requires the direct cooperation of private groups or individuals who oppose the program and must bear a disproportionate share of its direct costs. Thus, for example, the federal government's threat to cut off all federal and state aid to local school districts was effective in bringing about compliance with *Brown* in the South.

However, even gradual prodding of subordinate units requires external monitoring of their activities, development of increasingly precise indicators of their performance, presence of a fixer, and an active external support constituency. While both were uphill efforts, Title I and desegregation of southern schools clearly suggest that implementation can be advanced toward quite demanding statutory objectives.

The last pattern, the **Rejuvenation Scenario** (Figure 8.4) combines two elements from previous patterns; a poor statutory base and start-up implementation process similar to that of the Gradual Erosion Scenario, but also a much longer time horizon. Thus the enacting legislation may contain ambiguities, compromises, and contradictions resulting from lack of a clear vision on the part of the enactors or, more likely, from the bargaining and

Figure 8-4   The Rejuvenation Scenario

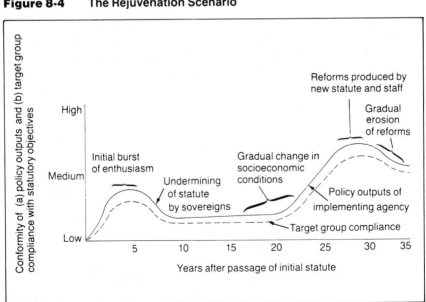

negotiating characteristic of the development of most legislation in our pluralistic society. While proponents of the implementation effort may be able to dominate the initial staffing of the agency and thus aggressively interpret its ambiguous mandate, their efforts are soon undermined by unsympathetic sovereigns and they leave the agency. The agency then settles into a long period of quiet and generally ineffectual activity.

Eventually, however, changing socioeconomic conditions substantially increase the number of proponents of the program's implementation and proponents can then substantially strengthen the program's legislative mandate. This period of reform is also marked by significant changes in agency personnel, with the result that, for a period, the agency aggressively seeks to change target group behavior. After several years, however, declining support and rising opposition mean that the agency must again pursue more cautious policies, although the agency is not nearly so ineffectual as it was during its long period of inactivity.

This scenario resembles the most recent experience of the Federal Trade Commission and, in certain very general respects, the Atomic Energy Commission.[10] It highlights, also, the fact that we seldom ever start from scratch in addressing a public issue. Rather, through reorganization, infusion of new resources and leadership, and legislative redirection, we reinvigorate existing government structures. The longer an agency is in existence, obviously, the more likely it is to go through such a metamorphosis.

The task at hand

As we stated at the outset, the underlying pedagogical purposes of this text were to bring greater clarity to understanding the overall process of the implementation of legal objectives; to synthesize a rather disparate array of possible implementation paths and studies into a small set of key scenarios; and, in doing so, to provide perspective on the implementation process for both the analyst (the student) and the practitioner.

For the analyst, the task at hand is now to challenge, extend, and refine our model of the critical variables affecting policy implementation. For practitioners, the challenge is, on the one hand, to bear in mind the set of historical, social, and institutional constraints under which they must inevitably labor, and on the other, to use their knowledge of the six conditions to analyze and to improve public programs.

For the pessimists among us, of course, the road is somewhat easier. They can take comfort in their belief that little of merit will ever be enacted into law, and if by chance it should happen to be, that the implementation effort will surely succumb to the path of gradual erosion. For optimists, who remain open to the possibilities of both the effective and cumulative incrementalist implementation paths, the challenge is to improve our understanding of the conditions under which these patterns occur. For the activists, the challenge is to increase the incidence with which they occur.

It is for the optimists and activists that we provide a checklist of questions that should be asked in the design and orchestration of any implementation effort. These questions emanate from each of the key points on our analysis and the answers to them should underscore the potential strengths and trouble spots of the implementation of any ambitious public policy.[11] Note that they deal not only with statutory design but also with the need to develop political support among important members of the policy subsystem if program objectives are not to be undermined over time. For the purposes of this exercise, we shall simplify the situation somewhat by making the following assumptions concerning the tractability of the problem: (a) that the statute seeks a rather substantial change in the target group behavior, and (b) that there is a reasonably valid causal theory relating changes in such behavior to the "solution" of the problem being addressed; in other words, the principal difficulty facing statutory framers is obtaining compliance from target groups. The questions to ask are these:

1.   What is the general policy to be implemented? Are the statutory objectives (and standards) precise and, if multiple, are they clearly ranked in importance? Moreover, if the statute is assigned to an existing agency, does it indicate the relative priority of these new objectives in the totality of the agency's programs?

2.   Are the principal factors affecting program objectives understood and does the statute give implementing officials sufficient jurisdiction over target groups and other points of leverage to attain, at least potentially, the desired goals?

3.   Does the statute provide sufficient financial resources to the implementing institutions to enable them to conduct the necessary technical analyses, to apply the general objectives to thousands of specific cases, and to monitor target group compliance?

4.   Does the statute minimize the number of veto points within and among implementing institutions and does it provide sufficient sanctions and inducements to enable supportive officials to overcome resistance among their colleagues and among target groups? If the statute deals with a regulatory function, does it provide for tax breaks or other forms of compensation to members of target groups who are hit particularly hard by adjudicatory decisions?

5.   Are the decision rules contained in the statute consistent with statutory objectives? For example, do they place the burden of proof on target groups? Do they give as much authority as possible within implementing institutions to those officials most likely to support statutory objectives? Do they make the granting of permits or licenses contingent upon specific findings consistent with statutory objectives?

6.   Does the statute assign the responsibility for implementation to institu-

tions or agencies which strongly support the statute's objectives and are likely to grant the program high priority? Specifically, can (should) a new agency to administer the program be created or else can the program be assigned to a prestigious existing agency which supports the objectives and is looking for a new mission?

7.   Does the statute maximize the opportunities for supporters outside the implementing agencies to participate actively in the implementation process? Specifically, does it provide standing for supporters to intervene actively in agency proceedings and to appeal agency decisions to the courts? Does the statute provide for evaluation studies by prestigious independent organizations to monitor the extent to which agency decisions and the impacts of those decisions are consistent with statutory objectives? Finally, is it possible to centralize legislative oversight in the hands of supportive legislators?

8.   What is the probability that changes in socioeconomic conditions or in technology during the foreseeable future are likely to undermine political support for statutory objectives? If the achievement of these objectives is contingent upon technological innovation, what steps does the statute take to foster such research and development?

9.   What can be done to counter the short attention span the mass media and the general public give to the issue? In particular, is it possible to convince some of the more important media to hire specialist reporters to cover the general issue addressed by the statute?

10.   What steps can be taken to activate any latent supportive constituencies and to assure that supportive groups have the necessary staff and other resources to monitor and to participate actively in the implementation process?

11.   What can be done to assure that legislative and executive sovereigns who support the statute will actively monitor and intervene in the implementation process? In particular, is anyone available to serve as a fixer and does he or she have the staff and other resources to do so effectively? Moreover, what can be done to assure that subsequent legislation in policy areas relevant to the statute does not undermine statutory objectives and that attempts to revise the statute do not emasculate it?

12.   Can anything be done to appoint implementing officials who are not only committed to the achievement of statutory objectives but also have above-average managerial and political skills?

The answers to these questions should provide a reasonable estimate of the probability that the policy decisions of implementing agencies will be consistent with statutory objectives and that target groups will actually comply with those decisions until the objectives are attained.

A concluding remark

It has been our purpose throughout these pages to emphasize the complex and varied nature of the implementation process while, at the same time, suggesting a general framework through which implementation can be understood and explored. To the extent that the framework provides a meaningful way of viewing implementation and the examples chosen provide sufficient illustrative material for both student and practitioner, we shall consider our effort worthwhile. If the emphasis on statutory structuring and the identification of conditions crucial to successful implementation precipitates further thinking and empirical research, our greatest ambition in writing this text will be realized. In sum, it has not been our purpose to present the final word on implementation so much as to provide a starting point for understanding and a challenge to further inquiry.

For further reflection

1. Berman's conclusion that "adaptive strategies" are required for most implementation efforts flows largely from his work in monitoring federal educational programs. See Paul Berman, "Thinking About Programmed and Adaptive Implementation," in *Why Policies Succeed or Fail*, ed. Helen Ingram and Dean Mann, Sage Yearbook in Politics and Public Policy, vol. 8 (Beverly Hills: Sage Publications, 1980), pp. 205–27. Identify as many different federal policy areas as possible—at least ten— according to your estimation of whether they are more amenable to "adaptive" or "top down/programmed" strategies of implementation.

2. Legislation (or other authoritative directives) calling for major change in the status quo can be initiated by federal, state, or local governments. At which level of initiation is a policy more likely to be implemented most successfully? Why? At which level, and under what conditions, is the passage of non-incremental policy most likely to occur? Why?

3. *A Group Project:* Categorize the federal programs launched (or given their major impetus) during the mid-1960s according to the four scenarios described in this chapter—effective implementation, gradual erosion, cumulative incrementalism, rejuvenation. At a minimum, consider the following programs:

    ☐ Title I of the Elementary and Secondary Education Act
    ☐ Civil Rights Act of 1964
    ☐ Voting Rights Act of 1965
    ☐ Model Cities
    ☐ Manpower training
    ☐ Appalachian redevelopment
    ☐ Clean Air Act of 1963
    ☐ Community action programs of the war on poverty
    ☐ Medicare and Medicaid

4. Compare and constrast the implementation checklist presented in this

chapter with that developed by Eugene Bardach in *The Implementation Game* (Cambridge, Mass.: MIT Press, 1977), pp. 264–66.

Notes

1. Alvin W. Gouldner, "Metaphysical Pathos and the Theory of Bureaucracy," *American Political Science Review* 49 (June 1955): 507.
2. Paul Berman, "Thinking About Programmed and Adaptive Implementation: Matching Strategies to Situations," in *Why Policies Succeed or Fail,* ed. Helen Ingram and Dean Mann (Beverly Hills: Sage Publications, 1980), pp. 205–27.
3. Aaron Wildavsky, *Speaking Truth to Power: The Art and Craft of Policy Analysis* (Boston: Little, Brown and Company, 1979), p. 43.
4. Though pessimists are in the majority today, if gauged by the volume of publication, other voices have been raised. A positive view of the accomplishments of the Great Society is presented by Sar Levitan and Robert Taggart, "The Great Society Did Succeed," in *Making Change Happen?* ed. Dale Mann (New York: Teachers College Press, 1978), pp. 308–25. and Henry Aaron, *Politics and the Professors: The Great Society in Perspective* (Washington, D.C.: The Brookings Institution, 1978).
5. Sec. 201, Elementary and Secondary Education Act of 1965.
6. This is a revised and extended list of that developed in Paul Sabatier and Daniel Mazmanian, "The Conditions of Effective Implementation: A Guide to Accomplishing Policy Objectives," *Policy Analysis* 5 (Fall 1979): 503–4.
7. Kenneth Culp Davis, *Discretionary Justice* (Urbana: University of Illinois Press, 1969).
8. See also Paul Sabatier, "Social Movements and Regulatory Agencies: Toward a More Adequate—and Less Pessimistic—Theory of 'Clientele Capture,'" *Policy Sciences* 6 (Fall, 1975): 301-42.
9 The Gradual Erosion Scenario is quite close to the Bernstein rise-capture-decay cycle of regulatory agencies described in his now classic study: Marver Bernstein, *Regulating Business by Independent Commission* (Princeton: Princeton University Press, 1955).
10. See, for example, Alan Stone, *Economic Regulation and the Public Interest* (Ithaca: Cornell University Press, 1977); Harrison Wellford, "The FTC's New Look: A Case Study of Regulatory Revival," in *Consumer Health and Product Hazards: Cosmetics and Drugs, Pesticides, Food Additives,* ed. Samuel Epstein and Richard Grundy (Cambridge, Mass.: MIT Press, 1974), pp. 324–67.
11. For other schemes of making implementation estimates, tailored much more to middle-level program managers within an agency, see Eugene Bardach, *The Implementation Game: What Happens After a Bill Becomes a Law* (Cambridge, Mass.: MIT Press, 1977), pp. 254–83 and Harold Luft, "Benefit Cost Analysis and Public Policy Implementation" *Public Policy* 24 (Fall 1976): 437–62. The twelve questions presented were developed initially in Paul Sabatier and Daniel Mazmanian, "The Implementation of Public Policy: A Framework for Analysis," in *Effective Policy Implementation,* ed. Daniel Mazmanian and Paul Sabatier (Lexington, Mass.: Lexington Books, 1981), pp. 25–26.

Postscript

NOTE: The following is a slightly revised version of an article by Paul A. Sabatier which appeared in the *Journal of Public Policy* 6 (January 1986): 21-48. The authors would like to thank Cambridge University Press for permission to reprint the article.

As indicated in the **PREFACE**, this chapter first reviews two major traditions in the implementation literature and then synthesizes some of their best features into a conceptual framework for examining policy change over a 10-20 year period. This shift from policy implementation to long-term policy change is one of several approaches which implementation scholars of the late 1970s and early 1980s have taken since publication of the first edition of this book. In our view, it is one of the more promising ones. (For further developments, see the symposium on "Policy Change and Policy-Oriented Learning" in the Fall 1988 issue of *Policy Sciences*.)

Top-down and bottom-up approaches to implementation research: a critical analysis and suggested synthesis

The last fifteen years has witnessed an enormous amount of research on policy implementation. While the early work was primarily American—motivated in part by perceived failures in Great Society programs—much of the most interesting recent work has been done in Western Europe. For general reviews, see Yin (1980), Barrett and Fudge (1981), Alexander (1982), and Sabatier and Mazmanian (1983a).

Most of the early American studies were analyses of a single case and came to very pessimistic conclusions about the ability of governments to effectively implement their programs (Derthick, 1972; Pressman and Wildavsky, 1973; Murphy, 1973; Bardach, 1974). The second generation of studies were more analytical and comparative in perspective (Goggin, 1986). They sought to explain variation in implementation success across programs and governmental units by reference to specific variables and conceptual frameworks (Van Meter and Van Horn, 1976; Sabatier and Mazmanian, 1979, 1980). But they maintained the same "top-down" perspective as earlier writers, i.e. they started with a policy decision (usually a statute) and examined the extent to which its legally-mandated objectives were achieved over time and why.

In the late 1970s and early 1980s, however, a quite different approach emerged in response to the perceived weaknesses of the "top-down" perspective. Rather than start with a policy decision, these "bottom-uppers" started with an analysis of the multitude of actors who interact at the operational (local) level on a particular problem or issue. In the process, the familiar policy stages of formulation, implementation, and reformulation tended to disappear. Instead, the focus has been on the strategies pursued by various actors in pursuit of their objectives. Such studies have shown that local actors often deflect centrally-mandated programs toward their own ends (Lipsky, 1971; Berman and McLaughlin, 1976; Hanf and Scharpf, 1978; Ingram, 1978; Elmore, 1979; Browning et al, 1981; Barrett and Fudge, 1981; Hjern and Hull, 1982; Hanf, 1982).

This chapter will first examine the "top-down" and "bottom-up" approaches in greater detail, including an analysis of the strengths and weaknesses of each. It will then suggest a synthetic framework which integrates most of the strengths of the respective approaches and applies it to a longer time frame than in most implementation studies.

Top-down approaches: a not entirely disinterested evaluation

In analyzing the two approaches, we shall focus on a representative scholar for each: Daniel Mazmanian and Paul Sabatier for the top-downers, Benny Hjern et al for the bottom-uppers.[1] While this neglects the views of other scholars, it assures that the work of a leading proponent of each "school" will be subjected to detailed analysis.

Presentation

The essential features of a top-down approach are that it starts with a policy decision by governmental (often central government) officals and then asks:[2]

1) To what extent were the actions of implementing official and target groups consistent with (the objectives and procedures outlined in) that policy decision?

2) To what extent were the objectives attained over time, i.e. to what extent were the impacts consistent with the objectives?

3) What were the principal factors affecting policy outputs and impacts, both those relevant to the official policy as well as other politically significant ones?

4) How was the policy reformulated over time on the basis of experience?

The work of Sabatier and Mazmanian serves as a useful example of the top-down approach because it has been around for several years; it has been subjected to extensive empirical testing; and it is viewed by at least a few completely disinterested observers (Alterman, 1983; Goggin, 1984) as a leading proponent of this point of view.

The Sabatier and Mazmanian framework (1979, 1980) took as its point of departure the first generation of implementation research with its very pessimistic conclusions (Pressman and Wildavsky, 1973; Murphy, 1973; Bardach, 1974; Jones, 1975; Berman and McLaughlin, 1976; Elmore, 1978). Sabatier and Mazmanian first identified a variety of legal, political, and "tractability" variables affecting the different stages of the implementation process (see Figure 2.1, p. 22).

They then sought to synthesize this large number of variables into a shorter list of six sufficient and generally necessary conditions for the effective implementation of legal objectives:

1)   Clear and consistent objectives.

     Taken from Van Meter and Van Horn (1975), clear legal objectives were viewed as providing both a standard of evaluation and an important legal resource to implementing officials.

2)   Adequate causal theory.

     Borrowing the fundamental insight of Pressman and Wildavsky (1973) that policy interventions incorporate an implicit theory about how to effectuate social change, Sabatier and Mazmanian pointed to the adequacy of the jurisdiction and policy levers given implementing officials as a means of ascertaining those causal assumptions.

3)   Implementation process legally structured to enhance compliance by implementing officials and target groups.

     Borrowing again from Pressman and Wildavsky (1973), the authors pointed to a variety of legal mechanisms including the number of veto points involved in program delivery, the sanctions and incentives available to overcome resistance, and the assignment of programs to implementing agencies which would be supportive and give it high priority.

4)   Committed and skillful implementing officials.

     Recognizing the unavoidable discretion given implementing officials, their commitment to policy objectives and skill in utilizing available resources were viewed as critical (Lipsky, 1971; Lazin, 1973; Levin, 1980). While this could partially be determined by the initial statute, much of it was a product of post-statutory political forces.

5)   Support of interest groups and sovereigns.

     This simply recognized the need to maintain political support throughout the long implementation process from interest groups and from legislative and executive sovereigns (Downs, 1967; Murphy, 1973; Bardach, 1974; Sabatier, 1975).

6)   Changes in socio-economic conditions which do not substantially undermine political support or causal theory.

This variable simply recognized that changes in socio-economic conditions, e.g. the Arab oil boycott or the Vietnam War, could have dramatic repercussions on the political support or causal theory of a program Hofferbert, 1974; Aaron, 1978).

In short, the first three conditions can be dealt with by the initial policy decision (e.g. a statute), whereas the latter three are largely the product of subsequent political and economic pressure during the subsequent implementation process.

Although Sabatier and Mazmanian took seriously the arguments of Lipsky (1971), Berman (1978; 1980), and Elmore (1978) concerning the substantial limitations of programmed/hierarchical control, they did not accept the pessimists' conclusion concerning the inevitability of "adaptive" implementation in which policy-makers are forced largely to acquiese to the preferences of street-level bureaucrats and target groups. Instead, they sought to identify a number of legal and political mechanisms for affecting the preferences and/or constraining the behavior of street level bureaucrats and target groups both in the initial policy decision and then subsequently over time. For example, policy-makers normally have some ability to select one set of implementing officials over another; to affect the number of clearance points; to provide appropriate incentives and sanctions; to affect the balance of constituency support; etc. And, as Pressman and Wildavsky (1973) clearly showed, policy-makers can strongly affect the implementation process by basing a program on a valid causal theory rather than a dubious one. In short, while Sabatier and Mazmanian rejected hierarchical *control*—in the sense of tightly constrained behavior—as impossible, they argued that the behavior of street level bureaucrats and target groups could be kept within acceptable bounds over time if the six conditions were met (Sabatier and Mazmanian, 1979: 489-92, 503-4).

Over the next five years, Sabatier and Mazmanian sought to have the framework tested—by themselves and others—in a variety of policy areas and political systems. The results, summarized in Table 1, indicate that the framework has been applied over twenty times. These cases have involved ten policy areas, including strong representation from land use control, education, and environmental protection. While a majority of cases have been American, many of these have focused on state or local policy initiatives rather than on the implementation of federal policy. In addition, there have been eight cases, primarily in higher education, involving six European countries.

It is now time to assess the results of this research program. This will be done, first, from the standpoint of one of the authors and then from the perspective of their "bottom-up" critics.

A Critical Self-Appraisal

One ought, of course, to be skeptical of self-evaluations. Authors are often tempted to select cases which fit their theories. In this instance, however, only

TABLE 1
Empirical Applications of the Sabatier and Mazmanian Framework

I. Original Research by Sabatier and/or Mazmanian.

   1. California Coastal Conservation Act, 1972-80 (Sabatier and Mazmanian, 1983b)
   2. Bay Conservation and Development Act, 1965-72 (Sabatier and Klosterman, 1981)
   3. French Coastal Decrees of 1976 and 1979 (Sabatier, 1984)

II. Secondary Analysis of Others' Research by Sabatier and/or Mazmanian.

   1. British Open University, 1969-79 (Cerych and Sabatier, 1986)
   2. French Instituts Universitaires de Technologie, 1967-79 (Cerych and Sabatier, 1986)
   3. Norwegian Regional Colleges, 1970-79 (Cerych and Sabatier, 1986)
   4. University of Tromsø (Norway), 1969-79 (Cerych and Sabatier, 1986)
   5. German Gesamthochschule, 1970-79 (Cerych and Sabatier, 1986)
   6. Swedish 25/5 Scheme (Cerych and Sabatier, 1986)
   7. Polish Preferential University Admissions (Cerych and Sabatier, 1986)
   8. 1970 U.S. Clean Air Act, 1970-79 (Mazmanian and Sabatier, 1983)
   9. U.S. School Desegregation, South and North, 1955-75 (Mazmanian and Sabatier, 1983)
   10. 1965 U.S. Elementary and Secondary Education Act, Title I, 1966-67 (Mazmanian and Sabatier, 1983)
   11. 1970 New Towns Act (U.S.), 1970-78 (Mazmanian and Sabatier, 1983)

III. Utilization by Other Scholars

   1. Model Cities, Revenue Sharing, and Block Grants in SF Bay Area (Browning et al, 1981)
   2. Variety of Federal Civil Rights Programs (Bullock, 1981; Bullock and Lamb, 1984; Nuccio, 1987)
   3. Evolution of U.S. Welfare (AFDC) Policy since 1935 (Goodwin and Moen, 1981)
   4. 1965 ESEA, Title I, 1966-79 (Kirst and Jung, 1981)
   5. Groundwater Management in Several New York Counties (Jones, 1984)
   6. U.S. Hazardous Waste Policy (Lester, 1985; Davis, 1985; Wiley, 1985; Lester and Bowman, 1989; Davis and Lester, 1988)
   7. U.S. Coastal Zone Management (Lowry, 1985)
   8. Environmental Policy (Mann, 1982)
   9. U.S. Family Planning Legislation (McFarlane, 1989)
   10. Wetlands Regulation (Rosenbaum, 1981)
   11. Implementation of Court Decisions (Baum, 1981)

seven of the twenty-four cases were selected by Mazmanian and Sabatier, thus affording some protection against biased case selection.[3] That still leaves the potential for biased data selection or interpretation of results, but the reader can decide for himself after examining the case evidence.

These caveats notwithstanding, experience has demonstrated some real strengths in the Sabatier/Mazmanian framework.

First, the importance it attaches to legal structuring of the implementation process—one of its major innovations—has been confirmed in numerous studies (Rosenbaum, 1981; Sabatier and Klosterman, 1981; Bullock and Lamb, 1984; McFarlane, 1989). This is particularly gratifying since one of the most frequent criticisms of the framework has been that the emphasis on structuring is unrealistic, i. e. that the cognitive limitations of policy-makers and the need for compromise at the formulation stage preclude careful structuring (Majone and Wildavsky, 1978; Barrett and Fudge, 1981). The evidence suggests that, while fairly coherent structuring is difficult, it occurs more frequently than critics realize and, when present, proves to be very important.

For example, the framework emphasized the importance of selecting implementing institutions supportive of the new program and suggested creating new agencies as a specific strategy. This turned out to be possible in six of the twenty-odd cases studied—the California coastal commissions, BCDC, Open University, French Instituts Universitaires de Technologie (IUTs), Norwegian Regional Colleges, and University of Tromso—and in many other cases formulators expressly selected sympathetic existing institutions. When this was not possible, e.g. compensatory education in the U.S., it proved to be a serious impediment to effective implementation.

Likewise, two of the major contributions borrowed from Pressman and Wildavsky (1973)—veto points and causal theory—were confirmed in many studies. In the case of the coastal commmissions, for example, the agencies' greater success in protecting scenic views than in providing public access to the beach can largely be explained by reference to the number of veto points: In particular, the coastal commissions had all the legal authority necessary to protect scenic views, while actually providing public access required the cooperation of at least a half-dozen other agencies (Chap. 7). The superior ability of U.S. air pollution authorities to regulate automotive emissions than to reduce vehicle miles traveled can be attributed to a greater understanding of, and control over, the factors involved (Chap. 4). The much greater success of the British Open University than the French IUTs in reaching projected enrollments can be partially attributed to the better theory utilized by policy formulators in the former case (Cerych and Sabatier, 1986). While Bowen (1982) rightly cautions that the analysis of veto points is more complicated than envisaged by Pressman and Wildavsky, their contributions remain of the first order.

Perhaps the best evidence of the potential importance of legal structuring is that the two most successful cases studied to date—the California coastal commissions (at least in the short run) and the British Open University—were also the best designed institutions. That is, they structured the process to provide reasonably consistent objectives, a good causal theory, relatively few veto points, sympathetic implementing officials, access of supporters to most decisions, and adequate financial resources.

Second, the six conditions of effective implementation have proven to be a useful checklist of critical factors in understanding variations in program performance and in understanding the strategies of program proponents over time. While the relative importance of specific factors has varied across cases—with implementing agency support being probably the most consistently critical one—all except clear and consistent objectives have been important in many cases. There is also some evidence that interest group support may be more critical in the U.S. than in many European countries—presumably reflecting the greater autonomy of administrative agencies in countries like Great Britain, France, and the German Federal Republic.

Third, the relatively manageable list of variables and the focus in the framework on the formulation-implementation-reformulation cycle encouraged many of our case authors to look at a longer time-frame than was true of earlier implementation studies (i.e. ten years instead of four). This, in turn, led to a discovery of the importance of learning by propram proponents over time as they became aware of deficiencies in the original program and sought improved legal and political strategies for dealing with them. The best example is the American compensatory education case, where serious deficiencies revealed by early evaluation studies enabled program proponents to greatly stengthen the legal structure and constituency support over time (Kirst and Jung, 1982; Chap. 6). For other examples of learning over time, one can cite the supporters of the French IUTs who greatly improved their understanding of the factors affecting student choices over time (Cerych and Sabatier, 1986).

Fourth, our focus on legally-mandated objectives—particularly when combined with the ten-year time span for assessing program effectiveness—helped produce a less pessimistic evaluation of governmental performance than was true of the first generation of implemenation studies. On the one hand, the focus on legally-mandated objectives encouraged scholars to carefully distinguish the objectives contained in legal documents from both the political rhetoric surrounding policy formulation and the tendency of critics to evaluate a program on the basis of what they mistakenly perceived to be its objectives—the criticism of the "failure" of the Open University to meet the needs of working class students being a case in point.[4] In addition, the longer time-frame used in many of these studies meant that several which were initially regarded as failures—U.S. compensatory education and the French IUTs—were regarded in a more favorable light after proponents had had the benefit of a decade of learning and experimentation (Kirst and Jung, 1982; Chap. 6; Cerych and Sabatier, 1986).

On the other hand, several years' experience with testing the Sabatier/Mazmanian framework has also revealed some significant flaws—quite apart from the more serious methodological criticisms of the "bottom-uppers."

First, the emphasis they placed on "clear and consistent policy objectives" was a mistake. Experience has confirmed the critics' charge that very few programs meet this criterion, either initially or after a decade (Majone and Wildavsky, 1978; MacIntyre, 1985). Instead, the vast majority incorporate a multitude of partially-conflicting objectives. This does not, however, preclude the possibility for assessing program effectiveness. Instead, it simply means that effectiveness needs to be reconceptualized into the ''acceptability space'' demarcated by the intersection of the ranges of acceptable values on each of the multiple evaluative dimensions involved. This can be illustrated by the case of the Norwegian regional colleges: They were supposed to serve students from the local region and to foster regionally-relevant research at the same time that they were also mandated to be part of a national educational system in which the transfer of student credits among institutions and the evaluation of faculty research by peers in other institutions had to be protected. While the institutions after a decade were receiving ''excellent'' ratings on very few of these dimensions, the evidence suggests they were satisfactory on all of them (Cerych and Sabatier, 1986).

On a related point, most implementation scholars have followed Van Meter and Van Horn (1976) in assuming that, *ceteris paribus*, the probability of effective implementation of a reform is inversely related to the extent of envisaged departure from the status quo ante. In their study of European higher education reforms, however, Cerych and Sabatier (1986) provide evidence that the relationship is not linear but rather curvilinear. They suggest that very incremental reforms—e.g. the Swedish 25/5 Scheme for adult admission to universities— simply do not arouse enough commitment to get much done, while those such as the German *Gesamthochschulen* which envisage a comprehensive reform of the entire system arouse too much resistance to get off the ground.[5] Instead, those reforms—e.g., the British Open University— which are ambitious enough to arouse intense commitment from proponents but rather limited in their effects on the entire (e.g. higher education) system stand the best chance of success.

Second, while Sabatier and Mazmanian encouraged a longer time-frame and provided several examples of policy-oriented learning over time, their framework did not provide a good conceptual vehicle for looking at policy change over periods of a decade or more (Goodwin and Moen, 1981; Browning et al., 1981; Goggin, 1984; Lowry, 1985). This is primarily because, as we shall see below, it focused too much on the perspective of program *proponents*, thereby neglecting the strategies (and learning) by other actors which would provide the cornerstone for a more dynamic model.

The assessment thus far has been from the point of view of the authors or other sympathizers of a top-down perspective. It is now time to examine the more fundamental methodological criticisms raised by ''bottom-uppers,'' most notably, Benny Hjern.

The Bottom-Up Critique

The fundamental flaw in top-down models, according to Hjern and Hull (1982), Hanf (1982), Barrett and Fudge (1981), Elmore (1979) and other bottom-uppers, is that they start from the perspective of (central) decision-makers and thus tend to neglect other actors. Their methodology leads top-downers to assume that the framers of the policy decision (e.g. statute) are the key actors and that others are basically impediments. This, in turn, leads them to neglect strategic initiatives coming from the private sector, from street level bureaucrats or local implementing officials, and from other policy subsystems. While Sabatier and Mazmanian are not entirely guilty of this—in particular, their focus on causal theory and hierarchical integration encourages the analyst to examine the perspectives of other actors—this is certainly a potential Achilles' heel of their model.

A second, and related, criticism of top-down models is that they are difficult to use in situations where there is no dominant policy (statute) or agency, but rather a multitude of governmental directives and actors, none of them preeminent. As this is often the case, particularly in social service delivery, this is a very telling criticism. While Sabatier and Mazmanian can recognize such situations—through the concepts of (inadequate) causal theory and (poor) hierarchical integration—they have very little ability to predict the outcome of such complex situations except to say that the policy they are interested in will probably not be effectively implemented.

A third criticism of top-down models is that they are likely to ignore, or at least underestimate, the strategies used by street level bureaucrats and target groups to get around (central) policy and/or to divert it to their own purposes (Weatherly and Lipsky, 1977; Elmore, 1978; Berman, 1978). A related point is that such models are likely to neglect many of the counterproductive effects of the policies chosen for analysis. While a really skillful top-downer can attempt to deal with such deficiencies, there is little doubt that these, too, are important criticisms.

Finally, there are a whole series of arguments that the distinction between policy formulation and policy implementation is misleading and/or useless (Nakamura and Smallwood, 1980; Barrett and Fudge, 1981; Hjern and Hull, 1982; Hjern, 1982). These include the following: The distinction ignores the fact that some organizations are involved in both stages and/or that local implementating officials and target groups often simply ignore central legislators and administrators and deal directly with each other; since it is difficult to isolate policy decisions, it is preferable to talk about action and reaction (Barrett and Fudge, 1981); and because policies change as they get implemented, it is better to talk about policy evolution (Majone and Wildavsky, 1978).

This criticism strikes me as much less persuasive than the previous three. On the one hand, there are certainly cases, such as the Swedish 25/5 Scheme (Cerych and Sabatier, 1986), where there is no discernible policy "decision" but rather a series of very incremental steps over time. But in the vast majority of the cases using the Sabatier and Mazmanian framework, it was not only possible but also highly desirable to retain the distinction between formulation and implementation. In fact, of the twenty-four cases, the 25/5 Scheme was the only one in which anyone even remotely skilled in legal analysis would find it difficult to discern an initial major policy decision. As for the arguments that some organizations are involved in both formulation and implementation, so what? The same organizations also try to influence local and central government; does this suggest that distinction between levels of government ought also to be rejected as useless? Finally while local officials and target groups may sometimes ignore the legal authority of central officials, if such officials were really as insignificant as Hjern et al suggest then why do the very same local officials and interest groups spend thousands of hours and millions of dollars every year trying to influence them?

Furthermore, obliterating the distinction between formulation and implementation will have two very significant costs (Sabatier and Mazmanian, 1983a). First, it makes it very difficult to distinquish the relative influence of elected officials and civil servants—thus precluding an analysis of democratic accountability and bureaucratic discretion, hardly trivial topics. Second, the view of the policy process as a seamless web of flows without decision points (Majone and Wildavsky, 1978; Barrett and Fudge, 1981) precludes policy evaluation (because there is no policy to evaluate) and the analysis of policy change (as there is never a defined policy at t_0 which changes into another defined policy at t_1).

In sum, while the first three criticisms are reasonably persuasive, the fourth is not. The bottom-uppers have thus been able to advance some rather telling arguments against the top-down approach. Have they also been able to accomplish the more difficult task of developing a more viable alternative?

Bottom-up approaches: the promised land?

In discussing the bottom-up perspective, the focus will be on the work of Benny Hjern and his colleagues—David Porter, Ken Hanf, and Chris Hull—who, while at the Science Center in Berlin during the period from roughly 1975 to 1983, developed a coherent methodology for conducting implementation analysis.[6] It is this willingness to propose an intersubjectively reliable alternative to top-down approaches which distinguishes Hjern et al. from many bottom-up critics (e.g. Barrett and Fudge, 1981) and is one of the principal reasons their work has been chosen for analysis.

Presentation

Hjern et al. began with an acute awareness of the methodological weaknesses of the top-down approach, a commitment to the development of an intersubjectively reliable methodology, and a concern with policy areas—e.g. manpower training—involving a multitude of public and private organizations.

TABLE 2
Comparison Between Top-Down and Bottom-Up Approaches

	Top-Down (Sabatier & Mazmanian)	Bottom-Up (Hjern et al.)
Initial Focus	(Central) Government decision, e.g., new pollution control law	Local implementation structure (network) involved in a policy area, e.g., pollution control
Identification of major actors the process	From top-down and from govt. out to private sector (although importance attached to causal theory calls for accurate understanding of target group's incentive structure)	From bottom (govt. and private) up
Evaluative criteria	Focus on extent of attainment of formal objectives (carefully analyzed). May look at other politically significant criteria and unintended consequences, but these are optional.	Much less clear. Basically anything the analyst chooses which is somehow relevant to the policy issue or problem. Certainly does not require any careful analysis of official govt. decision(s).
Overall Focus	How does one steer system to achieve (top) policy-maker's intended policy results?	Strategic interaction among multiple actors in a policy network.

In contrast to the top-down approach—which starts from a policy decision and focuses on the extent to which its objectives are attained over time and why—the bottom-up approach of Hjern et al. starts by identifying the network of actors involved in service delivery in one or more local areas and asks them about their goals, strategies, activities, and contacts. It then uses the contacts as a vehicle for developing a networking technique to identify the local, regional, and national actors involved in the planning, financing, and execution of the relevant governmental and non-governmental programs. This provides a mechanism for moving from street level bureaucrats (the "bottom") up to the "top" policy-makers in both the public and private sectors (Hjern et al., 1978; Hjern and Porter, 1981; Hjern and Hull, 1985). Table 2 compares some of the central features of top-down and bottom-up approaches.

The study of Swedish manpower training programs, for example, by Hjern et al. (1978) started with the interaction of unions, governmental employment agencies, local governments, and industrial firms in several areas, and then moved from there via a networking technique to identify the people actually involved in planning, financing, and executing the relevant programs. They concluded that program success was far more dependent upon the skills of specific individuals in "local implementation structures" than upon the efforts of central government officials.

In addition to their study of manpower training programs in Sweden and the German Federal Republic, Hjern et al. have sought to apply this technique to a variety of programs designed to foster the economic viability of small firms in the Federal Republic and several other countries (Hjern and Hull, 1985). They have also encouraged the application of their approach to Swedish energy policy (Wittrock et al, 1982), English manpower training (Davies and Mason, 1982), Dutch pollution control (Hanf, 1982), and Swiss economic development (Ackermann and Steinmann, 1982). It should be noted, however, that—with the exception of Hanf—these latter papers are more united by a bottom-up perspective than by any serious effort to employ the networking methodology first outlined by Hjern and Porter (1981).

Evaluation

The approach developed by Hjern et al. has several notable strengths.

First, they have developed an explicit and replicable methodology for identifying a policy network ("implementation structure"). In the small firms study, for example, they started with a random sample of firms in an area, and then interviewed key officials in each firm to ascertain their critical problems, the strategies developed to deal with each, and the persons contacted to execute each of those strategies. They then used those contacts via a networking technique to identify the "implementation structure" (Hull and Hjern, 1982). In the case of financial problems, for example, the structure would include local (and perhaps regional) banks, officials in agencies with financial assistance programs, and, in the most successful case, an official in a local redevelopment agency who had extensive contacts he could direct firms to. It is this intersubjectively reliable methodology which separates Hjern et al from the vast majority of bottom-up (and even top-down) researchers.

Second, because Hjern et al. do not begin with a governmental program but rather with actors' perceived problems and the strategies developed for dealing with them, they are able to assess the relative importance of a variety of governmental programs vis-a-vis private organizations and market forces in solving those problems. In contrast, a top-down approach is likely to overestimate the importance of the governmental program which is its focus. For example, Hanf's (1982) bottom-up analysis of pollution control in the Netherlands concluded that energy policies and the market price of alternative fuels had more effect on firms' pollution control programs than did governmental pollution control programs--a conclusion which would have been difficult for a top-downer to reach.

Third, because Hjern et al. do not start with a focus on the attainment of formal policy objectives, they are free to see all sorts of (unintended) consequences of governmental and private programs.

Fourth, this approach is able to deal with a policy/problem area involving a multitude of public (and private) programs, none of them preeminent. In contrast, such cases present substantial difficulties for top-down approaches.

Finally, because of their focus on the strategies pursued by a wide range of actors, bottom-uppers are better able to deal with strategic interaction over time than are top-downers—who tend to focus on the strategies of program proponents, while neglecting those of other actors.

For all these strengths, however, the Hjern et al approach also has its limitations.

First, just as top-downers are in danger of overemphasizing the importance of the Center vis-a-vis the Periphery, bottom-uppers are likely to overemphasize the ability of the Periphery to frustrate the Center.

More specifically, the focus on actors' goals and strategies—the vast majority of whom are at the Periphery—may underestimate the Center's *indirect* influence over those goals and strategies through its ability to affect the institutional structure in which individuals operate (Kiser and Ostrom, 1982). For example, if Hjern et al. had studied the California coastal commmissions, they would have taken as given that the vast majority of coastal officials were very sympathetic to environmental protection—without ever realizing that the distribution of officials' preferences was a consequence of the prior efforts of the framers of the coastal law to structure the situation in such a way—via the distribution of appointments between state and local governments—to maximize the probability of that outcome. Likewise, Hjern et al. would simply take as granted that Actor A had certain resources without inquiring into the reasons s/he had them. In short, one of the most basic shortcomings of the Hjern et al. approach is that it takes the present distribution of preferences and resources as given, without ever inquiring into the efforts of other actors to structure the rules of the game.

Second, in a related point, Hjern et al. take the present participants in an implementation structure as given without examining the prior efforts of various individuals to affect participation rates. For example, their networking methodology would simply have revealed that environmental groups were frequent litigants in American air pollution cases—thus neglecting the extensive efforts of drafters of the 1970 Clean Air Act to provide such groups with legal "standing" (formal rights of intervention) to participate in such litigation.

This brings us to a third, and more fundamental, limitation with the Hjern et al approach: Its failure to start from an explicit theory of the factors affecting its subject of interest. Because it relies very heavily on the perceptions and activities of participants, it is their prisoner—and therefore is unlikely to analyze the factors *indirectly* affecting their behavior or even the factors directly affecting such behavior which the participants do not recognize. Hjern et al. suffer from all of the limitations—as well as the advantages—of "grounded theory" (Glaser and Strauss, 1967). Their networking methodology is a useful starting point for identifying many of the actors involved in a policy area, but it needs to be related via an explicit theory to social, economic, and legal factors which structure the perceptions, resources, and participation of those actors.

Scharpf (1978) and Thrasher (1983) have attempted to use exchange theory toward this end, but that hasn't been followed by Hjern et al. Likewise, Barrett and Fudge (1981) and Barrett and Hill (1984) have toyed with a number of approaches—mostly related to bargaining—but thus far haven't come close to an explicit conceptual framework. Until they do, the implicit assumptions which are guiding their data collection will remain difficult to discern.

Finally, it is worth observing that top-downers and bottom-uppers have been motivated by somewhat different concerns and thus have developed different approaches. Top-downers have been preoccupied with (a) the effectiveness of specific governmental programs and (b) the ability of elected officials to guide and constrain the behavior of civil servants and target groups. Addressing such concerns requires a careful analysis of the formally-approved objectives of elected officials, an examination of relevant performance indicators, and an analysis of the factors affecting such performance. Bottom-uppers, on the other hand, are far less preoccupied with the extent to which a formally enacted policy *decision* is carried out and much more concerned with accurately mapping the strategies of actors concerned with a policy *problem*. They are not primarily concerned with the implementation (carrying out) of a policy per se but rather with understanding actor interaction in a specific policy sector.

Where do we go from here?

Having identified the strengths and weaknesses of the two approaches, there are at least two strategies which can be pursued. The first is to the indicate the conditions under which each is the more appropriate approach. The second is to develop one or more syntheses of the competing approaches.

Comparative Advantage

The top-down approach is useful, first, in cases where there is a dominant public program in the policy area under consideration or where the analyst is solely interested in the effectiveness of *a* program. In cases like the California coastal commissions or the Open University—where a single public agency clearly dominated the field—the top-down approach is appropriate. On the other hand, in policy areas such as manpower training and employment development—which necessarily involve a multitude of public and private actors—the bottom-up approach is more appropriate. One might in fact be tempted to demarcate entire policy areas—e.g. highways, social security, income taxation—where there is a dominant public agency, but this should only be done with caution as unions and other private actors may turn out to be more important than anticipated.

On a more general note, the top-down approach is more useful in making a preliminary assessment of which approach to use: To the extent that the scores on the six conditions of effective implementation are relatively high and the investigator is primarily interested in the *mean* policy outputs and outcomes, then the top-down approach is appropriate. On the other hand, in cases where the scores on the six conditions are relatively low and one is interested in inter-local variation, then the bottom-up approach should be employed. When scores on the six conditions are moderate or mixed, the appropriate methodology depends on whether one is primarily interested in mean responses or in assessing inter-local variation. The top-down is more appropriate for the former because it focuses on the extent to which the overall system is structured/constrained. The bottom-up focuses on local implementation structures, and thus is better for assessing the dynamics of local variation. One could, of course, aggregate across numerous bottom-up studies to obtain a mean response, but this would normally be prohibitively expensive.

The top-down approach is more useful for making these preliminary assessments because of its greater theoretical development. The identification of specific variables and causal relationships makes predictions possible. On the other hand, the bottom-up approach of Hjern et al. (or Barrett and Fudge) has not yet developed much of a substantive theory and thus is poorly equipped to make predictions.

In summary, the top-down approach appears to have a comparative advantage in situations in which (1) there is a dominant piece of legislation structuring the situation or in which (2) research funds are very limited, one is primarily interested in mean responses, and the situation is structured at least moderately well. In contrast, the bottom-up approach is more appropriate in situations where (1) there is no dominant piece of legislation but rather large numbers of actors without power dependency, or where (2) one is primarily interested in the dynamics of different local situations.

Syntheses

A preferred alternative to these either-or choice situations is to synthesize the best features of the two approaches. To date, there have been at least three such efforts.

The most ambitious has been the study of the implementation of programs designed to reduce sulfur dioxide emissions in several European countries directed by Peter Knoepfel and Helmut Weidner. The conceptual framework for the study was explicitly designed to be a synthesis (Knoepfel and Weidner, 1982a).

But it is also very complicated and, at times, difficult to understand. Unfortunately, the full results of their massive research program are available only in German and thus probably will not receive the dissemination they merit.[7]

A second approach, developed by Richard Elmore (1985), attempts to combine his previous work on "backward mapping"—one of the bottom-up classics—with what he terms "forward mapping," essentially a top-down perspective. He argues that policy-makers need to consider both the policy instruments and other resources at their disposal (forward mapping) *and* the incentive structure of ultimate target groups (backward mapping) because program success is contingent on meshing the two. Elmore's paper is primarily concerned with aiding policy practitioners by indicating the need to use multiple perspectives in designing and implementing policies. At that very practical level, it is excellent. It does not purport, however, to provide a model of the policy process which can be used by social scientists to explain outcomes in a wide variety of settings.

The third approach, to be outlined below, explicitly attempts to develop such a general model of the policy process which combines the best features of the bottom-up and top-down approaches, while also applying them to a longer time frame than is the case in most implementation research.

An advocacy coalition framework of policy change

One of the major contributions of Mazmanian and Sabatier (1983) was their contention that the relatively short time-span (4-5 years) used in most implementation studies not only led to premature judgments concerning program failure but also missed some very important features of the policy process, namely, the extent of policy-oriented learning.

For example, early studies of Federal compensatory education programs (Title I of ESEA) concluded that the program was bringing about very little change because of ambiguous objectives, dubious causal theories, resistance of implementing officials, and the inability of proponents to organize at the local level (Murphy, 1973; McLaughlin, 1975). But later studies incorporating a 10-15 year time-span portrayed a fair amount of improvement on the part of both school officials and students' educational achievement (Kirst and Jung, 1982; Mazmanian and Sabatier, 1983: Chap. 6). Over time, objectives were clarified; research resulted in more adequate causal theories; and supportive constituencies were fostered at both the state and local levels. This suggested a process of policy learning by program proponents, as they discovered deficiencies in the existing program and then developed a series of strategies to deal with them.

While this approach did a good job of illustrating learning by proponents, its top-down assumptions made it difficult to focus equally on learning by opponents. This deficiency can be addressed, however, by incorporating bottom-uppers' techniques for ascertaining the strategies—and, by extension, the learning from experience—of a wider variety of actors concerned with a program. This points to a synthesis which combines top-down and bottom-up approaches in the analysis of policy change over periods of a decade or more.

Elements of the Synthesis

The elements of such a conceptual framework are at hand. Consistent with the bottom-uppers, one needs to start from a policy *problem* or subsystem—rather than a law or other policy *decision*—and then examine the strategies employed by relevant actors in both the public and private sectors at various levels of government as they attempt to deal with the issue consistent with their objectives. The networking technique developed by Hjern et al. can be one of the methods for determining the actors in a subsystem, although it needs to be combined with other approaches indicating the actors who are indirectly (or even potentially) involved.

Likewise, the concerns of top-down theorists with the manner in which legal and socio-economic factors structure behaviorial options need to be incorporated into the synthesis, as do their concerns with the validity of the causal assumptions behind specific programs and strategies. This leads to a focus on (1) the effects of socio-economic (and other) changes external to the policy network/subsystem on actors' resources and strategies; (2) the attempts by various actors to manipulate the legal attributes of governmental programs in order to achieve their objectives over time; and (3) actors' efforts to improve their understanding of the magnitude and factors affecting th eproblem—as well as the impacts of various policy instruments—as they learn from experience.

Attention thus shifts from policy implementation to policy change over periods of 10-20 years. The longer time span creates, however, a need to aggregate actors into a manageable number of groups if the researcher is avoid severe information overload. After examining several options, the most useful principle of aggregation seems to be by belief system. This produces a focus on "advocacy coalitions," i.e. actors from various public and private organizations who share a set of beliefs and who seek to realize their common goals over time.

In short, the synthesis adopts the bottom-uppers' unit of analysis—a whole variety of public and private actors involved with a policy problem—as well as their concerns with understanding the perspectives and strategies of all major categories of actors (not simply program proponents). It then combines this starting point with top-downers' concerns with the manner in which socio-economic conditions and legal instruments constrain behavior. It applies this synthesized perspective to the analysis of policy change over periods of a decade or more. This time-frame is required to deal with the role of policy-oriented learning—a topic identified as critical in several top-down studies, although by no means inherent to that approach. Finally, the synthesis adopts the intellectual style (or methodological perspective) of many top-downers in its willingness to utilize fairly abstract theoretical constructs and to operate from an admittedly simpli-

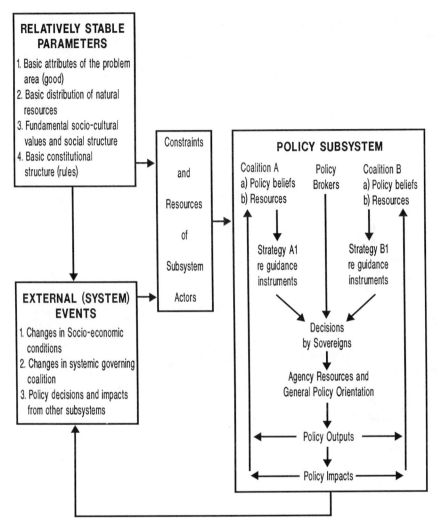

Figure 1. General Model of Policy Evolution Focusing on Competing Advocacy Coalitions Within Policy Subsystems

fied portrait of reality. It is primarily concerned with theory construction rather than with providing guidelines for practitioners or detailed portraits of particular situations.

Overview of the Framework

The advocacy coalition framework starts from the premise that the most useful aggregate unit of analysis for understanding policy change in modern industrial societies is not any specific governmental organization but rather a policy subsystem, i.e. those actors from a variety of public and private organizations who are actively concerned with a policy problem or issue such as higher education or air pollution control (Heclo, 1978; Jordan and Richardson, 1983; Milward and Wamsley, 1984; Rose, 1984; Sharpe, 1985).

Figure 1 presents a general overview of the framework. On the left side are two sets of exogenous variables—the one fairly stable, the other dynamic—which affect the constraints and resources of subsystem actors.

Air pollution policy, for example, is strongly affected by the nature of air quality as a collective good, by the geographical contours of air basins, and by political boundaries which are usually quite stable over time. But there are also more dynamic factors, including changes in socio-economic conditions and in system-wide governing coalitions, which provide some of the principal sources of policy change. These are all features drawn from top-down models which "structure" policy-making.

Within the subsystem, the framework draws heavily upon the bottom-up approach. It assumes, however, that actors can be aggregated into a number of advocacy coalitions—each composed of politicians, agency officials, interest group leaders, and intellectuals who share a set of normative and causal beliefs on core policy issues. At any particular point in time, each coalition adopts a strategy(s) envisaging one or more changes in governmental institutions perceived to further its policy objectives. Conflicting strategies from different coalitions are mediated by a third group of actors, here termed "policy brokers," whose principal concern is to find some reasonable compromise which will reduce intense conflict. The end result is legislation or governmental decrees establishing or modifying one or more governmental action programs at the collective choice level (Kiser and Ostrom, 1982; Page, 1985). These in turn produce policy outputs at the operational level (e.g agency permit decisions). These outputs at the operational level, mediated by a number of other factors (most notably, the validity of the causal theory underlying the program), result in a variety of impacts on targeted problem parameters (e.g ambient air quality), as well as side effects.

At this point the framework requires additional elements not normally central to implementation studies. Some aspects of public policy clearly change far more frequently than others. In order to get a conceptual handle on this, the framework distinguishes the *core* from the *secondary* aspects of a belief system or a governmental action program. Recall that coalitions are seeking to get their beliefs translated into governmental programs, so the two concepts can be analyzed in similar categories. The extent to which a specific program incorporates the beliefs of any single coalition is, however, an empirical question and will reflect the relative power of that coalition within the subsystem.

Table 3 represents a preliminary attempt to identify the principal topics addressed in the Deep Core, the Policy Core, and the Secondary Aspects of a belief system. (Only the latter two are relevant to governmental action programs.) It suggests that coalitions will be very reluctant to alter their beliefs concerning core issues such as the proper scope of governmental vs. market activity; their orientation on basic policy conflicts; the relative distribution of authority among different levels of government; or their identification of social groups whose welfare is most critical. For example, Federal air pollution policy in the U.S.—which essentially reflects the beliefs of the environmental coalition—accords government a very important role in this policy area; places greater priority on public health than on economic development; gives the Federal Government on unusually preeminent role over states and localities; and places a high priority on protecting the welfare of susceptible health populations, e.g. people suffering from emphysema. These are topics on which neither the environmental coalition nor Federal law have changed very much since 1970 (See Chap. 4).

On the other hand, there has been a great deal of change in the secondary attributes of Federal air pollution programs which are instrumental to achieving the core aspects. These include such topics as the appropriate deadlines for meeting particular emission standards; the relative importance of various sources of pollutants affecting air quality; the most valid methods for measuring ambient air quality; the proper enforcement budget of implementing agencies; the perceived feasibility of particular pollution control technologies; and the precise effects of particular concentrations on specific populations. While these have all been the subject of vigorous debate, they represent rather marginal, instrumental choices within the context of core beliefs.

The framework argues that the core aspects of a governmental action program—and the relative strength of competing advocacy coalitions within a policy subsystem—will typically remain rather stable over periods of a decade or more. Major alterations in the policy core will normally be the product of changes external to the subsystem—particularly large-scale socio-economic perturbations or changes in the systemwide governing coalition. An example of the latter would be the change in Britain from Parliaments dominated by moderate socialists and conservatives to a system dominated by Mrs. Thatcher's wing of the Conservative Party with a *fundamentally* different conception of the proper scope of governmental activity.

While changes in the policy core are usually the result of external perturbations, changes in the secondary aspects of a governmental action program are often the result of policy-oriented learning by various coalitions or policy brokers. Following Heclo (1974:306), policy-oriented learning refers to relatively enduring alterations of thought or behavioral intentions which result from experience and which are concerned with the attainment or revision of policy objectives. Policy-oriented learning involves the internal feedback loops depicted in Figure 2, as well as increased knowledge of the state of problem parameters and the factors affecting them. For example, a decade of experience and research in U.S. air pollution programs has indicated that efforts to reduce vehicle miles traveled by commuters through the use of, e.g. parking surcharges, have only very modest effects on air quality, impose very substantial costs on commuters, and therefore are no longer a feasible policy option (See Chap. 4). Since the vast majority

TABLE 3
Structure of Belief Systems of Policy Elites[a]

	Deep (Normative) Core	Near (Policy) Core	Secondary Aspects
Defining characteristics	Fundamental normative and ontological axioms	Fundamental policy positions concerning the basic strategies for achieving normative axioms of deep core.	Instrumental decisions and information searches necessary to implement policy core.
Scope	Part of basic personal philosophy. Applies to all policy areas.	Applies to policy area of interest (and perhaps a few more).	Specific to policy area/subsystem of interest.
Susceptibility to change	Very difficult; akin to a religious conversion.	Difficult, but can occur if experience reveals serious anomalies.	Moderately easy; this is the topic of most administrative and even legislative policy-making.

Illustrative components	1) The nature of man
	  i) Inherently evil vs. socially redeemable.
	  ii) Part of nature vs. dominion over nature
		1) Proper scope of governmental vs. market activity.
		2) Proper distribution of authority among various units (e.g. levels) of government.
			1) Most decisions concerning administrative rules, budgetary allocations, disposition of cases, statutory interpretation, and even statutory revision.

iii) Narrow egoists vs. contractarians.

2) Relative priority of various ultimate values: freedom, security, power, knowledge, health, love, beauty, etc.

3) Basic criteria of distributive justice: Whose welfare counts? Relative weights of self, primary groups, all people, future generations, non-human beings, etc.

3) Identification of social groups whose welfare is most critical.

4) Orientation on substantive policy conflicts, e.g. environmental protection vs. economic development.

5) Magnitude of perceived threat to those values.

6) Basic choices concerning policy instruments, e.g. coercion vs. inducements vs. persuasion.

7) Desirability of participation by various segments of society:
   i) Public vs. elite participation.
   ii) Experts vs. elected officials.

8) Ability of society to solve problems in this policy area:
   i) Zero-sum competition vs. potential for mutual accomodation.
   ii) Technological optimism vs. pessimism.

2) Information concerning program performance, the seriousness of the problems, etc.

a The Policy Core and Secondary Aspects also apply to governmental programs.

of policy debates involve secondary aspects of a governmental action program—in part because actors realize the futility of challenging core assumptions—such learning can play an important role in policy change. In fact, a principal concern of the framework is to analyze the institutional conditions conducive to such learning and the cases in which cumulative learning may lead to changes in the policy core.

A more extensive exposition of the framework can be found in Sabatier (1986). This overview should, however, indicate how it synthesizes important elements from both top-down and bottom-up perspectives within the implementation literature. But the framework also borrows from a number of other literatures, including those on long term policy change (Heclo, 1974; Derthick, 1979; Browning et al., 1985; Hogwood and Peters, 1983), coalition stability (Dodd, 1976; Hinckley, 1981), elite belief systems (Putnam, 1976), and the utilization of policy research (Weiss, 1977).

Summary

This chapter has examined the strengths and weaknesses of top-down and bottom-up approaches to implementation analysis. It has then indicated situations where each has a comparative advantage. A more promising strategy, however, is to synthesize the best features of each into a new approach. The last part of this chapter has outlined a synthesis addressed to understanding the dynamics of policy change over periods of a decade or more.

Notes

1. This is really a focus on two scholars: Paul Sabatier, including his collaboration with Dan Mazmanian and Ladislav Cerych, and Benny Hjern, including his collaboration with David Porter, Ken Hanf, and Chris Hull. The principal selection criterion is the extent of theoretical and/or methodological development. Sabatier et al. was chosen instead of Pressman and Wildavsky (1973) or Van Horn (1979; Van Meter and Van Horn, 1976) because his work built on theirs and was subjected to more extensive empirical testing. Hjern was selected rather than other "bottom-uppers" (Lipsky, 1971; Berman, 1978; Barrett and Fudge, 1981; Barrett and Hill, 1984) because of Hjern's superior methodology.

2. Note that the top-down approach is very similar to classic studies of program/policy evaluation (Weiss, 1972), although placing greater emphasis on the factors affecting policy outputs and program outcomes.

3. The cases in the *Effective Implementation* book were selected not because of any knowledge of the case on the part of the editors but rather because we knew the authors were first-class scholars who had ongoing research projects involving policy implementation. As for the cases involving European higher education reforms, these were all selected by Cerych before he had any knowledge of the Sabatier/Mazmanian framework.

4. For example, the OU was criticized in 1971 for failing to meet its mandate of reducing the social inequalities in the British higher education system. While that had been one of the goals articulated in the early stages of the formulation process, it was *not* included in the final charter and, in fact, the OU was expressly to serve students on a "first come, first serve" basis. Thus an affirmative action program for working class students would have violated the OU's charter (Cerych and Sabatier, 1985).

5. The Swedish 25/5 Scheme was a proposal instituted over several years in the early 1970s which waived normal university entrance requirements for adults over 25 years of age with 5 years work experience. The German Gesamthochschulen was a massive reform launched in the early 1970s which originally sought to completly transform German higher education. For discussions of each, see Cerych and Sabatier (1986).
6. These comments are based primarily upon extended discussions with Benny Hjern during the 1981-82 academic year which I spent at the University of Bielefeld. They are also based upon his key articles (Hjern et al, 1978; Hjern and Porter, 1980; Hjern and Hull, 1982), his review of the *Effective Implementation* book (Hjern, 1982), and his manuscripts on Swedish manpower training and on the "helping small firms" project (Hjern and Hull, 1985).
7. The German versions should be available from Weidner at the International Institute for Environment and Society, Science Center, Berlin. For discussions in English of some of the results, see Knoepfel (1981) and Knoepfel and Weidner (1982b).

Bibliography

Aaron, Henry (1978). *Politics and the Professors*. Washington, D.C.: Brookings Institution.

Ackermann, Charbel and Steinmann, Walter (1982). "Privatized Policy Making," *European Journal of Policy Research* 10 (June): 173-185.

Alexander, Robert (1982). "Implementation: Does a Literature Add Up to a Theory?" *Journal of the American Planning Association* (Winter): 132-155.

Alterman, Rachelle (1983). "Implementation Analysis: The Contours of an Emerging Debate," *Journal of Planning Education and Research* 3 (Summer): 63-65.

Bardach, Eugene (1974). *The Implementation Game*. Cambridge: MIT Press.

Barrett, Susan and Fudge, Colin, eds. (1981). *Policy and Action*. London: Methuen.

_____ and Hill, Michael (1984). "Policy, Bargaining and Structure in Implementation Theory," *Policy and Politics* 12: 219-240.

Baum, Lawrence (1981). "Comparing the Implementation of Legislative and Judicial Policies," in *Effective Policy Implementation*, ed. by D. Mazmanian and P. Sabatier. Lexington, Mass: D.C. Heath, pp. 39-62.

Berman, Paul (1978). "The Study of Macro-and Micro-Implementation," *Public Policy* 26: 157-184.

_____ (1980). "Thinking about Programmed and Adaptive Implementation," in *Why Policies Succeed or Fail*, ed. by Helen Ingram and Dean Mann. Beverly Hills: Sage.

_____ and McLaughlin, Milbrey (1976). "Implementation of ESEA Title I," *Teacher College Record* 77 (Feb.): 397-415.

Bowen, Elinor (1982). "The Pressman-Wildavsky Paradox," *Journal of Public Policy* 2 (February): 1-22.

Bowman, Ann and Lester, James (1986). "Subnational Policy Implementation: Testing the Sabatier-Mazmanian Model," *Administration and Society*, forthcoming.

Browning, Rufus, Marshall, Dale, and Tabb, David (1981). ''Implementation and Political Change: Sources of Local Variation in Federal Social Programs,'' in *Effective Policy Implementation*, ed. by D. Mazmanian and P. Sabatier. Lexington, Mass.: D.C. Heath, pp. 127-146.

——————————— (1985). *Protest Is Not Enough*. Berkeley: University of California Press.

Bullock, Charles (1981). ''Implementation of Equal Education Opportunity Programs: A Comparative Analysis,'' in *Effective Policy Implementation*, ed. by D. Mazmanian and P. Sabatier. Lexington, Mass.: D.C. Heath, pp. 89-126.

——————————— and Lamb, Charles, eds. (1984). *Implementation of Civil Rights Policy*. Monterey, Ca.: Brooks Cole.

Burnham, Walter Dean (1970). *Critical Elections and the Mainsprings of American Politics*. New York: Norton.

Cerych, Ladislav and Sabatier, Paul (1986). *Great Expectations and Mixed Performance: The Implementation of European Higher Education Reforms*. Stoke-on-Trent, United Kingdom: Trentham Books.

Davies, Tom and Mason, Charles (1982). ''Gazing Up from the Bottoms: Problems of Minimal Response in the Implementation of Manpower Policy,'' *European Journal of Political Research* 10 (June): 145-158.

Davis, Charles (1985). ''Perceptions of Hazardous Waste Policy Issues among Public and Private Sector Administrators,'' *Western Political Quarterly* 38 (Sept.): 447-463.

——————————— and Lester, James, eds. (1988). *Dimensions of Hazardous Waste Politics and Policy*. Westport, Conn.: Greenwood Press.

Derthick, Martha (1972). *New Towns In-Town*. Washington: Urban Institute.

——————————— (1979). *Policymaking for Social Security*. Washington: Brookings.

Dodd, Lawrence (1976). *Coalitions in Parliamentary Governments*. Princeton: Princeton University Press.

Downs, Anthony (1967). *Inside Bureaucracy*. Boston: Little, Brown, and Company.

Elmore, Richard (1978). ''Organizational Models of Social Program Implementation,'' *Public Policy* 26 (Spring): 185-228.

——————————— (1979). ''Backward Mapping,'' *Political Science Quarterly* 94 (Winter): 601-616.

——————————— (1985). ''Forward and Backward Mapping,'' in *Policy Implementation in Federal and Unitary Systems*, ed. K. Hanf and T. Toonen. Dordrecht: Martinus Nijhoff, pp. 33-70.

Glaser, Barney and Strauss, Anselm (1967). *The Discovery of Grounded Theory*. Chicago: Aldine.

Goggin, Malcolm L. (1984). ''Book Review of *Implementation and Public Policy*, Daniel A. Mazmanian and Paul A. Sabatier, eds.,'' *Publius* 14 (Fall): 159-160.

——————————— (1986). The ''Too Few Cases/Too Many Variables' Problem In Implementation Research,'' *Western Political Quarterly*, forthcoming.

Goodwin, Leonard and Moen, Phyllis (1981). "The Evolution and Implementation of Federal Welfare Policy," in *Effective Policy Implementation*, ed. D. Mazmanian and P. Sabatier. Lexington: Heath, pp. 147-168.

Hambleton, Robin (1983). "Planning Systems and Policy Implementation," *Journal of Public Policy* 3 (October): 397-418.

Hanf, Kenneth (1982). "The Implementation of Regulatory Policy: Enforcement as Bargaining," *European Journal of Political Research* 10 (June 1982): 159-172.

_____ and Scharpf, Fritz, eds. (1978). *Interorganizational Policy Making: Limits to Coordination and Central Control*. London: Sage.

Heclo, Hugh (1974). *Social Policy in Britain and Sweden*. New Haven: Yale Univ. Press.

_____ (1978). "Issue Networks and the Executive Establishment," *The New American Political System*, ed. Anthony King. Washington, D.C.: American Enterprise Institute.

Hinckley, Barbara (1981). *Coalitions and Politics*. New York: Harcourt, Brace, Jovanovich.

Hjern, Benny (1982). "Review of *Effective Policy Implementation*, Daniel A. Mazmanian and Paul A. Sabatier, eds.," *Journal of Public Policy* 2(3): 301-308.

_____ and Porter, David (1981). "Implementation Structures: A New Unit of Administrative Analysis," *Organization Studies* 2: 211-227.

_____ and Hull, Chris (1982). "Implementation Research as Emprical Constitutionalism," *European Journal of Political Research* 10 (June 1982): 105-116.

_____ (1985). "Helping Small Firms Grow," Unpublished book-length manuscript, Management Institut, Science Center, Berlin.

_____, Hanf, Kenneth and Porter, David (1978). "Local Networks of Manpower Training in the Federal Republic of Germany and Sweden," in *Interorganizational Policy Making: Limits to Coordination and Central Control*. London: Sage, pp. 303-344.

Hofferbert, Richard (1974). *The Study of Public Policy*. Indianapolis: Bobbs-Merrill.

Hogwood, Bryan and Peters, G. Guy (1983). *Policy Dynamics*. New York: St. Martin's.

Hull, Chris and Hjern, Benny (1982). "Helping Small Firms Grow," *European Journal of Political Research* 10 (June): 187-198.

Ingram, Helen (1977). "Policy Implementation through Bargaining: Federal Grants in Aid." *Public Policy* 25 (Fall 1977).

Jones, Charles (1975). *Clean Air*. Pittsburgh: University of Pittsburgh Press.

Jones, Susan (1984). "Application of a Framework for Implementation Analysis to Evaluate Groundwater Management Policy in Two New York Counties," Unpublished Master's Thesis, Department of City and Regional Planning, University of North Carolina, Chapel Hill.

Jordan, A.G. and Richardson, J.J. (1983). "Policy Communities: The British and European Political Style,'' *Policy Studies Journal* 11 (June): 603-615.

Kirst, Michael and Jung, Richard (1982). "The Utility of a Longitudinal Approach in Assessing Implementation: Title I, ESEA," in *Studying Implementation*, ed. by Walter Williams. Chatham, N.J.: Chatham House, pp. 119-148.

Kiser, Larry and Ostrom, Elinor (1982). "The Three Worlds of Action," in *Strategies of Political Inquiry*, ed. E. Ostrom. Beverly Hills: Sage, pp. 179-222.

Knoepfel, Peter (1981). "Conceptualizing Comparative Policy Analysis," *Architecture and Behavior* 1: 287-305.

_____ and Weidner, Helmut (1982a). "A Conceptual Framework for Studying Implementation," in *The Implementation of Pollution Control Programs*, ed. by Paul Downing and Kenneth Hanf. Tallahassee: Policy Sciences Program.

_____ (1982b). "Implementing Air Quality Control Programs in Europe," *Policy Studies Journal* 11 (Sept.): 104-115.

_____ and Hanf, Kenneth (1980). "Analytical Framework and Research Guidelines for the National Teams," Unpublished manuscript, International Institute for Science and Society, Science Center, Berlin, 120 pp.

Lazin, Frederick (1973). "The Failure of Federal Enforcement of Civil Rights Regulations in Public Housing, 1963-71," *Policy Sciences* 4: 263-274.

Lester, James (1985). "Hazardous Waste and Policy Implementation: The Subnational Role," *Harardous Waste* 2 (Fall).

_____ and Bowman, Ann O'M. (1989). "Implementing Intergovernmental Policy: Testing the Sabatier-Mazmanian Model," *Polity* 21 (Summer).

Levin, Martin (1980). "Conditions Contributing to Effective Implementation and Their Limits." Unpublished manuscript, Brandeis University.

Lipsky, Michael (1971). "Street Level Bureaucracy and the Analysis of Urban Reform," *Urban Affairs Quarterly* 6: 391-409.

Lowry, Kem (1985). "Assessing the Implementation of Federal Coastal Policy," *Journal of the American Planning Association*, 51 (Summer): 288-298.

McFarlane, Deborah (1989). "Testing the Statutory Coherence Hypothesis: The Implementation of Federal Family Planning Policy in the States," *Administration and Society* 20 (February): 395-422.

MacIntyre, Angus (1985). "The Multiple Sources of Statutory Ambiguity," in *Administrative Discretion and the Implementation of Public Policy*, ed. Hibbeln and Shumavon. New York: Praeger, pp. 66-88.

Majone, Giandomenico (1980). "Policies as Theories," *Omega* 8: 151-162.

_____ and Aaron Wildavsky (1978). "Implementation as Evolution," in *Policy Studies Review Annual—1978*, ed. Howard Freeman. Beverly Hills: Sage.

Mann, Dean, ed. (1982). *Environmental Policy Implementation*. Lexington, Mass: D.C. Heath.

Mazmanian, Daniel A. and Paul A. Sabatier, eds. (1981). *Effective Policy Implementation*. Lexington, Mass.: D.C. Heath.

_____ (1983). *Implementation and Public Policy*. Chicago: Scott Foresman and Co.

Milward, H. Brinton and Wamsley, Gary (1984). "Policy Subsystems, Networks, and the Tools of Public Management," in *Public Policy Formation and Implementation*, ed. Robert Eyestone. Boston: JAI Press.

Murphy, Jerome (1973). "The Education Bureaucracies Implement Novel Policy: The Politics of Title I of ESEA," in *Policy and Politics in America*, ed. Allan Sindler. Boston: Little, Brown.

Nakamura, Robert and Smallwood, Frank (1980). *The Politics of Policy Implementation*. New York: St. Martin's.

Nuccio, Kathleen (1987). "The Equal Employment Opportunity Commission," Unpublished Ph.D. Dissertation, School of Social Work, Bryw Mahr College.

Page, Ed (1985). "Laws an an Instrument in Center-Local Relations," *Journal of Public Policy* 5 (2): 241-265.

Pressman, Jeffrey and Wildavsky, Aaron (1973). *Implementation*. Berkeley: Univ. of California Press.

Rose, Richard (1984). "From Government at the Center to Nationwide Government," Studies in Public Policy No. 132, University of Strathclyde, Glasgow.

Rosenbaum, Nelson (1981). "Statutory Structure and Policy Implementation: The Case of Wetlands Regulation," in *Effective Policy Implementation*, ed. by D. Mazmanian and P. Sabatier. Lexington, Mass: D.C. Heath, pp. 63-86.

Sabatier, Paul (1975). "Social Movements and Regulatory Agencies," *Policy Sciences* 8: 301-342.

_____ (1984). "Implementing Coastal Zone Management Laws in the U.S. and Europe," in *International Comparisons in Implementing Pollution Laws*, ed. by P. Downing and K. Hanf. Boston: Kluwer-Nijhoff.

_____ (1986). "Policy Analysis, Policy-Oriented Learning and Policy Change: An Advocacy Coalition Framework." Manuscript submitted to *Knowledge: Creation, Diffusion, Utilization*.

_____ and Klosterman, Barbara (1981). "A Comparative Analysis of Policy Implementation under Different Statutory Regimes," in *Effective Policy Implementation*, ed. D. Mazmanian and P. Sabatier. Lexington: Heath, pp. 169-206.

_____ and Mazmanian, Daniel (1979). "The Conditions of Effective Implementation," *Policy Analysis* 5 (Fall): 481-504.

_____ (1980). "A Framework of Analysis," *Policy Studies Journal* 8: 538-560.

_____ (1983a). "Policy Implementation." in *Encyclopedia of Policy Studies* ed. by Stuart Nagel. N.Y.: Marcel Dekker, 1983, pp. 143-169.

_____ (1983b). *Can Regulation Work? The Implementation of the 1972 California Coastal Initiative*. N.Y.: Plenum.

Scharpf, Fritz (1978). "Interorganizational Policy Studies," in *Interorganizational Policy-Making*, ed. K. Hanf and F. Scharpf. London: Sage, pp. 345-370.

Sharpe, L.J. (1985). "Central Coordination and the Policy Network," *Political Studies* 33: 361-381.

Thrasher, Michael (1983). "Exchange Networks and Implementation," *Policy and Politics* 11: 375-391.

Van Horn, Carl (1979). *Policy Implementation in the Federal System*. Lexington, Mass.: D.C. Heath.

Van Meter, Donald and Van Horn, Carl (1975). "The Policy Implementation Process: A conceptual Framework," *Administration and Society* 6 (Feb.): 445-488.

Weatherly, Richard and Lipsky, Michael (1977). "Street Level Bureaucrats and Institutional Innovation: Implementing Special-Education Reform," *Harvard Educational Review* 47 (2): 171-197.

Weiss, Carol (1972). *Evaluation Research*. Englewood Cliffs: Prentice Hall.

_____, ed. (1977). *Using Social Research in Public Policy Making*. Lexington, Mass.: D.C. Heath.

Wiley, Karen (1986). "Control of Technology in a Federal System: The EPA, the States, and Hazardous Waste Management," Paper presented at the Annual Meeting of the American Political Science Assn., Washington, D.C.

Wittrock, Bjorn et al. (1982). "Implementation Beyond Hierarchy: Swedish Energy Research Policy," *European Journal of Political Research* 10 (June): 131-143.

Yin, Robert (1980). *Studying the Implementation of Public Programs*. Boulder: Solar Energy Research Insitute.

Acknowledgments

Chapter 2

D. Mazmanian and P. Sabatier, "A Multivariate Model of Public Policy-Making," *American Journal of Political Science* 24 (August 1980), 439-68. Reprinted by permission.

P. Sabatier and D. Mazmanian, "The Implementation of Public Policy: A Framework of Analysis," *Policy Studies Journal,* Special Issue 1980. Copyright © 1980 Policy Studies Organization. Reprinted by permission.

Chapter 3

"Reprinted from Administration Hara-Kiri: Implementation of the Urban Growth and New Community Development Act, by Helene V. Smookler in volume no. 422 dated November 1975 of *The Annals of the American Academy of Political and Social Science."* © 1975 *by* The American Academy *of* Political *and* Social Science.

Chapter 4

From Ann F. Friedlaender, Ed., *Approaches to Controlling Air Pollution,* p. 353. Copyright © 1978 by The Massachusetts Institute of Technology.

Chapter 5

Charles S. Bullock, III, "Implementation of Selected Equal Education Opportunity Programs." Paper presented at the annual meeting of the American Political Science Association, Washington, D.C., August 28-31, 1980, Tables 1 and 3.

Chapter 6

From Joel S. Berke and Michael W. Kirst, *Federal Aid to Education,* p. 26. Copyright © 1972 by D. C. Heath and Company.

Michael Kirst and Richard Jung. "The Utility of a Longitudinal Approach in Assessing Implementation: A Thirteen-Year View of Title I, ESEA." *Educational Evaluation and Policy Analysis,* September-October, Volume 2, Number 5, 1980, pp. 17–34.

Chapter 8

Alvin Gouldner, "Metaphysical Pathos and the Theory of Bureaucracy," *American Political Science Review,* 49, June 1955, 507. Reprinted by permission.

P. Sabatier and D. Mazmanian, "The Conditions of Effective Implementation," *Policy Analysis,* 5:4, Fall 1979, 481-504. Copyright © 1979 by The Regents of the University of California. Reprinted by permission.

Index

Index

329